WITHDRAWN

Advances in

THE STUDY OF BEHAVIOR

VOLUME 20

Advances in
THE STUDY OF
BEHAVIOR

Edited by

PETER J. B. SLATER
Department of Biology and Preclinical Medicine
University of St. Andrews
Fife, Scotland

JAY S. ROSENBLATT
Institute of Animal Behavior
Rutgers University
Newark, New Jersey

COLIN BEER
Institute of Animal Behavior
Rutgers University
Newark, New Jersey

MANFRED MILINSKI
Abteilung Verhaltensökologie
Zoologisches Institut
Universität Bern
Hinterkappelen, Switzerland

VOLUME 20

ACADEMIC PRESS, INC.
Harcourt Brace Jovanovich, Publishers

San Diego   New York   Boston
London   Sydney   Tokyo   Toronto

ACADEMIC PRESS, INC.
San Diego, California 92101

United Kingdom Edition published by
ACADEMIC PRESS LIMITED
24-28 Oval Road, London NW1 7DX

LIBRARY OF CONGRESS CATALOG CARD NUMBER: 64-8031

ISBN   0-12-004520-6   (alk. paper)

PRINTED IN THE UNITED STATES OF AMERICA
91 92 93 94   9 8 7 6 5 4 3 2 1

Contents

Social Behavior and Organization in the Macropodoidea
PETER J. JARMAN

The *t* Complex: A Story of Genes, Behavior, and Populations
SARAH LENINGTON

The Ergonomics of Worker Behavior in Social Hymenoptera
PAUL SCHMID-HEMPEL

"Microsmatic Humans" Revisited: The Generation and Perception
of Chemical Signals

BENOIST SCHAAL AND RICHARD H. PORTER

Lekking in Birds and Mammals: Behavioral and Evolutionary Issues

R. HAVEN WILEY

Contributors

Numbers in parentheses indicate the pages on which the authors' contributions begin.

PETER J. JARMAN (1), *Department of Ecosystem Management, University of New England, Armidale, New South Wales 2351, Australia*

SARAH LENINGTON (51), *Institute of Animal Behavior, Rutgers University, Newark, New Jersey 07102*

RICHARD H. PORTER (135), *Department of Psychology and Human Development, Vanderbilt University, Nashville, Tennessee 37203*

BENOIST SCHAAL (135), *Ecole Pratique des Hautes Etudes, Laboratoire de Psycho-biologie de l'Enfant, URA 315 CNRS, 75005 Paris, France*

PAUL SCHMID-HEMPEL (87), *Zoologisches Institut der Universität, CH-4051 Basel, Switzerland*

R. HAVEN WILEY (201), *Department of Biology, The University of North Carolina at Chapel Hill, Chapel Hill, North Carolina 27599*

Preface

As it has for 25 years, *Advances in the Study of Behavior* continues to serve the increasing number of scientists who are engaged in the study of animal behavior by presenting their theoretical ideas and research to their colleagues and to those in neighboring fields. We hope that the series will continue to serve, ". . . as a contribution to the development of cooperation and communication among scientists in our field." Traditional areas of animal behavior research have achieved new vigor by the links they have formed with related fields and by the closer relationship that now exists between those studying animal and human subjects. Though lately behavioral ecology and sociobiology have tended to overshadow other areas, the range of scientists studying behavior is greater today than ever before: from ecologists and evolutionary biologists, to geneticists, endocrinologists, pharmacologists, neurobiologists and developmental psychobiologists, as well as ethologists and comparative psychologists.

It is our intention, not to focus narrowly on one or a few of these fields, but to publish articles covering the best behavioral work from a broad spectrum, as the range of articles in the present volume shows. The skills and concepts of scientists in such diverse fields necessarily differ, making the task of developing cooperation and communication among them a difficult one. But it is one that is of great importance, and one to which the Editors and publisher of *Advances in the Study of Behavior* are committed. We will continue to provide the means to this end by publishing critical reviews, by inviting extended presentations of significant research programs, by encouraging the writing of theoretical syntheses and reformulations of persistent problems, and by highlighting especially penetrating research that introduces important new concepts.

With this twentieth volume we are very pleased to welcome Dr. Manfred Milinski of the University of Bern as an Associate Editor. His expertise and his base on continental Europe will help us to ensure that the series retains both its strong international coverage and its breadth of subject matter.

Social Behavior and Organization in the Macropodoidea

PETER J. JARMAN

DEPARTMENT OF ECOSYSTEM MANAGEMENT
UNIVERSITY OF NEW ENGLAND
ARMIDALE, NEW SOUTH WALES 2351, AUSTRALIA

I. INTRODUCTION

The superfamily Macropodoidea (the macropods), the great metatherian (marsupial) radiation of terrestrial herbivores, is found naturally only in Australia and Papua New Guinea, where about 56 species have historically existed. They evolved in isolation from the eutherian ungulates, although alongside rodents for the last four or five million years.

It has often been asserted that macropods play an ecological role akin to that of ungulates in Eurasia, Africa, and the Americas and, taken broadly, that is a useful comparison. Like ungulates, macropods speciated rapidly in the Miocene or Pliocene, perhaps in response to increasing aridity and the spread of grasslands and shrub steppe communities. Like ungulates, they evolved morphological, physiological, and behavioral adaptations to the opportunities offered by these new habitats. And, like ungulates, they evolved under predation from an array of mammalian, avian, and reptilian predators (see Jarman and Coulson, 1989). These similarities give macropods, in addition to their own intrinsic fascination, an heuristic role as evolutionary parallels upon which theories of the evolution of eutherian large herbivores can be tested. Yet, there are also differences between the metatherian and eutherian radiations, and the need to explain these may also test adaptive explanations.

The superficial ecological and sociobehavioral resemblances between macropods and eutherian herbivores such as bovids, cervids, or leporids are so great that one may forget how far distant were their common ancestors. I want to emphasize this point. The macropods are much more closely "related" to the large carnivorous marsupial thylacine *Thylacinus cynocephalus* or the small, insectivorous *Antechinus* and *Sminthopsis* species than they are to any of the eutherian herbivores, with whom they have had no phylogenetic links since the days of the dinosaurs.

This review describes the social behavior and organization of the macropods,

1

and suggests, where appropriate, adaptive explanations for it. Knowledge of the social systems of most macropods is still incomplete. Consequently, critical tests of adaptive explanations have rarely been made. Nevertheless, enough macropod species have now been studied, at least at the level of describing their sociality in the field, and sufficient progress has been made since previous reviews (e.g., Kaufmann, 1974a; Russell, 1984), to justify this attempted synthesis.

Social organization is imposed on a population by its members' reactions to each other and to their environment. It is in large part the outcome of social behavior, and I assume that sociality, social behavior, and social organization have evolved in parallel. There is thus no obvious sequence in which to discuss them, and in this article I review macropod sociality first, considering which species are found in groups and how grouping is affected by environmental variables. I then review the forms of social behavior, discussing how macropod species communicate and interact and how the behavior patterns involved are distributed across the array of species. Then I review their forms of social organization. Finally, I discuss the apparent adaptiveness of macropod social organization.

II. THE MACROPODOIDEA: TAXONOMY, MORPHOLOGY, GROWTH, AND REPRODUCTION

The superfamily Macropodoidea contains two families, the Potoroidae, i.e., the potoroos, bettongs, and rat kangaroos, and the Macropodidae, containing hare wallabies, nailtail wallabies, rock wallabies, other wallabies, tree kangaroos, wallaroos, and kangaroos. The families are separated primarily on features of dentition and cranial morphology. Such features apart, similarly sized species in the two families are ecologically and physiologically, and in some respects behaviorally, similar.

Macropods occur in almost all terrestrial habitats in Australasia. Species richness is lowest in rainforest and alpine or hot arid desert, and is greatest in the savanna and woodland zone. Potoroids, which are absent from New Guinea, are most species-rich in Australia south of the tropic, where they occupy habitats from rainforest to desert. Macropodids are most species rich in the middle latitudes of eastern Australia. The richest extant macropod community contains 10 sympatric species, and these are generally ecologically separated by choice of habitat (Jarman *et al.,* 1987; Southwell, 1987) and diet (Jarman, 1984). All macropods are primarily herbivores, but some potoroids and hare-wallabies also eat invertebrates regularly but in small quantities. Reproductive or storage organs of plants and fungi feature in the diets of many smaller macropods. Larger species eat predominantly leaves (rather than stems) of forbs and grasses.

Sacculation of the stomach, allowing microbial digestion, is most developed in the larger, grazing macropods and least in the potoroids, which have a more tubiform stomach (Hume, 1982). Dental morphology reflects the potoroid's highly selective feeding on storage organs and new leaves of angiosperms and fruiting bodies of subterranean fungi, as well as the range of macropodid diets, from new leaves eaten by the smaller species, through a mixed diet of grasses and browse taken by many medium-sized wallabies, to kangaroos' diets consisting almost entirely of mature or young green leaves of grasses (Jarman, 1984; Sanson, 1989).

Colloquial and binomial names of all macropod species mentioned in the text are given in Table I, together with the maximum known weights of males and females.

The extant potoroid species range in size from 0.6 to 3 kg, and the macropodids from just under 1 to nearly 100 kg. In both families the species under about 4 kg (i.e., all the extant potoroids, most of the hare-wallabies, and some small rock-wallabies) are homomorphic; macropodids above that weight are heteromorphic (= sexually dimorphic; Jarman, 1983) in size and shape.

Only the red kangaroo and the common wallaroo are sexually dimorphic in coloring. Interestingly, in at least some populations of the red kangaroo, not all the males are "male" colored nor all the females "female" colored, reversals of dimorphic coloring occurring in as many as 30% of individuals (Oliver, 1986). In this species it would be truer to say that certain color morphs are more common in one sex than the other, rather than being sex-linked.

Heteromorphism in size in the medium-sized and larger species results from two processes: males grow at a faster rate than females, or continue to grow rapidly for longer; and males also develop the size and musculature of most elements of their forelimbs to an exaggerated extent. Since the forelimbs play an important part in fighting in most of these species, this is the equivalent of exaggeration of weaponry through growth of horns, antlers, and associated neck musculature in eutherian bovids or cervids (Jarman, 1983, 1989a). Like many ungulates, males of some macropods develop dermal shields, thickened skin over the belly and neck which presumably protects them to some extent from damaging blows from opponents in fights (Jarman, 1989b). Physical development of a fully adult macropod male therefore involves the full growth of weapons, musculature, and defenses, and this growth takes many years. The heteromorphic macropods, like some ungulates, should be able to use the state of growth of weaponry (i.e., of length and muscularity of forelimbs) to assess a male's stage of development.

In all closely studied macropod species, both sexes continue to grow after physiological reproductive maturity. The continuation is least in the homomorphic species, the potoroids and smallest macropodids, in which growth in both sexes apparently ceases (or is imperceptible) a few months after physiological reproductive maturity. Males of the medium-sized and large macropodids continue to grow for at least some years after maturity. In species in which males

TABLE I

Species of Macropods Referred to in the Text, Their Colloquial and Binomial Names[a] and Maximum Weights of Males and Females (if Known)[b]

Name		Weight (kg)	
Colloquial	Binomial	Male	Female
Family Potoroidae, the potoroos, bettongs, and rat-kangaroos			
Rufous bettong	*Aepyprymnus rufescens*	3.2	3.5
Tasmanian bettong	*Bettongia gaimardi*	~1.7	
Burrowing bettong	*Bettongia lesueur*	1.1	1.1
Brush-tailed bettong	*Bettongia penicillata*	~1.3	
Musky rat kangaroo	*Hypsiprymnodon moschatus*	0.7	0.6
Long-footed potoroo	*Potorous longipes*	2.2	1.8
Long-nosed potoroo	*Potorous tridactylus*	1.7	1.6
Family Macropodidae, kangaroos, wallaroos, and wallabies			
Lumholtz's tree kangaroo	*Dendrolagus lumholtzi*	10.0	7.0
Spectacled hare wallaby	*Lagorchestes conspicillatus*	4.3	4.2
Rufous hare wallaby	*Lagorchestes hirsutus*	1.6	1.6
Antilopine wallaroo	*Macropus antilopinus*	49.0	20.0
Black-striped wallaby	*Macropus dorsalis*	19.0	8.5
Tammar wallaby	*Macropus eugenii*	9.0	6.9
Western gray kangaroo	*Macropus fuliginosus*	72.0	39.0
Eastern gray kangaroo	*Macropus giganteus*	75.5	40.0
Whiptail wallaby	*Macropus parryi*	26.0	15.0
Common wallaroo	*Macropus robustus*	58.0	25.0
Red-necked wallaby	*Macropus rufogriseus*	27.0	16.0
Red kangaroo	*Macropus rufus*	93.0	37.0
Bridled nailtail wallaby	*Onychogalea fraenata*	6.0	5.0
Unadorned rock wallaby	*Petrogale inornata*	~4.0	
Brush-tailed rock wallaby	*Petrogale penicillata*	7.6	6.6
Quokka	*Setonix brachyurus*	3.3	2.7
Red-legged pademelon	*Thylogale stigmatica*	6.8	4.1
Red-necked pademelon	*Thylogale thetis*	9.2	4.8
Swamp wallaby	*Wallabia bicolor*	22.0	16.5

[a]After Strahan (1983).
[b]From sources given in Jarman (1989b).

can exceed 20 kg, male growth persists throughout life (Jarman, 1989a), although an individual's rate of growth may fluctuate. Field observations suggest that individual male eastern gray kangaroos grow neither steadily nor to a prescribed pattern; rather, an individual may grow in spurts with periods of stasis between. The same may be true of red-necked wallabies (personal observation; C. N. Johnson, personal communication).

Females of some medium-sized and large macropodid species may grow throughout life, and this seems to be true of some of the larger rock wallaby species (e.g., brush-tailed rock wallaby) and swamp wallabies. However, females of several of the medium-sized and large *Macropus* species, although they continue to grow for a year or two after reproductive maturity, thereafter grow imperceptibly (Jarman, 1989a).

I have emphasized the diversity of forms of growth in the macropods because I believe that they are related to each species' and sex's reproductive strategy and to intrasexual, and sometimes intersexual, behavior. Moreover, I want to abolish the common assumption that large mammals must necessarily grow, like humans, to an asymptotic "adult" weight. Many large mammals, both eutherian and metatherian, grow persistently. The selective pressures on individuals in such species differ from those on individuals in species whose growth ceases at or soon after maturity. The macropods contain examples of both styles of growth, asymptotic and persistent.

Reproduction in macropods is, of course, intriguingly different from that of eutherians, and demands some forms of female–young behavior that are unknown in eutheria. However, there are also parallels to eutherian mother–young behavior, which are discussed later.

Australia and Papua New Guinea range latitudinally from the monsoonal tropics in the north, where rainfall is highly predictable and occurs in summer, through middle latitudes where rainfall is less seasonal or predictable, to southern "Mediterranean" regions with predictable winter rainfall. Finally, at the southern latitudinal extremes in Tasmania, there is a climate of year-round rain, but with seasonality induced by temperature differences between summer and winter. Most of the continent that is more than 500 km from a coast has low and unpredictable rainfall and primary productivity which is driven by availability of soil moisture; macropods in those regions are faced with unpredictably fluctuating food resources.

The very few macropod species that reproduce strictly seasonally live in the most southern latitudes and "Mediterranean" zone of southern Australia. They include the tammar wallaby, whose reproductive physiology has been particularly well studied (see Tyndale-Biscoe and Renfree, 1987, for a review). Elsewhere, macropods breed aseasonally, perhaps with a bias toward some months of the year. In the arid zone, macropods breed opportunistically when primary production makes breeding possible. Such species enter anestrus during drought, emerging from that state when resource availability improves.

Females of small macropod species first show estrus and mate when quite young. Indeed, in some bettong species among the potoroids and possibly the diminutive rufous hare-wallaby among the macropodids (K. A. Johnson and G. Lundie-Jenkins, personal communication), females may first conceive just before they are weaned. Females of many other small species first conceive within weeks of weaning. However, females of the largest species delay the onset of breeding for many months, up to 2 years in the case of eastern gray kangaroos, after weaning.

No matter how long or short the delay, females of all species grow substantially beyond the weight at which they first breed. Breeding usually starts at half or less than half the maximum weight achieved by females in the larger species, but more commonly at over two-thirds the asymptotic female weight in potoroids and the smallest macropodids.

Their behavior indicates that male macropods can detect the approach of estrus 3 to 8 (or even 10) days before it occurs. One or a few matings occur at estrus. If these lead to conception and implantation of the blastula, birth occurs about 30 days later in most species. This is a day or two less than the interval between successive estruses; thus, gestation does not interfere with the timing of the estrous cycle.

However, not all conceptions lead to immediate implantation. If the female is already suckling a juvenile in the pouch, implantation of the blastula will be delayed. This embryonic diapause is controlled through the hormonal consequences of the mother's lactating in response to the sucking of the current pouch-young. About 4 weeks before the pouch-young is due to leave the pouch permanently, the blastula implants and gestation ensues. The female denies her pouch-young reentry to the pouch a day or so before she gives birth to the next infant. This then makes its way unaided into the pouch, finds a teat, and clamps its mouth around it. A day or two after that event, in several species which can breed continuously, the female may once again enter estrus.

All extant macropod species give birth to only one young at a time, except for the most primitive living species, the musky rat-kangaroo, which commonly has twins. Nevertheless, a female macropod may be supporting three dependent young simultaneously: an unimplanted blastula or developing embryo, a pouch-young, and a young-at-foot which, although excluded from reentering the pouch, is still putting its muzzle into the pouch to suck. Moreover the mother may be producing milk of two different compositions (from two of her four teats) to support the differing nutritional demands of her sucking young.

Times taken for growth and maturation are related to specific body weight, the smaller macropod species maturing sooner than the larger (Lee and Ward, 1989). Males show spermatogenesis when a few weeks (in the smallest species) or months (in the largest species) older than are females at first estrus, but males of the medium-sized and large species are usually socially inhibited from participating actively in reproduction.

Longevities of macropods in the wild have rarely been recorded. Larger species seem capable of living to between 15 and 20 years, while the smallest species might enjoy 8 to 10 years (but the latter figures are only guesses). Fecundity is rarely better than 1.1 young per breeding female per year in the largest species, but may reach nearly 3 young per breeding female per year in the smallest species, at least in captivity.

In most of the medium-sized and large macropods mortality seems to fall more heavily in their early years on males, since the sex ratio in the adult population is nearly always female-biased. In some populations of some *Macropus* species the sex ratio of pouch-young departs from parity, favoring males. The extent of this departure is geographically patterned in eastern gray and red kangaroos, and relates to rainfall (Johnson and Jarman, 1983). The sex ratio of the offspring may vary with the mother's age or reproductive history in red-necked wallabies (Johnson, 1985) and eastern gray kangaroos (Stuart-Dick, 1987). Although the mechanisms for varying the pouch-young sex ratio are unknown, the phenomenon is clear; its part in the adaptiveness of individual reproductive behavior in macropods needs to be explained.

This brief introduction to the macropods has tried to give enough information about their ecology, physiology, morphology, and population dynamics for the reader to appreciate the superfamily's range of adaptations, and how the species' social organization and behavior reflect those attributes.

III. Sociality in the Macropods

The tendency of a species, or of socially distinct classes within it, to form groups may be called the species' sociality. Other aspects of grouping, such as its diurnal, seasonal, or situational variability, contribute to this general descriptor. Sociality partly results from interindividual social behavior, but also arises from individuals' responses to components of the environment other than their conspecifics.

Sociality in the macropods relates quite closely to the size, diet, and habitat of a species. Studies of grouping exist for only a few species, but group sizes in the field have now been described for most macropod species. There is a general tendency for the smallest species to be found solitarily, or in twos or threes at most, and for the largest species to be in groups of 5 to 20 animals (Jarman and Coulson, 1989; Fig 1).

A. Interspecific Comparisons

Current theories about the adaptiveness of grouping in relation to a species' size, consequent metabolic demand, diet, dispersion of food items, and means of avoiding predation can be used to predict the relationships between these attributes that we might find in the macropods. In a greatly condensed form, these theories (e.g., Jarman, 1974) predict that species large enough to have a chance of escaping from a detected hunting predator and able to subsist on abundant food items that are therefore of relatively low quality (such as grass leaves) but require minimal searching time should readily form groups. In contrast, small species must be solitary in order to hide from predators, which they cannot outrun, and they cannot afford the competition that would arise from being in groups while seeking their rare, scattered, and individually valuable food items, which have to be of high nutritional value.

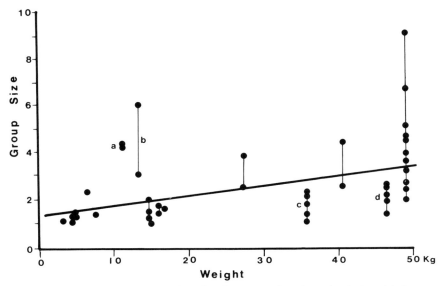

FIG. 1. Regression of mean group-size values for macropod species against body weight (average of male and female weights). The plotted regression is $y = 0.0407x + 1.366$, where y is group size and x is body weight. Values and regression from Jarman and Coulson (1989). a, Black-striped wallaby; b, whiptail wallaby; c, common wallaroo; and d, red kangaroo.

Enough is now known about macropods' diets for these to be compared with group size (Jarman, 1984; Norbury *et al.*, 1989). The potoroids and comparably small (<3 kg) macropodids feed on the most highly nutritious parts of plants and fungi: the leaf or flower buds, newly emerged leaves, fruits, seeds, and roots, tubers, rhizomes, or other storage organs. Most of these items need to be sought diligently; some grow underground and must be dug out. Many potoroids are specialists in finding fruiting bodies of hypogean (underground) fungi. All these small species most commonly forage solitarily. In contrast, all the species that can sustain themselves on plentiful, green but mature leaves of grasses are larger and have a propensity to forage in groups which, in a few species, may number 20 or 30 individuals and still be cohesive and coordinated. Species that feed on browse (i.e., leaves of dicotyledonous plants) or browse mixed with grasses, fruit, or fungi are of medium size and tend to forage either solitarily or in very small (<4 individuals) groups.

The regression of group size on body size is significant (Jarman and Coulson, 1989), despite much scatter about the line (Fig. 1). Some notable outliers are the burrowing bettong, some rock-wallabies, and the black-striped wallaby, which form social groups larger than their body size would predict, and the common wallaroo and red kangaroo, which form unexpectedly small groups for their large body sizes.

These exceptions illustrate some of the environmental variables that affect grouping. All rock wallaby species use natural rock cavities as daytime shelter, but the availability of suitable cavities is limited and groups of individuals share them. Black-striped wallabies shelter in the daytime in patches of particularly structured (usually quite dense) undergrowth in or adjacent to more open habitats. Each patch tends to be used by a group of black-striped wallabies. Thus, each of these species tends to form unexpectedly large groups because of the spatial distribution of their daytime sheltering resource, rather than because of a primary relationship between body size, metabolic rate, dietary requirements, the dispersion of appropriate food items, and avoidance of predators while feeding.

The smaller-than-expected group sizes shown by the common wallaroo and red kangaroo, on the other hand, may reflect the scattered dispersion of food items in their habitats, which are, respectively, boulder-strewn hillside and semi-arid or arid shrublands. The surprise here is to find such relatively large species feeding on such scattered items.

Macropod species, like other terrestrial mammalian herbivores, differ in their susceptibility to predation in part as a result of body size. Small species fall prey to a wider range of predators, including birds and reptiles, than large species. Large species, being faster, have a better chance of evading a detected predator than do small species. Thus, small species need to avoid detection by predators, while large species need to maximize their probability of detecting predators.

All the potoroids and smaller macropodids spend the daytime [when birds of prey such as wedge-tailed eagles (*Aquila audax*) are active] hidden either in nests or burrows (potoroids) or under cover of vegetation. Potoroids emerge from and return to their nests at dusk and dawn rather than at any critical thresholds of temperature or insolation, making it unlikely that nests are used primarily for thermoregulation, as has sometimes been suggested. For these species, the 24 hr are divided into contrasting periods of near-inactivity in a nest or squat during daylight, and of potential movement, foraging, and interaction outside the nest at night. Thus, use of nests or squats imposes temporal organization on the individual's daily activities.

By contrast, in the large, partly diurnally active, species which forage and rest in groups, individuals, at least in some situations, use the alertness of other group members to increase their average foraging time, and decrease their time spent alert (Southwell, 1981; Jarman, 1986). The daily schedule of activity seems relatively little affected by anti-predator considerations, but may be strongly affected by the need to seek shade when ambient temperature or radiant heat loads are high.

Macropod species vary in their sociality in relation to their size, the dispersion of their food items, and the ways in which they minimize their individual risk of predation in much the same way as the African bovids (Jarman, 1974, 1984; Norbury *et al.*, 1989). These aspects of sociality set a context for their social behavior and organization. However, further insight into their mechanisms of social organization come from looking at intraspecific variation in some aspects of sociality.

B.   INTRASPECIFIC VARIATION IN SOCIALITY

A quarter of a century ago, Caughley (1964) suggested that, since the processes of group formation appeared to involve random association and dissociation of individuals, macropod group sizes should reflect population density. This prediction has been amply fulfilled in the past 10 years by studies of some of the largest species. The group sizes found in populations of eastern and western gray kangaroos, red kangaroos, and common wallaroos correlate positively with their densities (Johnson, 1983; Southwell, 1984a,b; Jarman and Coulson, 1989). In the eastern gray kangaroo, group flux, the rate at which group composition changes as animals leave and join, rises with population density (Southwell, 1984b) and initial group size (Jarman and Coulson, 1989). These studies emphasize how readily groups change in this species, the only one for which such data have been published. In a moderately dense population, a group of 10 kangaroos had a 0.2 probability of changing composition in the next 3 min (Jarman and Coulson, 1989).

Habitat can have an intraspecific effect on grouping. Eastern and western gray kangaroo populations found in denser habitats and in more xeric habitats tend to form smaller groups than those in more mesic and more open habitats (Southwell, 1984a; Coulson and Raines, 1985; Heathcote, 1987; G. M. Coulson, unpublished data, in Jarman and Coulson, 1989).

In contrast to its response to population density and habitat, group size varies within a population rather little with season or time of day. Large samples (Southwell, 1981; Taylor, 1982; Jarman and Coulson, 1989; J. L. Clarke, personal communication) show that eastern gray kangaroo groups tend to be smaller at night than in the day. In summer, the group size of animals resting in the middle of the day may be affected by the size of the patches of shade available to them.

Eastern gray kangaroos tend to forage in smaller groups in winter than in spring or summer (Southwell, 1981; Taylor, 1982; Jarman and Coulson, 1989). The degree of synchrony of reproduction in the population affects this seasonal variation. Females of group-forming macropod species tend to isolate themselves when their joey is about to quit the pouch. If a high proportion of females reach that stage simultaneously, their tendency to be isolated will temporarily reduce the typical group size by lowering the number of animals available to form groups.

These examples show that an individual macropod's responses toward its

environment (and perhaps its own reproductive state) are expressed in its sociality. Moreover, they show that sociality varies with the situation. The tendency to form groups may have a genetic basis, but the size of those groups clearly
does not. This emphasizes the role that individual social behavior must play in
group formation and persistence.

IV.   BEHAVIORAL INTERACTIONS: FORM AND FUNCTION

A.   COMMUNICATION IN MACROPODS

The macropods' modes of communication are those to be expected for her-
bivorous mammals, with visual and olfactory signaling being more frequently
used than auditory or tactile.

Visual signals indicate gender and social status of males in heteromorphic
macropods, and aspects of intent in dyadic interaction in all species. Only in the
common wallaroo is coloration an obvious and invariable indicator of sex. In
other heteromorphic macropods, the subtle differences in coloring between the
sexes are insufficient for long-range signaling of gender in most light conditions.
Enlarged shoulders and forelimbs distinguish larger males, but younger males
and females may still be indistinguishable at a distance, as they are in all ages of
the homomorphic potoroids and small macropodids.

Males of the heteromorphic macropods use their enlarged forelimb girdles for
visual signaling (presumably of potential fighting ability) at moderate to long
range, adopting poses, reminiscent of human body-builders, which best display
their muscularity and size. They also visually display their height. The homomorphic species give no comparable signals.

At close range, both sexes in all species use postures and gestures to signal
intention to approach, attack, or retreat, and their consequential counterparts,
threat and submission. These visual signals are most obvious among males of the
largest heteromorphic species and have often gone unrecognized in females.
Postural signals of dominance and submission are used inter- and intrasexually by
both sexes of potoroids (e.g., brush-tailed bettongs; M. Lissowsky, personal
communication).

All macropod species have postures of alertness which, particularly when
adopted abruptly or exaggeratedly, communicate alertness or alarm to conspecifics and allospecifics that are in sight. Many species accompany these
postures with foot thumps and, in a few species, snorts or hisses (see Coulson,
1989).

The forms of their visual signals distinguish macropods from some radiations
of eutherian herbivores. For example, no macropod male gains distinct dimorphic coloring at puberty or the attainment of socially dominant status, as
occurs in several bovids [e.g., blackbuck (*Antilope cervicapra*) or sable antelope
(*Hippotragus niger*)]. Female reproductive state is never signaled by perineal

skin coloring and swelling as in many primates [e.g., chimpanzee (*Pan troglodytes*)]. Despite their upright, genital-exposing posture, no male macropod has a contrastingly colored scrotum as seen in some primates [e.g., vervet monkeys (*Cercopithecus aethiops*)]. Macropods lack any color contrasts forming a "tail flag," so common in bovids, cervids, and leporids. Indeed, their tails serve little signal function.

While they share the common postural/gestural importance of the relative positions and orientations of ears, head, and neck, macropods can subtly vary the conformation of the trunk (thorax plus abdomen) more than can bovids or cervids, being more similar in this respect to primates. Macropod visual signaling tends to emphasize the size, shape, and posture of the whole trunk and limbs. This may enable a macropod to indicate its gender and status, while doing something additional such as feeding, in a way that is denied to those cervids and bovids which signal with gestures or postures of the head and cranial weapons.

Macropods are generally fairly silent, certainly when compared with some other metatherians. Few of their vocalizations carry any great distance. However, vocalizations may be more important than we have hitherto supposed in mother–young communication.

Macropods communicate olfactorily using either secretions from dispersed skin glands on the throat, chest, and perhaps forearms (mainly the medium and large species of macropodids), or the products of paracloacal glands (seen most clearly in potoroids, but probably also used by macropodids), or the rich aroma produced by enurination (both families). Skin and paracloacal glands produce scents which can be deposited, usually but not only by males (Fig. 2a), and play a part in long-range signaling. Olfaction plays a strong role in short-range communication, being used to check individual status, reproductive condition, and identity (Russell, 1985; Coulson, 1989).

The small homomorphic species generally lack the few loud vocalizations and long-range visual signals of the medium-sized and large heteromorphic species. However, they deposit secretions from their paracloacal glands more obviously. The rufous hare-wallaby, one of the smallest macropodids, sometimes sprays urine onto vegetation during social encounters (G. Lundie-Jenkins, personal communication). These small species largely lack specifically masculine displays centered on male weaponry.

B. DYADIC INTERACTIONS

Compared with eutherian bovids, cervids, lagomorphs, or primates, macropods in the wild at first sight appear very noninteractive, rates of overt, obvious interactions being quite low. Despite a full repertoire of behavior patterns appropriate to dyadic interactions, even the most social macropods devote little time to overt interacting. However, "covert" interactions are almost continuous,

a

bi   **ii**

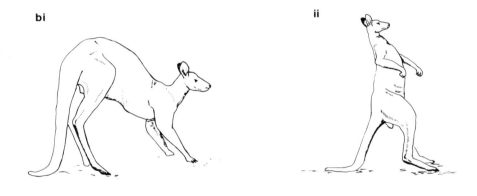

FIG. 2. Scent-marking, displays, and fighting in large kangaroo males. (a) Eastern gray kangaroo male rubbing secretions from skin glands on his chest onto a tree. Note his erect, S-shaped penis. (b) Eastern gray kangaroo male displaying to another male (not shown) (i) in the stiff-legged walk, and (ii) standing very tall. Both postures emphasize the actor's length of legs, and the second displays his height; these equate with his "reach" when fighting. (c) Eastern gray kangaroo males in the early stages of a fight (or when sparring), wrestling with their forelimbs. They are standing on the toes of their hind feet, and their heads are thrown back, protecting their eyes. (d) Red kangaroo males in a fully escalated fight. In each picture the male on the left is delivering a strong kick to his opponent's belly. In i the opponent was himself starting to kick and, in such a position, is easily unbalanced. In ii the opponent holds off the kicker with extended forelimbs.

c

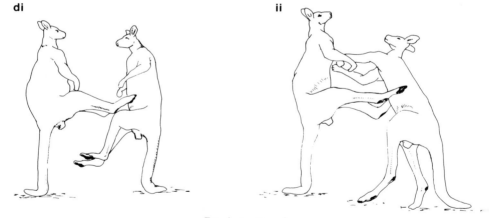

FIG. 2. (*continued*)

determining relative positions, spacing, and interindividual separations within groups. Macropod social systems are not based on territoriality or the permanent exclusion of some classes from groups, so they lack interactions that drive away individuals. Such interactions form an extremely obvious part of the repertoire of many eutherian herbivores.

C.   MOTHER–YOUNG INTERACTIONS

In macropods, mother and young can interact during stages in the young one's development that are not matched in eutheria, namely, the brief perinatal stage, the phases when the infant is permanently attached to a teat, when it is detached from the teat and getting into and out of the pouch, and when it is finally being denied reentry to the pouch. After this last stage, the infant returns to suck but is no longer carried by its mother.

Interactions between mother and young macropod at birth are simple. The mother adopts a birth posture, licks a strip of fur between her cloaca and her pouch, and keeps still. The infant when born struggles free of the enclosing membranes, then uses its well-developed forelimbs and paws, which are capable of grasping, to haul itself up through the damp fur to the pouch opening and into the pouch without direct help from the mother. There it finds a teat and fastens its mouth around it. The mother ingests the very small quantity of birth membranes and fluids.

While the infant is permanently attached to the teat, the mother's interactions with it are limited to cleaning the pouch and ingesting the joey's urine and feces. It is not known whether she grooms the joey itself. Interactions become more complex once the infant detaches itself from the teat and first begins to put its head out of the pouch and then leaves the pouch for the first time. Mother and joey then interact in three ways: through her cleaning the pouch and grooming the joey, through her controlling the joey's exits from the pouch, and through behavior that ensures the joey's return to the pouch.

While the mother will put her muzzle into her pouch to groom or clean feces and urine from the joey (which will defecate and urinate in response to grooming around the cloaca), she grooms most intensely those parts that protrude from the pouch, as well as the whole joey when it emerges.

The mother appears to control emergence, allowing it, especially at first, only when and where she can assure safety. Thus the female eastern gray kangaroo first allows the joey to emerge when she has been able to survey the surroundings thoroughly and when other kangaroos are not moving close to her (Stuart-Dick, 1987). The mother nuzzles and grooms the joey, discourages its movements away, and quite soon encourages it back into the pouch. Similarly, the rufous bettong joey first emerges in the nest in the daytime, typically while the mother is grooming it (personal observation). She relaxes the pouch opening and the joey gradually slides or rolls out as she grooms. Like the eastern gray kangaroos, the rufous bettong joey may be groomed intensely while it is out but is soon encouraged to return to the pouch.

These two examples, which lie at the extremes of macropod sociality, are interestingly different. The eastern gray kangaroo mother chooses the circumstances for emergence of her joey with care, minimizing the chances of disturbance by either kangaroos or predators. Living a mobile existence in habitat in which she can move freely and see well (but be seen well too) makes this both necessary and possible; she neither needs nor regularly uses particularly structured cover. The bettong mother, although restricted in the daytime to its nest, does not have to make any further choices about when and in what circumstances to release the joey from the pouch.

The growing joey leaves the pouch more often and for longer bouts, interacting with its mother more actively. It is suckled and groomed and sometimes grooms in return, explores, and plays with its mother (but usually not other kangaroos). When out of the pouch, the joey may spend time with its head back in the pouch; although it may then be sucking and may withdraw its head with the elongated teat in its mouth, it can also simply stand with its head in the pouch.

Return to the pouch requires cooperation. The mother must adopt the right posture (belly clear of the ground, for example) and must tense the pouch muscles sufficiently to form a rim over which the joey can somersault, but not so contracted as to close the pouch opening. The joey must be willing to enter, which it shows by first putting its head into the pouch. It then pulls back against the lower rim of the opening with its forepaws, pushes off from the ground with the hindfeet, and does a head-first, forward roll into the pouch. It is not lifted into the pouch by the mother.

The gray kangaroo pouch-infant must stand in front of its mother, facing toward her, to reenter the pouch. Stuart-Dick (1987) has described how the mother gradually trains the infant to reenter quickly. From the earliest movements of the joey away from the mother, she gives a soft, clucking vocalization as the joey returns to her and, standing crouched, leans forward slightly, and may hold her arms apart, to facilitate the infant's finding and reentering the pouch. The pair may repeat a sequence of exits from and reentries to the pouch, especially as the joey starts to explore. After descending from the pouch, the joey moves away from the mother's front, around her, and, as she vocalizes, back to stand in front of her and somersault into the pouch as she leans forward. As the joey grows, these excursions increase in length and duration and they become interrupted by autogrooming and playing with the mother.

Rufous bettong joeys interact with the mother very similarly, even though they are confined in their movements by the nest. They emerge from the pouch and clamber over and around the mother. However, the joey is not assiduously trained to return to the pouch; before she leaves the nest at dusk to feed, the mother crouches, raising her back as high as possible, and the joey scrambles back into the pouch.

Compared with the eastern gray kangaroo, the rufous bettong joey spends a far higher proportion of its time when out of the pouch playing with the mother (who, being in the nest, is neither feeding nor surveying the surroundings), nibbling her ears or tail-tip, and attempting to climb onto her back or over her. This clambering is generally focused on the mother's neck and shoulders, as it is in eastern gray kangaroos (although they tend to wrestle with the mother's head more). No macropod carries its young on its back, but this facet of play strongly resembles climbing and clinging of young phalangerids, koalas, and some dasyurids. It is well tolerated by the mother.

The interactions of eastern gray kangaroo and rufous bettong mothers and pouch-infants differ in that the young eastern gray kangaroo will rest out of the pouch or move with the mother while she feeds from quite an early stage; the rufous bettong joey leaves the pouch only in the daylight hours when both are in the nest. It reenters the pouch before the mother leaves the nest at dusk to start feeding. Thus, until the start of the next (young-at-foot) phase of its development, the rufous bettong young has no experience of following its mother in the open, while the eastern gray kangaroo young becomes adept at following and returning to its mother and reentering her pouch very rapidly in an emergency. The rufous bettong young need never do that.

The juvenile changes from a pouch-infant to a young-at-foot when it is permanently excluded from the pouch. Yet it continues to need to suck. This denial of reentry while giving it access to a teat seems to test the mother–young relationship in eastern gray kangaroos. The young one may try to reenter, but finds itself rebuffed by its mother if it inserts more than its muzzle. She stops calling it to her and never adopts the reentry-invitation posture. Stuart-Dick (1987) has argued that the risk that the juvenile, on being repelled by its mother, might follow other kangaroos and get lost explains the tendency of females at this stage to isolate themselves from other adult kangaroos.

Traumatic as the change may be, within a few days the young-at-foot stops attempting to reenter the pouch and settles to a new relationship with its mother, grazing for itself but still returning to suck several times a day. It stays close to its mother and coordinates its activities with hers, but it also begins to interact with other conspecifics. For eastern gray kangaroos this is a long-lasting phase, in which male and female offspring differ slightly in their interactions with their mothers. Mothers more actively maintain association with daughters than sons through allogrooming (Stuart-Dick and Higginbottom, 1989).

Macropod species differ strongly in the form of mother–young relationships during this young-at-foot stage. Juveniles of several species of medium-sized macropodid species, exemplified by the red-necked wallaby (Johnson, 1987a), tammar wallaby (in captivity; Russell, 1989), swamp wallaby, and red-necked pademelon (personal observation), spend most of their time apart from their mothers for at least the first few days after permanent emergence from the pouch. The mother leaves the juvenile "lying out" where it is concealed from aerial predators and usually remote from conspecifics. The two reunite when the mother returns to the young's hiding place, which she does a few times daily to suckle it. The young-at-foot may emerge and approach her. Mother and young appear to confirm each others' identities olfactorily, usually with nasonasal contact. After a long suckling bout the young-at-foot may play with the mother much as do eastern gray kangaroos (Johnson, 1987a) before the mother again leaves it.

The phase of pouch-life during which the young rufous bettong can enter and leave the pouch (i.e., from first exit to last reentry) lasts for only a few days and nearly all exits and reentries occur within the nest (personal observation). Then the female leaves the nest at dusk (in captivity the young may occasionally emerge first) with the young very close behind. Whenever she stops, the young stops and sits on her tail or touching her rump-to-rump. It follows closely while she forages and returns to the nest with her. Occasionally, both in captivity and in the wild, the young is left in the nest while the mother forages.

Young brush-tailed bettongs pass through three developmental phases after permanently leaving the pouch. At first they leave and reenter the nest with the mother, whom they follow as closely as do rufous bettongs. Then, over the next few nights, the young-at-foot leaves the nest with its mother but returns by itself. Eventually it leaves and returns to the nest by itself, although still associating closely with the foraging mother (M. Lissowsky, personal communication). In the wild its opportunities for interaction with conspecifics are limited, and in captivity interactive play is rare.

These styles of changing to become young-at-foot differentiate the macropods into three categories: (1) open-country, large species having the equivalent of ungulate "follower" young which continue to associate, move, and interact playfully with the mother from the time of permanent emergence; (2) medium-sized species occupying more closed habitat which, for the first few days, leave the young-at-foot "lying out," visiting it rarely to suckle it; (3) the small pot-oroids in which the infant is denied reentry to the pouch when it first leaves the nest, yet remains closely associated with the mother.

D. FEMALE–FEMALE INTERACTIONS

Among macropod species female–female interactions become increasingly aggressive with decreasing body size (and sociality). Females of some medium-sized and small macropodids and potoroids may interact agonistically rapidly and violently; indeed, in captivity female potoroids occasionally kill each other. Females of the small, asocial species converge with males in their degree and form of aggressiveness. In potoroids, the sexes share the same limited repertoire of agonistic displays and aggressive acts. In contrast, females of the large, social macropods, although capable of most of the males' rich repertoire of agonistic displays, typically do not use it, confining their agonistic interactions to noncontact "threat-stares" and "nose-jabs." These are backed up on rare occasions with physical contact, but this is likely to be no more than a push with the forepaws.

Females of all macropod species have discernible postures of dominance and submission, which are particularly vivid in the potoroids. Ganslosser (1989) and

Coulson (1989) review the repertoires and contexts for female–female agonistic interactions.

Adult female macropods spend little time allogrooming, although it is known in most species (Coulson, 1989). The antilopine wallaroo and black-striped wallaby (Croft, 1982; Heathcote, 1989), both social species, are exceptions. Allogrooming has not yet been shown to play any important part in female social organization.

The most important consequences of interactions between females are simply whether they aggregate and coordinate their activities, or whether they separate, on meeting. Their "decision" follows visual or olfactory inspection, and only rarely, in the larger species, are any further interactions evident. Those that do aggregate continue to make decisions about their relative spacing and position within the group, transmitting and receiving signals about levels of agonistic intent through postures and gestures which are often too subtle to be noticed by casual observers. Yet, it is this exchange of information about the individual female's responses to the closeness, behavior, and perhaps identity of her neighbors in the group which is the behavioral foundation for group-living in the social macropods.

E. Male–Male Interactions

Adult male macropods interact with other males, actively and overtly, with three major consequences: they achieve spacing within groups, they obtain knowledge about identity and (hierarchical) status, and they determine access to a female in or approaching estrus or, rarely, to another resource. Adult males do not usually play, unlike subadult male peers in social species.

Males obtain information about each other visually and olfactorily. In the heteromorphic species, persistent growth and specific development of the forelimbs and shoulders indicate a male's fighting potential (Jarman, 1989a). Males in such species have several displays which reveal their size and forelimb development. These include standing or walking with the limbs stretched to their maximum (Fig. 2bi), standing upright on the hindlegs or rearing up on the tips of the hind feet and the tail (Fig. 2bii), and holding the arms stiffly across the chest, down the side, or up in the air (Coulson, 1989; Ganslosser, 1989).

Such displays are combined into sequences whose fullness depends to some extent on the interactors' ages. Young males are less likely to use stiff-legged walking and tall-standing displays. They are also most unlikely to use any of the behavior patterns by which large males spread scent from their chests onto objects, such as logs or tussocks of grass; this includes so-called grass-pulling displays.

Some medium-sized and large heteromorphic species also have submissive postures, notably a low crouch; eastern gray kangaroos also give a submissive vocalization, one of the few loud vocalizations given by this species (personal observation). At close range, males of this species may also give a threatening growl.

The potoroids and small, homomorphic macropodids lack this full array of agonistic displays (Coulson, 1989; Ganslosser, 1989). In particular, they do not give any of the displays that reveal height, or length, or muscular development of forelimbs. Two male potoroids that meet do not progress through an extensive sequence of displays which allow mutual assessment of fighting ability or weaponry; instead, they have a small range of threat gestures (which may include growling), each of which may develop directly into an attack, but they seem to lack the preattack displays of the heteromorphic macropodids.

A macropod male's weapons are his teeth and his fore- and hind-feet. He lacks cranial weapons akin to horns or antlers and exaggerated teeth akin to canine or incisor tusks. Species differ in the ways in which they bring these weapons to bear on their opponent. Potoroids and the smallest macropodids fight by wrestling, biting, and attempting to kick with the hindfeet by jumping at, onto, or over the opponent, who defends himself by lying on his side or back (Fig. 3b), kicking out with his hind-feet. Forefeet are used to ward off attack and to grapple. The tail plays no part.

Medium-sized and large macropodids do not usually lie down and kick in a fight; indeed, opponents attempt to keep upright, trying to avoid being thrown to the ground by the wrestling (Fig. 2c) or kicks (Fig. 2d) of the other. Tree-kangaroos (*Dendrolagus* species) kick little, but use their powerful forelimbs for wrestling (Ganslosser, 1989). Only the largest *Macropus* species are able to use the stiffened tail as a prop, leaning back on it to deliver two-footed kicks. They accompany this by using the forelimbs to hold off an opponent, rather than to draw the opponent close enough to be bitten.

The predictability of sequences of behavioral acts during fighting in macropod species increases with body size. Actions in potoroid fights are rather unpredictable; they wrestle, scratch, and bite without predictable sequence or reciprocity. At the other extreme, gray or red kangaroo fights look slower and more predictable because these males trade relatively few but potentially highly damaging blows, rather than inflicting a myriad of small bites and scratches. A male of these large species orients himself carefully in relation to his opponent before delivering a kick, and similarly aligns himself to receive the retaliatory kick; rarely do the opponents kick simultaneously.

The predictable sequences and reciprocity of behavioral acts in the fighting of the large species, which has been called "ritualized" in contrast to the "non-ritualized" fighting of the potoroids, arises easily from an escalation of sparring; indeed, I see no break in the continuum between the two. But, very occasionally, "in situations which tend to be highly competitive" (Ganslosser, 1989), such as in the presence of an estrous female, or when a male eastern gray kangaroo tries to supplant the most dominant male in the population (personal observation), such males will fight in an utterly violent, "nonritualized" fashion, without carefully reciprocated blows. They may wrestle each other to the ground, jump on a felled opponent, and pursue it vigorously if it flees, striking at it with fore- and hindfeet. Such observations make the derived nature of the "ritualized" fighting of larger macropodid species very obvious.

F. MALE–FEMALE INTERACTIONS

Interactions between male and female macropods almost always concern reproduction, and involve the male checking the female's estrous status, attempting to be her close consort, or directly courting or mating with her. The female either complies with or rejects this behavior. Only rarely do male and female macropods interact in nonsexual ways, such as by allogrooming.

To check a female's estrous status, a male attempts to smell her general body odor, or her pouch, cloaca, or urine; he may also taste her urine. For a male to smell her pouch area or cloaca, a macropodid female must cooperate by letting him approach closely and by standing crouched (exposing the cloaca) or upright (exposing the pouch). If she is lying when he approaches, he may force her to her feet to gain such access. Females of several species of macropodids respond to the male's sniffing or nuzzling at the cloaca by urinating. He will catch some of the urine in his mouth and display flehmen (Coulson and Croft, 1981; personal observation).

Females of large, heteromorphic species do not oppose inspection by males larger than themselves (which means most of the adult males), although they will move away from males and leave a group if continually disturbed by inspecting males. However, females of some medium-sized species, such as swamp wallaby and brush-tailed rock wallaby, grow to be larger than the smaller adult males in the population and will usually physically fend off importunate small males with threats and pushes with the forepaws.

Potoroid females take this a step further and show full-blown aggression to any male trying to inspect them. The female is as big as the male and there is no great difference in their muscularity or claws (Jarman, 1989a). The sexes share the repertoire of agonistic displays and actions. Thus, a male trying to inspect a female is faced by an animal quite capable of injuring him. A female rufous bettong, for example, when approached by a male, throws herself down on her side or back, with her belly toward him, and growls (Fig. 3). If he continues to approach, she may lash out at his head with her poised hind feet. The male approaches her diagonally, "drumming" (Coulson, 1989) with his leading foot. The male's preparedness to push home his dangerous inspection increases as the female enters the last week before estrus (personal observation). I have not seen urine-tasting in this species. Females are intolerant of prolonged inspection.

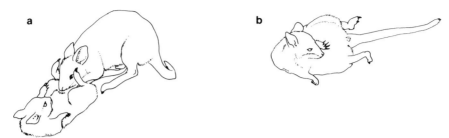

FIG. 3. Postures of rufous bettongs. (a) A male cautiously sniffs the pouch opening of a cooperating but still potentially aggressive female. (b) The defensive posture, used by both sexes; the aggressor would be to the right of the picture.

However, a male may avoid some of the dangers of attack by sniffing the nest occupied by a female, or a female while she is still in her nest. In the latter case, he will still be received with growls, but the female may be less able to ward him off. However, potoroos lack both the foot-drumming display of the male and the kicking of the female (J. H. Seebeck, quoted in Coulson, 1989); however, females of the small macropodid rufous hare-wallaby do lie down and kick at males (G. Lundie-Jenkins, personal communication).

To consort closely with a female, a male must displace any closer males and move with and be accepted by the female. Consorting usually starts a week or so before her estrus. A female rufous bettong is normally intolerant of a male close to her and, early in his consorting, the male follows behind the female, being growled at or even attacked. As her estrus approaches, he spends more time alongside her (Fig. 4). In heteromorphic macropodids, large males can approach a female at any time and can to some extent dictate her movements. Thus, a large male eastern gray kangaroo will move in front of a female and block her path. As a consorting male, he is as likely to feed in front of her as beside or behind her, and may position himself between her and other males. During consorting he reconfirms her estrous status by repeated inspections.

Keeping other males away from a female involves the male–male agonism described above. However, large males of some heteromorphic species also scent-mark females. This is done by rock-wallabies (W. Davies, quoted in Rus sell, 1985) and eastern gray kangaroos (personal observation), and may yet be detected in other species. Male potoroos and rock-wallabies have been recorded urinating on females (J. H. Seebeck and A. B. Horsup, quoted in Coulson, 1989).

Direct courtship is similar throughout the macropods. In almost all species the male approaches the female from behind and scratches or pulls at the female's tail, rump, or flanks with both forepaws. She may either move forward, turn and threaten the male, or stand still. If she does the last, he moves forward, strad-

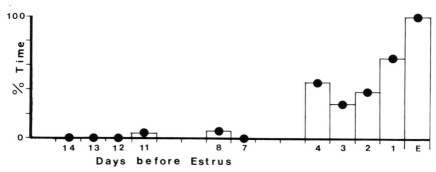

FIG. 4. The proportion of time spent by a male rufous bettong within 1 m of a female, during the first hour after emergence from the nest at dusk, in the 2 weeks leading up to estrus and on the night of estrus (E). Data from animals in captivity in large pens (P. J. Jarman, unpublished data).

dling her rump with his hind legs and clasping her around the abdomen while thrusting. Intromission generally lasts less than a minute (but is sometimes prolonged) and, in the larger species, the male may lift the female off the ground or dance from foot to foot as ejaculation approaches. In rufous bettongs the female may, immediately after ejaculation, swing around, dislodging the male, and drive him away. In the heteromorphic species, male and female may continue to consort after copulation and will sometimes mate a few more times.

V. SOCIAL ORGANIZATION

A. DISPERSAL

Individual macropods occupy home ranges which are, in the short term, stable and spatially well defined. The red kangaroo, once described as characteristically nomadic (Bailey, 1971), has more recently been shown to occupy small stable ranges, except during drought or after patchy drought-breaking rain, when it is temporarily nomadic (Denny, 1985). Individuals of other macropod species relocate their home ranges, i.e., disperse only a very few times, if at all, in their lives.

Johnson (1989), reviewing dispersal in macropods, follows Greenwood (1980) in recognizing natal dispersal as the movement of an individual between its places of birth and breeding, and breeding dispersal as movement between one breeding attempt and another. Individuals that do not show natal dispersal are called philopatric. Of the eight species discussed by Johnson (1989), natal dispersal appeared negligible in the tammar wallaby and quokka, occurred in both sexes in the long-nosed potoroo, and occurred predominantly in males in the brush-tailed bettong, red-necked wallaby, eastern gray kangaroo, whiptail wallaby, and red kangaroo. Natal dispersal was male-biased in the brush-tailed rock-wallaby. Johnson (1989) reported breeding dispersal among some males of the long-nosed potoroo, and both male and female tammar wallabies and red kangaroos. The tammars and red kangaroos shifted home range after fire and during drought; another study of tammars found no shifts in range (Johnson, 1989).

Most macropods are sedentary as adults, and subadult males are more likely to disperse than females. At some stage after weaning, generally between the ages of 2 and 4 years, a young red-necked wallaby or eastern gray kangaroo male expands his range for a few weeks or months, exploring new country before settling to a new, normally sized, home range. Male eastern gray kangaroos may repeat this process as adults, sometimes late enough to have had a chance to mate (personal observation). However, most macropod males disperse and establish a home range before breeding and then remain in the same place throughout their breeding life.

Females of most species also settle, before first breeding, in a life-long range. However, except for the long-nosed potoroo, they settle in a range which is likely to be contiguous with that of their mother, in contrast to the patrifugous males. Although female red-necked wallabies and eastern gray kangaroos are usually patricolous (philopatric), more female wallabies disperse as subadults than do kangaroos (Stuart-Dick and Higginbottom, 1989). An eastern gray kangaroo female may share her home range with more of her daughters than does a red-necked wallaby, which may be important for the relative sociality of the two species.

Male-biased natal dispersal of macropods does not arise from the aggressive behavior of larger males (Johnson, 1989). We do not know what proximate factors trigger the exploration, range expansion, and final adoption of a new range by the young male. The consequence is to enhance the probability of outbreeding.

B.   HOME-RANGE SIZE AND OVERLAP

Sizes of home ranges vary greatly among macropod species and seem influenced by habitat and the dispersion of resources as well as the species' body size. Long-nosed potoroos have ranges of 5 to 20 ha in open woodland (Kitchener, 1973) but only 1.4 to 2.0 ha in dense forest (Bennett, 1987a; Seebeck and Rose, 1989). Other potoroids of open woodland or pasture, such as rufous and brush-tailed bettongs, have ranges of 20 to 35 ha (Christensen, 1980; Schlager, 1981).

The macropodids of dense forest, such as pademelon species, have ranges of 10 ha or less (Johnson, 1977), while those of open country, such as eastern gray kangaroos, range over a few square kilometers (Jarman and Taylor, 1983). M. J. S. Denny (in Lavery, 1985) reported red kangaroos using ranges of 200 km^2, although when sedentary their ranges are far smaller (Oliver, 1986). Home-range sizes of red-necked wallabies (Johnson, 1987b) and eastern gray kangaroos (personal observation) are larger in winter than summer, responding to changes in resource availability.

Males usually have larger ranges than females (Croft, 1989), and in most species a male's range overlaps those of several females. A female's range usually overlaps with those of at least a few, and sometimes many, other females. Exceptions are the long-nosed potoroo, in which females may have exclusive ranges (Seebeck and Rose, 1989), and the long-footed potoroo, in which monogamous pairs occupy nonoverlapping home ranges (Scotts and Seebeck, 1988). In all other species, solitariness must result from active avoidance of other females. Similarly, in no species does the sharing of a common range mean that females are inevitably found together in groups, although the number of females whose ranges overlap will set an upper limit to the size of group they can form.

With the exception of the long-nosed and long-footed potoroos, a male macropod's range overlaps those of other males. Some males of a few species defend part of their range against other males. Male brush-tailed bettongs defend a nesting, but not a feeding, area (Sampson, 1971; Christensen, 1980), and larger male brush-tailed rock-wallabies drive smaller males from areas containing refuges occupied by females (Batchelor, 1980).

Subordinate males of other macropods are not completely excluded from any areas, despite strong dominance hierarchies. Thus males, like females, of most macropod species share their ranges with a number of other males. Both sexes therefore have a social environment which is molded more by population density and home-range size than by spatial exclusion.

Home-range size affects the number of conspecifics with which an individual interacts. Males usually have larger ranges then females, even in homomorphic species, suggesting that males expand their range, beyond that needed for food and shelter, to gain access to more females. Large male red-necked pademelons use larger nocturnal feeding ranges than do smaller males (Johnson, 1980), thereby improving their chances of contacting females at night. Home-range area increases with body size in male red-necked wallabies (Johnson, 1987b) and eastern gray kangaroos (personal observation), the largest adult males in the population ranging over twice the area used by the smallest ones, whose ranges are similar to those of females.

Large males may move further than smaller males or females. Clarke et al. (1989) recorded one large male eastern gray kangaroo traveling 5.6 km through his range in 24 hr; females and smaller males typically moved about 1 km a day. In his travels the large male contacted most of the females within his range.

C. DISTRIBUTION OF SOCIAL CATEGORIES

Despite lack of territoriality in most macropod species, a few studies have shown that social categories are not equally likely to be found in any one habitat or place. Females with young about to quit the pouch most commonly differ from the norm in habitat choice. Females of several of the larger species isolate themselves at this stage, often in less preferred habitat; red-necked wallabies prefer to be close to the edges of dense cover (Johnson, 1987b) but eastern gray kangaroos avoid both cover and highly preferred feeding areas (Stuart-Dick, 1987; personal communication).

Red kangaroo females are likely to enter estrus soon after the young quits the pouch. Johnson and Bayliss (1981) used this fact to explain the partial separation of such females which, accompanied by large males, preferred one habitat, from the rest of the population, which occupied other habitats.

Classes of males may differ in their locations without the immediate presence of near-estrous females. Medium-sized red-necked wallaby males tended to avoid the areas occupied by high densities of females and large males (Johnson, 1987b). Medium-sized eastern gray kangaroo males, in contrast, were more likely to be found where females were most concentrated (Jarman and Southwell, 1986). Smaller brush-tailed rock-wallaby males were less likely to occur on cliffs occupied by large males (K. P. Joblin, personal communication).

However, these separations of social categories are only partial: smaller males in these species are not totally excluded by the presence or aggression of larger males. No classes of juveniles are excluded from any areas or habitats. The macropods are, on the whole, far less strongly organized by the differential distribution of social categories than are many ungulates.

D.   COMPOSITION OF, AND ORGANIZATION WITHIN, GROUPS

If the outcome of interactive behavior leads individuals of specific social categories to associate with or avoid individuals of the same or other categories, then the society becomes organized. An unorganized society would arise if the social categories of the interactants had no effect on the outcome of their interactions.

Organization can be discerned, without necessarily watching many interactions, by the extent of two phenomena: the nonrandom composition of groups (i.e., the extent to which social categories associate with each other within groups or avoid being members of the same group), or the nonrandom location of social categories relative to each other within a group. A caveat must be added. Compositional organization may be influenced by social categories being kept apart by differing resource requirements. Spatial organization within groups is less strongly influenced by this. Both phenomena have recently been explored in macropod species.

A species may be relatively asocial yet still display compositional organization when it does form groups of two or more. The long-footed potoroo, the only macropod reported to be monogamous and territorial (Scotts and Seebeck, 1988), is so poorly known in the wild that we do not know whether it habitually forages solitarily or in pairs. The other potoroids (except the burrowing bettong or boodie) are primarily solitary, but may all be seen at times in twos or threes. The groups of two in the rufous bettong rarely consist of a mother and young-at-foot (Seebeck *et al.*, 1989), because the young-at-foot stage lasts only 3 or 4 weeks, and the young may be left alone in a nest for part of the night. Young-at-foot grow very fast and may not be recognized in the field as unweaned young (I. Wallis, personal communication). Those considerations apart, in field populations of rufous bettongs 13% (Southgate, 1980) to over 50% (J. L. Clarke, personal communication; A. Dennis, personal communication) of sightings were of pairs of animals, and A. Dennis (personal communication, supported by I. Wallis, personal communication) feels that many of these were persistent male–female pairs.

The burrowing bettong in captivity carries persistent association a stage further. A male escorts a group of females and defends them against other males. In the wild this bettong lives in communal warrens of up to 40 animals (Seebeck *et al.*, 1989), which appears to include several males. Organization and composition of their groups in the wild remain unknown.

The smallest macropodids are also poorly known in the wild. The hare-wallabies and bridled nailtail wallaby, all of which shelter in the day in squats, almost always do so solitarily (except for females with young-at-foot), but may loosely aggregate on rich patches of food when foraging at night. Pairs are most commonly formed by a mother with dependent young or a male consorting with a female (bridled nailtail wallaby; P. Tierney, in Lavery, 1985).

Pairings of these sorts are the basic social units in all the medium-sized macropods in which groups form and even in such large species as red kangaroos (Russell, 1979) and common wallaroos (Croft, 1981a). However, groups containing more than one adult of the same sex become increasingly common with increasing size of macropodid species. These may arise simply from the animals' tendency to aggregate and form cohesive, interacting groups, but nonrandomness in their composition implies that some social categories respond to the presence of other categories in the group.

A widespread nonrandomness in group composition in medium-sized and large macropods is the tendency for the largest males to be seen alone and, thus, to be underrepresented in larger groups. This has been observed in red-necked wallabies (Johnson, 1985), whiptail wallabies (Kaufmann, 1974b), antilopine wallaroos (Croft, 1987), common wallaroos, (Croft, 1981a; Taylor, 1981), red kangaroos (Russell, 1979; Croft, 1981b; Johnson and Bayliss, 1981), and eastern gray kangaroos (Jarman and Southwell, 1986; Taylor, 1981; Heathcote, 1987). Unlike the solitariness of females, which shun conspecifics when their young are about to quit the pouch, this appears not to be avoidance of conspecifics but rather to arise because these large males spend much time moving between groups, checking females. This is discussed below (Section V,E).

The eastern gray kangaroo population studied by Jarman and Southwell (1986) exemplifies compositional organization in these species. Males, including the largest males when they are not solitary, tend to be with other males. Although there were enough males in the studied population for at least one male to have been with each group which contained females, 40% of females had no male with them. The number of males in a female-containing group, when any male was present, averaged 3.1; had males been randomly allocated to groups there would have been 2.2 males present. Significantly, too many female groups lacked males, while others contained unexpectedly large numbers of males. As in other gregarious *Macropus* species, males may form groups without females (e.g., Johnson, 1983). Clearly, males both congregate with other males and are commonly attracted to certain females.

Reproductive categories of females differed little in their tendency to be alone, with other females but no male, or with males, except for females with young-at-foot, which were more often alone or without males than were the others. When in groups, females with no young, or with small pouch-young, or young-at-foot showed a weak tendency to associate with others of their category; females with large pouch-young avoided their own category.

Female categories did not differ in the number or mix of social categories of males accompanying them, except for females in or approaching estrus. Such females had more males with them than had other females, and more of these males were medium or large rather than small. These females were also rarely alone, and were strikingly often the only female in the group with the males (in 31% of sightings compared with 4% for most other females). In this study, estrous females were usually of the category with small pouch-young. Yet, males did not treat that whole category particularly differently from other categories of females, reflecting the small proportion of her time for which a female is in estrus.

The male categories used in this analysis are based on size and development, which also indicate a male's probable position in the hierarchy (see later). Large males, which tend to be alone, were underrepresented in groups with females. Irrespective of their category, and whether there was one or more of them, males accompanied almost identical mixes of female categories. These differed from the structure of the whole female population in containing fewer females with young-at-foot (because they isolated themselves, avoiding conspecifics) and more females with small pouch-young (the category most likely to enter estrus).

The study population usually contained, at any one time, one large male who was dominant over all others. He was more often alone or with females with small or medium-sized pouch-young than were other large males, and less often the only male with females without young. The dominant male's association with, or dissociation from, female categories departed further from random expectation than did those of other males.

Although this summary has emphasized the differences between categories, the outstanding feature of the analysis is that categories differed rather little in the composition of the groups in which they occurred. The extra solitariness of females with young-at-foot was not absolute, and the presence of an estrous female made only a small, although significant, difference to the average number and mixture of categories of the males in her group. The most dominant male merely exaggerated general trends among males toward association with female categories, although his tendency to be alone was distinctly greater than that of other large males. Thus, compositional organization is relatively lightly imposed by social behavior. Even in this highly social species of macropod, behavior of individuals or categories toward each other does not necessarily exclude any categories from participating in groups.

Spatial relationships of social categories within groups of macropods may further demonstrate social organization. Categories of eastern gray kangaroos appear to select their nearest neighbors nonrandomly (Table II). Females with young-at-foot and their young-at-foot are so consistently nearest neighbors that both categories rarely have any other as nearest neighbor. Subadults select either other subadults or females (other than those with young-at-foot) as nearest neighbors, and avoid all adult male categories. Females with medium-sized or large pouch-young avoid or are avoided by large and medium-sized males, but associ-

TABLE II

THE TENDENCIES OF SOCIAL CATEGORIES OF EASTERN GRAY KANGAROOS TO BE NEAREST NEIGHBORS IN GROUPS, EXPRESSED AS PROBABILITY VALUES FOR THE SIGNIFICANCE (FROM CHI-SQUARED TESTS) OF THEIR ASSOCIATION (+) OR DISSOCIATION (−)[a]

| | Nearest neighbors | | | | | | | |
	LM	MM	SM	FSY	FLY	FYF	SA	YAF
LM	=	+++	---	+++	---	=	---	---
MM		++	=	++	---	--	--	---
SM			+++	++	++	---	--	---
FSY				=	=	---	+++	---
FLY					+++	---	+++	---
FYF						---	---	+++
SA							+++	--
YAF								---

[a]Significant departures from random association are represented by one symbol if $p < .05$, two if $p < .01$, and three if $p < .001$; = indicates that the association is random. The social categories are LM, large adult males; MM, medium adult males; SM, small adult males; FSY, adult females with no or small pouch-young; FLY, females with medium-sized or large pouch-young; FYF, females with young-at-foot; SA, subadult; and YAF, young-at-foot. Data from P. J. Jarman, unpublished.

ate with small males and subadults. Females with no or small pouch-young, the category most likely to enter estrus, associate with all categories of males and subadults. Small adult males associate with their own category and avoid large males. Medium-sized males associate with their own category and large males; large males neither associate with nor avoid each other.

The mean separation between nearest neighbors in most class dyads of eastern gray kangaroos (Table III) tends to be between 6 and 9 m. Young-at-foot are closer to neighbors than are other classes because they are habitually very close (mean of 3 m) to their mothers and only rarely will any other animal be a nearer neighbor. Subadults also tend to be close (4 to 6 m) to their nearest neighbors. Females with no or small pouch-young were, on average, quite close to whichever class was their nearest neighbor. Males, especially large males, kept moderately separated as neighbors. Despite these trends for social categories to show minor differences in their separation, as nearest neighbors, from other categories, such data leave a strong impression of a kangaroo group consisting of rather evenly spaced individuals. Category-specific interactions, with a few exceptions, do not strongly influence spatial organization within groups.

Eastern gray kangaroos also show spatial organization within groups in the orientation of group members toward each other, both when they are nearest neighbors and when separated by other animals. As might be expected, young-at-foot and their mothers orient significantly nonrandomly in relation to each other. When nearest neighbors, medium-sized and small males and females with no or small pouch-young orient strongly nonrandomly with their own category. The only category toward which large males showed nonrandom orientation when nearest neighbors was that of females with no or small pouch-young, the category most likely to enter estrus.

Such cases of nonrandom mutual orientation confirm that eastern gray kangaroos, as well as showing slight compositional organization of the groups in which they occur, react to other group members to bring about organization in their mutual orientation and, to a lesser extent, spacing. I feel, from casual observation of whiptail wallabies, common wallaroos, and red kangaroos, that similar organization will be found to arise from social behavior in most of the gregarious macropods.

E.   MATING SYSTEMS OF MACROPODS

Each mating system, the set of behavior patterns whereby individuals gain matings, has a spatial and a temporal dimension, since the behavior tends to vary with locality and across time [as encapsulated in Wittenberger's (1979) spatiotemporal classification], and an associative dimension comprising the sex and numbers of the focal animal's reproductive partners. The optimal system for males of a species frequently differs from that for females.

TABLE III
MEAN NEAREST-NEIGHBOR DISTANCES FOR DYADS OF SOCIAL CATEGORIES OF
EASTERN GRAY KANGAROOS[a]

	Nearest neighbor							
	LM	MM	SM	FSY	FLY	FYF	SA	YAF
LM	8	8	9	6	11	4	5	5
MM		7	7	6	8	4	6	5
SM			6	7	9	6	6	6
FSY				7	7	7	6	6
FLY					9	7	6	6
FYF						12	6	3
SA							5	4
YAF								5

[a]Records were taken of the spacings between individuals in foraging groups; the animals were well habituated to close approach by observers (P. J. Jarman, unpublished data). Means are rounded to the nearest meter; they are from samples of between 100 and 600 cases (except for females with young-at-foot and young-at-foot, which both tended to be isolated from other kangaroos). Social category abbreviations as in Table II.

In a recent review, Clutton-Brock (1989) usefully divides consideration of each sex's mating system into the mating bond and the defense system. The two are functionally interdependent and are separated here merely for convenience. Clutton-Brock (1989) emphasizes that mating systems are the outcome of individual behavioral strategies and are thus not species typical, but may be varied according to the situation. He also typified mating systems as representing "different forms of mate guarding adapted to the spatial and temporal distribution of receptive females which, in turn, depends on variation in resource distribution, predation pressure, the costs of social living and the activities of other males" (Clutton-Brock, 1989, p. 340). This usefully describes major components of the male mating systems in macropods. However, their mating systems are also adapted to optimize the individual male's access to information about the reproductive status of females.

The range of mating bonds displayed by macropods is limited. Only the long-footed potoroo appears to be obligately and persistently monogamous (Seebeck et al., 1989), one male and one female sharing a common territory. The long-nosed potoroo may illustrate situational variation in expression of mating bonds since Heinsohn (1968) described males as having exclusive ranges, each overlapping those of several females, while Bennett (1987a,b) found that the average individual of either sex used a range overlapping those of at least four other individuals of each sex (in Seebeck et al., 1989). This species is probably facultatively monogamous, or polygynous, or even promiscuous. Disappointingly little is known about the field behavior of either potoroo species. We do not know how mating bonds form, nor do we know how territory is defended, if, indeed, it is.

Bettongia and *Aepyprymnus* display an assortment of mating systems. Like the potoroos, these species (except the burrowing bettong) build nests, occupy them solitarily, and defend them, at least while occupied, against adults of either sex. However, rufous bettong nests may be used sequentially by several individuals. Southgate (1980) reported rufous bettong ranges which overlapped between but not within the sexes; however, other studies have shown much overlap within sexes as well (A. Dennis, personal communication; I. Wallis, personal communication; personal observation). There is thus no clear evidence for territoriality. A. Dennis (personal communication, supported by I. Wallis, personal communication) reports persistent male–female pairs. The species may therefore practise nonterritorial monogamy, with polygyny or promiscuity in some populations.

Captive rufous bettongs illustrate two important aspects of macropod male mating systems: the acquisition of knowledge about females, followed by a temporary consortship as a form of mate-guarding. In pens containing one adult male and two to five adult females, each male tended to emerge from his nest at dusk a few minutes before any females. He then usually patrolled the pen, sniffing at each of the other nest sites and the females they contained. Usually, having checked a female olfactorily, he would then leave her. However, for the week preceding her estrus, he would spend an increasing amount of time each night accompanying her. On the night of her estrus he would visit her nest first, and would wait for her to emerge (rarely trying to enter the nest before she had emerged) when they would mate. The progressive consorting with a female in the week prior to her estrus (Fig. 4) may be mate-guarding, although it could also familiarize the female with that male. The nightly checking of females and their nests must give the male information about females in his range (assuming that this occurs in the wild), allowing him to modify his behavior to maximize his probability of detecting a female approaching estrus and to court her.

Male brush-tailed bettongs defend either their whole range when at low density (Sampson, 1971), or a preferred nesting area at high density (Christensen, 1980). Female ranges overlap those of several other females and one or more males. Except when in courting pairs, adults of this species and of Tasmanian bettongs are solitary. By contrast, the burrowing bettong lives in communal warrens. In captivity a burrowing bettong male defends access by other males to a group of females (Stodart, 1966), but not by defending a territory. Whether in the wild such a harem shares a burrow with others, and how stable its membership is, remain to be studied. The male's mating bond appears to be one of unimale polygyny whereas that of the female is serial monogamy.

The smaller macropodids are even less well known than the potoroids, and we can only guess at their mating systems. The rufous hare wallaby (G. Lundie-Jenkins, personal communication) and spectacled hare wallaby (J. Courtenay, personal communication), although solitary in the wild and given to scent-marking, show no symptoms of spatial exclusivity or territoriality in either the wild or captivity. Females share a pen with minimal aggression, although males can be violently aggressive to each other. Their mating system is probably not obligate long-term monogamy, since there is no evidence that pairs share a nest or regularly forage together in the wild. The bridled nailtail wallaby also spends the day squatting solitarily under vegetation and forages at night (P. Tierney, personal communication). Home ranges overlap both inter- and intrasexually. However, this species is heteromorphic and larger males can supplant smaller males who are accompanying females, suggesting a mating system that is either polygynous or promiscuous.

The quokka, another small but heteromorphic macropodid, lives at high density with much inter- and intrasexual overlap of home ranges and habitual use of rest sites by individuals. Kitchener (1973) described stable male–female pairs. Larger males defend access to daytime shelter, which they share with females (Kitchener, 1973). Since this is one of the few highly synchronous, seasonally breeding macropods, it would be useful to have these early observations confirmed.

The rock wallabies characteristically spend the day on or near a cliff or boulder scree, where they can avoid predators (especially eagles) by sheltering in interstices. A few females, with or without a large male, usually share a refuge. The unadorned rock wallaby has been reported (Dwyer, 1972; W. Davies, in Russell, 1984; Horsup, 1986) to live in stable harems each one male with one or more females. In colonies of brush-tailed rock wallabies (K. Joblin, personal communication), each refuge (a complex, cavelike space between rocks) is occupied by one or a few females and a large male guards access to one or a few such refuges, driving away any small males who intrude. K. Joblin (personal communication) also found that at each refuge the largest female was either the only or the most frequent one to rear young to independence, suggesting that a size-based dominance hierarchy among females plays a part in the females' breeding strategy.

Less is known about mate bonding or defense at night when rock wallabies disperse from their refuges to forage. In unadorned rock-wallabies the male and females from one refuge commonly forage together (A. Horsup, personal communication), but in brush-tailed rock wallabies animals may leave the refuge singly and can be seen foraging alone (personal observation). So, although male rock wallabies display a mating system which involves exclusion of other males from an area in which a number of females are habitually found in the daytime, a system which can be described as unimale polygyny, we do not yet know how this defensive strategy operates at night. If Joblin's observations on apparent suppression of the breeding of subordinate females can be confirmed, this will be an important addition to our knowledge of the breeding systems of macropod females.

The behavior of tree kangaroos is sadly unknown in the wild. Lumholtz's tree kangaroo adults are almost invariably seen singly (Proctor-Gray, 1985). Their heteromorphism suggests a male mating system of polygyny or promiscuity; their frequent deposition of scent does not necessarily indicate spatial defense.

The black-striped wallaby is an exception within its genus (see below) in appearing to live in closed-membership groups of several females with one or a few males. The groups not only share a common daytime resting area, usually in dense cover, but also forage together at night. However, the evidence for the persistence and exclusivity of membership of these groups is slender, being largely that, at low density, groups can regularly be seen at the same dispersed, discrete sites. Also, C. N. Johnson (personal communication) regularly saw two marked females together in a group at one site over several months. However, in a more dense population, the discreteness and cohesion of groups was much less obvious and their ranges clearly overlapped (personal observation). It is too early to classify the systems of the species.

The other macropodid species, in the genera *Thylogale*, *Wallabia*, and *Macropus*, are all heteromorphic. Despite varying from commonly solitary to highly gregarious, they share basically similar mating systems in which ranges overlap both inter- and intrasexually and group membership is open. Male access to estrous females is largely hierarchically determined. Males of these species grow (at a decelerating rate) throughout life and faster than females (i.e., they are holobiotically heteromorphic; Jarman, 1983, 1989a). Females of the species that have been studied are not permanently accompanied by, let alone bonded to, any male. For 5 to 10 days before estrus, a female is attractive to males, who compete to consort closely with her. In estrus she may range widely and be followed by half a dozen males (in the most gregarious species) of various sizes, the largest usually closest to her. Both sexes mate promiscuously.

Overlap in ranges may mean that a male competes with anything up to 20 other males for access to an estrous female. Males achieve mating success by being the most dominant (which usually means the largest) male with the estrous female. No males of these species employ territoriality to secure their access spatially, although Johnson (1985) found that the largest male red-necked wallabies controlled separate domains within which each secured most of the matings. In other species the local male hierarchy produces one alpha male who, for the period of his tenure, is the most likely male to mate (e.g., Kaufman, 1974b; Jarman and Southwell, 1986). Since males of these species may secondarily disperse as large adults (eastern gray kangaroos, personal observation), an adult male can always choose either to fight his way to the top of his local hierarchy or to move to a new locality where his chances are relatively better.

A dominant male can displace subordinate males from a female that is in or approaching estrus, or may interrupt mating, and can even break a consortship which has been established over several days. The system is based very much on defense of access to the female at the time of mating.

Given that males do not guard females before their proestrous phase, a major part of these species' male mating strategies concerns improving the probability of detecting a female in or approaching estrus. The ways in which they do this vary with the ecology of the species, especially the patterns of resource use by females. For example, in most of these species, males have larger ranges than females, and in some of them the size of male range increases with body size or with rank (e.g., Johnson, 1987b; Jarman and Southwell, 1986). Large male red-necked pademelons have larger nocturnal foraging ranges than small males in the pasture to which females are attracted. I have observed large red kangaroo males spending longer than other males at resources, such as water, which are essential to females.

The most dominant eastern gray kangaroo male spends more time alone than any other male as he moves extensively between groups of females (Jarman and Southwell, 1986). Thus, either by having a large range, or by choosing which habitat or locality to be in, or by moving extensively within his range and checking most females he contacts, a male maximizes his chances of detecting estrous females.

In the red kangaroo (Johnson and Bayliss, 1981) and red-necked wallaby (Johnson, 1987b), large males with females of the category most likely to enter estrus occupied slightly different habitats or areas from smaller males, perhaps through some displacement of the smaller males. This is neither a total displacement nor an inevitable consequence of hierarchical antagonism. It does not happen in the eastern gray kangaroo in which males, especially the largest ones, choose preferentially to be close to females with no or small pouch-young, the class most likely to come into estrus (Section V,C).

The female counterpart of these male mating strategies is less obvious. In many species females discourage inspection by males who are smaller than themselves, by threatening them, cuffing at them, or just moving away. They can also be more or less ready to accept a close consort. When a female is in estrus she often moves very widely. Whether or not this is induced simply by the harassment of males trying to court her, the effect is that the female covers much of her range, with a very visible train of males behind her, and is unlikely to be overlooked. This, and the long proestrous period in which she is attractive to males, are likely to maximize the probability of her being detected by a locally dominant male. A largely unexplored facet of the breeding system of macropods (and of most other mammalian taxa) is the way in which females may influence the reproduction of other females. Macropods illustrate three possibilities. In the long-footed potoroo, and some populations of long-nosed potoroo, females may hold territories which exclude other females from both that territory's food and shelter and the opportunity to meet and court males there. Each female in the monogamous pairs of long-footed potoroos may therefore be preemptively securing all current matings with her male.

Observations of brush-tailed rock-wallabies (K. Joblin, personal communication) suggest that a larger and more dominant female limits the successful reproduction of subordinate females sharing her refuge. These observations, if substantiated, indicate that a daughter may pay, in lost reproduction, for not dispersing to find an unoccupied refuge. Johnson (1985) observed that female red-necked wallabies who shared their home range with several closely related females (as well as unrelated females) were less reproductively successful than females with only unrelated females in their range.

However, the presence of female kin can be reproductively beneficial. Among eastern gray kangaroos (R. I. Stuart-Dick and P. J. Jarman, unpublished data), females who have living mothers tend to reproduce for the first time at a younger age, are more likely first to have a female offspring, and are much more likely to rear that offspring to weaning than are females whose mothers die before their daughter first breeds. These differences are matched by a tendency for closely related females to occur in the same subgroup within a large group, to follow each other when leaving or joining groups, to orient similarly within groups, and to interact agonistically at much lower rates than unrelated females (P. J. Jarman and R. I. Stuart-Dick, unpublished observation).

VI. THE SOCIAL SYSTEMS OF MACROPODS

A. CORRELATES OF SOCIAL BEHAVIOR AND ORGANIZATION IN MACROPODS

Some characteristics of the social behavior and organization of the macropods are too general for their adaptiveness to be investigated by comparison within the superfamily. However, others vary enough for a comparative approach, seeking covariation between values of characters, or the clustering of character states, to be taken. Such an approach, taken by Croft (1989) and Norbury et al. (1989), confirms, in general terms, the expected relationships between species' size, type and dispersion of food items, habitat, antipredator behavior, grouping, and dimorphism (Jarman, 1983, 1984).

However, almost any variable can be taken as a starting point for a comparative consideration of the adaptiveness of social behavior and organization. Here I want to investigate two relationships: that between use of shelter, a basic aspect of resource-related behavior, and social systems; and that between male fighting style, a highly derived aspect of dyadic, intrasexual behavior, and mating systems.

The clusters of characteristics of species which are distinguished initially by their typical uses of shelter are shown in Table IV. All potoroids (except the musky rat kangaroo) spend the day in nests which they build; burrowing bettongs regularly, and rufous bettongs occasionally, place their nests in burrows which they dig. Macropodids of the same size (up to 3 or 4 kg) use naturally occurring shelter. Hare wallabies and nailtail wallabies squat under dense vegetation (and the rufous hare wallaby may dig a short burrow in hot weather), while small rock wallabies shelter in rock crevices, interstices, and caves. In contrast to nests and, to a lesser extent, squats, rock shelters do not need to be made by the animal, but may be of limited availability. All these species, staying in or close to their shelters from dawn to dusk, use them, I believe, primarily to escape either detection alone (nests and squats) or both this and direct attack (rock shelters) by aerial and terrestrial predators.

The two types of shelter and their use clearly distinguish the behavior of species toward predators. Nest- and squat-using species are assiduous in being concealed from dawn to dusk. They usually sit tight until closely approached by a terrestrial predator (or a human), bursting from their shelter when the disturber is within 1 or 2 m, and running fast and directly to another nest or squat. Each individual has several such shelters and evidently knows how to reach one from another quickly. Rufous bettongs may also use hollow logs as refuge when pursued, and Schlager (1981) watched a rufous bettong, while building a nest, first exploring and then repeatedly moving back and forth along a route from the nest site to a nearby hollow log. The antipredator behavior of this species relies on avoidance of detection (by being in shelter in daylight, and keeping still), followed by an explosive emergence when a predator is very close, and then rapid disappearance into another, known shelter.

By contrast, the rock wallaby may spend much of the day near its refuge, but not actually out of sight. However, on sighting a predator, it retreats rapidly to the rock shelter, where it is invulnerable to eagles, and terrestrial predators can approach it only with difficulty. K. Joblin (personal communication) found that brush-tailed rock wallabies' refuges were so structured that animals could leave by any one of several exits if a predator entered.

A nest or squat screens the occupant visually, but gives it no physical protection from attack. Because they are used solitarily, the occupant is the only one to make movements into, within, and out of the shelter, which might reveal its presence to a predator hunting visually. It also controls the moment for explosive exit, rather than risking being a later animal to emerge from a suddenly revealed, communal shelter. By contrast, a rock shelter protects its occupants from physical attack. Its efficacy is, within limits of the shelter's capacity, unaffected by the number of animals sharing it, although individuals might compete to ensure that they would not be blocked by another when trying to enter in a hurry.

These differences in types of shelters and their use seem to be reflected socially. Because nests and squats militate against gregarious use, males of those

TABLE IV
CORRELATIONS BETWEEN THE USE OF TYPES OF SHELTER BY SPECIES OF MACROPODS AND OTHER ASPECTS OF THOSE SPECIES' SOCIAL ORGANIZATION AND BEHAVIOR

Structure used for shelter or refuge	Timing of use	How available?	Type of use	Defense?	Animals using shelter	Mating systems	Male defense of mating	Dimorphism	Behavior of young after permanent emergence while mother forages
Nest or dug burrow	Dawn to dusk	One adult builds several	Repeated	Yes	One adult	Monogamous, polygynous, or promiscuous	Spatial defense and consorting	Homomorphic	Follows mother closely or stays in or returns to nest
Squat	Most daylight hours	One adult chooses several	Repeated	Yes	One adult	Polygynous or promiscuous	Not known	Homo- or heteromorphic	Not known

Dense vegetation or rocky refuge	Most daylight hours in or near shelter	Not abundant	Permanent	Yes	Several adults in persistent groups	Monogamous or polygynous	Spatial defense and consorting	Heteromorphic	Left in or at refuge at first, then follows mother
Some use of dense vegatation	Mainly middle of day	Quite abundant	Irregular	No	One or a few adults plus newly emerged young-at-foot	Promiscuous	Hierarchical rank and consorting	Heteromorphic	Left lying out at first then follows mother
No use of cover except for shade	Times of high insolation	Abundant	Ephemeral	No	One to many transient adults	Promiscuous	Hierarchical rank and consorting	Heteromorphic	Follows mother more or less closely from start

species cannot monopolize a female by sharing and defending her nest during the day (although the male may remain nearby). Females of the homomorphic potoroids may be sufficiently aggressive toward males to deter them from entering nests which have cost time and effort to build. In contrast, rock-wallaby females can use a shelter gregariously, providing an opportunity for a male to preempt diurnal access to females by excluding other males. Most rock wallaby species are heteromorphic and males may scent-mark both the surrounds of a shelter and females themselves. Although potoroid males may not be able to monopolize females by sharing their nests, they may use the nests as clues for predictably locating and olfactorily monitoring females. It would be interesting to know whether male potoroids and hare wallabies scent-mark near females' nests and squats.

A nest, squat, or rock refuge potentially allows an unweaned juvenile, once excluded from the pouch, to shelter rather than follow its mother, with the risks attached to this. Since the mother will know where to find it, it also has a reduced need to learn to return to its mother. However, it must learn its way to its refuge. As it matures it needs to establish itself at a refuge or to find or build its own squats or nests. There are opportunities here for nonlactational maternal investment. I have recorded a female rufous bettong ceasing to use a set of established nests when she weaned an offspring that then continued to use them exclusively, and a rock wallaby female may allow a daughter to remain on her refuge. Dispersing subadults may have difficulty establishing themselves at rocky refuges or developing a set of nests or squats.

The comparable clustering of characteristics of the medium-sized and large macropods derives from their lack of precisely located shelters and their relatively greater freedom of movement. Some medium-sized species, but not the largest, still use shelter to avoid detection by predators, particularly when a juvenile quits the pouch. Juvenile red-necked and red-legged pademelons, swamp wallaby, red-necked wallaby, and tammar wallaby (this last species in captivity, E. M. Russell, personal communication) are left "lying out," where vegetation provides visual shelter, by a foraging mother who returns to suckle them infrequently. This phase lasts a few days before the juvenile follows the mother as a young-at-foot.

By contrast, the young of eastern and western gray kangaroos, red kangaroo, common and antilopine wallaroos, and whiptail wallaby follow the mother from the time they permanently leave the pouch. Before this event, the mother tends to isolate herself from conspecifics, and the young learns to monitor the movements of its mother and follow her, while she remains alert to its movements and will move to rejoin it. Movements of the mother and young of these species may be more evenly reciprocal than in other macropods. Their interactions may also involve a greater range of vocalizations. It is in such species that female young are most regularly philopatric and females are most likely to share their range with all their daughters. Interestingly, females of these species delay the onset of their breeding for longer than other macropod species.

For these largest macropod species, freedom from geographically fixed shelters allows complete freedom of movement, and shelters do not dictate their group size. It is these species that have been shown sometimes to benefit, in terms of reduced individual alertness, from grouping. Their form of open-membership grouping is very fluid, group composition often changing several times an hour, with group size reflecting population density. In such a society males do not use territory to preempt matings, but use their hierarchical rank to displace others from consorting with estrous or near-estrous females.

Without contested boundaries, a male's range can be as large as he is able to cover intermittently. Within this he could obtain all matings if he were sufficiently dominant and perfectly informed of the impending estruses. His range is likely to be a compromise between area covered and frequency of monitoring the status of females within it.

Males of these species have emphasized hierarchical behavior and evolved the most exaggerated dimorphism known in terrestrial mammals; a female red or gray kangaroo, at first estrus, may be courted and mated by a male six times her own weight. They have evolved a range of displays of size, height, muscular development, and weaponry quite unknown among the homomorphic species.

The social organization of these largest species is free grouping, modified by interindividual (seen as interclass) differences in ability to benefit by being solitary or in a group. The male mating systems play little part in determining group composition, except for the lowered frequency of group membership of the highly mobile largest males.

The fighting styles of the different macropods correlate with species-typical size, but styles might also cluster with other broadly species-typical factors, such as the frequency of encountering other males or the degree of socially induced delay in onset of male reproduction (i.e., the ratio of the proportions of a male's life typically spent breeding and not breeding). The former might affect the relative value of using nonfighting displays to delay escalation to full fighting, and the latter the relative cost of foregoing reproduction through losing a fight.

The largest and smallest macropod species do indeed differ in fighting styles (Table V). In the largest, a male encounters other males frequently (indeed, he spends most of his time accompanied by other males); he may dominate the population reproductively for a brief and final portion of his adult life. Males of these species escalate through a range of sequentially ordered displays before full-scale fighting. In the smallest species, males meet other males infrequently and do not associate with them, yet may be socially competent to breed for most of their lives. These have few prefighting displays, tending to attack rather quickly if at all.

The largest species, being social, have frequent opportunities for intermale

TABLE V

STYLES OF FIGHTING AND DISPLAYS IN THREE GROUPS OF MACROPODS

Species	Dimorphism	Components of fighting	Reciprocity of blows	Continuity of fights	Prefight displays	Male/male play and sparring as subadults and adults
Potoroids, except *Hypsiprymnodon*	Homomorphic	Jump onto back; scrabble; bite; lie and kick or jump over and kick out	Blows independent	Almost no breaks in fight	Brief vocal and postural displays	Almost none
Wallabia, Thylogale, Petrogale, and small *Macropus* species	Moerately heteromorphic	Wrestle, roll and bite; jump over and kick out; grapple upright with forelimbs and rake with hind feet	Blows only partly reciprocated	Occasional breaks in fight	Sometimes postural displays of intent to fight	Limited opportunity
Large *Macropus* species	Strongly heteromorphic	Grapple with forelimbs; rarely bite; prop on stiff tail and jab with hind feet. Only jump onto opponent if he is knocked down	Generally reciprocated blows	Short or long breaks in which males groom and display	Large repertoire of displays of forelimb size or height; also scent-marking, e.g., grass-pulling display	Frequent opportunity through changes in group membership

play (as subadults) and sparring. They grow throughout life. Much of their sparring and serious fighting aims to unbalance or knock down an upright opponent, and greater height and weight are valuable assets. A male's ability to use his thick and stiffened tail as a prop both counteracts his opponent's attempts to push him down and backward and allows him the full advantage of his height. In these species, prefighting dominance displays emphasize height (Fig. 2bii) as well as development of weaponry.

In contrast, the smallest species may gain most from agility and speed, rather than height and weight; I do not know whether they have any prefighting displays of speed and agility. If these fighting attributes are difficult to display without being put into practice (i.e., if there is no physical "sign" which immediately identifies its bearer as being particularly agile without a fight occurring), I would not expect the species to have male mating strategies in which a male's defense of access to an estrous female depended simply on other males recognizing and deferring to his dominance.

The thick, stiffened tail, although essential for upright fighting in which hindleg blows are fully reciprocated, probably did not evolve just for fighting, since it characterizes females as well, who do not "prop" on the tail to fight. They, like the males, use it as a fifth leg when slowly walking or "pentapedally crawling." Smaller species take the body's weight on the forelimbs alone while moving the hindlimbs forward. While the evolution of the "propping" tail poses a question for adaptive morphologists rather than ethologists, it exemplifies the way in which the adaptation of an organ system for one function (here, locomotion) opens the way for a behavioral change (fighting style) which may itself cause social changes (male emphasis on hierarchical position determining access to estrous females).

B. FURTHER ECOLOGICAL FACTORS AND THE EVOLUTION OF MACROPOD SOCIAL SYSTEMS

Among the larger, social species of macropods the grouping of females responds to variations in ecological parameters. Except when their young are about to quit the pouch, females tend to associate while foraging, the size and rates of flux of groups varying with population density, habitat, and dispersion of food items. Some smaller species (e.g., quokka and many rock-wallabies) may shelter in groups but forage more solitarily. The very smallest, which build their own nests or find their own squats, both shelter and forage solitarily. Females in these three kinds of species have rather different opportunities for long-term investment in their nondispersing offspring (mainly daughters).

While the smallest can do little more than pass on a set of squats or nests, and rock-wallabies may allow continued use of the maternal refuge, the larger species can invest in daughters through continued association in foraging groups. Since their responsiveness to food-item dispersion implies some competition within the group, persistent association between mother and daughters might allow competitive differentiation between kin and nonkin. The finding (R. I. Stuart-Dick, personal communication) that levels of agonistic interactions are lower between female kin than nonkin in foraging groups of eastern gray kangaroos shows that this occurs. This promises to be an exciting area for future research.

The interactions of adult male macropods with females are mostly to do with reproduction, being either to court or mate with a female or to gain knowledge, by inspection, about the potential for courting or mating with that female. Again, we find size-related differences between species. Inspection of a female by a male rufous bettong (the best-known small macropod) is strongly resisted and dangerous for him, but he can inspect predictably located nests instead. Inspection of females of the largest species is easy for males, who are many times bigger than they are and can force them to stop and expose their pouches. Such females even urinate readily when inspected by large males. This is convenient for males of large, social species who may want to inspect many females daily and hence must inspect each one quickly. The contrast is between the easy inspection of many, spatially unpredictable females in the large, social species, and the very risky inspection of a few, spatially predictable females in the small, solitary species.

Male macropods may use any spatial predictability in the occurrence of potentially estrous females to improve their probability of contacting them. They may preferentially occupy the preferred habitat, the nocturnal feeding area, the ephemeral food source, the water source, or refuges or nest sites used by females. Some of these (nests or refuges) are specific to individual females, others (feeding or drinking sites) are specific to a special category or population. The less spatially predictable the females are (as in the largest, social, open-country species), the more must the male rely on extensive traveling to contact them.

In many species, individual males vary in the reproductive tactics they use and their tactical success. This general form of mating system, depending heavily on contact with and knowledge of females, is potentially highly responsive to variations in the population's ecology, but requires males to be more aware of factors affecting the distribution of females than is the case in the social systems of most large eutherian herbivores.

All macropod females seem to signal the approach of estrus several days in advance and to accept a male consort to some extent during that time. All have brief estruses. Females of all larger species are likely to move widely when consorting and may attract a train of several males. Even estrous female potoroids may attract more than one male. So, macropod females can rely to a great extent on intermale competition to select a mate for them. Yet there are some signs of active female choice, at least in the rejection of small males, and this remains a topic for further research.

This review of the social behavior and organization of macropods would be incomplete without mention of some features that are missing in the superfamily. With the possible exceptions of black-striped wallabies and some rock wallabies (at least in the daytime), no macropod species shows closed-membership grouping. Certainly none has evolved highly complex and tightly closed societies comparable to those of many primates. Nor is there persistent and obligate association between female kin; even in eastern gray kangaroos the associations are facultative. Nor do coalitions of related or unrelated males enter into any of the mating strategies. Male macropods, with the exception of rock-wallaby males in the daytime and some potoroid males in some circumstances, do not use territoriality to exclude other males from females (thus preempting matings), nor do they gather and defend harems.

Each of these prompts the question: Why not? In no case can one fall back on the outmoded excuse that metatheria are evolutionarily inferior to eutheria. If any generalization rings true for the macropods, it is that they are behaviorally flexible. None of the eutherian behavioral traits listed above allows for flexibility.

Macropods have evolved on a continent where their kinds of resources have been and are relatively unpredictable in their availability. This is a difficult generalization to support with firm data but, on the whole, rainfall-induced primary productivity in Australia varies less predictably through time and space than on a continent of comparable latitudinal range and size such as North America or Africa south of the Sahara. I would argue that the effect of this has been to favor the evolution of social behavior and organization which is only loosely tied to spatial and temporal predictability of individuals and of food and water. The evidence suggests that many of the behavioral and social differences between macropods and their eutherian counterparts ultimately arise from these environmental differences.

VII. SUMMARY

There have been increasing numbers of field studies, over the past decade, of the Macropodoidea, the kangaroos, wallabies, and rat kangaroos, the most species-rich modern array of metatherian herbivores. As a result it is now possible to make interspecific comparisons of their social behavior and organization. Although ecologically and ethologically comparable to the bovids and cervids, macropods nevertheless have their own peculiarities. Species-specific social patterns correlate (as in bovids and cervids) with body size, dimorphism, diet, and habitat: large, grazing macropods of open country are heteromorphic and found in larger groups than small, homomorphic species that feed highly selectively and live in dense cover. Intraspecific comparisons have shown that individual alertness in gregarious species diminishes with group size. Nearly all gregarious macropods form open-membership groups, and both the rate of change of group membership and average group size reflect population density.

Communication is more often visual or olfactory than auditory or tactile. Allogrooming is rare except that of a dependent juvenile by its mother. The initial behavior of the mothers is to ensure the swift and appropriate return of the joey to the pouch but later they change to allow suckling but not reentry to the pouch. Species differ in the behavior of the permanently emerged young-at-foot: some are left "lying out" or in a secure refuge, while others follow the mother at all times. Interactions between males relate largely to dominance. Males of small, homomorphic species tend to keep apart, being briefly aggressive when they meet. Males of large, heteromorphic species readily associate but form hierarchies based on fighting ability, which is demonstrated either in sparring or, less often, in fully escalated fights, or in visual and olfactory displays. Males of such species grow throughout life, and most visual displays show their height, length of limbs, and forearm musculature.

Males associate with females to check their estrous status and, if appropriate, to court and mate with them. Males can detect approaching estrus about a week in advance, and then compete to escort the female during that proestrous phase. A more dominant male can displace a subordinate that is consorting with a female at any stage of courting or mating. A male's reproductive success depends on his dominance and his knowledge of the estrous status of females. Species show many ways by which males maximize their knowledge of females: by associating with the category of females most likely to enter estrus, by checking females frequently and assiduously, and by being where females are likely to visit. These happen with minimal displacement of other males. In the gregarious species, categories of animals differ rather little in the compositions of the groups in which they occur, although there are stronger tendencies for categories to select their nearest neighbors.

With the exceptions of two potoroids that appear to be monogamous and rock wallabies that may be polygamous, male and female mating systems in macropods are promiscuous. The use by many small macropod species of built nests or natural shelters affects their social systems. The macropods' social systems rarely depend on territoriality or harem formation, usually being based on free association between classes and the relative fighting ability of males in the presence of an estrous female. Such systems may suit the seasonally unpredictable Australian environment.

Acknowledgments

I would like to thank the many scientists who have, over the years, shared their knowledge of macropod behavior with me, in particular, Eleanor Russell, Dave Croft, and Udo Ganslosser, and my macropod colleagues at the University of New England who are too numerous to list here. I especially thank those who have allowed me to quote their unpublished findings. Working with interested, sharing colleagues has been one of the greatest pleasures in studying macropods in Australia. This article was written while I was a sabbatical visitor on the population biology floor of the School of Biological Sciences, University of East Anglia, Norwich, U.K., and I gratefully acknowledge the facilities granted me there. I thank Peter Slater, Colin Beer, and anonymous referees for the editorial improvements that they suggested.

References

Bailey, P. T. (1971). The red kangaroo, *Megaleia rufa* (Desmarest) in north-western New South Wales. 1. Movements. *CSIRO Wildl. Res.* **16**, 11–28.

Batchelor, T. A. (1980). The social organization of the brush-tailed rock-wallaby (*Petrogale penicillate penicillata*) on Motutapu Island, M.Sc. Thesis, University of Auckland, New Zealand.

Bennett, A. (1987a). Biogeography and ecology of mammals within a fragmented forest environment in south-western Victoria. Ph.D. Thesis, University of Melbourne, Australia.

Bennett, A. (1987b). Conservation of mammals within a fragmented forest environment: The contributions of insular biogeography and autecology. *In* "Nature Conservation: The Role of Remnants of Native Vegetation" (D. A. Saunders, G. W. Arnold, A. A. Burbidge, and A. J. Hopkins, eds.), pp. 41–52. Surrey Beatty and Sons, New South Wales, Australia.

Caughley, G. (1964). Social organization and daily activity of the Red Kangaroo and the Grey Kangaroo. *J. Mammal.* **45**, 429–436.

Christensen, P. E. S. (1980). The biology of *Bettongia penicillata* Gray 1837, and *Macropus eugenii* (Desmarest, 1817) in relation to fire. *For. Dept. West. Aust., Bull.* **91**, 1–90.

Clarke, J. L., Jones, M. E., and Jarman, P. J. (1989). A day in the life of a kangaroo: Activities and movements of Eastern Grey Kangaroos *Macropus giganteus* at Wallaby Creek. *In* "Kangaroos, Wallabies and Rat-Kangaroos" (G. Grigg, P. Jarman, and I. Hume, eds.), pp. 611–618. Surrey Beatty and Sons, New South Wales, Australia.

Clutton-Brock, T. H. (1989). Mammalian mating systems. *Proc. R. Soc. London, Ser. B* **236**, 339–372.

Coulson, G. M. (1989). Repertoires of social behaviour in the Macropodoidea. *In* "Kangaroos, Wallabies and Rat-Kangaroos" pp. 457–473. Surrey Beatty and Sons, New South Wales, Australia.

Coulson, G. M., and Croft, D. B. (1981). Flehmen in kangaroos. *Aust. Mammal.* **4**, 139–140.

Coulson, G. M., and Raines, J. A. (1985). Methods for small-scale surveys of grey kangaroo populations. *Aust. Wildl. Res.* **12**, 119–125.

Croft, D. B. (1981a). Social behavior of the euro, *Macropus robustus*, in the Australian arid zone. *Aust. Wildl. Res.* **8**, 13–49.

Croft, D. B. (1981b). Behaviour of red kangaroos, *Macropus rufus* (Desmarest, 1822) in north-western New South Wales, Australia. *Aust. Mammal.* **4**, 5–58.

Croft, D. B. (1982). Some observations on the behaviour of the Antilopine wallaroo *Macropus antilopinus* (Marsupialia: Macropodidae). *Aust. Mammal.* **5**, 5–13.

Croft, D. B. (1987). Socio-ecology of the Antilopine wallaroo, *Macropus antilopinus*, in the Northern Territory, with observations on sympatric *M. robustus woodwardii* and *M. agilis*. *Aust. Wildl. Res.* **14**, 243–255.

Croft, D. B. (1989). Social organization of the Macropodoidea. *In* "Kangaroos, Wallabies and Rat-Kangaroos" (G. Grigg, P. Jarman, and I. Hume, eds.), pp. 505–525. Surrey Beatty and Sons, New South Wales, Australia.

Denny, M. J. S. (1985). The red kangaroo and the arid environment. *In* "The Kangaroo Keepers" (T. H. Lavery, ed.), pp. 55–72. Univ. of Queensland Press, Australia.

Dwyer, P. D. (1972). Social organization of a population of rock-wallabies, *Petrogale inornata. Aust. Mammal.* **1,** 72.

Ganslosser, U. (1989). Agonistic behaviour in Macropodoids—a review. *In* "Kangaroos, Wallabies and Rat-Kangaroos" (G. Grigg, P. Jarman, and I. Hume, eds.), pp. 475–503. Surrey Beatty and Sons, New South Wales, Australia.

Greenwood, P. J. (1980). Mating systems, philopatry and dispersal in birds and mammals. *Anim. Behav.* **28,** 1140–1162.

Heathcote, C. F. (1987). Grouping of eastern grey kangaroos in open habitat. *Aust. Wildl. Res.* **14,** 343–348.

Heathcote, C. F. (1989). Social behaviour of the black-striped wallaby, *Macropus dorsalis,* in captivity. *In* "Kangaroos, Wallabies and Rat-Kangaroos" (G. Grigg, P. Jarman, and I. Hume, eds.), pp. 625–628. Surrey Beatty and Sons, New South Wales, Australia.

Heinsohn, G. E. (1968). Habitat requirements and reproductive potential of the macropod marsupial *Potorous tridactylus* in Tasmania. *Mammalia* **32,** 30–43.

Horsup, A. B. (1986). The behaviour of the allied rock wallaby *Petrogale assimilis* (Macropodinae). B.Sc.(Hons.) Thesis, James Cook University of North Queensland, Australia.

Hume, I. D. (1982). "Digestive Physiology and Nutrition of Marsupials." Cambridge Univ. Press, Cambridge.

Jarman, P. J. (1974). The social organisation of antelopes in relation to their ecology. *Behaviour* **48,** 215–267.

Jarman, P. J. (1983). Mating system and sexual dimorphism in large, terrestrial mammalian herbivores. *Biol. Rev. Cambridge Philos. Soc.* **58,** 1–36.

Jarman, P. J. (1984). The dietary ecology of macropod marsupials. *Proc. Nutr. Soc. Aust.* **9,** 82–87.

Jarman, P. J. (1986). Group size and activity in eastern grey kangaroos. *Anim. Behav.* **35,** 1044–1050.

Jarman, P. J. (1989a). Sexual dimorphism in macropods. *In* "Kangaroos, Wallabies and Rat-Kangaroos" (G. Grigg, P. Jarman, and I. Hume, eds.), pp. 433–447. Surrey Beatty and Sons, New South Wales, Australia.

Jarman, P. J. (1989b). On being thick-skinned: Dermal shields in large mammalian herbivores. *Biol. J. Linn. Soc.* **36,** 169–191.

Jarman, P. J., and Coulson, G. (1989). Dynamics and adaptiveness of grouping in macropods. *In* "Kangaroos, Wallabies and Rat-Kangaroos" (G. Grigg, P. Jarman, and I. Hume, eds.), pp. 527–547. Surrey Beatty and Sons, New South Wales, Australia.

Jarman, P. J., and Southwell, C. J. (1986). Grouping, associations and reproductive strategies in eastern grey kangaroos. *In* "Ecological Aspects of Social Evolution" (D. I. Rubenstein and R. W. Wrangham, eds.), pp. 399–428. Princeton Univ. Press, Princeton, New Jersey.

Jarman, P. J., and Taylor, R. J. (1983). Ranging of eastern grey kangaroos and wallaroos on a New England pastoral property. *Aust. Wildl. Res.* **10,** 33–38.

Jarman, P. J., Johnson, C. N., Southwell, C. J., and Stuart-Dick, R. (1987). Macropod studies at Wallaby Creek. I. The area and animals. *Aust. Wildl. Res.* **14,** 1–14.

Johnson, C. N. (1983). Variations in group size and composition in red and western grey kangaroos, *Macropus rufus* (Desmarest) and *M. fuliginosus* (Desmarest). *Aust. Wildl. Res.* **10,** 25–31.

Johnson, C. N. (1985). Ecology, social behaviour and reproductive success in a population of red-necked wallabies. Ph.D. Thesis, University of New England, Australia.

Johnson, C. N. (1987a). Relationships between mother and infant red-necked wallabies (*Macropus rufogriseus banksianus*). *Ethology* **74,** 1–20.

Johnson, C. N. (1987b). Macropod studies at Wallaby Creek. IV. Home range and movement of the red-necked wallaby. *Aust. Wildl. Res.* **14,** 125–132.

Johnson, C. N. (1989). Dispersal and philopatry in the macropodoids. *In* "Kangaroos, Wallabies and Rat-Kangaroos" (G. Grigg, P. Jarman, and I. Hume, eds.), pp. 593–601. Surrey Beatty and Sons, New South Wales, Australia.

Johnson, C. N., and Bayliss, P. G. (1981). Habitat selection by sex, age and reproductive class in the red kangaroo in western New South Wales. *Aust. Wildl. Res.* **8,** 465–474.

Johnson, C. N., and Jarman, P. J. (1983). Geographical variation in offspring sex ratios in kangaroos. *Search* **14,** 152–154.

Johnson, K. A. (1977). Ecology and management of the red-necked pademelon, *Thylogale thetis,* on the Dorrigo plateau of northern New South Wales. Ph.D. Thesis, University of New England, Armidale, Australia.

Johnson, K. A. (1980). Spatial and temporal use of habitat by the red-necked pademelon, *Thylogale thetis* (Marsupialia: Macropodidae). *Aust. Wildl. Res.* **7,** 157–166.

Kaufmann, J. H. (1974a). The ecology and evolution of social organization in the kangaroo family (Macropodidae). *Am. Zool.* **14,** 51–62.

Kaufmann, J. H. (1974b). Social ethology of the whiptail wallaby, *Macropus parryi,* in northeastern New South Wales. *Anim. Behav.* **22,** 281–369.

Kitchener, D. J. (1973). Notes on home range and movement in two small macropods, the potoroo (*Potorous apicalis*) and the quokka (*Setonix brachyurus*). *Mammalia* **37,** 231–240.

Lavery, H. J., ed. (1985). "The Kangaroo Keepers." Univ. of Queensland Press, Australia.

Lee, A. K., and Ward, S. J. (1989). Life histories of macropodoid marsupials. *In* "Kangaroos, Wallabies and Rat-Kangaroos" (G. Grigg, P. Jarman, and I. Hume, eds.), pp. 105–115. Surrey Beatty and Sons, New South Wales, Australia.

Norbury, G. L., Sanson, G. D., and Lee, K. A. (1989). Feeding ecology of the Macropodoidea. *In* "Kangaroos, Wallabies and Rat-Kangaroos" (G. Grigg, P. Jarman, and I. Hume, eds.), pp. 169–178. Surrey Beatty and Sons, New South Wales, Australia.

Oliver, A. J. (1986). Social organisation and dispersal in the red kangaroo. Ph.D. Thesis, Murdoch University, Western Australia.

Proctor-Gray, E. (1985). The behavior and ecology of Lumholtz's tree-kangaroo, *Dendrolagus lumholtzi* (Marsupialia: Macropodidae). Ph.D. Thesis, Harvard University, Cambridge, Massachusetts.

Russell, E. M. (1979). The size and composition of groups in the red kangaroo, *Macropus rufus.* *Aust. Wildl. Res.* **6,** 237–244.

Russell, E. M. (1984). Social behaviour and social organization of marsupials. *Mammal Rev.* **14,** 101–154.

Russell, E. M. (1985). The metatherians: Order Marsupialia. *In* "Social Odours in Mammals" (R. E. Brown and D. W. Macdonald, eds.), pp. 45–104. Oxford University Press, Oxford.

Russell, E. M. (1989). Maternal behaviour in the Macropodoidea. *In* "Kangaroos, Wallabies and Rat-Kangaroos" (G. Grigg, P. Jarman, and I. Hume, eds.), pp. 549–569. Surrey Beatty and Sons, New South Wales, Australia.

Sampson, J. C. (1971). The biology of *Bettongia penicillata* Gray, 1837. Ph.D. Thesis, University of Western Australia.

Sanson, G. D. (1989). Morphological adaptations of teeth to diets and feeding in the Macropodoidea. *In* "Kangaroos, Wallabies and Rat-Kangaroos" (G. Grigg, P. Jarman, and I. Hume, eds.), pp. 151–168. Surrey Beatty and Sons, New South Wales, Australia.

Schlager, F. E. (1981). The distribution, status and ecology of the rufous rat-kangaroo, *Aepyprymnus rufescens,* in northern New South Wales. M. Nat. Res. Thesis, University of New England, Australia.

Scotts, D. J., and Seebeck, J. H. (1988). Studies of *Potorous longipes* (Marsupialia: Potoroidae); with preliminary recommendations for its conservation in Victoria. *Arthur Rylah Inst. Tech. Rep. Ser.* No. 62.

Seebeck, J. H., and Rose, R. W. (1989). Potoroidae. *In* "Fauna of Australia" (G. R. Dyne and D. W. Walton, eds.), Vol. 1B, Chapter 30. Australian Government Publishing Service, Canberra.

Seebeck, J. H., Bennett, A. F., and Scotts, D. J. (1989). Ecology of the Potoroidae—a review. *In* "Kangaroos, Wallabies and Rat-Kangaroos" (G. Grigg, P. Jarman, and I. Hume, eds.), pp. 67–88. Surrey Beatty and Sons, New South Wales, Australia.

Southgate, R. (1980). Factors affecting the spatial and temporal use of habitat by the rufous rat-kangaroo *Aepyprymnus rufescens*. B. Nat. Res. Thesis, University of New England, Armidale, Australia.

Southwell, C. J. (1981). Sociobiology of the eastern grey kangaroo, *Macropus giganteus*. Ph.D. Thesis, University of New England, Armidale, Australia.

Southwell, C. J. (1984a). Variability in grouping in the eastern grey kangaroo, *Macropus giganteus*. I. Group density and group size. *Aust. Wildl. Res.* **11**, 423–435.

Southwell, C. J. (1984b). Variability in grouping in eastern grey kangaroo, *Macropus giganteus*. II. Dynamics of group formation. *Aust. Wildl. Res.* **11**, 437–449.

Southwell, C. J. (1987). Macropod studies at Wallaby Creek. II. Density and distribution of macropod species in relation to environmental variables. *Aust. Wildl. Res.* **14**, 15–33.

Stodart, E. (1966). Observations on the behaviour of the marsupial *Bettongia leseuri* (Quoy & Gaimard) in an enclosure. *CSIRO Wildl. Res.* **11**, 91–101.

Strahan, R. (1983). "The Australian Museum Complete Book of Australian Mammals." Angus & Robertson, Sydney, Australia.

Stuart-Dick, R. I. (1987). Parental investment in the eastern grey kangaroo. Ph.D. Thesis, University of New England, Armidale, Australia.

Stuart-Dick, R. I., and Higginbottom, K. B. (1989). Strategies of parental investment in Macropodoids. *In* "Kangaroos, Wallabies and Rat-Kangaroos" (G. Grigg, P. Jarman, and I. Hume, eds.), pp. 571–592. Surrey Beatty and Sons, New South Wales, Australia.

Taylor, R. J. (1981). The comparative ecology of the eastern grey kangaroo and wallaroo in the New England tablelands of New South Wales. Ph.D. Thesis, University of New England, Armidale, Australia.

Taylor, R. J. (1982). Group size in the eastern grey kangaroo, *Macropus giganteus*, and the wallaroo, *Macropus robustus*. *Aust. Wildl. Res.* **9**, 229–237.

Tyndale-Biscoe, C. H., and Renfree, M. B. (1987). "Reproductive Physiology of Marsupials." Cambridge Univ. Press, Cambridge.

Wittenberger, J. F. (1979). The evolution of mating systems in mammals and birds. *In* "Handbook of Behavioural Neurobiology" (P. Marler and J. G. Vandenbergh, eds.), Vol. 3, pp. 271–349. Plenum, New York.

The t Complex: A Story of Genes, Behavior, and Populations

SARAH LENINGTON

INSTITUTE OF ANIMAL BEHAVIOR
RUTGERS UNIVERSITY
NEWARK, NEW JERSEY 07102

I. INTRODUCTION

For much of the past century the house mouse (*Mus musculus*) has served as the mammalian *Drosophila*. It has been an all-purpose organism for the study of genetics at levels ranging from molecular processes to behavioral genetics to the genetics of populations. Increasingly, these levels of analysis are being integrated, creating new insights regarding the interaction of genes, behavior, and population structure. The t complex of the mouse has been one genetic system which has been particularly amenable to such an integration. In this article I review the major molecular, behavioral, and population features of the t complex as an illustration of the relevance of data gathered at one level of analysis for interpretations at other levels.

II. HISTORICAL BACKGROUND

A. HISTORY OF DISCOVERY OF THE t COMPLEX

The t complex was first discovered in 1927 by a Russian scientist (Dobrovolskaia-Zawadskaia, 1927) who was studying the effect of mutations in mice on carcinogenesis. One of the mice in her laboratory produced a short-tailed offspring. Subsequently, the symbol $T/+$ has been used to indicate the genotype of mice carrying the mutation affecting tail length and $+/+$ to indicate the genotype of wild-type mice without the mutation. The genetic locus affecting tail length was called the "T locus." Mice whose genotype was $T/+$ when mated with wild-type $+/+$ mice produced, as expected, 50% normal-tailed ($+/+$) progeny and 50% short-tailed ($T/+$) progeny. Breeding two $T/+$ mice with each other indicated that T, when homozygous, was lethal as all T/T embryos died before birth. However,

51

things did not stay simple. Dobrovolskaia-Zawadskaia caught wild mice and bred them to $T/+$ mates in the laboratory. In addition to the usual normal-tailed and short-tailed progeny, completely tailless progeny were produced by this cross. This indicated that the wild mice were carrying another gene affecting tail length (which was later referred to as "t"). The t allele carried by the wild mice was considered to be recessive to the wild-type ($+$) allele since wild mice all have normal length tails. Dobrovolskaia-Zawadskaia concluded that she was seeing mice of four different genotypes: $+/+$ and $+/t$ mice with normal tails, $T/+$ mice with short tails, and T/t mice with no tails.

Dobrovolskaia-Zawadskaia's principal interest was in the genetics of cancer, not the genetic characteristics of a peculiar mutation. Consequently, she gave her stock of these mice to L. C. Dunn at Columbia University and went back to her cancer research. Dunn then spent the next several decades unraveling the basic characteristics of what has now become known as the "t complex."

B. CLASSICAL GENETICS OF THE t COMPLEX

The t complex quickly became of interest to both classical geneticists and population geneticists. One of the characteristics that made it particularly interesting to classical geneticists was the distorted transmission of t alleles (now referred to as "t haplotypes") in heterozygous males (Chelsey and Dunn, 1936). When a female is heterozygous for t (either T/t or $+/t$), her t-carrying chromosome is transmitted in the normal Mendelian fashion, i.e., 50% of her progeny get t and 50% get the alternative chromosome. However, when a male heterozygous for t is mated, typically nearly all (90–100%) of his progeny inherit his t chromosome.

The fact that a high percentage of the progeny of a $+/t$ male inherited his t chromosome was found not to be due to embryonic mortality, but rather to preferential fertilization. The t complex is by no means the only example of a gene showing such distorted transmission. Indeed, every organism that has ever been well studied genetically has one or more genes that show similar distortions of transmission (Zimmering et al., 1970), referred to variously as "meiotic drive," "segregation distortion," or "transmission ratio distortion." However, as a mammalian example, with potential for elucidating sperm function in mammals, the t complex attracted particular attention.

It was also discovered that t haplotypes did not just affect tail length and sperm function, but were also usually recessive lethals. Like their T/T counterparts, mice homozygous for t typically died before birth. The effect of t haplotypes on embryonic viability raised the possibility that this complex might have an important function in regulating embryonic development (Dunn and Gluecksohn-Schoenheimer, 1939), and led to a large amount of research on the development effects of the t lethal factors (reviewed in Sherman and Wudl, 1977).

Matters became more complicated when it was discovered that there were some *t* haplotypes that were not recessive lethals but were rather semilethal: most mice homozygous for these *t* haplotypes survived, but all *t/t* males were sterile (although females were fertile). So, there were apparently two different classes of *t* haplotypes: lethals and semilethals (sometimes also called male sterile haplotypes). This basic description of the classical genetic properties of the *t* complex led to what remains today one of the classic problems in population genetics.

C. Population Genetics

1. Identification of t Haplotypes in Wild Mice

The effect of *t* haplotypes on tail length was used to identify the *t* complex genotype of wild mice. Until recently, when DNA probes specific for *t* haplotypes became available, identification of genotype could only be accomplished through progeny testing in which a wild mouse is mated to a short-tailed mate (*T/+*). If the wild mouse is *+/+*, only normal-tailed (*+/+*) and short-tailed (*T/+*) progeny are produced. If, however, the wild mouse is *+/t*, normal-tailed (*+/+*, *+/t*), short-tailed (*T/+*), and tailless (*T/t*) progeny are produced. Thus, by examining litters for the presence of tailless young, *t* complex genotype can be determined. Use of this procedure led to widespread screening of wild populations for *t* haplotypes. Determination of genotype was faster in males than in females owing to the transmission ratio distortion associated with *t* haplotypes. Because *+/t* males usually transmit their *t* chromosome to a high proportion of their progeny, *+/t* males can be quickly discriminated from *+/+* males. Consequently, much of the early work on the population genetics of *t* haplotypes was based only on data from *+/t* males (reviewed in Lenington *et al.*, 1988b).

2. Population Genetics Problem

The early surveys carried out by Dunn and co-workers (Dunn and Morgan, 1953; Dunn, 1957; Dunn *et al.*, 1960) and confirmed by later surveys (Bennett, 1979; Figueroa *et al.*, 1988; Klein *et al.*, 1984; Lenington *et al.*, 1988b) indicated that about 25% of wild house mice are heterozygous for *t* (but see below). Bruck (1957) constructed a mathematical model to predict the equilibrium frequency of *t* haplotypes: this was based on selection against lethal alleles reducing their frequency but being counteracted by the transmission distortion in heterozygous males, which favors their spread. Transmission distortion is an extremely powerful factor in increasing gene frequency even in the face of the allele favored by the distorted transmission having strong negative effects on fitness. Hence, this model predicted that about 75% of wild mice should be heterozygous when in fact only about 25% heterozygotes are found in wild populations.

Later models constructed by Dunn and Levene (1961) and Lewontin (1968) for male sterile alleles gave similar results. This discrepancy between observed and predicted frequencies led to a search for additional factors over and above the known effects on embryonic mortality and male sterility that might be responsible for reducing the frequency of *t* alleles in natural populations.

One solution was proposed by Lewontin (1962) and Lewontin and Dunn (1960), who argued that, if mice live and breed in small populations, genetic drift might play a key role in controlling gene frequency. In populations containing lethal haplotypes (Lewontin and Dunn, 1960), drift could only lead to fixation of the wild-type haplotype and the frequency of the *t* haplotype would thereby be decreased. In populations containing semilethal haplotypes (Lewontin, 1962), drift could produce populations in which either haplotype was fixed. However, because males homozygous for semilethal haplotypes are sterile, mice living in populations in which the *t* haplotype was fixed would not be able to reproduce. Hence, these populations would go extinct and the frequency of semilethal haplotypes would also be reduced. Computer simulations of these two situations gave expected values for the equilibrium frequency of *t* haplotypes that were very close to the observed. Petras (1967) later pointed out that any process leading to genetic homogeneity within populations would have the same effect and proposed that inbreeding could produce the same results as genetic drift. With the collection of data that seemed to indicate that mice do indeed live in small, closed populations (Anderson, 1964), the "*t* allele problem" was considered solved. The frequency of *t* haplotypes appeared to be controlled by selection at three levels: gametic selection (manifested by transmission distortion), individual selection (lethality and male sterility), and interdemic or group selection (the extinction of whole populations whose male members are homozygous for *t*). Indeed, the *t* complex was considered to be the only good example of group selection in natural populations (Williams, 1966). This picture of the genetics and population genetics of the *t* complex remained intact with minor modifications until the mid 1970s when new molecular and behavioral data changed the picture dramatically.

III.   THE GENETIC STRUCTURE OF THE *t* COMPLEX

A.   SIZE OF THE *t* COMPLEX

Improved mapping of the *t* complex led to the recognition that it is not just a single genetic locus, but rather a large ($20–30 \times 10^3$ kilobases of DNA) segment of chromosome 17 (Silver, 1985). Thus, the *t* complex contains not just one but a large number of genes, and indeed comprises more than 1% of the entire mouse genome. A map of the *t* complex is presented in Fig. 1.

The *t* complex is associated with a series of four inversions (Artzt *et al.*, 1982; Hammer *et al.*, 1989; Hermann *et al.*, 1986) which prevent recombination and

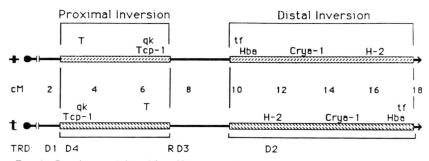

FIG. 1. Genetic maps (adapted from Hammer *et al.*, 1989) of the wild-type *Mus domesticus* and *t* haplotype forms of the *t* complex. The shaded boxes represent the proximal and distal inversions. There are two additional inversions, not shown on this map (Hammer *et al.*, 1989). Map distances from the centromere are indicated in centimorgans (cM). The phenotypic markers Brachyury (*T*), quaking (*qk*), and tufted (*tf*) are shown along with the four distorter loci (*D1–D4*), the responder locus (*R*), the H-2 complex, *tcp-1*, *Crya-1*, and the locus of an α-hemoglobin pseudogene, *Hba*. Reprinted with permission of the author.

thus, despite its size, it is usually transmitted to progeny as a single genetic unit. When the size of the *t* complex was recognized, the name of the chromosomal region was changed from "locus" to "complex," and the genetic structure of the region was characterized by the term "haplotype" rather than "allele."

B. LETHAL FACTORS

The early genetic work on the *t* complex had indicated that there was not just one type of lethal factor, but several (Dunn and Suckling, 1956). These factors could be classified into a number of complementation groups each producing fetal death at a different point in embryonic development (reviewed in Sherman and Wudl, 1977). Lethal factors from three complementation groups (t^0, t^{w1}, t^{w5}) are found in North American wild mice. Many more complementation types are found in Eurasian mice (Dunn *et al.*, 1973; Klein *et al.*, 1984). With improved mapping of the *t* complex it was determined that these various lethal factors were not alternative alleles at a single locus, but rather each mapped to a different part of the *t* complex (Artzt, 1984; Artzt *et al.*, 1982). Usually, however, a given chromosome contains only one lethal factor. These factors are lethal only when homozygous with themselves (Bennett, 1975), so that, for example, t^{w5} is lethal only if both chromosomes carry t^{w5}. If a mouse, instead, carries one chromosome with t^{w1} and another chromosome with t^{w5}, the mouse survives, but all such "compound heterozygote" males are sterile (Bennett, 1975). As with semilethal haplotypes, compound heterozygote females are fertile.

C. Transmission Ratio Distorting Genes

Transmission ratio distortion in males is controlled by genetic factors that are distinct from the lethal factors. There seem to be at least four distorter loci (abbreviated *tcd-1* through *tcd-4*) (Silver and Remis, 1987) which act additively to increase the magnitude of distortion, and also one responder locus (*tcr*)(Lyon, 1984). Presence of *tcr* alone without the distorter genes result in a lower than Mendelian transmission of *t*, i.e., less than 50% (Lyon, 1984), and indeed, occasionally wild males are caught whose *t* haplotype is transmitted at a low ratio (Guenet *et al.*, 1980; Lenington and Heisler, 1991).

Transmission ratio distortion seems to occur because *t*-bearing sperm produce a substance which, in a manner that is not well understood, interferes with the functioning of +-bearing sperm. Studies using artificial insemination and chimeric mice (Olds-Clarke and Peitz, 1986; Seitz and Bennett, 1985) indicate that this substance is transferred during the process of sperm formation when + and *t* sperm are still in contact. Thus, presumably, if a female were to copulate with both a +/+ and a +/*t* male, + sperm from the +/*t* male would be adversely affected, whereas + sperm from the +/+ male would not. The action of the toxic substance seems to be time dependent, starting at ejaculation, so that the greater the interval between ejaculation and fertilization the greater the proportion of + sperm that are deactivated and the higher the transmission of the *t* haplotype (Braden, 1958). This finding provides the potential for mice to modify the transmission of *t* haplotypes behaviorally by modifying the time of copulation relative to ovulation (see below).

In addition to the mapped genetic factors affecting transmission distortion, there are also numerous modifiers which have not been well studied, but which are located throughout the mouse genome (Bennett *et al.*, 1983). In one instance, the same chromosome was found to be transmitted at frequencies ranging from 35 to 75%, depending on the male's genetic background (Bennett *et al.*, 1983). Transmission of *t* in wild males is not quite as high as that often reported for laboratory males. On average, wild males carrying lethal haplotypes have a transmission ratio of 85–90%, and those carrying semilethal haplotypes have an even lower transmission ratio, about 70–75% (Lenington and Heisler, 1991).

D. Male Sterility

The genes responsible for male sterility seem to be indistinguishable from those responsible for transmission ratio distortion (Lyon, 1986; 1987). When a mouse is homozygous for chromosomes carrying genes that disrupt the functioning of sperm carrying the homologous chromosome, the two types of sperm inactivate each other and male sterility results.

E.   Tail Length Factors

Although the *t* complex was originally defined by and named for its effect on tail length, the tail length factors have turned out to be a very minor part of the genetic structure. Tail phenotype is affected by genes present at least two loci (Bode, 1984; Nadeau *et al.*, 1989) which are confined the proximal region of the *t* complex.

F.   Major Histocompatibility Complex

A fascinating finding in the last decade, with numerous implications for behavioral work, has been the close association between the *t* complex and the major histocompatibility complex (MHC). The MHC was originally discovered because of its effect on graft rejection and assumed great importance because of its effects on immune response in general. In the past 15 years it has also been realized that genes within the MHC in both mice and rats mediate a chemical communication system that may be used in mate choice, kin recognition, and individual recognition (Yamazaki *et al.*, 1976, 1979, 1983; Brown, 1983; Brown *et al.*, 1987; Egid and Brown, 1989).

The *t* complex and the MHC may be considered to be components of the same genetic system. On chromosomes containing + haplotypes the MHC maps to the distal end of the *t* complex. However, on chromosomes containing *t* haplotypes, an inversion puts the MHC in the middle of the *t* complex (Artzt *et al.*, 1982). Several lethal factors are found in very close association with the MHC (Artzt, 1984). Indeed, mapping studies have shown that the most commonly occurring lethal haplotype in North American wild mouse populations, t^{w5}, is inseparable from the MHC (Shin *et al.*, 1984).

The MHC is highly polymorphic in mice. Over 100 MHC haplotypes have been identified on chromosomes carrying the wild-type *t* haplotype (Klein, 1986). However, only a few MHC haplotypes have been identified on *t* chromosomes (Hammerberg and Klein, 1975; Nizetic *et al.*, 1984). These MHC types on *t* chromosomes are similar to each other (Shin *et al.*, 1982) and seem to be unique to *t* haplotypes. The MHC types found on *t* chromosomes have not been found on + chromosomes (Silver, 1985).

The *t* complex, like the MHC, also mediates a communication system. Indeed, there seems to be interaction between the two genetic systems in their effects on the behavior of mice (Lenington and Egid, 1989; Lenington *et al.*, 1988a).

G.   Other Genes within the *t* Complex

The region of chromosome 17 comprising the *t* complex contains numerous other genes the function of which is mostly either unknown or poorly understood. However, recently this region has been shown to contain genes which are involved in normal testicular development in mice (Washburn and Eicher, 1989). It also contains the α-crystillin locus (*Crya-1*) (Skow *et al.*, 1987) and a locus (*Tcp-1*) coding for a testicular expressed protein (Silver, 1985; Willison *et al.*, 1986).

IV. *t* Haplotypes in Natural Populations

In recent years, considerably more information has become available on the distribution of *t* haplotypes in natural populations. In our laboratory we have sampled mice from a large number of populations because we needed wild mice for behavioral research. We have usually determined genotype by progeny testing. In addition, the development of molecular probes specific for regions of the *t* complex has made it possible to survey wild populations using molecular techniques to determine genotype. The picture that has emerged from these recent studies is, not surprisingly, far more complex than the earlier data suggested.

A. Geographic Distribution

Mice carrying *t* haplotypes have been captured on all continents (Erhart *et al.*, 1989; Lenington *et al.*, 1988b). These haplotypes have been reported to occur in at least four species of the genus *Mus* (*musculus, domesticus, bactrianus,* and *molossinus*) (Delarbre *et al.*, 1988; Hammer *et al.*, 1989; Klein *et al.*, 1984; Tutikawa, 1955).

Mus domesticus is distributed throughout western Europe, and all house mice in North America are derived from this species. There is considerably more polymorphism within the *t* complex in European populations of *M. domesticus* than in North American populations, probably because North America was colonized by a small population of mice from Europe (Klein *et al.*, 1984). Only three lethal factors (t^{w5}, t^{w1}, and t^0) have been found in North American populations, whereas European populations contain lethal factors from at least 10 complementation groups. In addition, the amount of polymorphism associated with the MHC within *t* haplotypes is far greater for European *M. domesticus* than for North American.

There is a similar reduction in the polymorphism associated with *t* haplotypes present in *M. musculus* populations. This species is found in eastern Europe. A stable hybrid zone exists along much of the border between the ranges of *M. domesticus* and *M. musculus*. Only two lethal factors (t^{w73} and t^0) have been found in *M. musculus* (Klein *et al.*, 1984; Forejt *et al.*, 1988). With regard to the rest of the *t* chromatin, *M. musculus* haplotypes share some alleles with their *M. domesticus* counterparts (e.g., $tcp-1^a$). However, some DNA sequences identified on *M. musculus* haplotypes are unknown in *M. domesticus* (Forejt *et al.*, 1988).

B. FREQUENCY IN POPULATIONS

The frequency of complete *t* haplotypes has been found in most surveys to be about 20–25% (Lenington *et al.*, 1988b; Klein *et al.*, 1984; Figueroa *et al.*, 1988). This does not mean, however, that all populations have a frequency of *t* in this range. There is considerable variation among populations and the modal frequency is low (<20%) (Lenington *et al.*, 1988b), while a few populations have a frequency of over 50%. Frequency of *t* haplotypes may be higher in populations in which the predominant haplotype is a semilethal than in populations in which it is lethal (Lenington *et al.*, 1988b).

Frequency of *t* haplotypes appears to vary by sex. The frequency of *t* haplotypes in wild females appears to be only about half that in males (Lenington *et al.*, 1988b). On average, about 30% of wild-caught males carry *t* haplotypes whereas only 16% of wild-caught females are +/*t*.

Estimates of the frequency of *t* haplotypes have, however, been greatly complicated by the discovery of partial haplotypes. As mentioned above, the *t* complex contains a long sequence of DNA. Use of molecular probes to screen wild mouse populations has shown that some mice carry "partial haplotypes," i.e., they have chromosomes which carry some, but not all, of the genes identified as part of the *t* complex (Erhart *et al.*, 1989; Figueroa *et al.*, 1988). Such partial haplotypes will only be detected by progeny testing if they carry the tail interaction factor located in the proximal portion of the *t* complex. However, many partial haplotypes only carry *t*-specific genes for the distal portion of the complex and hence will not be detected by progeny testing (Erhart *et al.*, 1989). The origin of these partial haplotypes is currently a matter of speculation (see below). However, they have appeared at high frequency (up to 47% of mice tested) in some surveys of mouse populations (Erhart *et al.*, 1989; Figueroa *et al.*, 1988). Many may be associated with low transmission (Lyon, 1984; Lyon and Zenthon, 1988), and at present it is not obvious how partial haplotypes will be accommodated into a theory regarding the maintenance of *t* haplotypes in wild populations. However, they clearly confound all current theories and make it difficult even to know what figure to cite as the empirical frequency for *t* haplotypes.

V. EFFECT OF THE *t* COMPLEX
ON BEHAVIOR AND FITNESS

One hypothesis proposed to account for the lower than expected frequency of *t* haplotypes in wild populations is heterozygote disadvantage. If +/+ mice have higher fitness than $+/t$ mice, the frequency of t will be reduced through individual selection. All of the studies described below have as their focus determination of fitness differences between $+/+$ and $+/t$ mice.

A.   ORIGINS OF ANIMALS USED IN THE STUDIES

In this section I distinguish between three different categories of mice that have been used to investigate the effect of t complex genotype on behavior and fitness. The three categories are laboratory strains (either inbred or outbred), wild-caught mice (those caught directly from the wild), and "wild-derived" mice (those bred from wild parents). These may be one or more generations removed from their wild origins. Almost all the work done in our laboratory has been with wild-derived mice. Using these sacrifices genetic control in that the animals differ at many genetic loci, not just the t complex. However, it seemed important to use wild mice to be able to generalize from our results to processes occurring in natural populations. Therefore, in the studies discussed below, we have used mice from 34 different populations covering a wide area of North America, ranging from Maine to Colorado. Thus, we hope we have randomized the variability for which we have been unable to control.

All of our work with wild mice has been conducted with animals carrying all of the haplotypes found in wild North American populations. In these studies we have pooled data from all $+/t$ mice regardless of the specific haplotype carried. Obtaining these mice and progeny testing them has been such a time-consuming task that it has not been possible to obtain data in which would allow comparison among different t haplotypes. However, although we have looked for behavioral differences associated with specific haplotypes we have never detected any. This is not to imply that quantitative differences in behavior do not exist, only that large obvious qualitative differences between mice carrying different t haplotypes probably do not occur.

B.   VIABILITY

1.   Juvenile Viability

Dunn *et al.* (1958) examined relative juvenile viability of wild-derived $+/+$ and $+/t$ mice by mating $+/t$ females to $+/+$ males. Wild-type homozygotes and $+/t$ progeny should be produced from such a cross in a 1:1 ratio. Both males and females were progeny tested to determine genotype. However, during this progeny testing, many more males produced young when bred to $T/+$ mates than did females, and so Dunn *et al.* confined their analysis to the data from males. They found about twice as many $+/t$ as $+/+$ individuals among the males that survived to sexual maturity and produced enough progeny to determine genotype. They concluded that the viability of $+/t$ males was higher early in life than of $+/+$ males. However, these data might also reflect fertility differences between $+/+$ and $+/t$ males, since progeny testing was the only way to determine the genotype of males. Consequently, these data do not definitively show differences in juvenile viability. Among the small number of females for which genotype could be determined, the two genotypes were present in equal proportions.

The finding mentioned above that the frequency of *t* haplotypes in wild populations is higher in males than females may be relevant to the issue of genotypic differences in viability. Both trapping bias (Lenington and Franks, 1985) and fertility differences (Lenington *et al.*, 1988b) were ruled out as explanations for the phenomenon. Thus, the sex difference in frequency may be indirect evidence that either the viability of $+/t$ males is higher than that of $+/+$ males or the viability of $+/t$ females is lower than that of $+/+$ females under natural conditions. This sex difference in gene frequency was present among both mice trapped as juveniles and those trapped as adults, so the viability differences are manifested early in life. Therefore, at present it seems likely that there are some sex-specific juvenile viability differences associated with *t* complex genotype. At present it is unclear in which sex the viability differences are manifested.

2. *Adult Viability*

Franks and Lenington (1986) measured viability of adult wild-derived males and females in a seminatural environment. No genotypic differences in adult viability were found for either sex.

C. COMMUNICATION

At the beginning of our research on behavioral correlates of *t* complex genotype, it seemed that there may have been strong selection for females to avoid mating with males who carried *t* haplotypes. For such mating preference to occur it is obviously necessary for females to be able to discriminate between males who do and those who do not carry *t* haplotypes. Hence, the bulk of the behavioral research on the *t* complex has involved its role in communication between wild mice.

Mice have been tested for their ability to discriminate either between soiled bedding from cages of mice of differing genotypes (Lenington *et al.*, 1988a) or between intact mice of differing genotypes (Lenington, 1983; Williams, 1989). Test animals are placed in a choice apparatus (Fig. 2) in which the amount of time they spend near each of the two stimulus animals or bedding sets is recorded. An animal's preference is defined as the odor near which it spends the most time. The strength of preference is a measure based on the proportion of time it spends near the preferred odor.

Genes within the *t* complex are associated with a urinary odor cue (Drickamer

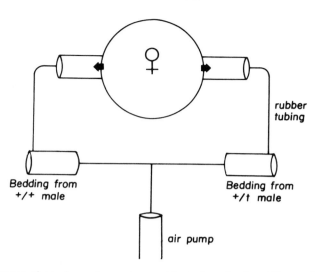

FIG. 2. Diagram of one form of apparatus used in testing mice for ability to discriminate *t* complex genotype. The test animal is placed in the central chamber and allowed access to each of two side cylinders. Soiled bedding from the cage of two stimulus animals differing in genotype is placed in the two lower cylinders. Air is blown over the soiled bedding and into the two side cylinders. The amount of time the test animal spends in each of the two side cylinders is recorded. When whole animals are used as stimuli instead of soiled bedding, the apparatus is the same except that at the end of the side cylinders there is a compartment into which stimulus animals are placed. The stimulus animal is separated from the test animal by perforated plexiglass, so the test animal can smell and hear, but not touch, the stimulus animals.

and Lenington, 1987). Both males and females appear to be able to discriminate the genotype of opposite sexed conspecifics based on odor alone, and have preferences for odors of +/+ individuals. However, preferences of males for odors of females are weaker and less consistent than are those of females for male odors (Williams, 1989), and hence discrimination by females has received more attention than that by males.

Among females, only those carrying *t* haplotypes show strong, consistent preferences for the odors of +/+ males. Females homozygous for the + haplotype have shown preferences in some studies (Lenington, 1983; Lenington and Egid, 1985, 1989) but not in others (Williams, 1989; Coopersmith, personal communication). In general, the preferences of +/+ females appear to be influenced in complex ways by a number of environmental factors including the genotype of their parents (Lenington and Egid, 1989), the population background of both stimulus males and test females (Williams, 1989), and the relative dominance status of the stimulus males (Coopersmith, personal communication). Heterozygous females, in contrast, show strong preferences for the odors of

+/+ males which are independent of parental genotype and which are manifested even with a wide variety of environmental manipulations (Lenington, 1983; Lenington and Egid, 1985, 1989; Williams, 1989). Their preferences appear to become stronger when in estrus (Williams, 1989), indicating that the odor preference probably reflects mating preference.

The strength of preference of +/*t* females seems to be independent of the particular *t* haplotype carried by the female. No difference in strength of preference was found among females heterozygous for t^0, t^{w1}, or t^{w5} (Williams, 1989). Wild-derived +/*t* females carrying semilethal haplotypes also have preferences of the same magnitude as those carrying lethal haplotypes (Lenington and Egid, 1985; J. R. Williams, unpublished data). In addition, the strength of preference appears to be similar in wild-derived and inbred laboratory females. Finally, the strength of preference does not differ among inbred laboratory strain females of differing genetic backgrounds (Williams, 1989).

The limitation of consistent preferences for +/+ males to +/*t* females indicates that genes on *t* chromosomes probably influence the manifestation of preference by females. Mice carrying recombinant chromosomes have been used to map the locations within the *t* complex of genes influencing the odor cue in males and the preference in females. As discussed above, inversions within the *t* complex suppress recombination in +/*t* mice. However, in compound heterozygous females (those with two *t* haplotypes each carrying a different lethal factor), the genes are properly aligned so that recombination can occur at normal rates (Fig. 3). Two types of progeny can be produced through such recombination: those carrying two lethal factors on one chromosome and those carrying a complete *t* haplotype (containing the tail interaction factor, transmission ratio-distorting factors, *t*-specific MHC) but lacking lethal factors. Comparison of the behavior of mice carrying each of these chromosomes allows one to determine whether genes associated with the lethal factors are necessary for the behavior in question. If mice carrying these two recombinant chromosomes differ, lethal

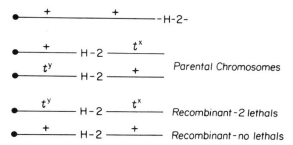

FIG. 3. Schematic diagram of parental chromosomes and recombinant two-lethal and no-lethal chromosomes.

factors or genes closely associated with them must be responsible for the differences. Mice carrying each of these chromosomes were bred with wild mice to put the recombinant chromosomes on a wild genetic background. The two types of mice will be referred to for the remainder of the article as "two-lethal" (i.e., $+ + / t^{w12} t^{w32}$) and "no-lethal." Females and males were tested for their preferences between opposite sexed mice carrying these two chromosomes.

Females had strong preferences for odors of no-lethal males, indicating that lethal factors or genes closely associated with them are necessary for the odor cue (Lenington and Egid, 1985). Male mice, in contrast, showed no preference for females carrying either type of chromosome (Egid and Lenington, 1985), indicating that genes producing the odor cue in females are not associated specifically with lethal factors.

When females carrying the two types of recombinant chromosomes were tested for preference between $+/+$ and $+/t$ males, only two-lethal females had preference for $+/+$ males; no-lethal females did not prefer $+/+$ males (Lenington et al., 1988a). This result indicated that the presence of lethal factors was necessary for the expression of preference in females. However, wild $+/t$ females (carrying only one lethal factor) had preferences for $+/+$ males that were similar in strength to those manifested by two-lethal females. Thus, the effect of lethal factors on a single chromosome was not additive. In contrast, preferences of t^{w5}/t^{w1} (compound heterozygote) females were much stronger than those of two-lethal $(+ + / t^{w12} t^{w32})$ females (Lenington et al., 1988a). In other words, the effect of two lethal factors associated with two complete t haplotypes was stronger than the effect of two lethal factors associated with only one complete haplotype. These data indicate that a second gene, independent of the lethal factors, also plays a role in the expression of female preference.

In order to try to identify more precisely the location of this second gene, we tested females carrying the partial haplotype t^{w18} for their preference between $+/+$ and $+/t$ males. The t^{w18} haplotype was originally derived from a wild-caught female carrying t^{w5} (Dunn, 1957). This haplotype carries a unique lethal factor which differs in complementation type from all other lethal factors. It also appears to lack the distal part of the t complex, including the t-specific MHC (Artzt et al., 1982; D. Bennett, personal communication). Females whose genotype was $+/t^{w18}$ showed no preference for males of either genotype. The 12 t^{w18} females spent an average of 52% (SD = 62%) of their time in the arm of the test apparatus near the $+/+$ male. This did not differ significantly from 50% ($t = 0.17$; df = 11; $P > 0.05$).

Two possible hypotheses might account for this result. First, the t^{w18} lethal factor, per se, may not be associated with genes influencing female preference. However, the finding mentioned above that, among mice carrying complete haplotypes, preference is independent of the specific lethal factor carried, reduces the likelihood of this possibility. A second, more likely, possibility is that the second gene necessary for the expression of preference is located within the distal portion of the *t* complex.

An informative experiment to test this second hypothesis would be to test females who carried a no-lethal haplotype on one 17th chromosome and t^{w18} on the other. Neither chromosome when paired with a + chromosome results in the expression of female preference. However, the model proposed above hypothesizes that one of the genes necessary for preference is found on the t^{w18} chromosome in association with the lethal factor. The second should be found on the no-lethal chromosome since the distal portion of the *t* complex is intact on this chromosome. Hence a mouse that carries both such chromosomes has both genes necessary for the expression of preference for +/+ males. We have only tested two such females but both showed strong +/+ preferences. One spent 72% of the test period near the +/+ male and the other spent 89%.

The association of female preference with lethal factors, combined with the independence of the magnitude of preference from the particular type of lethal factor, has implications for a controversy regarding the molecular structure of the *t* complex. There has been considerable debate about whether the various lethal factors are genetically and functionally related or simply an independent collection of mutations (Silver, 1985). At present prevailing opinion seems to favor the interpretation of the lethals as independent mutations. It has been pointed out that the number of lethals within the *t* complex is no greater than would be expected in any similar sized region of mouse DNA (Silver, 1985; Lyon, 1986). However, the behavioral data seem to indicate that many of the lethal factors or genes closely associated with them produce the same behavioral phenotype. If the behavioral data are an indication of an underlying genetic similarity, lethal factors may have had a less independent origin than is currently supposed.

D. Use of Odor Cues Associated with the *t* Complex

The data presented above indicate that mice can perceive information regarding *t* complex genotype. Given that they have this information, it is pertinent to ask how it is used. It seems to be used in several behavioral contexts. The system analyzed genetically above is probably used in mating preference. The other contexts in which *t* complex recognition described below (puberty acceleration, pregnancy block, parental behavior) may represent manifestations of the same communication system, or, alternatively, the cues and responses used in these contexts may be modulated by a totally different set of genes on the 17th chromosome.

1. Mate Choice

Mating preference relative to *t* complex genotype has not been tested for directly. The ideal experiment would be to give a test animal a choice between tethered mates, but such data have not been collected. Despite this gap, however, it seems likely that the preferences of $+/t$ females for odors of $+/+$ males reflect mating preferences, particularly as these preferences are stronger among estrous than diestrous females. Restriction of genes for mating preference to t chromosomes functions to protect both $+/+$ and $+/t$ females from the deleterious effects of mating with $+/t$ males. Heterozygous females mating with $+/t$ males would suffer an immediate decrement in fitness owing to the production of t/t progeny. It is obviously adaptive for them to prefer $+/+$ mates. Homozygous, $+/+$, females suffer no such immediate decrement from mating with a $+/t$ male but their fitness would be reduced in the next generation if their $+/t$ daughters chose $+/t$ mates. However, their $+/t$ daughters inherit genes on the t chromosome derived from their father and these affect their preferences for mates. Hence, these $+/t$ daughters are less likely to chose $+/t$ males as mates and, consequently, $+/+$ females who mate with $+/t$ males may suffer little if any adverse effect on fitness.

2. Acceleration of Puberty

It has been known for some time that juvenile female mice that are exposed to male odors achieve puberty at an earlier age than those not so exposed (Vandenbergh, 1969). Recently (Drickamer and Lenington, 1987), it was found that urine from $+/+$ males is significantly better at accelerating puberty in females than is urine from $+/t$ males (although the latter accelerates puberty more than exposure to saline).

3. The Bruce Effect and Individual Recognition

Female mice, early in pregnancy, have a tendency to abort their litters if the stud male is removed and they are exposed to the odor of a strange male (the Bruce effect). In a study of the effect of genes within the MHC on a female's ability to discriminate stud from strange male, it was found using congenic mice that if the stud and strange male were identical at the MHC, the probability that a female would abort her litter was much less than if they had different MHC types (Yamazaki et al., 1983). In a study carried out in our laboratory on t complex effects on pregnancy block using wild-derived mice, it was found that, if both stud and strange male are $+/t$, females do not abort their litters (□□ Coopersmith, unpublished data) (Table I). Sixty percent of females produced litters when both stud and strange male were $+/t$. In contrast, for all other genotypic combinations of stud and strange male the proportion of females producing litters was much lower.

The low rate of abortion when both stud and strange male are $+/t$ may be due to the similarity of MHC types on t-carrying chromosomes. Interestingly enough, the inhibition of pregnancy block is accomplished even though $+/t$ stud and $+/t$ strange males may not be carrying the same haplotype. Heterozygous

TABLE I
PROPORTION OF FEMALES PRODUCING LITTERS AFTER BEING EXPOSED TO
STRANGE MALES DIFFERING IN *t* COMPLEX GENOTYPE

Genotype of stud male	$+/+$	$+/t$	$+/+$	$+/t$
Genotype of strange male	$+/+$	$+/+$	$+/t$	$+/t$
Total number of females	47	37	31	43
Proportion producing litters	0.21	0.32	0.35	0.60

$+/t$ mice that do not carry the same haplotype are similar but *not* identical at the MHC on their *t* chromosomes. The large amount of variability within the MHC on $+$ chromosomes virtually guarantees that the two males will differ at the MHC on their homologous chromosome. Apparently, the similarity between the two *t* chromosomes is sufficient to suppress pregnancy block as a response to the strange male. Indeed, these data may imply a more important role for the 17th chromosome in individual and/or kin recognition than was implied by the earlier data of Yamazaki *et al.* (1983). They used mice that were genetically homogeneous, differing only at the MHC. Under these circumstances, their data showed that additional genetic similarity at the MHC between stud and strange male was sufficient to suppress pregnancy block, and genetic differences at the MHC between the two males were sufficient to elicit the blocking effect. The data obtained in our laboratory indicate that even when the males are genetically highly heterozygous, difference or similarity between the males on only one of the two 17th chromosomes is sufficient to elicit or suppress the block. A stimulus which is perceived even against a noisy background is likely to be more salient than one perceived only against a homogeneous background. The data on pregnancy block by no means demonstrate that *t*-associated MHC cues are used for kin and/or individual recognition. However, if they are, it is possible that the similarity among *t* complex genes may cause errors to be made in such discrimination.

4. Parental Behavior

Lactating female mice seem to be able in some instances to discriminate between the odors of pups differing in *t* complex genotype (Egid, 1986; Schwartz, personal communication). Females were tested for pup discrimination by recording the proportion of time they spent near pups of differing genotypes when placed in a simple choice apparatus. As in the tests with adult stimulus animals, the females were presented with two pups differing in genotype, and the amount of time a female spent near each pup was recorded.

A subset of females that were tested for pup preference was also tested to determine which pup was retrieved first in a retrieval test. Nineteen of the 26 females tested first retrieved the same pup as they had spent the most time near in the discrimination test. Hence it seems possible that the behavior manifested in the pup discrimination test may be a measure of maternal preference.

The females' behavior was related to pup sex as well as pup genotype. They showed no preference when presented with a choice between $+/+$ and $+/t$ males (Egid, 1986; Schwartz, personal communication), but strong preferences for $+/+$ when the choice was between $+/+$ and t/t males (it will be recalled that t/t males are sterile). Females also appear to have a strong preference for $+/+$ over t/t females (Schwartz, personal communication).

Responses of lactating females to female $+/+$ and $+/t$ pups were more problematic. In one study (Egid, 1986), females seemed to prefer $+/+$ over $+/t$ female pups. Preliminary data from a second study, however, have failed to replicate this as the females showed no preference between $+/+$ and $+/t$ female pups (Schwartz, personal communication).

Female mice are known to cull litters when food becomes scarce (Perrigo, 1987). If parental investment is distributed nonrandomly with respect to t complex genotype, maternal behavior could influence gene frequency in wild populations.

E. DOMINANCE AND AGGRESSION

1. Aggression in Males

The data on dominance and aggression of mice differing in t complex genotype highlight the problems that arise when attempting to generalize data obtained in experiments conducted in restricted settings to more naturalistic situations. In four studies (Martin and Andrewartha, 1962; Lenington, 1983, and unpublished data; Levine et al., 1980) $+/+$ males were allowed to fight in an arena or in laboratory cages against $+/t$ opponents. The results of these studies are summarized in Table II. "Dominance" in these studies was assessed in a variety of ways. Some studies (Lenington, 1983; and unpublished data) called the mouse performing the greatest number of attacks "dominant." Levine et al. (1980) and Martin and Andrewartha (1962) assessed dominance on the basis of which mouse survived the paired encounter. Despite the variety of methodologies, these data seem to indicate a clear advantage for $+/t$ wild and wild-derived males in aggressive encounters with $+/+$ males. The data have to be interpreted with some caution, however. The first reason for caution is that the effect may be dependent to some extent on the genetic background of the males. Laboratory strain males, or hybrids between laboratory strain and wild-derived mice, do not seem to show an aggressive advantage for $+/t$ males (Table II).

A more important reason for caution is that the aggressive advantage for $+/t$ males seen in arenas does not translate itself in a straightforward way into

TABLE II
STUDIES OF AGGRESSION IN +/+ AND +/*t* MICE

Genetic background of mouse	Number of fights won by +/+	Number of fights won by +/*t*	Reference
Wild caught	0	4	S. Lenington (unpublished data)
Wild derived	6	10	Martin and Andrewartha (1962)
	0	11	Lenington (1983)
	4	11	
	4	17	S. Lenington (unpublished data)
Laboratory strain or hybrids between laboratory	8	8	Martin and Andrewartha (1962)
strain and wild	10	15	Levine *et al.* (1980)
	10	2	S. Lenington (unpublished data)

dominance among mice living under more natural social conditions. Behavior of +/+ and +/*t* mice was studied in a seminatural environment (Franks and Lenington, 1986) in which 20 trials were run using 6–10 mice/trial. Each trial lasted for 20 days during which data were collected on mating and aggressive behavior. No difference was found in this study between the probability that a +/+ or a +/*t* male would be dominant. Eight of the 20 trials had +/*t* dominant males and 12 had +/+ dominant males. However, there were profound differences in aggressive behavior between +/+ and +/*t* dominant males. Heterozygous males, when dominant, were highly likely to kill subordinate males whereas dominant +/+ males were not. Furthermore, among surviving subordinate males, none ever copulated with a female in trials with a dominant +/*t* male. In contrast, half the subordinates in trials with dominant +/+ males copulated with females. Consequently, dominant +/*t* males seemed to be more aggressive and exert more "social control" over their companions than did dominant +/+ males. This result is consistent with the finding of Lenington (1983) that dominant +/*t* males had a significantly higher rate of attack than did dominant +/+ males.

The association of *t* haplotypes with male aggressive behavior is of particular interest in view of recent data indicating that genes within this region of chromosome 17 are involved in normal male testicular development (Washburn and Eicher, 1989). In addition, as discussed above, the MHC is closely associated with the *t* complex. Genes within the MHC have been shown to affect cortisone levels, male testosterone levels, and male tissue responsiveness to testosterone (Ivanyi *et al.*, 1976; Ivanyi, 1978). Testosterone has been shown to facilitate male aggressive behavior in mice (Beeman, 1947; Luttge *et al.*, 1974). Consequently, differences in aggressive behavior between $+/+$ and $+/t$ males may reflect differences in MHC haplotypes found on $+$ and t chromosomes.

In summary, it seems likely that $+/t$ wild males are more aggressive than $+/+$ males. Whether, however, this increased aggression is translated into differences in dominance status or only more subtly into differences in consequences for subordinate males is uncertain.

2. Aggression in Females

The relationship between female dominance and t complex genotype has only been studied in a seminatural environment (Franks and Lenington, 1986), but the data, in contrast to those on males, were very clear-cut. The consequences of possession of a t haplotype for aggressive behavior in females are the opposite of those in males. In the 20 trials, $+/t$ females were dominant in only 4 and $+/+$ females in the remaining 16. Thus, possession of a t haplotype seems to reduce severely a female's chance of being dominant in relation to $+/+$ females.

F. FERTILITY

1. Male Fertility

Several studies (Franks and Lenington, 1986; Johnston and Brown, 1969; Levine *et al.*, 1980) have compared production of offspring of $+/+$ males with that of $+/t$ males. All except the study of Johnston and Brown, however, were designed in such a way that male fertility in the strict sense was confounded with social interactions among males and female preferences for mates of a particular genotype. For example, in the study by Franks and Lenington (1986), matings took place in large social groups. Therefore greater offspring production by males of one genotype may not simply reflect genetic effects on fertility directly but rather may result from male dominance interactions or female mating preference. In the study by Johnston and Brown, $+/+$ and $+/t$ (heterozygous for semilethal haplotypes) wild-derived males were mated in single male–female pairs with females of all genotypes. The relevant comparison for purposes of assessing fertility is matings with $+/+$ females. Matings to $+/t$ and t/t females confounded fertility of $+/t$ males with embryonic mortality as well as female mating preference. There was no difference in fertility of males of the two genotypes when mated with $+/+$ females.

2. Female Fertility

Franks and Lenington (1986) found that, in a seminatural environment, $+/t$ females were much less likely than $+/+$ females to go into behavioral estrus. This effect persisted even when female dominance rank (which is an important predictor of estrus behavior) was controlled. Among those females that did copulate with males, $+/t$ females were much less likely to become pregnant than were $+/+$ females. In the study mentioned above, Johnston and Brown (1969) found that fertility of $+/t$ females mated to $+/+$ males was slightly lower than that of $+/+$ females.

VI.   Behavior and Male Transmission Ratio

A.   Behavior That Reduces the Transmission of *t* Haplotypes

One of the most striking characteristics of *t* haplotypes is their association with transmission ratio distortion. Although it is commonly claimed that complete *t* haplotypes are transmitted at a high ratio ($\sim$90%), this ratio is by no means immutable. The first hint that the transmission ratio of individual males could be altered behaviorally came with the work of Braden (1958). Mice normally copulate about 6 hr prior to ovulation (Braden, 1957). Braden timed the mating of males with females such that copulation took place either at the normal time or just prior to the expected time of ovulation. Male transmission ratio was typically high in the first group. However, in the second group (that mated just before ovulation) the transmission ratio distortion normally associated with *t* haplotypes disappeared. In this group, males transmitted their *t* haplotype at the expected Mendelian ratio of 50%. This study led to the conclusion that the action of the substance which led *t* sperm to interfere with the functioning of $+$-bearing sperm was time dependent. The longer the interval between copulation and ovulation, the more $+$ sperm were deactivated, and the higher was the probability that an egg would be fertilized by a *t*-bearing sperm. The substance is transmitted during the process of sperm formation when $+$ and *t* sperm are still in contact. Studies with artificial insemination (Olds-Clarke and Peitz, 1986) have shown that the transmission of $+$ sperm from $+/+$ males is unaffected by the presence of *t* sperm. Only recently, however, has it been demonstrated that male transmission ratio may be altered by normal behavioral interactions of mice.

Our laboratory has conducted a large-scale breeding program with mice over a 10-year period. In the process, we have accumulated a large body of data on the transmission of *t* haplotypes in wild breeding pairs. It is possible to use birth dates of litters to classify them as having been produced as a result of cycling estrus (CE) or postpartum estrus (PPE) matings. We have found that, among litters produced as a result of CE matings, male transmission ratio is high: 79% (SD = 21%). However, when these same males sired litters as a result of PPE matings, the magnitude of their transmission ratio distortion decreased to 59% (SD = 32%). This difference was highly statistically significant (Lenington and Heisler, 1991). Reduction of transmission ratio distortion associated with PPE matings was also found in inbred laboratory mice, and hence it appears to be independent of genetic background.

It is not known whether or not this phenomenon is a result of time of mating. In order to determine whether matings in PPE and CE differed in the relation of time of mating to ovulation, we videotaped the mating behavior of mice in PPE and CE. Females were killed 3 hr after mating and their oviducts were examined for the presence of ova. If PPE matings typically occur close to the time of ovulation, one would expect to see ova after PPE matings but not after CE matings. Only five mating sequences (two CE and three PPE) were videotaped. Shed ova were found in the oviducts of one of the two females mating in CE and one of the three females mating in PPE. The data are obviously very limited, but it does not appear that PPE matings occur substantially closer to the time of ovulation than do CE matings.

There seemed to be however, a striking difference in mating behavior between PPE and CE matings. Copulatory behavior in the two CE matings lasted 175 and 63 min each. In the three PPE matings it lasted 25, 8, and 3 min each. Data from other rodent species also indicate that PPE is shorter in duration than CE (Carter *et al.*, 1986; Young, 1970).

It is known that the pattern of copulatory behavior in rodents may affect sperm transport and fertility by eliciting neuroendocrine reflexes in the female. These neuroendocrine reflexes can alter the biochemical milieu in the female reproduction tract in such a way as to affect sperm transport (Adler and Toner, 1986). Biochemical differences between $+$- and t-bearing sperm may result in the two types of sperm responding differently to changes in the female's reproductive tract. Consequently, this behavioral difference may differentially affect the transport of each sperm type. Regardless of the underlying mechanism causing the decrease in transmission of t with PPE matings, however, any factor that alters the frequency of PPE mating will have an effect on the frequency of t in mouse populations.

B.   FACTORS THAT AFFECT THE FREQUENCY
OF POSTPARTUM ESTRUS LITTERS

We have used mice trapped from a large number of localities. When we have made pairs in the laboratory, both male and female have sometimes come from the same population. On other occasions, they have come from different, and often widely separated, populations. We have found that when the male and female come from the same population the frequency of PPE matings is much higher than when they come from different populations (Lenington and Heisler, 1991). This difference is substantial. When male and female come from the same population, 63% of litters are conceived during PPE. In contrast, when male and female come from different populations, only 40% of the litters born have been conceived during PPE. As a consequence, the percentage of progeny that inherit a $+/t$ male's haplotype is on average lower when male and female come from the same population (64%) than when they differ in population background (83%). We do not know how the alteration in frequency of PPE mating is controlled. In the videotaping study mentioned above, copulation often did not occur postpartum. In situations in which copulation did not occur in the 36-hr period after parturition, male and female simply sat on opposite sides of the cage and ignored each other. No interactions took place that would suggest that females were rejecting the advances of males or that males were avoiding solicitations by females.

VII. EVOLUTION OF THE *t* COMPLEX

All *t* haplotypes show a high degree of genetic similarity. Hence all are postulated to have arisen from a common ancestor (Silver, 1985; Forejt *et al.*, 1988). Theories about the origin of *t* haplotypes fall into two general categories: extrinsic theories postulating that *t* haplotypes arrived in mouse populations by introgression from another species, and intrinsic theories, postulating that *t* haplotypes arose by a process of evolution within an ancestral species of *Mus*.

A. EXTRINSIC THEORY

It is possible the *t* haplotypes were derived by genetic introgression from another species (Silver, 1985; Delarbre *et al.*, 1988). The introgressed chromosome could have behaved normally in the parental species but become associated with distorted transmission in the new species. Such a situation has been reported in tobacco (Cameron and Moav, 1957). In this case, a chromosome from one species was experimentally introduced into another. Although the chromosome was transmitted normally in the first species, when transferred to the second, it was transmitted in a high ratio through the male gametes. However, *t* haplotypes in *M. domesticus* and in *M. musculus* carry an invariant form of *Tcp-1* (*Tcp-1*[a]) (Forejt *et al.*, 1988; Willison *et al.*, 1986). *Tcp-1*[b] is found on $+$ chromosomes. If *t* haplotypes arose by introgression, one would also expect to find the *Tcp-1*[a] gene sequence in other European species of *Mus* (*spretus, castaneus, abbotti,* and *spicilegus*). *Tcp-1*[a] gene sequences have been identified in *M. abbotti* and *spicilegus* (Delarbre *et al.*, 1988), but not in other European species of *Mus* (Willison *et al.*, 1986). However, neither *M. musculus* nor *M. domesticus* is known to hybridize under natural conditions with these other species (Bonhomme *et al.*, 1984).

B. INTRINSIC THEORY

1. Genetic Changes

The evolutionary scenario most often proposed for the evolution of *t* haplotypes involves selection acting at both the level of the chromosome and that of the individual. It seems likely that genes which affected sperm function (distorters and responders) appeared first on 17th chromosomes (Silver, 1988). These would be selected for at the level of the chromosome because of their ability to increase the transmission of the chromosome on which they were located. However, recombination would inevitably tend to break up this combination of genes, and thereby destroy their capacity to increase their own transmission. Therefore, there would be selection (again at the level of the chromosome) for this gene combination to be protected from recombination by becoming associated with inversions (Charlesworth and Hartl, 1978). Other genetic systems associated with distorted transmission (e.g., SD in *Drosophila*) are also associated with inversions (Hartl, 1975a). An apparently inevitable by-product of the genes for transmission distortion is the production of sterility in homozygous males (Lyon, 1986). Consequently, there would be selection at the level of the individual for mechanisms to reduce investment in these sterile males. The most effective way to reduce this investment is for *t/t* mice to die early in gestation, and hence there is selection for lethal factors (Lyon, 1986; Silver, 1988).

2. Age of the t Complex

Extrinsic and intrinsic theories have different implications for estimates of the age of *t* haplotypes. If *t* haplotypes arose by introgression, such introgression could presumably have occurred quite recently. The only way to estimate the time at which it took place is to estimate the amount of divergence among the various haplotypes themselves.

If *t* haplotypes arose by a process of selection in an ancestral mouse species this probably took place at least 2–4 million years ago (Hammer *et al.*, 1989; Silver, 1988). As mentioned above, *t* haplotypes have been found in four species of *Mus*. The intrinsic theory would predict that *t* haplotypes originated before the four species diverged (Delarbre *et al.*, 1988). Studies measuring recombination between *t* and + chromosomes in interspecific crosses between *M. domesticus* and *M. abbotti* or *M. spretus* indicate that one of the four inversions associated with *t* haplotypes occurred after the divergence between *M. spretus* and the other three *Mus* species, but before the divergence of *M. abbotti* from the lineage leading to *M. musculus* and *M. domesticus* (Hammer *et al.*, 1989). The other three inversions occurred within the lineage leading to *M. domesticus* and *M. musculus*.

3. Limitations of the Intrinsic Hypothesis

The intrinsic hypothesis describes a plausible origin for *t* haplotypes. It successfully accounts for the origin of the major features of the *t* complex: transmission distortion, male sterility, inversions, and lethality. However, there are several empirical findings and theoretical considerations that are unexplained by this hypothesis.

a. Existence of Semilethal Haplotypes. Because semilethal haplotypes are harder to characterize than lethal haplotypes they have been relatively neglected. However, they are very common in mouse populations. More populations contain lethal than semilethal haplotypes. However, when semilethal haplotypes are present in mouse populations, they tend to be present in higher frequencies than lethals (Lenington *et al.*, 1988b). Strong selection for lethality is inconsistent with a high frequency of semilethals in natural populations. No data are available on the outcome of competition between mice heterozygous for lethals and semilethals in the same population.

b. Restriction of Variability in M. musculus Haplotypes. As discussed above, much more polymorphism is found in *t* haplotypes from European *M. domesticus* populations than in those from *M. musculus* populations. If *t* haplotypes originated in a common ancestor of *M. musculus* and *M. domesticus,* one would expect equal amounts of polymorphism in the two lineages. One hypothesis proposed to account for the reduced variability of *M. musculus* haplotypes is that *t* haplotypes in *M. musculus* originated by introgression from *M. domesticus* (Forejt *et al.*, 1988; Willison *et al.*, 1986). A hybrid zone exists between the two species (Sage, 1981) and introgression is certainly a possibility. However, this theory is inconsistent with the data of Hammer *et al.* (1989) which argues for an origin of *t* haplotypes in a common ancestor of *M. musculus* and *M. domesticus.* At present there is no resolution of this inconsistency.

c. Partial Haplotypes. Two recent surveys have found a high frequency of partial haplotypes in populations of both *M. domesticus* and *M. musculus* (Erhart *et al.*, 1989; Figueroa *et al.*, 1988). Two hypotheses might account for this finding (Erhart *et al.*, 1989; Figueroa *et al.*, 1988). First, they may have arisen from recombination between + and *t* chromosomes. Despite the inversions associated with *t* haplotypes, recombination does occasionally occur and can produce partial haplotypes (Lyon and Phillips, 1959). Second, *t* haplotypes may have been assembled from gene sequences present as polymorphisms in ancestral mouse populations. These partial haplotypes may be descendants of these ancestral chromosomes. If partial haplotypes arise by recombination, their presence is compatible with both extrinsic and intrinsic theories for the evolution of *t* haplotypes. If they represent a persistent polymorphism, their existence is most compatible with the intrinsic theory for the origin of *t* haplotypes.

d. Modifiers of Transmission Ratio Distortion. Individual selection should select for modifiers of transmission distortion, reducing the level of distortion to a point where t haplotypes disappear from mouse populations (Prout et al., 1973). Modifiers of transmission distortion exist within the mouse genome (Bennett et al., 1983). Some seem to be located on the 17th chromosome and others are found elsewhere in the genome. The role of these modifiers in wild mouse populations has not been studied. However, the existence of such modifiers raises the inevitable question, still unanswered after four decades of work, of what controls the frequency of t haplotypes in natural populations.

VIII. MAINTENANCE OF t HAPLOTYPES IN WILD POPULATIONS

The question of the regulation of gene frequency in mouse populations has been approached from two directions. The classical problem has been based on the finding that the frequency of t haplotypes predicted by theoretical models is two or three times that actually observed in natural populations. Hence the classical question has been: What reduces the frequency of t haplotypes in natural populations? A more recent question on the maintenance of t haplotypes has been: Why do they exist at all? If transmission distortion can be reduced, t haplotypes should not in theory exist.

A. WHAT REDUCES THE FREQUENCY OF t HAPLOTYPES?

Three answers which are not mutually exclusive have been proposed for this question. The first is that the frequency of t haplotypes is reduced by processes that increase homozygosity within mouse populations (inbreeding, genetic drift) (Lewontin and Dunn, 1960; Lewontin, 1962; Petras, 1967). Increasing homozygosity of t haplotypes will result in a decrease in their frequency. The second hypothesis is that the frequency is reduced through heterozygote disadvantage, either through sexual selection or because of other differences in fitness between $+/+$ and $+/t$ mice (Franks and Lenington, 1986; Lenington, 1983, 1986; Levine et al., 1980). The third hypothesis is that transmission ratio distortion may be reduced in natural populations so reducing the frequency of t haplotypes (Erhart et al., 1989; Lenington, 1986; Lenington and Heisler, 1991; Levin et al., 1969).

1. Increasing Homozygosity

If either inbreeding or genetic drift played a major role in controlling gene frequency, it would be expected that over time any given mouse population would show a directional change in the frequency of t haplotypes (Lenington et al., 1988b). Such haplotypes would either tend to increase or decrease within a population. However, this expectation has not been borne out in populations that have been repeatedly sampled over periods of up to 4 years. Although there is considerable variation among populations in the frequency of t haplotypes, there also seems to be stability of frequency within a population (Lenington *et al.*, 1988b). This temporal stability in the frequency of *t* haplotypes argues against the hypothesis that genetic drift and/or inbreeding play a major role in diminishing their frequency.

2. Heterozygote Disadvantage

  a. Sexual Selection. The data relating *t* complex genotype to aspects of behavior indicate a complicated role for sexual selection as a regulator of gene frequency. Heterozygous males seem to have an advantage in aggressive encounters with other males, but a disadvantage relative to +/+ males with respect to female mating preference. Consequently, the effect of sexual selection on frequencies of *t* haplotypes will hinge on the relative importance of male aggression and female mating preference as determinants of male mating success. The most relevant data for this question are those obtained in the study by Franks and Lenington (1986) on mice in the seminatural environment. Their observations indicated that mating preference was not likely to be an important force controlling gene frequency in natural populations. In this setting, mating patterns (who mated and with whom) were primarily determined by dominance status. Virtually all mating was done by the dominant male and female. Once dominance rank was determined, there was little latitude left for mate choice on the part of either female or male. Hence, in contexts in which intermale aggression is reduced, female mating preference may give a reproductive advantage to +/+ males (as possibly indicated by the data of Levine *et al.*, 1980). However, in the face of intermale aggression, there is probably a selective advantage for +/t males.

  b. Other Differences in Fitness. The data on differences in fitness between +/+ and +/t animals indicate that selection is operating in differing directions in the two sexes. Heterozygous females have a lower fitness than do +/+ females, whereas the fitness of +/t males is either equal to or higher than that of +/+ males (Dunn *et al.*, 1958; Franks and Lenington, 1986; Johnston and Brown, 1969).

  Overall, in the study in the seminatural environment by Franks and Lenington (1986) +/t males fathered 33% more young than did +/+ males. Because a selective advantage for +/t males interacts with the transmission distortion favoring *t* chromosomes, even a small selective advantage for +/t males will have a very large effect on gene frequency. We used a theoretical model (Hartl, 1970) to predict the expected frequency of *t* haplotypes when selection differs between the sexes. Use of these data on the relative fitness of +/+ and +/t males and females gave an expected equilibrium frequency of +/t mice of 72%. This predicted value is very far from the observed value of 25%, and was no improvement over the equilibrium frequencies of 75–90% predicted by earlier theoretical models.

   c. Reduction of Transmission Ratio Distortion. Every model proposed for the
equilibrium frequency of *t* haplotypes is extremely sensitive to assumptions made
about the magnitude of the transmission ratio distortion (Fig. 4). Transmission
ratio distortion is lower in wild-caught males than the figures commonly reported
for laboratory strain males (laboratory stocks used in work on the *t* complex may
well have been inadvertently selected for high transmission of *t* haplotypes). In
addition, transmission ratio distortion is reduced in PPE matings. These findings
suggest that, overall, in natural populations the transmission of *t* haplotypes may
be much lower than the 90–95% figure used in estimating expected frequencies
for these haplotypes. Indeed, if *t* haplotypes are on average transmitted to only
about 60% of progeny as opposed to 90%, the classical models accurately predict
the observed frequency. The transmission of *t* haplotypes will depend on the
frequency of PPE matings in natural populations. At present, however, there are
no data on this point.

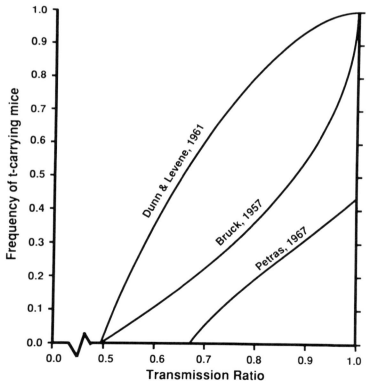

FIG. 4. Relationship between the equilibrium frequency of *t*-carrying mice and male transmission
ratio for three deterministic models.

However, the laboratory data on the frequency of PPE matings indicate that these may be more common in populations in which the male and female share the same genetic background (i.e., populations with low migration). This hypothesis predicts that the frequency of *t* haplotypes should only be high in populations with high rates of migration (owing to high transmission of *t* haplotypes) and low or nonexistent in populations with low rates of migration. Indeed, *t* haplotypes are commonly absent from isolated populations such as those on islands or in other situations with restricted migration (Lenington *et al.*, 1988b; Erhart *et al.*, 1989). Furthermore, in enclosed laboratory populations, male transmission ratio has been found to decline over time (Bennett *et al.*, 1983).

B. WHY DO *t* HAPLOTYPES CONTINUE TO EXIST?

Theoretical models indicate that if possession of a *t* haplotype were generally deleterious, unlinked suppressors of segregation distortion should increase in frequency in mouse populations, reducing male transmission ratio to the point where *t* haplotypes were eliminated. This situation is much less likely to occur if *t* haplotypes have a selective advantage (Eschel, 1985; Hartl, 1975b; Prout *et al.*, 1973). Genetic modifiers of transmission ratio distortion do exist within the mouse genome (Bennett *et al.*, 1983). In addition, mice have the capacity to reduce the magnitude of transmission ratio distortion by behavioral means. The persistence of *t* haplotypes in mouse populations in the face of mechanisms for their elimination suggests, however, that these haplotypes may have a selective advantage.

The data reviewed above indicate that the most likely selective advantage for *t* haplotypes is their effect on aggression in males. This chromosomal region, containing genes which profoundly alter sperm and testicular function, also seems to contain genes which enhance male aggressive behavior, and this could create a selective advantage for $+/t$ males. This selective advantage for $+/t$ males might potentially be related to the data on male transmission ratio. Male aggression may be less important in inbred populations in which individuals are closely related than in outbred populations (Kareem and Barnard, 1982). Indeed, the higher levels of aggression of $+/t$ males might enable them to establish themselves in new populations more easily than $+/+$ males.

If this is the case, it may not be coincidental that male transmission ratio varies with the extent of population outbreeding. It is possible that, under conditions of high migration, $+/t$ males behave in such a way as to maintain high transmission ratios, because of the advantages accruing to their sons. Under conditions of low migration, when possession of a *t* haplotype is no longer advantageous, their behavior may change in such a way as to minimize transmission of this otherwise deleterious haplotype.

A possible example of the natural history of *t* haplotypes within a population may be illustrated by the fate of those introduced onto Great Gull Island in Long

Island Sound (Fig. 5) (Anderson *et al.*, 1964). Mice on Great Gull Island, like most island populations of mice, did not carry *t* haplotypes. In 1957, Dunn and his co-workers introduced 6 + /*t* males to the island. Two years later the frequency of *t* haplotypes on the island was 84%. Over the next several years the frequency of *t* haplotypes declined and is now back to 0.00% (K. Artzt, personal communication). These data may reflect the processes outlined above. There may be an initial competitive advantage for + /*t* males in a context of recent migration. The frequency of PPE litters is low; male transmission ratio is high, and *t* haplotypes spread quickly. After some time, when no further migration occurs, the genetic background of + /*t* mice becomes similar to that of the other mice on the island. The frequency of PPE litters may then increase and male transmission ratio may decrease, leading to a decline and eventual loss of *t* haplotypes from the population.

IX. CONCLUSIONS AND DIRECTIONS FOR THE FUTURE

Genes within the *t* complex have a large number of pleiotropic consequences for behavior. In retrospect this is probably not surprising, given that the *t* complex comprises such a large proportion of the mouse genome. Because the *t* complex has been, and is continuing to be, extensively studied genetically, it is

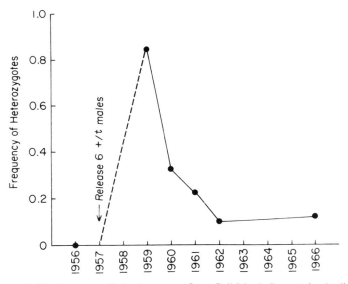

FIG. 5. The frequency of *t* haplotypes on Great Gull Island. See text for details.

possible, using this system, to identify with unusual precision the genetic correlates of behavior. Furthermore, it provides an almost unprecedented opportunity
to integrate physiology, genetics, and ecology with behavioral work on a wild
mammal. Behavior occupies a pivotal role in this synthesis. The work on genetics can elucidate the mechanisms underlying behavior. Understanding the behavioral consequences of *t* complex genotype can elucidate, in turn, the process
controlling the frequency of these genes in natural populations.

Much of the scenario proposed above regarding a selective advantage for *t*
haplotypes in natural populations is highly speculative. It would be of considerable interest to know whether $+/t$ males do in fact have an advantage as migrants
into new populations. It would also be important to determine whether the
frequency of *t* haplotypes is generally higher in populations with high rates of
migration than in populations where migration is low. Finally, the interpretation
that changes in the frequency of PPE litters are an adaptation to raise or lower
transmission ratios as a function of the demographic context hinges crucially on
the behavior of $+/+$ males. It is possible that all males, regardless of genotype,
have a high frequency of PPE litters in within population matings and a low
frequency in matings between populations. If this is the case, it is then unlikely
that the behavioral shift in frequency of PPE litters functions adaptively to
control transmission of *t* haplotypes.

An almost entirely neglected aspect of the *t* complex story has been the
neuroendocrine consequences of *t* haplotypes. The behavioral data indicate that *t*
complex genotype may have profound consequences for endocrine systems
and/or neural organization. Understanding these consequences could lead to
important insights about the pathways whereby genes modulate behavior.

X. Summary

The *t* complex in house mice has been an object of research and controversy
for over 60 years. There has been particular controversy about what factors
control the frequency of these deleterious genes in wild populations. This article
reviews the major behavioral, molecular, and population features of this unusual
genetic system. Behavior may be a major factor determining the frequency of *t*
haplotypes in wild mice. Genes within the *t* complex appear to have important
effects on mating preference, parental investment, and aggressive behavior.
There are probably two ways in which behavior regulates gene frequency. First,
it seems likely that there is selection for *t* haplotypes because possession of a *t*
mutation enhances male aggressive behavior. In all other respects, however,
possession of a *t* haplotype appears to lower fitness and mice appear to be
capable of behaviorally altering the transmission of these otherwise deleterious
genes to their progeny.

Acknowledgments

I wish to thank C. Barnard, J. S. Rosenblatt, and R. Trivers for helpful comments on this manuscript. Some of the work in this article was supported by PHS Grant #R012 HD 15977, and grants from the Charles and Johanna Busch Foundation.

References

Adler, N. T., and Toner, J. P., Jr. (1986). The effects of copulatory behavior on sperm transport and fertility in the rat. *In* "Reproduction: A Behavioral and Neuroendocrine Perspective" (B. Komisaruk, H. Siegal, M.-F. Cheng, and H. Feder, eds.), pp. 21–32. New York Academy of Sciences Press, New York.

Anderson, P. K. (1964). Lethal alleles in *Mus musculus:* Local distribution and evidence for isolation of demes. *Science* **145**, 177–178.

Anderson, P. K., Dunn, L. C., and Beasley, A. B. (1964). Introduction of a lethal allele into a feral house mouse population. *Am. Nat.* **98**, 57–64.

Artzt, K. (1984). Gene mapping in the T/t complex of the mouse. III. Lethal genes are arranged in three clusters on chromosome 17. *Cell (Cambridge, Mass.)* **29**, 565–572.

Artzt, K., Shin, H.-S., and Bennett, D. (1982). Gene mapping within the T/t complex of the mouse. II. Anomalous position of the H-2 complex in t haplotypes. *Cell (Cambridge, Mass.)* **28**, 471–476.

Beeman, E. A. (1947). The effect of male hormones on aggressive behavior in mice. *Physiol. Zool.* **20**, 373–405.

Bennett, D. (1975). The T-locus of the mouse. *Cell (Cambridge, Mass.)* **6**, 441–454.

Bennett, D. (1979). Population genetics of T/t complex mutations. *In* "Origins of Inbred Mice" (H. C. Morse, III, ed.), pp. 615–632. Academic Press, New York.

Bennett, D., Alton, A. K., and Artzt, K. (1983). Genetic analysis of transmission ratio distortion by t-haplotypes in the mouse. *Genet. Res.* **41**, 29–45.

Bode, V. C. (1984). Ethylnitrosurea mutagenesis and the isolation of mutant alleles for specific genes located in the t-region of mouse chromosome 17. *Genetics* **108**, 457–470.

Bonhomme, F., Catalan, J., Britton-Davidian, J., Chapman, V. M., Moriwaki, K., Nevo, E., and Thaler, J. (1984). Biochemical diversity and evolution of the genus *Mus. Biochem. Genet.* **22**, 275–303.

Braden, A. W. H. (1957). The relationship between the diurnal light cycle and the time of ovulation in mice. *J. Exp. Biol.* **34**, 177–188.

Braden, A. W. H. (1958). Influence of time of mating on segregation ratio of alleles at the T-locus in the house mouse. *Nature (London)* **181**, 786–787.

Brown, J. L. (1983). Some paradoxical goals of cells and organisms. *In* "Ethical Questions in Brain and Behavior" (D. W. Pfaff, ed.), pp. 111–124. Springer-Verlag, New York.

Brown, R. E., Singh, P. B., and Roser, B. (1987). The major histocompatibility complex and the chemosensory recognition of individuality in rats. *Physiol. Behav.* **40**, 65–73.

Bruck, D. (1957). Male segregation ratio advantage as a factor maintaining lethal alleles in wild populations of house mice. *Proc. Natl. Acad. Sci. U.S.A.* **43**, 152–158.

Cameron, D. R., and Moav, R. M. (1957). Inheritance in *Nicotiana tabacum.* XXVII. Pollen killer, an alien genetic locus inducing abortion of microspores not carrying it. *Genetics* **42**, 326–335.

Carter, C. S., Getz, L. L., and Cohen-Parsons, M. (1986). Social organization and behavioral endocrinology in a monogamous mammal. *Adv. Study Behav.* **16**, 109–145.

Charlesworth, B., and Hartl, D. L. (1978). Population dynamics of the segregation distorter polymorphism of *Drosophila melanogaster. Genetics* **89**, 171–192.

Chelsey, P., and Dunn, L. C. (1936). The inheritance of taillessness (anury) in the house mouse. *Genetics* **21**, 525–536.

Cox, T. P. (1884). Ethological isolation of local populations of house mice (*Mus musculus*) based on olfaction. *Anim. Behav.* **32**, 1068–1077.

Delarbre, C., Kashi, Y., Boursot, P., Beckman, J., Kourilsky, P., Bonhomme, F., and Gachelin, G. (1988). Phylogenetic distribution in the genus *Mus* of t-complex-specific DNA and protein markers: Inferences on the origin of t-haplotypes. *Mol. Biol. Evol.* **5**, 120–133.

Dobrovolskaia-Zawadskaia, N. (1927). Sur la mortification spontanée de la queue chez la souris mouveau-née sur l'existence d'un caractère (facteur héréditaire non-viable. *C. R. Seances Soc. Biol. Ses Fil.* **97**, 114–119.

Drickamer, L., and Lenington, S. (1987). T-locus effects on the male urinary chemosignal that accelerates puberty in female mice. *Anim. Behav.* **35**, 1581–1583.

Dunn, L. C. (1957). Studies of the genetic variability in populations of wild mice. II. Analysis of eight additional alleles at locus T. *Genetics* **42**, 299–311.

Dunn, L. C., and Gluecksohn-Schoenheimer, S. (1939). The inheritance of taillessness (anury) in the house mouse. II. Taillessness in a second balanced lethal line. *Genetics* **24**, 589–609.

Dunn, L. C., and Levene, H. (1961). Population dynamics of a variant t allele in a confined population of wild house mice. *Evolution (Lawrence, Kans.)* **15**, 385–393.

Dunn, L. C., and Morgan, W. C. (1953). Segregation ratios of mutant alleles from wild populations of *Mus musculus*. *Am. Nat.* **87**, 327–329.

Dunn, L. C., and Suckling, J. (1956). Studies of the genetic variability in wild populations of house mice. I. Analysis of seven alleles at locus T. *Genetics* **41**, 344–352.

Dunn, L. C., Beasley, A. B., and Tinker, H. (1958). Relative fitness of wild house mice heterozygous for a lethal allele. *Am. Nat.* **92**, 215–230.

Dunn, L. C., Beasley, A. B., and Tinker, H. (1960). Relative fitness of polymorphisms in populations of wild house mice. *J. Mammal.* **41**, 220–229.

Dunn, L. C., Bennett, D., and Cookingham, J. (1973). Polymorphism for lethal alleles in European populations of *Mus musculus*. *J. Mammal* **54**, 822–830.

Egid, K. (1986). Propensity of wild house mice, *Mus musculus*, to exhibit preferences for odors correlated with T locus genotype: An analysis of the basis for the cue and the preference. Unpublished Ph.D. Dissertation, Rutgers University, Newark, New Jersey.

Egid, K., and Brown, J. L. (1989). The major histocompatibility complex and female mating preferences in mice. *Anim. Behav.* **38**, 548–550.

Egid, K., and Lenington, S. (1985). Responses of male mice to odors of females: Effects on T and H-2 locus genotype. *Behav. Genet.* **15**, 287–295.

Erhart, M. A., Phillips, S. J., Bonhomme, F., Boursot, P., Wakeland, E., and Nadeau, J. (1989). Haplotypes that are mosaic for wild-type and t complex-specific alleles in wild mice. *Genetics* **123**, 405–415.

Eschel, I. (1985). Evolutionary genetic stability of Mendelian segregation and free recombination in the chromosomal system. *Am. Nat.* **125**, 412–420.

Figueroa, F., Neufeld, E., Ritte, U., and Klein, J. (1988). Specific DNA polymorphisms among wild mice from Israel and Spain. *Genetics* **119**, 157–160.

Forejt, J., Gregorova, S., and Jansa, P. (1988). Three new haplotypes of *Mus musculus* reveal structural similarities to t haplotypes of *Mus domesticus*. *Genet. Res.* **51**, 111–119.

Franks, P., and Lenington, S. (1986). Dominance and reproductive behavior of wild house mice in a seminatural environment correlated with T-locus genotype. *Behav. Ecol. Sociobiol.* **18**, 395–404.

Guenet, J. L., Condamine, H., Gaillard, J., and Jacob, F. (1980). t^{wPa-1}, t^{wPa-2}, t^{wPa-3}. Three recent haplotypes in the mouse. *Genet. Res.* **36**, 211–217.

Hammer, M. F., Schimenti, J., and Silver, L. (1989). Evolution of mouse chromosome 17 and the origin of inversions associated with t haplotypes. *Proc. Natl. Acad. Sci. U.S.A.* **86**, 3261–3265.

Hammerberg, C., and Klein, J. (1975). Linkage disequilibrium between H-2 and t complexes in chromosome 17 of the mouse. *Nature (London)* **258**, 296–299.

Hartl, D. I. (1970). A mathematical model for recessive lethal segregation distorters with differential viabilities in the sexes. *Genetics* **66**, 147–164.

Hartl, D. I. (1975a). Segregation distortion in natural and artificial populations of *Drosophila melanogaster*. In "Gamete Competition in Plants and Animals" (D. L. Malcahy, ed.), pp. 83–91. North-Holland, Publ., Amsterdam.

Hartl, D. L. (1975b). Modifier theory and meiotic drive. *Theor. Popul. Biol.* **7**, 168–174.

Hermann, B., Bucan, M., Mains, P. E., Frischauf, A., Silver, L., and Lerach, H. (1986). Genetic analysis of the proximal portion of the mouse t complex: Evidence for a second inversion within t haplotypes. *Cell (Cambridge, Mass.)* **44**, 469–476.

Ivanyi, P. (1978). Some aspects of the H-2 system, the major histocompatibility system, in the mouse. *Proc. R. Soc. London, Ser. B* **292**, 117–159.

Ivanyi, P., Hample, R., Mikova, M., and Starka, L. (1976). The influence of the H-2 system on blood serum testosterone. *Folia Biol. (Prague)* **22**, 42–43.

Johnston, P. G., and Brown, G. H. (1969). A comparison of the relative fitness of genotypes segregating for the t-allele in laboratory stock and its possible effects on gene frequency in the mouse populations. *Am. Nat.* **103**, 5–21.

Kareem, A. M., and Barnard, C. J. (1982). The importance of kinship and familiarity in social interactions between mice. *Anim. Behav.* **30**, 594–601.

Klein, J. (1986). "Natural History of the Major Histocompatibility Complex." Wiley, New York.

Klein, J., Sipos, P., and Figueroa, F. (1984). Polymorphism of t complex genes in European wild mice. *Genet. Res.* **44**, 39–46.

Lenington, S. (1983). Social preferences for partners carrying "good genes" in wild house mice. *Anim. Behav.* **31**, 325–333.

Lenington, S. (1986). Behavior as a phenotypic correlate of T locus genotype in wild house mice: Implications for evolutionary models. In "Reproduction: A Behavioral and Neuroendocrine Perspective" (B. Komisaruk, H. Siegal, M.-F. Cheng, and H. Feder, eds.), pp. 141–147. New York Academy of Sciences Press, New York.

Lenington, S., and Egid, K. (1985). Female discrimination of male odors correlated with male genotype at the T-locus in *Mus musculus*: A response to T-locus or H-2 locus variability? *Behav. Genet.* **15**, 37–51.

Lenington, S., and Egid, K. (1989). Family environment influences female preference for male odors correlated with t complex genotype. *Behav. Genet.* **19**, 257–266.

Lenington, S., and Franks, P. (1985). Trappability of wild mice under conditions of confinement in relation to T locus genotype and other variables. *J. Mammal.* **66**, 145–148.

Lenington, S., and Heisler. (1991). Submitted for publication.

Lenington, S., Egid, K., and Williams, J. (1988a). Analysis of a genetic recognition system. *Behav. Genet.* **18**, 549–564.

Lenington, S., Franks, P., and Williams, J. (1988b). Distribution of t-haplotypes in natural populations of wild house mice. *J. Mammal.* **69**, 489–499.

Levin, B. R., Petras, M. L., and Rasmussen, D. I. (1969). The effect of migration on the maintenance of a lethal polymorphism in the house mouse. *Am. Nat.* **103**, 647–661.

Levine, L., Rockwell, R. F., and Grossfield, J. (1980). Sexual selection in mice. V. Reproductive competition between $+/+$ and $+/t^{w5}$ males. *Am. Nat.* **116**, 150–156.

Lewontin, R. C. (1962). Interdeme selection controlling a polymorphism in the house mouse. *Am. Nat.* **96**, 65–78.

Lewontin, R. C. (1968). The effect of differential viability on population dynamics of t-alleles in the house mouse. *Evolution (Lawrence, Kans.)* **22**, 262–273.

Lewontin, R. C., and Dunn, L. C. (1960). The evolutionary dynamics of a polymorphism in the house mouse. *Genetics* **45**, 705–722.

Luttge, W. G., Hall, N. R., and Wallis, C. J. (1974). Studies on the neuroendocrine, somatic, and behavioral effectiveness of testosterone and its 5-alpha reduced metabolites. *Physiol. Behav.* **13**, 553–561.

Lyon, M. F. (1984). Transmission ratio distortion in mouse t haplotypes is due to multiple distorter genes acting on a responder locus. *Cell (Cambridge, Mass.)* **37**, 621–628.

Lyon, M. F. (1986). Male sterility of the mouse t-complex is due to homozygosity of the distorter genes. *Cell (Cambridge, Mass.)* **44**, 357–363.

Lyon, M. F. (1987). Distorter genes of the mouse t-complex impair male fertility when heterozygous. *Genet. Res.* **49**, 57–60.

Lyon, M. F., and Phillips, R. J. S. (1959). Crossing over in mice heterozygous for t-alleles. *Heredity* **13**, 23–32.

Lyon, M. F., and Zenthon, J. (1988). Differences in or near the responder region of complete and partial mouse t-haplotypes. *Genet. Res.* **50**, 29–34.

Martin, P. G., and Andrewartha, H. G. (1962). Success in fighting in two varieties of mice. *Am. Nat.* **96**, 375–376.

Nadeau, J. H., Varnum, D., and Burkart, D. (1989). Genetic evidence for two t complex tail interaction (*tct*) loci in t haplotypes. *Genetics* **122**, 895–903.

Nizetic, D., Figueroa, F., and Klein, J. (1984). Evolutionary relationships between the t and H-2 haplotypes in the house mouse. *Immunogenetics* **19**, 311–320.

Olds-Clarke, P., and Peitz, B. (1986). Fertility of sperm from t/+ mice: Evidence that +-bearing sperm are dysfunctional. *Genet. Res.* **47**, 49–52.

Perrigo, G. (1987). Breeding and feeding strategies in deer mice and house mice when females are challenged to work for their food. *Anim. Behav.* **35**, 1298–1316.

Petras, M. L. (1967). Studies of natural populations of *Mus*. II. Polymorphism at the T-locus. *Evolution (Lawrence, Kans.)* **21**, 466–478.

Prout, T., Bundgaar, J., and Bryant, S. (1973). Population genetics of modifiers of meiotic drive. I. The solution of a special case and some general implications. *Theor. Popul. Biol.* **5**, 155–162.

Sage, R. D. (1981). Wild mice. *In* "The Mouse in Biomedical Research" (H. L. Foster, J. D. Small, and J. G. Fox, eds.), Vol. 1, pp. 39–90. Academic Press, New York.

Seitz, A., and Bennett, D. (1985). Transmission ratio distortion of t is due to interactions between meiotic partners. *Nature (London)* **313**, 143–144.

Sherman, M., and Wudl, L. R. (1977). T complex mutations and their effects. *In* "Concepts in Mammalian Embryogenesis" (M. Sherman, ed.), pp. 136–234. MIT Press, Cambridge, Massachusetts.

Shin, H.-S., Stavnezer, J., Artzt, K., and Bennett, D. (1982). The genetic structure and origin of t-haplotypes analyzed with H-2 cDNA probes. *Cell (Cambridge, Mass.)* **29**, 969–976.

Shin, H.-S., Bennett, D., and Artzt, K. (1984). Gene mapping within the T/t complex of the mouse. IV. The inverted MHC is intermingled with several t-lethal genes. *Cell (Cambridge, Mass.)* **39**, 573–578.

Silver, L. M. (1985). Mouse t haplotypes. *Annu. Rev. Genet.* **19**, 179–208.

Silver, L. M. (1988). Mouse t haplotypes: A tale of tails and a misunderstood selfish chromosome. *Curr. Top. Microbiol. Immunol.* **137**, 389–391.

Silver, L. M., and Remis, D. (1987). Five of the nine genetically defined regions of mouse t haplotypes are involved in transmission ratio distortion. *Genet. Res.* **49**, 51–56.

Skow, L. C., Nadeau, J. N., Ahn, J. C., Shin, H.-S., Artzt, K., and Bennett, D. (1987). Polymorphism and linkage of the A-cristillin gene in t-haplotypes of the mouse. *Genetics* **116**, 107–111.

Tutikawa, K. (1955). Further studies on T locus in the Japanese wild mouse, *Mus musculus molossinus*. *Rep. Natl. Inst. Genet. (Jpn.)* **5**, 13–15.

Vandenbergh, J. G. (1969). Male odor accelerates female sexual maturation in mice. *Endocrinology (Baltimore)* **84**, 658–660.

Washburn, L. L., and Eicher, E. M. (1989). Normal testis determination in the mouse depends on genetic interaction of a locus on chromosome 17 and the Y chromosome. *Genetics* **123,** 173–179.

Williams, G. C. (1966). "Adaptation and Natural Selection." Princeton Univ. Press, Princeton, New Jersey.

Williams, J. R. (1989). Social and sexual preferences in wild house mice *Mus domesticus* based on genetic differences between conspecifics: Preferences based on t complex genotype and population membership. Unpublished Ph.D. Dissertation, Rutgers University, New Brunswick, New Jersey.

Willison, K. R., Dudley, K., and Potter, J. (1986). Molecular cloning and sequence analysis of a haploid expressed gene encoding t complex polypeptide 1. *Cell (Cambridge, Mass.)* **44,** 727–738.

Yamazaki, K., Boyse, E. A., Mike, V., Thaler, B. J., Mathieson, B. J., Abbott, J., Boyse, J., Zayas, Z. A., and Thomas, L. (1976). Control of mating preferences in mice by genes in the major histocompatibility complex. *J. Exp. Med.* **144,** 1324–1335.

Yamazaki, K., Yamaguchi, G. K., Barnowski, L., Bard, J., Boyse, E. A., and Thomas, L. (1979). Recognition among mice: Evidence from the use of a Y-maze differentially scented by mice of different major histocompatibility types. *J. Exp. Med.* **150,** 755–760.

Yamazaki, K., Beauchamp, G. K., Wysocki, C. J., Bard, J., Thomas, L., and Boyse, E. (1983). Recognition of H-2 types in relation to the blocking of pregnancy in mice. *Science* **221,** 186–188.

Young, W. C. (1970). Psychobiology of sexual behavior in the guinea pig. *Adv. Study Behav.* **2,** 1–110.

Zimmering, S., Sandler, L., and Nicoletti, B. (1970). Mechanisms of meiotic drive. *Annu. Rev. Genet.* **4,** 409–436.

The Ergonomics of Worker Behavior
in Social Hymenoptera

PAUL SCHMID-HEMPEL

ZOOLOGISCHES INSTITUT DER UNIVERSITÄT
CH-4051 BASEL, SWITZERLAND

I.   SOME PRELIMINARIES

A.   WHY STUDY SOCIAL HYMENOPTERA?

Of the 130,000 species of Hymenoptera that have been described (Parker, 1982) about 15,000 live socially. Among them, the ants (which comprise the vast majority of species), some bees, and many wasps have reached eusociality, characterized by cooperative brood care, overlapping generations, and division of reproductive activity. Eusociality poses some intriguing problems, such as the existence of nonreproductive individuals and other highly sophisticated "altruistic" traits, and like the polymorphic castes in ants and termites. The genetic theory of social behavior (Hamilton, 1964) has been by far the most successful attempt to explain these characteristics in evolutionary terms. Hamilton's concept of inclusive fitness has generated a considerable amount of interest in the biology and behavior of social insects. However, an unfortunate consequence of this success is that the study of behavior in this group has tended to concentrate on these ideas. "Traditional" questions about the organization of work in such societies (e.g., Jeanne, 1986a), or about their ecology in general, have become overshadowed by interest in kin selection and related issues. There is clearly much more to social insects than kin selection, haplodiploidy, or inclusive fitness. It is also often not sufficiently appreciated that social insects are a convenient group for investigating many other aspects of social behavior which are not necessarily tied to haplodiploid genetics, such as dominance, reproductive conflict, the significance of individuality, or the economics of individual and cooperative action. In the study of highly social mammals (e.g., carnivores or primates), such problems have always been major research questions. On the other hand, there can be little doubt that the new perspectives generated from rigorous application of first principles to social insect behavior have paved the way for promising new approaches to classical questions. In particular, attention has been

87

focused on the possibility of conflicts of interest among individuals within a social group.

Besides the many fascinating problems that social insects present, they are also an economically important group. A large fraction of the biomass in tropical biota consists of social insects, and some are potent soil builders, major pests, important pollinators, or may play an important role as predators in terrestrial ecosystems (see Wilson, 1971, 1985). Here, I concentrate on social species of Hymenoptera and on discussion of their ergonomics, broadly defined as the quantitative study of work, performance, and efficiency in animal societies (Wilson, 1968), with particular reference to a case study on nectar collection in the honeybee (*Apis mellifera* L.).

The natural history of social species of Hymenoptera shows many variations on a general theme (see accounts in Wilson, 1971; Michener, 1974; Brian, 1983). However for the following discussion, the life cycle can conveniently be divided into a founding stage, an ergonomic stage during which the colony grows, and a sexual stage when reproduction takes place (Fig. 1). Colonies are founded, either by a single inseminated queen (e.g., in leaf-cutting ants or

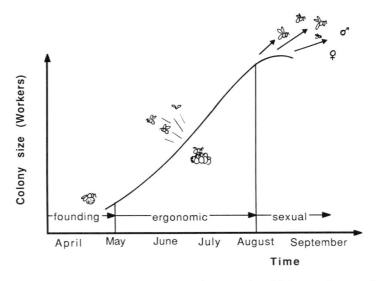

FIG. 1. Example of an idealized life cycle of an annual social insect colony, as found in bumblebees. The overwintered queen starts a colony in early spring and raises the first generation of workers by herself (the founding stage). After emergence of the first workers, almost all egg-laying is done by the queen, whereas activities of the workers ensure colony growth (during the ergonomic stage) and eventual reproduction (sexual stage). Mating takes place shortly after the young gynes leave the maternal nest; fertilized queens overwinter in the soil. This basic pattern is varied in many ways across different species of social insects.

bumblebees), by foundress associations (e.g., in some wasps), or by budding from parental colonies (e.g., in honeybees and stingless bees). During this stage, the crucial steps include dispersal and colonization of accessible nest sites. That the success of propagules may often depend primarily on success or failure in establishing a viable minimal colony size has been suggested by several studies (e.g., Bartz and Hölldobler, 1982; Rissing and Pollock, 1987).

Once established, colonies of social insects grow in worker numbers, rather than by an increase in the body size of individuals, although associated changes in worker size are known to occur (Rissing, 1987; Sutcliffe and Plowright, 1988). This pattern is a consequence of the holometabolous development of Hymenoptera, which means that the amount of food consumed by the larva is an important determinant of body size in the adult. Quite generally too, the development of female larvae into either workers or gynes (i.e., caste determination), is phenotypic rather than genotypic in determination. In ants, larval nutrition is particularly relevant, although other factors like pheromones or temperature may also have an effect (Wilson, 1985). In some rare cases, reproductive caste may be genetically influenced (Buschinger, 1975; Heinze and Buschinger, 1989).

Finally, colonies of social insects only reach sexual maturity after a period of colony development. At this time, sexually competent males and females are produced and these may or may not leave the colony to start another life cycle. During this stage, conflicts of interest, for example, between workers and queens over sex ratio of offspring (Trivers and Hare, 1976; Grafen, 1986), have been proposed and analyzed in more detail. It is clear that the behavior of individual workers cannot be considered in isolation from the background life cycle of the colony, but that the integration of these different levels is, as will be shown, rather intricate.

B.   WHY STUDY FUNCTIONS OF BEHAVIOR?

Behavior possesses both variation and heritability, and thus evolution through the forces of natural selection can occur. As with any other trait of an organism, several approaches to the study of behavior exist (Tinbergen, 1951). The functional approach to behavior has been intensively pursued over the past decade and has enjoyed success in explaining seemingly unrelated observations. However, controversy has surrounded this area almost since its inception (Maynard Smith, 1978; Oster and Wilson, 1978; Gould and Lewontin, 1979; Jamieson, 1986; Dupré, 1987), and the logic of this approach has not been appreciated by all (see Pierce and Ollason, 1987, and reply by Stearns and Schmid-Hempel, 1987). It therefore seems justified to devote a few comments to the reasoning used in this article.

The functional approach is concerned with the study of the value of a trait (behavioral or otherwise) for the survival and reproduction of the organism.

Study of the function of behavior is therefore a domain in its own right, closely related to ecology and evolutionary biology, rather than a simple extension of genetics or physiology. In the absence of information, heritable components for the trait of interest are assumed to exist, in the simple sense that like begets like. But, while the particular genetic or physiological machinery that produces the behavior under investigation is often ignored, this does not mean that basic principles of genetics or physiology are violated. The notion of the "value" of a behavior may sometimes be rather clear as, for example, when a parasitic wasp is laying eggs into the larvae of butterflies. Here, the behavior that maximizes rate of oviposition can readily be assessed in terms of its fitness value. However, more complicated cases are the rule and include most of the everyday activities of animals.

It is important to realize that there is no universal definition of fitness, but a broad array of different conceptions about how selective forces could act. For example, population geneticists are concerned with the consequences of differential selection on genotypes, genetic drift, mutation rate, and so forth, for the frequencies of interesting genes. Consequently, their definition of fitness relates to gene or genotype frequencies across generations (e.g., Crow, 1986). Sociobiologists, by contrast, are often interested in the conditions for the spread of rare, mutant genes in a population of wild genotypes and, in particular, of those coding for altruistic acts. Consequently, they use Hamilton's (1964) definition of inclusive fitness to determine whether or not the prevailing conditions are above or below the threshold for spreading. Ecologists may be interested in predicting the diet choice of predators under different ecological conditions, since it helps them to understand in more detail the nature of exploitative competition, or of other processes leading to community structure (Schoener, 1986). As a consequence, they consider energetic or nutritional value of foods in relation to the cost in time and energy of acquiring them to be an approximation to the predator's fitness. Thus, if one wants to study the function of a behavior, one must define what would constitute a satisfactory evolutionary explanation.

II. FUNCTIONAL APPROACHES TO WORKER BEHAVIOR

In social insects, the classical view assumes that selection on traits possessed by workers operates on variation among colonies, i.e., that colonies can be regarded as "superorganisms" (Wheeler, 1911; Oster and Wilson, 1978) whose members cooperate to gain reproductive success. Yet, populations of social insects are stratified in interesting ways with at least two levels: the colonies and the individuals within them. One would expect the degree of stratification to vary enormously in agreement with the vast biological diversity of the social insects. Nobody can seriously doubt that differences among colonies are crucially important for natural selection to take effect, but it is unclear to what extent within-colony variation is also subject to selective forces. Progress in the study of social insects is now extending the classical view in the light of accumulating evidence for within-colony conflicts (e.g., Bourke, 1988; Frumhoff and Schneider, 1987) and the existence of genetic heterogeneity of an as yet unexpected quality (e.g., Robinson and Page, 1988) (Fig. 2). Nevertheless, to consider the colony as being an economic unit is a useful starting point; complications due to conflicting selective forces can subsequently be added.

In this section, I selectively review some studies where the function of individual behavior has been analyzed. This will illustrate some recurrent problems, but is not intended to cover all of the species. The constraints on individual behavior through colony organization and social living, and how they in turn might affect the evolution of physiological parameters, will be the main interest rather than the physiological constraints per se.

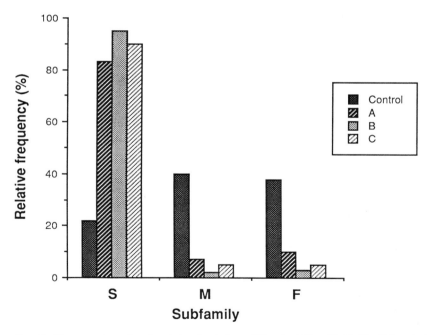

FIG. 2. The percentage of workers belonging to three different patrilines (S, M, F) within a single colony of honeybees and which were present in a control sample (taken randomly from all bees) and three arbitrary samples A, B, and C (taken from bees that specialize in undertaking, i.e., removing dead workers from the hive). Members of patriline S were overrepresented in the undertakers as compared to the control group. This difference persisted over 4 months. (Modified from Robinson and Page, 1988. Reproduced with permission.)

A. DIVISION OF LABOR

Inside a colony of social insects, individuals usually differ in the extent to which they perform various activities. Such division of labor has been studied repeatedly, with a major emphasis on documenting the behavioral patterns involved (e.g., Rösch, 1925; Lindauer, 1952; also reviews in Free, 1965; Wilson, 1971; Michener, 1974; Oster and Wilson, 1978; Brian, 1983). Other studies have analyzed the factors that affect such polyethism, for example, age dependence of the response to certain stimuli (see Wilson, 1971; Michener, 1974), genotypic variance (Winston and Katz, 1982; Frumhoff and Baker, 1988; Robinson and Page, 1988; Calderone and Page, 1988), or other correlates of individual variation in behavioral repertoire (Kerr and Hebling, 1964; Wilson, 1971; Jaycox *et al.*, 1974; Oster and Wilson, 1978; Calabi, 1988).

From a more functional viewpoint, it has been of interest to analyze how individuals shift their work in response to perturbation of the colony. For example, Winston and Fergusson (1985, in honeybees) and Wilson (1984, in ants) experimentally removed a number of workers to demonstrate that the remaining ones increase their activity. Similarly, workers of wax-deprived honeybee colonies carry out more of the activities associated with replacing missing cells than those in control colonies (Kolmes, 1985a); workers also switch tasks according to experimentally imposed variation in food availability or ambient temperature (Mirenda and Vinson, 1981; Meudec and Lenoir, 1982; Gordon, 1989a). Because in such experiments individuals shift their behavior in a way that may add to colony maintenance and survival, their work strategies are considered to be adaptive. Such observations also illustrate one of the problems in the study of highly social societies: plasticity in individual behaviors in relation to environmental contingencies should not only enhance the chances of survival and reproduction of the entire colony, but also of each member of the society. Thus, selection suspected to act on differences among individuals should often produce adaptations similar to those generated by selection among colonies.

A somewhat more difficult problem is to find and test a priori hypotheses about how labor should be divided among individuals. Yet, this is one of the problems to be solved if a deeper insight into the ergonomics of individual work strategies is to be gained. The most influential attempt to date is the work by Oster and Wilson (1978) on caste and ecology in social insects. They define caste rather broadly as a set of individuals that perform specialized labor in the colony for sustained periods of time. More narrowly, caste often denotes sets of individuals that differ both morphologically and in their behaviors from other such sets. Oster and Wilson (1978) suggested that variation in the relative frequencies of different castes among colonies or populations is a trait shaped by natural selection, such that the best caste ratio would ensure maximum production of daughter colonies. Because production of offspring colonies is rather difficult to measure, it is approximated by considering energy as a token for fitness.

Questions of caste structure have been studied in some detail in the ants. However, attempts to demonstrate the adaptive nature of caste ratios have produced ambiguous results. For example, artificial predation on ant colonies was observed to correlate with an altered ratio of minor and major workers in several ant species (Gentry, 1974; Herbers, 1980; Fowler, 1984). However, the observed variation often yields no clear pattern, so that the functional interpretations are not particularly stringent. For example, Walker and Stamps (1986) reported observations supporting ideas about adaptive caste ratios; in particular, the prediction that the number of soldiers (workers specializing in protecting the colony against enemies) should show a concave relationship with the number of workers during the sexual stage of the colony, but a convex one during the ergonomic stage. Yet, the observed curves do not unequivocally show this expected relationship. Similarly, Calabi and Traniello (1988) found a complete lack of ecological correlates with physical and temporal caste ratios in the ant *Pheidole dentata*, and, moreover, no relationship with reproductive success. The failure to find simple correlates for caste structure does not necessarily imply that it is not shaped by natural selection, but that we have not yet been able to understand the responsible forces in a predictable way. In addition, a lot of evidence suggests that flexibility in individual behavior is more important than caste distribution for variation in fitness components. Hence, the analysis of individual behavior in social insects gains additional importance.

Studies focusing on individual behavior in connection with division of labor do seem to have been more successful. For example, Seeley (1982) tested a spatial efficiency hypothesis of division of labor in honeybees. The underlying polyethism is largely age dependent (but see Robinson and Page, 1988), and spatial proximity of interrelated tasks and the individuals that fulfill them would conceivably increase the ergonomic efficiency of the colony by reducing time and energy needed to connect one task with the next. The distribution of worker groups that attend brood, store food, etc. did indeed conform with such a simple hypothesis. Similarly, Jeanne (1986b) studied nest-building behavior in the social wasp *Polybia occidentalis*. The analysis suggested that the division of labor with respect to collection of water and pulp, and actual cell construction among different individuals drastically reduces the time required to complete one construction cycle. This is achieved primarily by reducing the average waiting time for the transfer of material to the next individual. Wilson (1980) demonstrated that division of labor among various worker morphs in the leaf-cutting ant *Atta cephalotes* maximizes the amount of leaf material cut relative to costs of construction plus maintenance of the differently sized workers. Gordon (1986, 1987) has investigated the dynamics of work organization in the harvester ant

94   PAUL SCHMID-HEMPEL

Pogonomyrmex barbatus. In her experiments, artificial perturbation of nest
maintenance activities or foraging was shown to affect a variety of other activities, suggesting that if selection acts on foraging it will also affect other tasks.

A different approach to work strategies and division of labor is to analyze the
probability that, as a result of individual behavior, a particular set of interrelated
tasks will successfully be carried out by the colony as a whole (Oster and Wilson,
1978). Reliability theory, as routinely used in engineering to design complex
machinery such as airplanes, allows analysis of the performance of a system of
interacting components (Fig. 3). The organization of work in social insects is an
example of such a system, for it contains a mixture of parallel and serial processes. It is parallel in that many workers attend to the same task, e.g., foraging

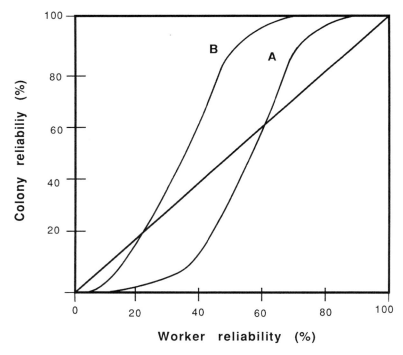

FIG. 3. The probability that a number of interdependent tasks is successfully completed by the
colony as a whole (*ordinate:* colony reliability) as a function of the probability that each individual
worker completes a single task (*abscissa:* worker reliability). For a solitary animal, the diagonal
would reflect the relationship between these two quantities. For a social insect, the dependence is
more complex and depends on the details of how tasks are organized. Line A approximates reliability
of successful resource collection by individually foraging workers (a purely parallel system), line B
success by group hunters (parallel–serial system). (After Herbers, 1981.)

or nest construction, at the same time. It is serial, as some tasks must be done one after another, e.g., bees collecting pollen and then feeding it to larvae. The way in which work is organized, i.e., the arrangement of component tasks in parallel or series, affects the overall reliability of the system (see Herbers, 1981) (Fig. 3). However, work arrangement in turn determines the required degree of reliability that each single component should have, given that the desired reliability of the whole system is specified. In general, arranging work in redundant systems requires less perfection of any single component than in nonredundant systems. The difference between these two organizations would of course disappear if the system is at zero or 100% reliability, but for many obvious reasons, e.g., constraints and trade-offs with other factors, natural selection on any one trait is not expected to lead to this level of perfection. Therefore, within the relevant domain, redundant organization could substantially add to the overall performance of the colony (Fig. 3). As a consequence, it is to be expected that selection on individual perfection in a particular task is not as strong for workers in social insects as compared to solitary living animals. Despite the obvious consequences for the analysis of functions of individual behavior, this approach does not seem to have been taken further in the literature. Note that redundancy does not necessarily imply the notion of specialization, i.e., the idea that some individuals should be better at a given task than others, nor of "satisfycing," i.e., that it would be sufficient when individual workers are just reliable enough. Introducing any degree of variance in the environment would actually make such a satisfying strategy rather vulnerable.

We can at this point take it that individual behavior patterns are in obvious and sensible ways integrated into the activities of the colony as a whole. It remains unclear, however, in which ways the observed patterns of caste structure and division of labor, as they result from the sum of individual behavior, add to fitness and whether they are superior to potential alternatives. This is certainly one of the biggest gaps in our understanding of social insects. Moreover, students of social insects accept that division of labor is a trait subject to evolution through natural selection (sensu Oster and Wilson, 1978). But, curiously enough, they have largely neglected the consequence that, in this case, selection should be demonstrated to act among variants of this trait in the population. In fact, almost no study takes account of variance in this trait among colonies within populations nor attempts to put it into the perspective of selective forces (see also Gordon, 1989b).

B.   FORAGING—THE PARADIGMATIC BEHAVIOR

Foraging is an everyday activity that is sufficiently complex to pose interesting problems and also frequent enough to be studied with modest means. Among the many tasks that individual workers carry out, foraging is in many ways also the most demanding. Collection of resources makes it necessary to leave the relative safety of the nest and is thus associated with increased exposure to predators and parasites (e.g., Porter and Jorgensen, 1981; Schmid-Hempel and Schmid-Hempel, 1984), thermal stress, or desiccation. Foraging is quite generally performed by older individuals, and from life tables it is clear that mortality rate increases considerably at the age at which this activity begins (see Sakagami and Fukuda, 1968; Wilson, 1971; Terada *et al.*, 1975; Winston and Katz, 1981; Wilson, 1985). As well as its relative ease of study, foraging thus exposes in a nutshell the problems associated with analyzing the ergonomics of individual behavior in social insects.

Foraging behavior has indeed received considerable attention in the literature, particularly in species of economic importance, such as pollinators (the bees) or pests of commercial crops (e.g., leaf-cutting ants). Many studies have concentrated on the mechanisms by which colony members are recruited to a profitable food source, for example, in work on tandem running, chemical trails (Hölldobler, 1978), or the highly sophisticated dance language used by the honeybee (von Frisch, 1965). Simultaneously, comparative analysis of foraging systems has produced a number of correlations that suggest an efficient use of various foraging methods. For example, among ants, workers in species exploiting scattered food sources often forage individually, whereas those utilizing persistent or aggregated food rely on trails or recruitment (e.g., Bernstein, 1975; Davidson, 1977; Wehner *et al.*, 1983; Shepherd, 1982; Traniello, 1983, 1989; Fresneau, 1985; Schmid-Hempel, 1987a).

Among the more rigorous attempts to study the function of recruitment and the involvement of individual behavior is the work by Taylor (1977) on the ants *Solenopsis invicta* and *Pogonomyrmex occidentalis*. In his experiments, the behavioral decision of interest is differential recruitment rate, i.e., the rate at which workers visit alternative food sources. Taylor (1978) assumed that recruitment rate should be adjusted such that resources are delivered to the colony at a maximum possible rate. The empirical evidence showed qualitative agreement with expectations from models based on this premise. The predictions, however, are so general that the empirical tests are hard to evaluate. Furthermore, in Taylor's models the individual workers are constrained to a "unit behavior": apart from choosing to go either to source A or to B, no other freedom is entrusted to them.

A somewhat different approach is to concentrate on the mechanisms by which individuals become attracted to a particular food source (e.g., the probability that an individual ant follows trail A or B), and to relate the recruitment patterns emerging from these individual rules (defined by the respective probabilities "chosen" by the animals) to efficient use. Models based on such probabilistic behavior are indeed capable of producing patterns of trail following and of individualistic, diffuse foraging that are close to observed behavior (Fig. 4)

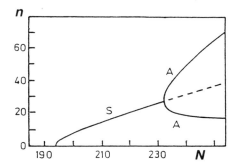

Fig. 4. The predicted number of recruited ants (*ordinate: n*) at one of two alternative, but identical, food sources as a function of the potential number of foragers available (*abscissa: N*). In the domain S, both sources are visited by an equal number of foragers. In domain A, an asymmetry with two stable points occurs. The model is mechanistic and assumes that foraging is regulated by the probability with which foragers follow either the trail to source X or Y. Observed dichotomous patterns can be closely mimicked with this kind of modeling. (From Pasteels *et al.*, 1987. Reproduced with permission.)

(Pasteels *et al.*, 1987; Deneubourg *et al.*, 1987; Goss *et al.*, 1989a,b). An inherent weakness of this approach is that it provides no a priori yardstick against which performance of different individual rules can be compared. In principle, though, it would be possible to find parameter values for each of these rules which, under given conditions, would yield maximum performance. The best performance of each rule could then in turn be compared with alternative ones to identify the best rule for a given environment (see also McNair, 1982). Compared with an approach such as that of Taylor (1978), these models are thus much more constrained in their assumptions about what animals can do, but they are not in contradiction to the "classical" optimization models (Krebs and McCleery, 1984). At present, these kinds of studies have not been properly related to analyses of optimal performance.

Ants have also been used to test models of diet choice for central-place foragers (Davidson, 1978; Rissing and Pollock, 1984; Bailey and Polis, 1987). In the standard procedure, two items of different quality (large versus small) are presented and individual choice is tested. Simple models (Orians and Pearson, 1979) would predict that foragers become more selective with distance, but in the ants studied so far this effect is not particularly strong. A partial explanation for this lack of distance sensitivity comes from the analysis by Lessells and Stephens (1983) of a single-prey loader system (i.e., where a forager takes but one prey during a foraging trip, as is normally the case in ants). Their models would indeed predict that foragers are not selective up to a critical threshold distance. However, because threshold distance is determined with respect to time and energy budgets, quantification of these parameters would be necessary to check whether the studied ants have simply foraged below this limit. Note that, apart from the constraints set by the necessity to return to the nest after each trip and by assuming that foragers carry out only one task at a time, i.e., the existence of a simple central-place foraging system, no additional reference to social living is made in these studies.

There is a class of foraging studies on social insects in which social living and the central-place structure are not taken into account at all. For example, Waddington and Holden (1979) investigated flower choice by foraging honeybees on arrays of artificial flowers by means of optimal diet models. Their unit of study is the average flower visit, preceded by an interflower flight, rather than the long-term repetition of cycles of traveling and handling times, or the entire roundtrip from and to the nest (see Stephens et al., 1986). Similarly, tests of predictions for residence time on inflorescences thought to maximize the net rate of energetic gains in bumblebees (Hodges, 1981, 1985; Pleasants, 1989) ignore the basic central-place structure of foraging systems in social insects. Neglecting this structure and social living may frequently only produce minor errors in the calculations, and thus useful predictions can nevertheless be gained.

C.   WORKER BEHAVIOR IN A VARIABLE WORLD

Most of the problems that organisms in their environment have to cope with are essentially stochastic. For example, food availability may fluctuate in space and time, and even become so variable that energetic shortfall results if the wrong source is exploited. Theoretical and empirical evidence has shown that such variance is important for animals and leads to behavior different from that expected if only the average situation was considered (e.g., Caraco et al., 1980; Stephens, 1981). Two aspects of a variable world are particularly important. The animal may behave so as to gain information about the state of the world, which can then be used in future actions (see Stephens, 1989). Such a situation exists when scouting honeybees search for profitable food sites, but this problem has not yet been analyzed by means of sampling models that seek to predict the best allocation of effort for gaining information about a food source (e.g., Stephens, 1987). Alternatively, the probability distribution of costs and benefits across a range of behavioral options may be known, but the animal has to decide about the risk of doing poorly versus the chance of doing well that is associated with each option, and then choose accordingly.

In the study of social insects, stochastic problems have not often been considered explicitly. Oster and Wilson (1978) analyzed the effect of uncertain environments on caste specialization. Under certain circumstances, increased environmental variability was expected to select for increased caste polymorphism (see Herbers, 1980). However, as Oster and Wilson have argued, flexibility in worker behavior would provide an equally good alternative to caste polymorphism. In fact, specialist or generalist workers are favored, depending on whether environmental variation is, respectively, unpredictable or predictable in space and time. It is known that individual behavioral specialization exists, even within a single task, and adds to task efficiency (e.g., Schmid-Hempel, 1984; Laverty and Plowright, 1988; Jeanne, 1988). Nevertheless, the predicted general trends in behavioral flexibility in relation to environmental uncertainty await further empirical work.

Foraging with respect to environmental variance has been discussed in more detail. The studies appear to be inspired primarily by progress in the study of vertebrates, in particular birds (Caraco et al., 1980). Consequently, the worker as an individual forager is the focus of interest and its relation to colony ergonomics has been neglected. For example, social bees and wasps have been found to avoid flowers that offer variable rewards, even if the expected average reward per flower is the same as in the alternative type (Real, 1981; Waddington et al., 1981). Because nectar feeders are usually also important pollinators of their food plants, such responses to variable rewards have consequences for gene flow and plant population structure (Ott et al., 1985). This is further substantiated by the observation that risk sensitivity is influenced by the spatial distribution of the resources (Real et al., 1982).

From the point of view of the bee or wasp, sensitivity to variance has been explained by avoidance of energetic shortfall (the z-score model of Stephens, 1981; Stephens and Charnov, 1982), variance discounting (i.e., a descriptive utility, indicating how undesirable variance is; Real, 1980), or, alternatively, by constraints on learning performance (Waddington et al., 1981). Risk of shortfall seems to explain some of the behavior of foraging birds (see Stephens and Krebs, 1986). However, the situation is slightly more complicated in social insects. Individual workers do not always provision themselves while foraging, but rather rely on the stores available in the nest. Hence, failure to meet a minimum resource requirement does not have the same consequences as for a solitary organism. Note that this does not imply that ineffective behavior of individuals is of no consequence for the colony's reproductive output, but rather that the additional options available in a social insect society, e.g., parallel action by other colony members and information sharing, should alter the effect of such "errors." There is a more technical point here, illustrated by the foraging studies of pollinators. In these studies (e.g., Real, 1980), bees are offered a choice between two flower types with equal average reward (e.g., 1 μl of nectar) but unequal variance (e.g., 1 μl in each flower versus 3 μl in every third). The expected average and variance in reward obtained per flower visit is then taken to be an appropriate utility measure that directs individual behavior. Yet, fitness is more likely to be related to variance in delivery rate of resources at the hive. The two measures—returns on a per flower basis versus returns on a per foraging cycle basis—diverge, by definition (Turelli et al., 1982), as well as when load effects occur (Schmid-Hempel *et al.*, 1985). Load effects distort the "symmetry" of the problem: large load increments collected at longer intervals (collected from more variable flowers) are energetically less costly to transport over a given cycle than small load increments collected at shorter intervals (collected from constant flowers with the same average reward). Hence, the expected benefit on the basis of an entire foraging cycle is actually higher for the more variable flowers, although mean reward per flower is kept the same (and we could conclude that bees avoid them in spite of a higher average return). The numerical discrepancy between these two measures may be small though, so that it would not matter in practice.

Thus, the behavior of workers in the face of a variable environment is evaluated through its effects on colony performance (see Nonacs and Dill, 1988). For example, what would be the consequences if the same amount of food is delivered in large packages rather than continuously over time? Such effects of variance are poorly understood, but may have important consequences (Plowright and Pendrel, 1977). The study by Barrow and Pickard (1985) also illustrates this point. They found that larval growth in bumblebees is reduced under temporally varying brood temperatures and thus results in reduced pupal and adult weights. On the other hand, colonies of social insects may be fairly resilient in the face of such variability, as suggested by studies where colonies are stressed and the effect on reproductives estimated (see Gentry, 1974; Schmid-Hempel and Heeb, 1990).

In a further class of studies, that will not be discussed in detail here, the behavior of workers in space is of interest. For example, spatial allocation of foraging effort is of obvious significance to the study of individual worker behavior. In the individually foraging ant *Cataglyphis bicolor,* Harkness and Maroudas (1985) have simulated foraging movements based on analogy to molecular diffusion. However, because the model is descriptive and also constrains the possible behavior of the animals, little can be said about efficient performance. In contrast, Schmid-Hempel (1984a) and Traniello (1987) have explicitly tested whether different search patterns of individual ants do actually provide higher benefits with respect to different distributions of food.

The study of adaptive, unconstrained spatial behavior is notoriously difficult, mostly because optimum performance, e.g., minimization of the time taken to encounter a food item, is difficult or almost impossible to calculate for all but the most simple cases (for a theory of search, see Stone, 1975). Hence, the two-dimensional analysis is usually replaced by an approach along a single dimension, e.g., distance effects in central-place systems, or the study of area-restricted searching. Many observations suggest that workers of social insects respond to a local increase in resource availability or to a recent find by increasing their search effort (e.g., Heinrich, 1979a; Pyke, 1978; Schmid-Hempel, 1984b). While most of this research has concentrated on foraging movements in feeding areas, use of space within the colony may also be of interest for studying behavioral adaptations (Cole, 1988).

Taken together, functional studies of the foraging behavior of social insects are still at an early stage compared to what has been achieved in birds or mammals (see Stephens and Krebs, 1986). Some of the obstacles to making progress include the difficulty of defining suitable goal functions and the existence of "erratic" individual behaviors, so familiar and sometimes so frustrating to every student of social insects. However, erratic behavior could in fact add to the colony's capability of discovering new food sources (Deneubourg, 1983) or facilitate exploitation of a wide range of different food types (Schmid-Hempel, 1984a; Traniello, 1988). It may thus consist of adaptive features worthy of study in themselves.

However, the analysis of individual behavior has generally been neglected in favor of colony performance. Colony integration is no doubt an important aspect, but various levels in a "hierarchy of decisions" exist. For example, consider the problem of a bee collecting nectar from flowers around her colony. Rich sources of nectar are very likely to occur in recognizable patches in the environment. The individual worker is thus faced with the problem of when and where to forage (i.e., which patch should be exploited at what time), what to collect (i.e., which plants to visit once a site is reached), and finally, how to exploit a given food source (e.g., what nectar load to collect). These decisions are not independent of one another, as it would make little sense to fly to a distant patch and not visit particularly profitable flowers worth the long trip. However, a series of decisions is involved in the process: the scouting activity of many workers will make information about concurrent food sources available. Such communication will usually lead to a concentration of foraging efforts at the more profitable sites (e.g., Seeley, 1986), and hence the "decision" of when and where to go would be made on this basis. But, once a worker is committed to a particular patch, there still exists the problem of how to use this source in an efficient way. This individual decision is not replaced by social foraging and will moreover influence the benfits obtained by the colony as a whole. The analysis of individual behavioral performance thus remains a problem in its own right.

III.   A CASE STUDY OF INDIVIDUAL BEHAVIOR

A.   FORAGING IN THE HONEYBEE

Foraging activities epitomize in a convenient manner the various aspects involved in the study of functions of worker behavior. The analysis is simpler if costs and benefits associated with behavior can be evaluated along similar axes. This is often the case for foraging animals, as energy and time are most often critical resources in short supply and can be readily measured. The situation may be much more complex in a system like that of a leaf-cutting ant (or a termite), where leaf material is collected in order to grow fungi that then in turn provide the necessary food. Here, organic matter, nutrients, or toxins contained in the leaves might become crucial and affect foraging decisions rather than time and energy alone. By contrast, social bees provide a convenient study example since they are highly dependent on energy contained in flower nectar.

Honeybees (*Apis mellifera* L.) form highly social societies with a pronounced division of labor (Seeley, 1985; Winston, 1987). In honeybees, the collection of resources is a major enterprise, involving thousands of foragers and covering areas up to 100 km^2 around the hive (Visscher and Seeley, 1982). Foragers collect pollen, which is used to raise new larvae, and nectar, the major energy source that drives the whole system (Michener, 1974; Heinrich, 1979b; Seeley, 1985). To fuel their own energy demand, workers usually provision themselves with (the concentrated) honey from the colony's store (Beutler, 1937). In many ways, therefore, energy, collected as nectar from flowers, is an important variable in the life of honeybees. This is also readily appreciated by comparing the enormous rates of energy consumption of walking or flying bees with other animals after correcting for body size (e.g., Casey, 1989; Rothe and Nachtigall, 1989; Wolf *et al.*, 1989). Furthermore, as a consequence of the division of labor, a foraging honeybee can be assumed to have no other task to attend to (e.g., nest defense, brood care), and hence there is a good chance that its behavior can be understood by using energy balances as a crucial measure of utility.

A hallmark of honeybee biology is the sophisticated recruitment system by means of the dance language (e.g., Lindauer, 1961; von Frisch, 1965; Gould *et al.*, 1985; Gould and Towne, 1987). Dance language and recruitment allow workers to exploit food sources that they themselves have never visited before—a major achievement in invertebrate behavioral evolution. Curiously enough, the economics of recruitment has only recently become more rigorously investigated (e.g., Seeley, 1986). On the level of individuals, a frequent observation in honeybees is that, even where sources of nectar do not diminish with time, the workers return to the hive with an only partially filled crop (Nuñez, 1966, 1970, 1982; Wells and Giacchino, 1968; Fukuda *et al.*, 1969). Such a behavior is also known from wasps (Pflumm, 1971) and hummingbirds (DeBenedictis *et al.*, 1978; Tamm, 1989). To explain this observation, Nuñez (1982) related individual behavior to colony economics by postulating a need to exchange information with other foragers in the hive. He argued that when workers exploit a food source, the associated prolonged absence from the hive may lead to a loss of information about alternative food sources, communicated by other members of the colony, and hence to an overall decline in the rate at which colonies can extract resources from the environment. As a result, it would pay individual workers to return earlier with only partially filled crops. While this hypothesis may in principle reflect the various benefits and costs involved in individual foraging, it appears that individual decisions based on this trade-off could generate higher rates of extraction only under some rather stringent conditions. For example, the extra amount of time or energy saved by returning earlier to the hive (with a partial instead of a full load) is required to yield higher returns when invested elsewhere, i.e., when allocated to following recruitment dances and locating and exploiting an alternative food source. But recruited workers have to invest considerably more time and energy to find the advertised opportunities, rather than simply follow a distance and direction (Seeley, 1983).

Simple models of central-place foraging, based on maximization of rate of energy extraction from food sources, predict that bees exploiting nondepleting flower patches should always gather full crop loads. Note that colonies of the honeybee are here regarded as "factory fortresses" (Oster and Wilson, 1978), designed to extract food at a maximum possible net rate (which is equivalent to delivery rate at the hive). Correct predictions can nevertheless be gained, if foraging costs that depend on the size of the gathered load are included (Kacelnik and Houston, 1984).

B. THE ECONOMIC USE OF ENERGY

The analysis of the foraging behavior of flower-visiting nectar-feeders offers several methodological advantages. For example, because plants advertise themselves to bees, this can also be exploited in experiments by marking food sources with colored "corollas." In the standard experimental paradigm discussed here, a patch of artificial flowers marked in this manner is offered at a distance from the hive with nectar available ad libitum. To mimic an entire flower field, three feeders, each containing an apparatus to deliver nectar to a tiny well at the top, are necessary. A sliding cover ensures that these "flowers" can be "closed" or "opened" to permit access according to the experimental schedule. The bees need only a few seconds to fly from one feeder to the next, but operating the sliding cover generates variation in the time between successive admissions to flowers. In this way, patches of different flower (inflorescence) densities can be mimicked rather accurately. Nectar may contain other, perhaps important, components besides sugar (e.g., amino acids; Baker and Baker, 1985), but in the experiments nectar is usually substituted for by sugar solution. The behavior of individual workers can now be studied rather easily, as honeybees are readily trained to collect "nectar" from such flowers, and, usually after two or three foraging cycles, the behavioral performance stabilizes and further cycles can be used for analysis.

Note that this experimental paradigm emphasizes stable performance after the animal has learnt about the situation. A different situation exists when the process of learning itself is of interest, for example, in the context of how animals track variable environments (Stephens, 1987). Furthermore, this basic paradigm refers to an intrinsically deterministic situation, because the foraging bee will always get the same amount of nectar reward on each visit to a flower, i.e., there is no variance in reward received. However, as should become clear in the remainder of this article, a great deal of insight can be gained even from exploring such simple paradigms.

Now suppose a bee visits n flowers in the patch and each time gets rewarded with a small quantity of nectar. An energetic equivalent of e units is contained in the diluted sugar solution in one flower. Hence, the total energy, G, collected in the form of nectar is $n \times e$. On the other hand, the animal incurs energetic expenditure, C, which can be calculated from the metabolic rates associated with various components of the foraging cycle (see Schmid-Hempel et al., 1985). As a consequence, a foraging bee that decides to visit n flowers will deliver net energy of value $G - C$ to the hive. To study the "design" of nectar collection, a goal function is formulated that should implement the local fitness measure hypothesized for the problem under study. Most standard models of foraging theory assume that animals should maximize their net rate of energy intake while foraging (Stephens and Krebs, 1986). This seems plausible, as time and energy are resources in short supply and efficient use of resources should relate to fitness. Hence, if T denotes the time invested in an average foraging cycle, it is hypothesized that nectar-collecting workers of the honeybee should maximize their net rate of energy delivery to the hive, i.e., they should maximize $r = (G - C)/T$ (the "net-rate model"). For the actual calculations of these quantities, it should be taken into account that flying becomes increasingly more expensive for the bee as nectar loads are accumulated and add to body weight. It is essentially this effect of variation in foraging costs that leads to predictions of partial crop filling even for nondepleting patches of flowers as used here. In fact, Schmid-Hempel et al. (1985) and Schmid-Hempel (1987b) have successfully used this model to predict crop loads of honeybees in the above experimental paradigm. However, while the *qualitative* expectations were also met for the above net rate model, the *quantitative* predictions were in line with the maximization of a different goal function, i.e., that of net energetic efficiency $e = (G - C)/C$ (the "net-efficiency model") (Fig. 5).

The present case study is therefore a particularly clear-cut example that shows the importance of different assumptions and the need for quantitative analysis. For example, Schmid-Hempel et al. (1985) have assumed that the stay in the hive is an integral part of the foraging cycle of bees. Inside the hive, workers unload their crop to receiver bees (e.g., Seeley and Levien, 1987) and prepare to fly out again. The situation is analogous to the unloading process of a bird that returns to the nest to feed its dependent young. However, in the latter case, duration of stay at the nest is rarely included in the analysis of foraging behavior (but see Kacelnik, 1984). The difference in approach reflects differences in biology: As an

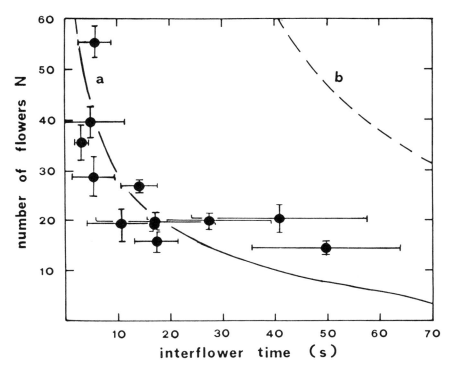

FIG. 5. Observed number of flower visits (*ordinate: N*) by honeybee workers collecting nectar from an array of artifical flowers mimicking a naturally flowering meadow when flower density in a patch is varied (*abscissa:* interflower flight time). Each dot is a different individual. Bars denote S.D. The broken line (b) indicates expected visits when bees maximize net rate of energy delivered to the hive, solid line (a) when net energetic efficiency is maximized (see text). The second model is found to generate robust predictions that are close to observations. (From Schmid-Hempel *et al.,* 1985. Reproduced with permission.)

additional complication, workers of social insects show division of labor, such that the time a forager spends in the hive is not part of another task, but most likely also a part of the foraging work. Needs such as nest maintenance, repelling intruders, and so forth are met by the many other workers that are active in parallel rather than by the forager itself. The situation should be quite different in birds, where tasks can only be met sequentially by the same individual, such that time at the nest may be best regarded as time off from foraging. Whether or not this distinction is real remains to be analyzed by evaluating the explanatory power of different scenarios. I note in passing that various degrees of biparental care or cooperative breeding among birds may offer interesting test cases to disentangle these factors and thus to analyze how animals structure their world.

Quantitative models can also be used for sensitivity analysis that helps us to identify crucial parameters. In the case of the nectar-collecting bees, it turns out that predictions are sensitive to the assumption of including the hive time in the foraging cycle. Yet, relaxing this assumption would still favor the same interpretation (Schmid-Hempel *et al.*, 1985). Furthermore, the increase in metabolic rate with nectar load was found to affect the predictions to a substantial degree. At the time of the study there were no appropriate data available in the literature, for the ecological importance of this parameter seems to have escaped the attention of physiologists (with the possible exception of Heinrich's 1975 study on bumblebee queens). In later research, this parameter has now been measured and found to agree quite well with the assumptions made in the original model (Wolf *et al.*, 1989). In addition, individual differences in this physiological constraint could be shown to exist, and these may be related to genetic variance of metabolic expenditure for which there is now evidence (Coelho and Mitton, 1988). This raises intriguing new possibilities about how work should be distributed among colony members. Furthermore, an evolutionary response to selection on physiological performance should be possible (see discussion in Section V,A). The study of the function of behavior can thus help one to identify important questions about mechanisms and constraints, and be fruitfully integrated with questions about proximate causation. In fact, in the case discussed here, clear links between ecologically relevant behavior (the exploitation of flowers in a patch) and constraints on individual performance (energy expenditure as determined by the physiological machinery) exist.

C.   DIFFICULTIES OF INTERPRETING A GOAL FUNCTION

In the case study described above, the "decision" about crop load taken by the bees was the trait of interest. We wished to understand this trait by testing alternative hypotheses about design, i.e., by comparing predictions from alternative goal functions. Successful predictions about crop load were generated by assuming that bees behave such as to maximize net energetic efficiency rather than to maximize net rate of energy delivery to the hive. Support for this conclusion actually comes from additional experiments (Schmid-Hempel, 1987b; Kacelnik *et al.*, 1986). Similarly, Waddington (1985) found that parameters characterizing the tempo of round dances of honeybees correlated with the gains and costs involved in exploiting experimental food sources in a way suggestive of the evaluation of a gain–cost ratio. Also, the recruitment response of entire honeybee colonies to alternative food patches seems to be approximated by this currency, i.e., that profitability of patches may be ranked according to the net efficiency criterion (Seeley, 1986). Interestingly, there is now evidence for a similar pattern in foraging birds (Welham and Ydenberg, 1988).

To repeat the obvious: agreement of observations with a particular theoretical expectation cannot exclude the possibility that alternative explanations not yet considered may actually be correct. For example, partial crop loads were expected to occur as a result of an increasing cost of nectar transportation. However, inferring causation from such observations alone can be fallacious, as the loading effect (Kramer and Nowell, 1980) may be due to other reasons, for example, the accumulation of an information deficit, as suggested by Nuñez (1982). Nevertheless, energetic costs of transporting nectar loads can be measured directly and provide an independent test of the assumption (Wolf *et al.*, 1989). Also, tests where individual bees were experimentally made heavier or kept at the same weight during nectar collection in the patch (Schmid-Hempel, 1986) have demonstrated the importance of transport costs. The latter study incidentally shows how mechanisms responsible for the "decision" of the animal can be experimentally approached within the same paradigm. Hence, it seems that in the case of the honeybee, a loading effect is indeed due to transport costs and that, according to the interpretation of the design function, the behavior of workers is sensitive to the associated energetic expenditures.

A corollary to this finding is that honeybee workers do not invest as much energy in an average foraging cycle as would be needed to maximize the net rate of energy delivery to the hive. Crop loads predicted by the net efficiency model are always lower than those of the net rate model, and this is due to the fact that metabolic expenditure increases more rapidly than expenditure of time as loads are accumulating. On the other hand, it would seem that a colony where a larger amount of net energy per unit time is delivered as a result of increased work efforts should grow more rapidly and be able to outcompete its neighbors.

At this point, it is important to return to the basic life cycle of entire colonies (Fig. 1). It is the ergonomic phase during which the colony grows in numbers that is of interest here, as it is then the individual members contribute by their work efforts to survival and growth of the entire society. Moreover, up to a point, there is generally a positive relationship between the size of the colony at reproduction and the number of reproductives that can be produced (Michener, 1964; Pomeroy and Plowright, 1982; Cole, 1984; Fowler, 1986). Hence, natural selection should favor rapid growth and consequent large size of the colony at the time of reproduction.

For the analysis of foraging strategies, this life history constraint has important consequences. Among other things, colony growth during the ergonomic phase depends on the rate at which resources are extracted from the surroundings and on how efficiently they can be converted into new workers, into new brood space, and so forth. However, in a highly eusocial insect, such as the honeybee, several generations of workers are usually produced before reproduction occurs. Hence, growth in worker numbers is not only affected by the rate at which resources are delivered to and converted inside the colony, i.e., by the birth rate of workers, but also by their mortality rate. As a first approximation, rate of

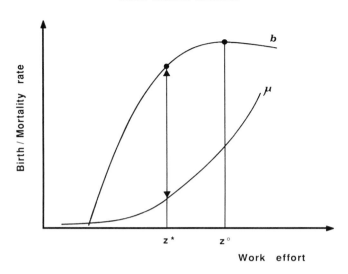

FIG. 6. Hypothetical dependence of birth rate (b) and mortality rate (μ) of workers on average work effort of foragers. Birth rate is maximized with work effort $z°$, but colony growth is maximized with z^*, i.e., where the difference ($b - \mu$) is maximal. Birth rate is assumed to depend in a simple way on the rate at which resources are delivered to the hive. (After Houston *et al.*, 1988.)

colony growth is the difference between rates of birth and of mortality of workers. Both quantities are obviously influenced by choice of foraging strategy. Indeed, it is possible to show that, with foraging-dependent mortality, less than maximum foraging efforts are expected to maximize rate of colony growth (Houston *et al.*, 1988) (Fig. 6).

The goal function found to generate correct predictions in the case study cited above is therefore interpreted as reflecting individual strategies designed to maximize colony growth. Yet, while the theoretical analysis by Houston *et al.* (1988) plausibly explains why workers should not work at maximum pace, empirical questions remain: Does variation in foraging efforts correlate with variation in life span? Is colony growth maximized by the choice to maximize net efficiency?

IV. Work Effort and Life Span

From the above studies, the individual behavior of workers in social insects is considered to reflect a balance between the benefits for colony growth and the costs in terms of worker life span. Similarly, trade-offs between reproductive effort and survival of the organism, i.e., the balance between allocating resources to either producing offspring or ensuring survival, have been found to be an essential component in the analysis of life history traits (e.g., Snell and King,

1977; Reznick, 1985; Partridge and Harvey, 1985). The situation in social insects is more complex, as different levels of organismal organization exist. At the level of the colony, allocation patterns involve the problem of production of new workers versus production of sexuals (Macevicz and Oster, 1976). A difficulty exists when studying individuals, as workers normally do not themselves reproduce (for a review of instances of worker reproduction, see Bourke, 1988). Nevertheless, the actions of individuals are still important as they contribute to colony growth and thus to the eventual production of sexuals.

An important implicit assumption is that an increase in behavioral activity should lead to a decrease in survival probability. Several attempts have been made to link the activity levels of workers, particularly foragers, to life span (Table I), but there are a number of problems with this. For example, it is known that the life span of workers in the honeybee has heritable components (Brückner, 1980; Winston and Katz, 1982; Milne, 1982, 1985) and is also affected by season and nutrition (Free and Spencer-Booth, 1959; Maurizio, 1961; Schmidt et al., 1987). It is also crucial to realize that trade-offs between activity and life span, as discussed in accounts of life history theory, refer to a process "within" each individual rather than "between" individuals. This has important empirical implications, because variation in individual "quality" could lead to counterintuitive observations. Suppose, for example, that there are large differences in the "quality" of individuals. In such a case, high-quality individuals could be more active than low-quality ones and still live longer. As a result, a positive relationship between work effort and life span across individuals may emerge, although the relevant trade-off within individuals still exits. Experimental manipulation is therefore needed.

Schmid-Hempel and Wolf (1988) and Wolf and Schmid-Hempel (1989) have tested individual honeybee workers from the same colony. Work effort was experimentally set by allocating individuals at random to different groups. Variation in effort was then generated by restricting the period of time these groups were allowed to forage each day. This procedure thus balanced some of the factors that could not be experimentally altered, i.e., individual differences due to nutrition or genetic quality, or "background" conditions set by the hive. However, contrary to the initial expectation that such an experimental reduction in foraging activity should lead to an increase in life span, no such effect was found (Fig. 7a). In contrast, when the foraging effort of workers in the different groups was experimentally increased, life span was indeed reduced (Fig. 7b). In these experiments, foraging effort was experimentally altered by gluing weights onto the thoraces of the bees, thus rendering effort again independent of individual "quality." Interestingly enough, effects on life spans were only observed with large extra loads, not with small or moderate ones. This was not due to lower active loading with small loads, as the weight of the average crop content was independent of experimental manipulation. A further decrease in life span

TABLE I

STUDIES ON FACTORS AFFECTING LIFE SPAN OF HONEYBEE FORAGERS

Method[a]	Result	Remarks	Reference
E: Survival of unfed bees under different light conditions	Live longer under dark > medium > bright light	Other conditions also vary (temperature, humidity)	Phillips (1922)
E: Reduced effort in comparison of laboratory versus field	Bees in laboratory live 1–2 weeks longer. Significance?	Field bees kept in hive, laboratory bees in small cages with constant light	Rockstein (1950)
E: Reduced effort for hive induced by blocking entrance	Bees foraging for half days live slightly longer than those foraging full days. Not significant	Difference between hives	Mauermayer (1954)
O: Increased foraging activity induced by more brood combs	Shorter life span under high brood rearing rates. Significant correlation	Differences among races. Connection with foraging assumed, i.e., more foraging with more brood	Hassanein and El-Banby (1960)
O: Survival in different seasons	Longevity reduced under active foraging periods. Significant correlation	Indirect evidence through weather data	Fukuda and Sekiguchi (1966)
O, E: Increased effort of bees in newly established swarms compared to bees in already established colonies	Longevity reduced to 12 days	Indirect evidence for importance of work. European honeybee differs from Africanized bee	Winston (1979)
E: Foraging effort varied through placing feeders for different lengths of time	Life spans shorter if feeders presented longer. Significance?	Comparison among hives and among years	Neukirch (1982)
E: Increased effort through removal of workers	Remaining bees live less long. Significant correlation	No direct measure of foraging effort. Different colonies	Winston and Fergusson (1985)
O: Correlation with pollen collection rate	Longevity decreases with pollen intake rate. Significant correlation	No direct measure of foraging effort. Comparison among hives	Wille et al. (1985)
E: Reduction of foraging by blocking entrance for different lengths of time and for different worker groups	No effect on life spans	Individuals within same hive. Various factors controlled	Schmid-Hempel and Wolf (1988)
E: Increased effort through permanent weights attached to thorax of bee	Reduction of life span at large weights. Significant correlation	Individuals within same hive. Various factors controlled	Wolf and Schmid-Hempel (1989)

[a]O, Observation; E, experiment.

beyond that of the group with 23 mg did not occur because of a change in the bees' behavior, i.e., they did reduce their activity.

The results of these studies suggest that foraging effort is indeed related to the life span of individual workers. There are, however, a number of points to make here. The experiments by Schmid-Hempel and Wolf could not distinguish between different sources of mortality and were not designed to do so. Rather, the findings represent "net curves," as set by the colony background and environmental conditions during the experiment, outlining an expected mortality–work load relationship. Nothing can be inferred about the relative importance of predators, parasites, or physiological deterioration in affecting life spans. While this limitation should be realized, such a net curve is actually an important constraint for behavioral decisions of the individual. This is because it should be largely irrelevant what the actual causes of mortality are, given their relative frequencies associated with different behavioral options. In a more narrow sense though, physiological deterioration may give the individual greater flexibility in adjusting work effort than would mortality risks through predators.

These experiments demonstrated furthermore that life span is in a nontrivial way related to average foraging effort: there seems to exist a threshold effort beyond which an effect does occur. Similar evidence is provided by reports where individual life spans have been studied in relation to a number of stress factors (Table I). For example, some other studies in the honeybee have sought to experimentally decrease the work effort of individuals by restraining their activity. Small effects usually result from such manipulations. If, on the other hand, work load is increased by a significant amount, e.g., by experimentally removing a fraction of the worker force, a negative effect on life span can usually be observed. Hence, it seems that at least in some social insects shorter life spans result from an increase above the normal activity level, but that variation below this limit has little effect (Fig. 8).

V.   The Evolutionary Ecology of Work Load
in Social Insects

In the preceding section, the relationship between work effort and worker life span was discussed in the context of foraging. To generalize the discussion, the term "work load" is suggested here: it is used in a similar sense to the notion of "tempo" suggested by Oster and Wilson (1978) to specify a measure of mean activity, but is intended to convey more clearly the importance of fitness costs associated with working. In addition, in Oster and Wilson's terminology, tempo also includes aspects of worker reliability that I wish to keep apart from the issue of work load.

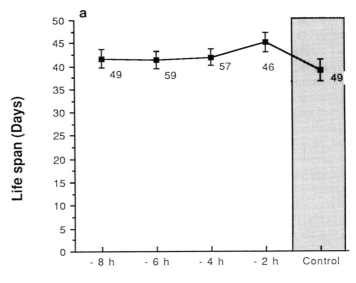

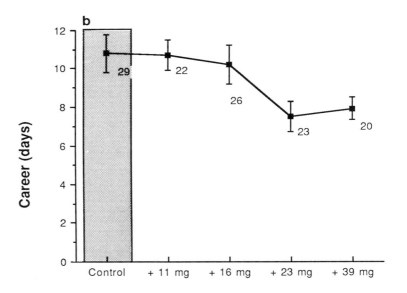

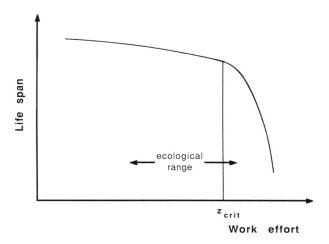

FIG. 8. An idealized curve relating work effort to life span of the individual. Over most of the ecological range, defined as that where the work effort is usually encountered by the species, little effect on life span is to be expected. Beyond a critical level, z_{crit}, detrimental effects will occur.

A.   INDIVIDUAL WORK LOAD

Foraging is clearly one of the physiologically most demanding tasks that workers of social insects can attend to, especially for a flying insect like a bee or wasp (e.g., Harrison, 1986; Wolf *et al.*, 1989). In addition, the foraging costs incurred during the growth period of the colony are likely to be an important determinant of fitness. For example, Eckert (1938) found that colonies of honeybees located far from their food sources did not grow as fast as those close to the source and this could lead to fewer swarms being produced (Winston, 1980; Seeley and Visscher, 1985). Hence, we can expect that selection acts to increase physiological performance to various degrees.

To a physiologist, performance is a multidimensional concept that may include limitations in flight speed, acceleration, load-carrying capacity, and so forth. For example, work output of the flight machinery is dependent on muscle mass as well as enzymatic activity, which in turn varies with temperature (Heinrich,

FIG. 7. (a) The effect of experimental reduction of average daily foraging activity on life span in workers of the honeybee. Individuals were assigned to five different groups and constrained to forage for 2, 4, 6, or 8 hr or not at all (controls) each day. No significant effect is found. Life span is measured from emergence to last observation. (After Schmid-Hempel and Wolf, 1988.) (b) The effect of an experimental increase in foraging effort. Workers in four groups carried permanent extra weights to different degrees. Reduction is significant, even when the heaviest group is excluded. Career is remaining life span after onset of treatment for randomly chosen bees. (After Wolf and Schmid-Hempel, 1989.)

1981). To achieve the necessary temperature for the flight machinery to operate, preflight warm-up may thus be needed. This requirement is related to ecological factors. For example, Stone and Willmer (1989) found that across species of bees warm-up rates and thoracic temperatures depend on the ambient temperatures at which the species are flying after the effects of phylogenetic similarity and body size have been controlled for. Similarly, Prys-Jones (1986) demonstrated that, in bumblebees, activities of substrate enzymes correlate with the prevalent foraging mode, as species that more often visit massed flowers have higher enzymatic activities per gram of muscle mass.

Physiological performance may not be as critical to walking animals such as the ants. Fewell (1988) estimated that foraging costs for workers of the ant *Pogonomyrmex occidentalis* are less than 0.1% of the caloric content of an average collected seed. Similarly, Nielsen *et al.* (1982) reported insignificant transport costs for small loads taken by *Camponotus herculeanus* (Formicidae). On the other hand, Bartholomew *et al.* (1988) reported a two- to threefold increase in metabolic expenditure for laden ants. From their measurements comparing the army ant *Eciton hamatum* and the leaf-cutter *Atta colombica,* they inferred a crucial role for foraging costs in the maintenance foraging columns. They consequently expected physiological adaptation to transportation of different kinds of loads. Across three different species of seed-harvester ants (*Pogonomyrmex spp.*), MacKay (1982) also concluded that the physiological machinery is selected to meet specific work requirements. In particular, high-altitude species show higher metabolic rates than low-altitude species. This observation is interpreted to show a potential for higher work capacities in species living under shorter productive seasons.

Physiological performance is somewhat loosely discussed here as the output of the physiological machinery that allows the animal to sustain a given work load (a work rate). Consequently, it appears that increased physiological performance should invariably be of selective advantage. But, because selection can act at the level of the colony and the individual, the situation is slightly more complex in social insects. In fact, several studies have related life span of workers to the amount of work performed (see Table I) and, in particular, to sustained physiological activity (e.g., Neukirch, 1982, for *Apis;* Calabi and Porter, 1989, for the fire ant *Solenopsis invicta*). Therefore, the question is rather, Why should selection favor increased physiological performance by individuals rather than a simple replacement schedule of worn-out workers? In general, replacement should be the inferior solution at any one time if the residual value of the individual worker is high. A number of factors may favor this. For example, construction costs for a new worker could be prohibitively high as a result of shortage of available nest space, material or brood area, or if a large standing worker force is needed to care for the brood. Individual experience could also increase worker value, e.g., through an increase in foraging success with age (Dobrzanska and

Dobrzanski, 1975; Heinrich, 1976; Rissing, 1981a; Schmid-Hempel and Schmid-Hempel, 1984). Furthermore, the spatiotemporal availability of major resources that affect prime components of fitness may be important. If such resources are ephemeral, critical periods of intense work may be needed to exploit them. Also, selection operating within a colony can place a large value on individuals. This can occur when colonies consist of heterogeneous worker (sub-)populations, e.g., with multiple mating of the queen. In this case, prolonged life span (as a consequence of increased performance) may be essential for individuals to enable them to provide nepotistic help for the sexual brood at times when reproduction occurs, which is usually late in the colony's life cycle (Page et al., 1989; Schmid-Hempel, 1990).

The evolution of physiological performance has to be separated from the evolution of longevity itself. For example, senescence is known to occur in the honeybee, as brain cells decline in number and become increasingly vacuolated (Rockstein, 1950). But to what extent a capacity to sustain high rates of physical activity is related to earlier senescence or shorter life span is unclear. Simple correlations between these quantities have to be viewed with some caution (LeBourg et al., 1984). Additional knowledge about demographic and ecological factors that select for a particular longevity is therefore needed (Strassmann, 1985; Dyer and Seeley, 1990).

It is interesting to note that the situation depicted here is quite similar to that of birds that provision their dependent young. This period of provisioning is critical to reproductive success and associated with excessive metabolic demand. Drent and Daan (1980) reported that parents sustain a maximum work load (the "maximum sustainable effort") at approximately four times the basal metabolic rate. Work above this level will lead to a decrease in body weight, and this is a good indicator of body condition and hence future survival probability in birds. Daan et al. (1991) have carried this further with a comparative study of altricial birds and, from observations of daily energy expenditure during provisioning and lean mass of metabolically active tissues, suggested that the necessity to sustain high work loads during such critical periods may have selected for the evolution of a large physiological machinery. Such a machinery would then allow the bird to sustain large work loads over extended periods of time, but would most likely also lead to the effect that survival probability rapidly declines when this threshold is exceeded.

Again, the honeybees provide a more thoroughly studied case within the social insects. For them, selection to increase sustainable work load by the individual workers may be driven by several of the above mentioned factors. For example, honeybees are thought to experience a boom and bust economy (Visscher and Seeley, 1982; Seeley, 1983, 1985) with transient but highly profitable food sources that presumably contribute a major part of the colony's income. They can be exploited due to the sophisticated communication and recruitment system.

Benefits in the context of intracolonial selection through nepotistic behavior may also be important (Page *et al.*, 1989). The particular importance of flight performance in honeybee workers is further demonstrated by the studies of Harrison (1986). He found that maximum mass-specific rates of oxygen consumption, together with an increase in enzymatic activity (similar to that found by Neukirch, 1982), were substantially higher in foragers than in hive bees, which concurred with an increase in behavioral foraging activity. Also, comparative studies of four species of *Apis* (*A. mellifera, A. florea, A. cerana,* and *A. dorsata*) (Dyer and Seeley, 1987, 1990) demonstrate intricate relationships. Across this group, *A. mellifera* (the European honeybee) and *A. cerana* are shown to have an excessive work "tempo" for their body size, i.e., to have a higher mass-specific metabolic rate, body temperature, flight speed, and foraging distance. The authors relate this to the different modes of nesting (the two species nest in cavities rather than in the open) which require different worker:brood ratios and hence should affect selection for sustainable work load in relation to life span. Moreover, the stepwise relationship between life span and foraging effort suggested by Figs. 7 and 8 would actually conform to the existence of a pronounced (rather than gradual) upper limit for sustainable work, provided mortality is largely determined by physiological wear (sensu Neukirch, 1982). In this case, effects of variation in foraging effort on life span should be small if workers are operating below the maximum sustainable work load (Fig. 7a). However, if working above this threshold, deterioration would rapidly occur (and perhaps in porportion to work load) (Fig. 7b).

On the other hand, physiological evolution could conceivably be dampened by substantial rates of mortality imposed by predators or parasites. There may in fact be no point in having a good physiological performance, if such enemies prevent workers from working at their limits. But suppose that predation affects all colonies in a population to the same degree. Under these conditions, a "mutant" colony, containing workers with above-average physiological work performance, would still be capable of growing disproportionally large and producing more sexuals. For this to be so, it is required that the effect of enemies is decoupled from physiological performance, such that increased foraging returns are not set off by a similar increase in predation rate. Whether or not these conditions are met is essentially an empirical problem that must be solved by careful field studies. Well-defended animals (e.g., social bees or wasps with a powerful sting) should be less vulnerable to predation (but perhaps not to parasites: Schmid-Hempel and Schmid-Hempel, 1988; Schmid-Hempel *et al.*, 1990). Hence, defense could render physiological performance even more important. A large number of studies have reported the identity of, and some general knowledge about, natural enemies of social insects (see accounts in Wilson, 1971; Kistner, 1982). Unfortunately, we know next to nothing about the relative quantitative effects of different mortality factors in natural populations (Table II).

TABLE II

EXAMPLES OF STUDIES WHERE MORTALITY FACTORS FOR WORKERS OF SOCIAL INSECTS HAVE BEEN ASSESSED

Species	Source of mortality	Remarks	Reference
Apis mellifera	Physiological wear out	Results of field and laboratory colonies agree	Neukirch (1982)
Apis mellifera *Bombus* spp.	Crab spider *Misumena vatia*. Expectation for average worker is 22–109 days to capture. Killed on 0–2% of flower visits	Time to capture estimated from frequency of flower visits and spider attacks on milkweed	Fritz and Morse (1985)
Bombus pascuorum	21% of nests killed by badger	Effect primarily on small nests	Cumber (1953)
Bombus spp.	Parasitoid flies (Conopidae) shorten life span by one half (7 days) in laboratory	High frequencies of parasites in natural populations	Schmid-Hempel and Schmid-Hempel (1988); Schmid-Hempel *et al.* (1990)
Polistes exclamans	Presence of pupal parasites explains variance in worker longevity	Enemies of adults not described	Strassmann (1985)
Pogonomyrmex spp.	72% of workers per year killed by horned lizard	Several populations	Whitford and Bryant (1979)
P. californicus	Workers killed in 7% of aggressive interactions with neighbors		DeVita (1979)
P. californicus	Horned lizard takes one forager group (400 workers) every 2.1 days	Predation selects for group foraging as compared with *P. rugosus* and *Veromessor*	Rissing (1981b)
Cataglyphis bicolor *Cataglyphis albicans*	Mortality rate 17% (C.b.) and 28% (C.a.) per day taken by spiders and robber flies	Confirmation indirectly from calculations, i.e., frequency of observed attacks could account for mortality rate	Schmid-Hempel and Schmid-Hempel (1984)

Physiological characteristics are related to, and ultimately shaped by, ecological conditions (see Heinrich, 1981; Willmer, 1985; Stone and Willmer, 1989). A full discussion of these interrelationships is clearly beyond the scope of this article. However, selection on physiological characteristics such as the level of sustainable work load could have subtle repercussions on the short-term behavioral strategies that were analyzed in more detail in Section III. Suppose that work load (e.g., the time or energy invested in foraging activity per average working day) can be characterized by a variable z which is related to mortality rate and net rate of resources obtained as shown in Fig. 9. A limit to sustainable work load is taken into account by defining a critical threshold, z_{crit}, beyond which a substantial increase in mortality rate occurs. As discussed before, to maximize colony growth we expect that the work load chosen by individuals should maximize the difference between the two curves b and μ in Fig. 9 (Houston et al., 1988). The two ecological conditions illustrated in Fig. 9 appear to be particularly relevant. In Fig. 9a the net benefit curve may peak at relatively low work efforts, for example, when resources are profuse and readily available. In this case, workers should be observed to work close to maximization of net rate of benefits, $z°$. In the situation shown in Fig. 9b, the net benefit curve peaks well beyond z_{crit} (the point that characterizes maximum sustainable work load), and hence we would expect workers to behave close to this limit. Which of the two situations is relevant depends of course on the prevailing ecological conditions, but it is precisely the situation in Fig. 9b that would also select for an increase in sustainable effort. The situation shown in Fig. 9a may also result from foraging efforts being small as compared to efforts associated with other activities, such as mating or territory defense. It is unlikely that workers of social bees or wasps (but perhaps not of ants and termites) must sustain other similarly demanding activities besides foraging. Furthermore, the resources exploited by an animal such as the honeybee may be of type b rather than of type a, because this characteristic is enhanced or even generated by the recruitment system which directs workers to the most profitable and profuse sources currently available (Seeley, 1983).

With respect to the case study of the honeybee discussed in the preceding sections, it is of course not clear why the axis z in Fig. 9b, reflecting a rather general notion of "work load," should be scaled so that working near point z_{crit} is equivalent to maximizing net energetic efficiency on the short-term behavioral scale for workers that exploit sources of nectar. This is because the work load defined here is not necessarily identical to the minute-to-minute rate of metabolic expenditure that was used to analyze the behavior of the foraging animal. In fact, the time scale over which work load (a rate) is evaluated with respect to the maximum sustainable load is rather difficult to derive.

Nevertheless, a biologically reasonable assumption is that daily energy expenditure is constrained (sensu Drent and Daan, 1980; Daan et al., 1990). Indi-

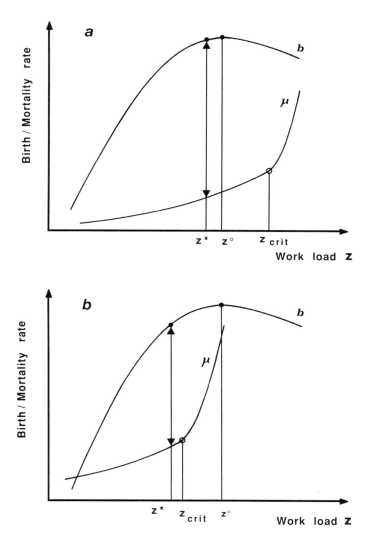

FIG. 9. Two situations, following Figs. 7 and 8, depict the hypothetical relationships between birth rate of workers (*b*) and mortality rate (μ) (*ordinate*) as a function of work load accepted by foragers (*abscissa: z*). (a) Colony growth is maximized by choice of z^* close to z°. (b) Maximum colony growth is achieved by choice of z^* close to z_{crit}. Case a depicts a situation with marginal food sources; case b is a particularly rich situation. Alternatively, internal differences of colonies could lead to corresponding differences in the benefit curves, producing similar relationships.

viduals working under the conditions of Fig. 9b should thus make the best use of this constraint and maximize benefits with respect to this daily limit. In terms of foraging energetics, this is likely to be the case when net energy gained (the assumed benefit) is maximized with respect to daily energy expenditure. In foraging experiments, the time scale is usually much shorter and refers to single foraging cycles. Yet, to maximize the gain/cost ratio for an entire day, this ratio should also be maximized for each single foraging cycle, for otherwise the worker would inevitably fall short of the maximum possible long-term (daily) result. Such a behavior was actually observed in the stable deterministic situation analyzed above (Schmid-Hempel *et al.*, 1985)—a situation that is presumably so simple for the animal that it can rather precisely cope with it. It is expected that this behavior is observed under "bonanza"-like conditions (Fig. 9b) that are thought to be typical for honeybees and are usually generated in foraging experiments. Under marginal conditions (Fig. 9a), however, the workers would be predicted to shift their behavior toward maximization of net rate of gain (while the actual work load involved nevertheless becomes smaller). Recent studies provide evidence that individual workers do in fact vary their behavioral strategies on such fine scales in relation to the value of resources (Cartar and Dill, 1990; Wolf and Schmid-Hempel, 1990). The observation that workers are sensitive to energy expenditure rather than time was interpreted by Schmid-Hempel *et al.* (1985) as the effect of a limited life time budget of energy expenditure available to each individual (sensu Neukirch, 1982). But there is an important point here, for a constraint imposed by maximum sustainable work load could produce similar behavior on the short-term to that produced with the constraint of a limited life time budget.

How generally the above scenario holds among the social insects awaits further study. The predictions emerging from the hypothesis can be tested; they link resource characteristics, individual life span, colony demography, and physiological performance. Of course, the evolution of a large physiological machinery in each individual represents just one of many possibilities to increase the chances of colony growth, survival, and reproduction. In addition, these issues should be distinguished from the empirical problem that, for example, investment of energy closely correlates with investment of time. Predictions from alternative "currencies" may therefore converge under certain parameter settings and thus become indistinguishable in an experiment (Houston, 1987). Note also that this convergence of predictions for different currencies does not imply that the fitness consequences for the animal, when adopting different policies, are the same.

B. CONFLICT OVER WORK LOAD

So far, the discussion has assumed that colonies of social insects are fully cooperative entities, with reproductive success equally distributed among their members. This view is certainly justified for many aspects of social insect biology and should focus on the relative strengths of selective forces on a variety of traits. Furthermore, it can serve as a sort of benchmark when one starts to study the problems involved. In many cases, however, evolutionary theory would lead us to suspect on a priori grounds that severe reproductive conflicts exist within colonies (Hamilton, 1964), resulting from polygyny (i.e., where several functional queens are present) and/or polyandry (i.e., with multiply mated queens). The potential for conflicts is suggested by instances of brood destruction (Ishay, 1964), dominance hierarchies for oviposition (Gamboa *et al.,* 1978; Cole, 1981; VanDoorn and Heringa, 1986), worker reproduction (Bourke, 1988), sex ratio shifts (Nonacs, 1986; Van der Have *et al.,* 1988), and of nepotism during the rearing of sexual brood (e.g., Klahn and Gamboa, 1983; Visscher, 1986; Page *et al.,* 1989).

Could such conflict also bear on the evolution of work load? Suppose that the daily work load accepted by individuals has heritable components and that a negative correlation with life span exists. In a colony with a queen that has mated with several males, "subfamilies" of workers would be present that differ in this trait. It can be shown that, under these conditions, a gene coding for low activity could spread in a population of hard-working colonies, and vice versa (Schmid-Hempel, 1990). The evolutionarily stable work load depends on the degree of genetic heterogeneity among colony members, the degree of nepotism, and so on. Nevertheless, workers would also be expected to work at a lower pace as compared to the cooperative solution.

This prediction of lower work loads seems at variance with our earlier discussion about selection on maximum sustainable effort. But it is not clear how often the queens have actually won in the evolutionary race (Fletcher and Ross, 1985; Schmid-Hempel, 1990), thus forcing the workers into cooperation and promoting selection for maximum performance (see also Ratnieks, 1988). In addition, conflict over work load may be regulated by the degree of inactivity rather than by work effort itself, i.e., activity levels once the workers have become active. In other words, workers may vary the time spent inactive, but work just as hard once they are engaged in an activity. A large degree of inactivity is indeed an often observed characteristic in social insects (Fig. 10), but the two issues could be due to entirely different selection pressures.

VI.   CONCLUSIONS AND PERSPECTIVES

The behavior of social insect workers has been analyzed in many ways. Here, I have concentrated on ergonomic aspects by discussing studies that have investigated how efficiently workers behave with respect to assumed fitness criteria. Most of these studies have addressed foraging behavior for obvious practical

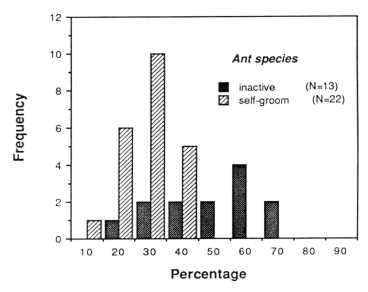

FIG. 10. Frequency distribution (*ordinate:* number of species) of the time spent inactive or in self-grooming as a percentage of all behavioral categories for various ant species. (After Schmid-Hempel, 1990.)

reasons. However, in principle, there seems to be no obstacle to extending this approach to other tasks in a colony (e.g., unloading by receiver bees; Seeley, 1989).

For a solitary animal, it is readily seen how individual behavior can affect fitness. The situation is of course more complex in social insects through the fact that reproductive conflicts within colonies exist (e.g., Page *et al.,* 1989), and that therefore several levels of selection are present. Complications also arise because the ergonomics of colonies exhibit additional features that lead to a pronounced nonlinear relationship between individual behavior and eventual colony success (see Fig. 3). Furthermore, colonies of social insects are remarkably well buffered against variation in external stress factors: all but heavy levels of perturbation yield only small effects on reproductive performance (e.g., Gentry, 1974; Kolmes, 1985b; Schmid-Hempel and Heeb, 1990).

Given these particular features of social insects, it appears that variation in individual behavior should often have little effect on eventual survival and reproduction at the level of the colony, and hence, depending on the genetic background, could not be subject to strong selection. Furthermore, it is likely that there are differences among the various activities in the degree to which they affect representation of relevant genetic factors in the next generation. Activities such as raising sexual offspring would clearly add a substantial amount to fitness, whereas the effect of fanning observed in bees (to cool a brood chamber) is more difficult to assess in this respect. We are not yet in a position to integrate these various issues. Linking short-term behavioral analysis and long-term consequences at the level of the population thus remains a major challenge for further research.

Throughout this article I have adopted the view that the behavior of individuals and the ergonomics of entire colonies are efficiently organized (sensu Oster and Wilson, 1978), and that the difficult question is to analyze in which precise way a trait of interest is efficient. One could, however, argue that social insects are not really maximally efficient in this sense, but just good enough to cope with environmental challenges (e.g., Kolmes, 1985b). It is largely a matter of empirical work to decide whether this version of the "satisfycing" concept is the most powerful explanation available for the observed patterns of behavior shown by social insects. There are, however, some reasons to believe that satisfycing does not adequately reflect the selective pressures. As was discussed before, several studies have successfully used the maximum efficiency approach. Failure to make correct predictions does not necessarily imply that the underlying concept is wrong, but shows that the design criteria have not yet been understood (note, however, that such models are not infallible: see Stearns and Schmid-Hempel, 1987). Finally, a satisfycing strategy would do very poorly in a stochastic world, for it is easy to see that, in the long run, those units with better performance should have a higher probability of persisting in the face of fluctuating environmental factors. The discussion around these issues demonstrates that large gaps still exist in our understanding of how individual behavior in social insects is linked to fitness components.

The functional study of social insects is currently undergoing a veritable adaptive radiation, triggered by an improved understanding of how selection works in such complex systems. Only a few of these diverse aspects have been discussed here, but they may delineate prospects for future studies. It is becoming increasingly clear that the various demographic, life history, and population biological factors discussed here are important if one is to understand the behavior of individual workers. In particular, the causal and functional explanation of variation in worker life spans seems to be a major problem whose solution is likely to add considerably to our understanding of social insects. Future studies must also take a new approach to the problem of division of labor, based on within-colony versus between-colony selection, studies of the evolutionary genetics of social insects, and the addition of the hitherto almost completely neglected population biology of social insects, in order to document, analyze, and understand variation at this level. Models based on concepts of optimality can help in this enterprise by identifying selective forces and pointing out important constraints imposed by physiology, ecology, or social organization. In this way, it should be possible to shed some of the unwarranted long-standing beliefs about peculiarities of social insect biology and replace them by unifying principles well known from other groups of organisms. This will allow us to put the truly astonishing diversity of social insects into proper perspective and integrate advances in this group with studies in other social organisms.

VII. Summary

Functional studies of behavior focus on efficient design with respect to a hypothesized fitness criterion. The situation is particularly complex in social insects, as selection can act at the level of individuals within colonies as well as at the level of colonies within populations. Existing research has often established a rather broad agreement with relatively unspecified expectations from models of adaptive behavior. Only a few studies have tested quantitative predictions more rigorously. Besides contributing to our understanding of social insect evolution in a more narrow sense, such rigorous studies help to identify important constraints set by sociality and physiology. In a case study described here, the nectar-collecting behavior of individual honey bees is discussed in relation to economic models and maximization principles, and it is shown that individual workers treat energy expenditure as a limiting factor. Integration of behavior into the colony occurs through its effects on colony growth and reproduction; it is suggested that behavioral strategies of workers reflect a balance between the benefits resulting from their work and the survival costs for the individual. From these observations, the more general hypothesis is formulated that, at least in some species of social insects, selection may have acted to increase the level of sustainable work effort in the workers through the evolution of a large physiological machinery. However, major difficulties still exist in linking individual behavior to its fitness consequences. Further progress in the study of social insect behavior is likely to result from developing testable models of social organization that take into account the evolutionary genetics of the group, from the study of various ecological stress factors that influence colony development and reproduction, and from an increased awareness of the importance of their population biology.

References

Bailey, K. H., and Polis, G. A. (1987). Optimal and central-place foraging theory applied to a desert harvester ant, *Pogonomyrmex californicus*. *Oecologia* **72,** 440–448.
Baker, H. G., and Baker, I. (1985). Studies of nectar-constitution and pollinator-plant coevolution. *In* "Coevolution of Animals and Plants" (L. E. Gilbert and P. H. Raven, eds.), pp. 100–140. Univ. of Texas Press, Austin.

Barrow, D. A., and Pickard, R. S. (1985). Larval temperature in brood clumps of *Bombus pascuorum* (Scop.). *J. Apic. Res.* **24**, 69–75.

Bartholomew, G. A., Lighton, J. R. B., and Feener, D. H. (1988). Energetics of trail running, load carriage size, and emigration in the column-raiding army ant, *Eciton hamatum*. *Physiol. Zool.* **61**, 57–68.

Bartz, S. H., and Hölldobler, B. (1982). Colony founding in *Myrmecocystus mimicus* Wheeler (Hymenoptera: Formicidae) and the evolution of foundress associations. *Behav. Ecol. Sociobiol.* **10**, 137–147.

Bernstein, R. A. (1975). Foraging strategies of ants in relation to variable food density. *Ecology* **56**, 213–219.

Beutler, R. (1937). Über den Blutzucker der Bienen. *Z. Vergl. Physiol.* **24**, 76–115.

Bourke, A. F. G. (1988). Worker reproduction in the higher eusocial hymenoptera. *Q. Rev. Biol.* **63**, 291–311.

Brian, M. V. (1983). "Social Insects." Chapman & Hall, London.

Brückner, D. (1980). Hoarding behaviour and life span of inbred, non-inbred, and hybrid honeybees. *J. Apic. Res.* **19**, 35–41.

Buschinger, A. (1975). Eine genetische Komponente im Polymorphismus der dulotischen Ameise *Harpagoxenus sublaevis*. *Naturwissenschaften*, **62**, 239.

Calabi, P. (1988). Behavioral flexibility in hymenoptera: A re-examination of the concept of caste. *In* "Advances in Myrmecology" (J. C. Trager, ed.), pp. 237–258. E. J. Brill Press, Leiden.

Calabi, P., and Porter, S. D. (1989). Worker longevity in the ant *Solenopsis invicta*: Ergonomic considerations of correlations between temperature, size and metabolic rates. *J. Insect Physiol.* **35**, 643–649.

Calabi, P., and Traniello, J. F. A. (1988). Social organization in the ant *Pheidole dentata*. Physical and temporal caste ratios lack ecological correlates. *Behav. Ecol. Sociobiol.* **24**, 69–78.

Calderone, N. W., and Page, R. E., Jr. (1988). Genotypic variability in age polyethism and task specialization in the honey bee, *Apis mellifera* (Hymenoptera, Apidae). *Behav. Ecol. Sociobiol.* **22**, 17–25.

Caraco, T., Martindale, S., and Whitham, T. S. (1980). An empirical demonstration of risk-sensitive foraging preferences. *Anim. Behav.* **28**, 820–830.

Cartar, R. V., and Dill, L. M. (1990). Colony energetic requirements affect the foraging currency of bumble bees. *Behav. Ecol. Sociobiol.* (in press).

Casey, T. M. (1989). Oxygen consumption during flight. *In* "Insect Flight" (G. Goldsworthy and C. H. Wheeler, eds.). CRC Press, Boca Raton, Florida.

Coelho, J. R., and Mitton, J. B. (1988). Oxygen consumption during hovering is associated with genetic variation of enzymes in honey-bees. *Funct. Ecol.* **2**, 141–146.

Cole, B. J. (1981). Dominance hierarchies in *Leptothorax* ants. *Science* **212**, 83–84.

Cole, B. J. (1984). Colony efficiency and the reproductivity effect in *Leptothorax allardycei* (Mann). *Insectes Soc.* **31**, 403–407.

Cole, B. J. (1988). Individual differences in social insect behavior: Movement and space use in *Leptothorax allardycei*. *In* "Interindividual Behavioral Variability in Social Insects" (R. L. Jeanne, ed.), pp. 113–116. Westview Press, Boulder, Colorado.

Crow, J. F. (1986). "Basic Concepts in Population, Quantitative, and Evolutionary Genetics." Freeman, New York.

Cumber, R. A. (1953). Some aspects of the biology and ecology of bumble-bees bearing upon the yields of red-clover seed in New Zealand. *N. Z. J. Sci. Technol.* **11**, 227–240.

Daan, S., Masman, D., and Groenewold, L. (1990). Avian basal metabolic rates: Their association with body composition and energy expenditure in nature. *Am. J. Physiol.* **259**, 333–340.

Davidson, D. W. (1977). Foraging ecology and community organization in desert seed-eating ants. *Ecology* **58**, 711–724.

Davidson, D. W. (1978). Experimental tests of the optimal diet in two social insects. *Behav. Ecol. Sociobiol.* **4**, 35–41.

DeBenedictis, P. A., Gill, F. B., Hainsworth, F. R., Pyke, G. H., and Wolf, L. L. (1978). Optimal meal size in hummingbird. *Am. Nat.* **112**, 301–316.

Deneubourg, J.-L. (1983). Probabilistic behavior in ants: A strategy of errors? *J. Theor. Biol.* **105**, 259–271.

Deneubourg, J.-L., Goss, S., Pasteels, J. M., Fresneau, D., and Lachaud, J.-P. (1987). Self-organization mechanisms in ant societies. (II) Learning in foraging and division of labor. *In* "From Individual to Collective Behavior in Social Insects" (J. M. Pasteels and J.-L. Deneubourg, eds.), pp. 177–198. Birkhaeuser, Basel.

DeVita, J. (1979). Mechanisms of interference and foraging among colonies of the harvester ant *Pogonomyrmex californicus* in the Mojave desert. *Ecology* **60**, 729–737.

Dobrzanska, J., and Dobrzanski, J. (1975). Ethological studies in the ant *Tetramorium caespitum* (Mayr). I. Foraging and building behaviour. *Acta Neurobiol. Exp.* **35**, 299–309.

Drent, R. H., and Daan, S. (1980). The prudent parent: Energetic adjustment in avian breeding. *Ardea* **68**, 225–252.

Dupré, J., ed. (1987). "The Latest on the Best." MIT Press, Cambridge, Massachusetts.

Dyer, F. C., and Seeley, T. D. (1987). Interspecific comparisons of endothermy in honey-bees (*Apis*): Deviation from the expected size-related patterns. *J. Exp. Biol.* **127**, 1–26.

Dyer, F. C., and Seeley, T. D. (1990). Nesting behavior and the evolution of worker tempo in four honey bee species. *Ecology* (in press).

Eckert, J. E. (1938). The flight range of the honey bee. *J. Apic. Res.* **47**, 257–285.

Fewell, J. (1988). Energetic and time costs of foraging in harvester ants, *Pogonomyrmex occidentalis*. *Behav. Ecol. Sociobiol.* **22**, 401–408.

Fletcher, D. J. C., and Ross, K. G. (1985). Regulation of reproduction in eusocial hymenoptera. *Annu. Rev. Entomol.* **30**, 319–343.

Fowler, H. G. (1984). Colony-level regulation of forager caste ratios in response to caste perturbations in the carpenter ant, *Camponotus pennsylvanicus* (De Geer) (Hymenoptera: Formicidae). *Insect Soc.* **31**, 461–471.

Fowler, H. G. (1986). Polymorphism and colony ontogeny in North American carpenter ants (Hymenoptera: Formicidae: *Camponotus pennsylvanicus* and *Camponotus ferrugineus*). *Zool. Jahrb., Abt. Allg. Zool. Physiol.* **90**, 297–316.

Free, J. B. (1965). The allocation of duties among worker honeybees. *Symp. Zool. Soc. London* **14**, 39–45.

Free, J. B., and Spencer-Booth, Y. (1959). The longevity of worker honeybees (*Apis mellifera*). *Proc. R. Entomol. Soc. London, Ser. A* **34**, 141–150.

Fresneau, D. (1985). Individual foraging and path fidelity in a ponerine ant. *Insectes Soc.* **32**, 109–116.

Fritz, R. S., and Morse, D. H. (1985). Reproductive success and foraging of the crab spider, *Misumena vatia*. *Oecologia* **65**, 194–200.

Frumhoff, P. C., and Baker, J. (1988). A genetic component to division of labour within honey bee colonies. *Nature (London)* **333**, 358–361.

Frumhoff, P. C., and Schneider, S. S. (1987). The social consequences of honey bee polyandry: The effects of kinship on worker interactions within colonies. *Anim. Behav.* **35**, 255–262.

Fukuda, H., and Sekiguchi, K. (1966). Seasonal change of the honey bee worker longevity in Sapporo, North Japan, with notes on some factors affecting the life span. *Jpn. J. Ecol.* **16**, 206–212.

Fukuda, H., Moriya, K., and Sekiguchi, K. (1969). The weight of crop content in foraging honeybee workers. *Annot. Zool. Jpn.* **42**, 80–90.

Gamboa, G. J., Heacock, B. J., and Wiltjer, S. L. (1978). Division of labour and subordinate longevity in foundress associations of the paper wasp *Polistes metricus* (Hymenoptera: Vespidae). *J. Kans. Entomol. Soc.* **51**, 343–352.

Gentry, J. B. (1974). Responses to predation by colonies of harvester ants, *Pogonomyrmex badius*. *Ecology* **55**, 1328–1338.

Gordon, D. M. (1986). The dynamics of the daily round of the harvester ant colony *Pogonomyrmex badius*. *Anim. Behav.* **34**, 1402–1419.

Gordon, D. M. (1987). Group-level dynamics in harvester ants: Young colonies and the role of patrolling. *Anim. Behav.* **35**, 833–843.

Gordon, D. M. (1989a). Dynamics of task switching in harvester ants. *Anim. Behav.* **38**, 194–204.

Gordon, D. M. (1989b). Caste and change in social insects. *Oxford Surv. Evol. Biol.* **6**, 55–72.

Goss, S., Fresneau, D., Deneubourg, J.-L., Lachaud, J.-P., and Valanzuela-Gonzalez, J. (1989a). Individual foraging in the ant *Pachycondyla apicalis*. *Oecologia* **80**, 65–69.

Goss, S., Pasteels, J. M., Deneubourg, J.-L., and Josens, G. (1989b). A model of noncooperative foraging in social insects. *Am. Nat.* **134**, 273–287.

Gould, J. L., and Towne, W. F. (1987). Evolution of the dance language. *Am. Nat.* **130**, 317–338.

Gould, J. L., Dyer, F. C., and Towne, W. F. (1985). Recent progress in the study of the dance language. *In* "Experimental Behavioural Ecology and Sociobiology" (B. Hölldobler and M. Lindauer, eds.), pp. 141–162. Sinauer, Sunderland, Massachusetts.

Gould, S. J., and Lewontin, R. C. (1979). The spandrels of San Marco and the Panglossian paradigm: A critique of the adaptationist programme. *Proc. R. Soc. London, B Ser.* **205**, 581–598.

Grafen, A. (1986). Split sex ratios and the evolutionary origins of eusociality. *J. Theor. Biol.* **122**, 95–121.

Hamilton, W. D. (1964). The genetical evolution of social behavior. *J. Theor. Biol.* **7**, 1–52.

Harkness, R. D., and Maroudas, N. G. (1985). Central place foraging by an ant (*Cataglyphis bicolor* Fab): A model of searching. *Anim. Behav.* **33**, 916–928.

Harrison, J. M. (1986). Caste-specific changes in honeybee flight capacity. *Physiol. Zool.* **59**, 175–187.

Hassanein, M. H., and El-Banby, M. A. (1960). Studies on the longevity of Carnolian, Caucasian, and Italian honeybee workers, with special reference to their foraging behaviour. *Bull. Soc. Entomol. Egypte* **44**, 291–308.

Heinrich, B. (1975). Thermoregulation in bumblebees. 2. Energetics of warm-up and free flight. *J. Comp. Physiol.* **96**, 155–166.

Heinrich, B. (1976). The foraging specializations of individual bumblebees. *Ecol. Monogr.* **46**, 105–128.

Heinrich, B. (1979a). Resource heterogeneity and patterns of movement in foraging bumblebees. *Oecologia* **40**, 235–245.

Heinrich, B. (1979b). "Bumblebee Economics." Harvard Univ. Press, Cambridge, Massachusetts.

Heinrich, B. (1981). Ecological and evolutionary perspectives. *In* "Insect Thermoregulation" (B. Heinrich, ed.), pp. 235–302. Wiley, New York.

Heinze, J., and Buschinger, A. (1989). Queen polymorphism in *Leptothorax spec. A:* Its genetic and ecological background (Hymenoptera: Formicidae). *Insectes Soc.* **36**, 139–155.

Herbers, J. M. (1980). On caste ratios in ant colonies: Population responses to changing environments. *Evolution (Lawrence, Kans.)* **34**, 575–585.

Herbers, J. M. (1981). Reliability theory and foraging in ants. *J. Theor. Biol.* **89**, 175–189.

Hodges, C. M. (1981). Optimal foraging in bumblebees: Hunting by expectation. *Anim. Behav.* **29**, 1166–1171.

Hodges, C. M. (1985). Bumblebee foraging: The threshold departure rule. *Ecology* **66**, 179–187.

Hölldobler, B. (1978). Ethological aspects of chemical communication. *Adv. Study Behav.* **8**, 75–115.

Houston, A. I. (1987). Optimal foraging by parent birds feeding dependent young. *J. Theor. Biol.*
    124, 251–274.
Houston, A. I., Schmid-Hempel, P., and Kacelnik, A. (1988). Foraging strategy, worker mortality
    and the growth of the colony in social insects. *Am. Nat.* **131**, 107–114.
Ishay, J. (1964). Observations sur la biologie de la guêpe orientale *Vespa orientalis. Insectes Soc.* **11**,
    193–206.
Jamieson, I. G. (1986). The functional approach to behavior: Is it useful? *Am. Nat.* **127**, 195–208.
Jaycox, E. R., Skowronek, W., and Gwynn, G. (1974). Behavioral changes in a worker honeybee
    (*Apis mellifera*) induced by injections of a juvenile hormone mimic. *Ann. Entomol. Soc. Am.*
    67, 529–534.
Jeanne, R. L. (1986a). The evolution of the organization of work in social insects. *Monit. Zool. Ital.*
    [N.S.] **20**, 119–133.
Jeanne, R. L. (1986b). The organization of work in *Polybia occidentalis:* Costs and benefits of
    specialization in a social wasp. *Behav. Ecol. Sociobiol.* **19**, 333–342.
Jeanne, R. L., ed. (1988). "Interindividual Behavioral Variability in Social Insects." Westview
    Press, Boulder, Colorado.
Kacelnik, A. (1984). Central-place foraging in starlings (*Sturnus vulgaris*). I. Patch residence time.
    J. Anim. Ecol. **53**, 283–300.
Kacelnik, A., and Houston, A. I. (1984). Some effects of energy costs on foraging strategies. *Anim.*
    Behav. **32**, 609–614.
Kacelnik, A., Houston, A. I., and Schmid-Hempel, P. (1986). Central-place foraging in honeybees:
    The effect of travel time and nectar flow on crop filling. *Behav. Ecol. Sociobiol.* **19**, 19–24.
Kerr, W. E., and Hebling, N. J. (1964). Influence of weight of worker bees on division of labor.
    Evolution (Lawrence, Kans.) **18**, 267–270.
Kistner, D. H. (1982). The social insects' bestiary. *In* "Social Insects" (H. R. Hermann, ed.), Vol. 3,
    pp. 1–244. Academic Press, London.
Klahn, J. E., and Gamboa, G. J. (1983). Social wasps: Kin discrimination between kin and non-kin
    brood. *Science* **221**, 482–484.
Kolmes, S. A. (1985a). A quantitative study of the division of labour among worker honey bees. *Z.*
    Tierpsychol. **68**, 287–302.
Kolmes, S. A. (1985b). An ergonomic study of *Apis mellifera* (Hymenoptera: Apidae). *J. Kans.*
    Entomol. Soc. **58**, 413–421.
Kramer, D. L., and Nowell, W. (1980). Central place foraging in the eastern chipmunk, *Tamias*
    striatus. Anim. Behav. **28**, 772–778.
Krebs, J. R., and McCleery, R. H. (1984). Optimization in behavioural ecology. *In* "Behavioural
    Ecology" (J. R. Krebs and N. B. Davies, eds.), pp. 91–121. Blackwell, Oxford.
Laverty, T. M., and Plowright, R. C. (1988). Flower handling by bumblebees—a comparison of
    specialists and generalists. *Anim. Behav.* **36**, 733–740.
LeBourg, E., Lints, F. A., and Lints, C. V. (1984). Does a relationship exist between spontaneous
    locomotory activity, fitness and lifespan in *Drosophila melanogaster? Exp. Gerontol.* **19**, 205–
    210.
Lessells, C. M., and Stephens, D. W. (1983). Central-place foraging: Single-prey loaders again.
    Anim. Behav. **31**, 238–243.
Lindauer, M. (1952). Ein Beitrag zur Frage der Arbeitsteilung im Bienenstaat. *Z. Vergl. Physiol.* **34**,
    299–345.
Lindauer, M. (1961). "Communication among Social Bees." Harvard Univ. Press, Cambridge,
    Massachusetts.
Macevicz, S., and Oster, G. F. (1976). Modeling social insect populations. II. Optimal reproductive
    strategies in annual eusocial insects colonies. *Behav. Ecol. Sociobiol.* **1**, 265–282.

MacKay, W. P. (1982). An altitudinal comparison of oxygen consumption rates in three species of *Pogonomyrmex* harvester ants. *Physiol. Zool.* **55**, 367–377.

Mauermayer, G. (1954). Investigations on the relation between the activity and length of life of honeybee workers. *Arch. Bienenkd.* **31**, 31–41.

Maurizio, A. (1961). Lebensdauer und Altern bei der Honigbiene *Apis mellifera. Gerontologia* **5**, 110–128.

Maynard Smith, J. (1978). Optimization theory in evolution. *Annu. Rev. Ecol. Syst.* **9**, 31–56.

McNair, J. N. (1982). Optimal giving-up times and the marginal value theorem. *Am. Nat.* **119**, 511–529.

Meudec, M., and Lenoir, A. (1982). Social responses to variation in food supply and nest suitability in ants (*Tapinoma erraticum*). *Anim. Behav.* **30**, 284–292.

Michener, C. D. (1964). Reproductive efficiency in relation to colony size in hymenopterous societies. *Insectes Soc.* **11**, 317–341.

Michener, C. D. (1974). "The Social Behavior of the Bees." Harvard Univ. Press, Cambridge, Massachusetts.

Milne, C. P., Jr. (1982). Early death of newly emerged honeybee workers in laboratory test cages. *J. Apic. Res.* **21**, 107–110.

Milne, C. P., Jr. (1985). An estimate of the heritability of worker longevity or length of life in the honeybee. *J. Apic. Res.* **24**, 140–143.

Mirenda, J. T., and Vinson, S. B. (1981). Division of labor and specification of castes in the red imported fire ant *Solenopsis invicta* (Buren). *Anim. Behav.* **29**, 410–420.

Neukirch, A. (1982). Dependence of life span of the honeybee (*Apis mellifera*) upon flight performance and energy consumption. *J. Comp. Physiol.* **146**, 35–40.

Nielsen, G., Jensen, T. F., and Holm-Jensen, I. (1982). The effect of load carriage on the respiratory metabolism of running worker ants of *Camponotus herculeanus* (Formicidae). *Oikos* **39**, 137–142.

Nonacs, P. (1986). Ant reproductive strategies and sex allocation theory. *Q. Rev. Biol.* **61**, 3–21.

Nonacs, P., and Dill, L. M. (1988). Foraging response of the ant *Lasius pallitarsus* to food sources with associated mortality risks. *Insectes Soc.* **35**, 293–303.

Nuñez, J. (1966). Quantitative Beziehungen zwischen den Eigenschaften von Futterquellen und Verhalten der Sammelbienen. *Z. Vergl. Physiol.* **53**, 142–164.

Nuñez, J. (1970). The relationship between sugar flow and foraging and recruiting behavior of honey bees (*Apis mellifera* L.). *Anim. Behav.* **18**, 527–538.

Nuñez, J. (1982). Honey bee foraging strategies at a food source in relation to its distance from the hive and rate of sugar flow. *J. Apic. Res.* **21**, 139–150.

Orians, G. H., and Pearson, N. E. (1979). On the theory of central place foraging. *In* "Analysis of Ecological Systems" (D. J. Horn, R. Mitchell, and G. R. Stair, eds.), pp. 155–177. Ohio State Univ. Press, Columbus.

Oster, G. F., and Wilson, E. O. (1978). "Caste and Ecology in the Social Insects." Princeton Univ. Press, Princeton, New Jersey.

Ott, J. R., Real, L. A., and Silverfine, E. M. (1985). The effect of nectar variance on bumblebee patterns of movement and potential gene dispersal. *Oikos* **45**, 333–340.

Page, R. E., Jr., Robinson, G. E., and Fondrk, M. K. (1989). Genetic specialists, kin recognition, and nepotism in honey-bee colonies. *Nature (London)* **338**, 576–579.

Parker, S. P., ed. (1982). "Synopsis and Classification of Living Organisms," Vol. 2. McGraw-Hill, New York.

Partridge, L., and Harvey, P. H. (1985). Costs of reproduction. *Nature (London)* **316**, 20.

Pasteels, J. M., Deneubourg, J.-L., and Goss, S. (1987). Self-organization mechanisms in ant societies (I). Trail recruitment to newly discovered food sources. *In* "From Individual to Collective Behavior in Social Insects" (J. M. Pasteels and J.-L. Deneubourg, eds.), pp. 155–176. Birkhaeuser, Basel.

Pflumm, W. (1971). Zum Sammelverhalten von Wespen. *Insectes Soc.* **18**, 155–160.

Phillips, E. F. (1922). The effect of activity on the length of life of honeybees. *J. Econ. Entomol.* **15**, 368.

Pierce, G. J., and Ollason, J. G. (1987). Eight reasons why optimal foraging theory is a complete waste of time. *Oikos* **49**, 111–118.

Pleasants, J. M. (1989). Optimal foraging by nectarivores: A test of the marginal value theorem. *Am. Nat.* **134**, 51–71.

Plowright, R. C., and Pendrel, B. A. (1977). Larval growth in bumblebees (Hymenoptera, Apidae). *Can. Entomol.* **109**, 967–973.

Pomeroy, N., and Plowright, R. C. (1982). The relation between worker numbers and the production of males and queens in the bumblebee *Bombus perplexus. Can. J. Zool.* **60**, 954–957.

Porter, S. D., and Jorgensen, C. D. (1981). Foragers of the harvester ant *Pogonomyrmex owyheei*—a disposable caste? *Behav. Ecol. Sociobiol.* **9**, 247–256.

Prys-Jones, O. E. (1986). Foraging behaviour and the activity of substrate cycle enzymes in bumblebees. *Anim. Behav.* **34**, 609–611.

Pyke, G. H. (1978). Optimal foraging: Movement patterns of bumblebees between inflorescences. *Theor. Popul. Biol.* **13**, 72–97.

Ratnieks, F. L. W. (1988). Reproductive harmony via mutual policing by workers in eusocial hymenoptera. *Am. Nat.* **132**, 217–236.

Real, L. A. (1980). Fitness, uncertainty, and the role of diversification in evolution and behavior. *Am. Nat.* **115**, 623–638.

Real, L. A. (1981). Uncertainty and plant–pollinator interactions: The foraging behavior of bees and wasps on artificial flowers. *Ecology* **62**, 20–62.

Real, L. A., Ott, J., and Silverfine, E. (1982). On the trade-off between the mean and the variance in foraging: Effect of spatial distribution and color preference. *Ecology* **63**, 1617–1623.

Reznick, D. (1985). Costs of reproduction: An evaluation of empirical evidence. *Oikos* **44**, 244–257.

Rissing, S. W. (1981a). Prey preference in the horned lizard: Influence of prey foraging method and aggressive behavior. *Ecology* **62**, 1031–1040.

Rissing, S. W. (1981b). Foraging specializations of individual seed-harvester ants. *Behav. Ecol. Sociobiol.* **9**, 149–152.

Rissing, S. W. (1987). Annual cycles in worker body size of the seed-harvester ant *Veromessor pergandei* (Hymenoptera: Formicidae). *Behav. Ecol. Sociobiol.* **20**, 117–124.

Rissing, S. W., and Pollock, G. B. (1984). Worker size variability and foraging efficiency in *Veromessor pergandei* (Hymenoptera: Formicidae). *Behav. Ecol. Sociobiol.* **15**, 121–126.

Rissing, S. W., and Pollock, G. B. (1987). Queen aggression, pleometrotic advantage and brood raiding in the ant *Veromessor pergandei* (Hymenoptera: Formicidae). *Anim. Behav.* **35**, 975–981.

Robinson, G. E., and Page, R. E., Jr. (1988). Genetic determination of guarding and undertaking in honey-bee colonies. *Nature (London)* **333**, 356–358.

Rockstein, M. (1950). Longevity in the adult worker honeybee. *Ann. Entomol. Soc. Am.* **43**, 152–154.

Rösch, G. A. (1925). Untersuchungen über die Arbeitsteilung im Bienenstaat. 1. Die Tätigkeiten im normalen Bienenstock und ihre Beziehungen zum Alter. *Z. Vergl. Physiol.* **2**, 571–631.

Rothe, U., and Nachtigall, W. (1989). Flight of the honeybee. IV. Respiratory quotients and metabolic rates during sitting, walking and flying. *J. Comp. Physiol. B* **158**, 739–749.

Sakagami, S. F., and Fukuda, H. (1968). Life tables for worker honeybees. *Res. Popul. Ecol.* **10**, 127–139.

Schmid-Hempel, P. (1984a). Individually different foraging methods in the desert ant *Cataglyphis bicolor* (Hymenoptera, Formicidae). *Behav. Ecol. Sociobiol.* **14**, 263–271.

Schmid-Hempel, P. (1984b). The importance of handling time for the flight directionality in bees. *Behav. Ecol. Sociobiol.* **15**, 303–309.

Schmid-Hempel, P. (1986). Do honeybees get tired? The effect of load weight on patch departure. *Anim. Behav.* **34**, 1243–1250.

Schmid-Hempel, P. (1987a). Foraging characteristics of the desert ant *Cataglyphis bicolor*. *In* "From Individual to Collective Behavior in Social Insects" (J. M. Pasteels and J.-L. Deneubourg, eds.), pp. 43–62. Birkhaeuser, Basel.

Schmid-Hempel, P. (1987b). Efficient nectar-collection by honeybees. I. Economic models. *J. Anim. Ecol.* **56**, 209–218.

Schmid-Hempel, P. (1990). Reproductive competition and the evolution of work load in social insects. *Am. Nat.* **135**, 501–526.

Schmid-Hempel, P., and Heeb, D. (1990). Resilience of colony development to variation in worker mortality in bumblebees, *Bombus lucorum* L. *Mitt. Schweiz. Entomol. Ges.* **63** (in press).

Schmid-Hempel, P., and Schmid-Hempel, R. (1984). Life duration and turnover of foragers in the ant *Cataglyphis bicolor* (Hymenoptera, Formicidae). *Insectes Soc.* **31**, 345–360.

Schmid-Hempel, P., and Schmid-Hempel, R. (1988). Parasitic flies (Conopidae, Diptera) may be important stress factors for the ergonomics of their bumblebee hosts. *Ecol. Entomol.* **13**, 469–472.

Schmid-Hempel, P., and Wolf, T. (1988). Foraging effort and life span of workers in a social insect. *J. Anim. Ecol.* **57**, 509–521.

Schmid-Hempel, P., Kacelnik, A., and Houston, A. I. (1985). Honeybees maximize efficiency by not filling their crop. *Behav. Ecol. Sociobiol.* **17**, 61–66.

Schmid-Hempel, P., Müller, C., Schmid-Hempel, R., and Shykoff, J. A. (1990). Frequency and ecological correlates of parasitism by conopid flies (Conopidae, Diptera) in populations of bumblebees. *Insectes Soc.* (in press).

Schmidt, J. O., Thoenes, S. C., and Levin, M. D. (1987). Survival of honeybees, *Apis mellifera* (Hymenoptera: Apidae), fed various pollen sources. *Ann. Entomol. Soc. Am.* **80**, 176–183.

Schoener, T. W. (1986). Mechanistic approaches to community ecology: A new reductionism? *Am. Zool.* **26**, 81–106.

Seeley, T. D. (1982). Adaptive significance of the age polyethism schedule in honeybee colonies. *Behav. Ecol. Sociobiol.* **11**, 287–293.

Seeley, T. D. (1983). Division of labor between scouts and recruits in honeybee foraging. *Behav. Ecol. Sociobiol.* **12**, 253–259.

Seeley, T. D. (1985). "Honeybee Ecology." Princeton Univ. Press, Princeton, New Jersey.

Seeley, T. D. (1986). Social foraging by honeybees: How colonies allocate foragers among patches of flowers. *Behav. Ecol. Sociobiol.* **19**, 343–354.

Seeley, T. D. (1989). Social foraging in honeybees: How nectar foragers assess their colony's nutritional status. *Behav. Ecol. Sociobiol.* **24**, 181–198.

Seeley, T. D., and Levien, R. A. (1987). Social foraging by honeybees: How a colony tracks rich sources of nectar. *In* "Neurobiology and Behavior in Honeybees" (R. Menzel and A. Mercer, eds.), pp. 38–52. Springer-Verlag, Berlin.

Seeley, T. D., and Visscher, P. K. (1985). Survival of honeybees in cold climates: The critical timing of colony growth and reproduction. *Ecol. Entomol.* **10**, 81–88.

Shepherd, J. D. (1982). Trunk trails and the searching strategy of a leaf-cutter ant, *Atta colombica*. *Behav. Ecol. Sociobiol.* **11**, 77–84.

Snell, T. W., and King, C. E. (1977). Lifespan and fecundity patterns in rotifers: The cost of reproduction. *Evolution (Lawrence, Kans.)* **31**, 882–890.

Stearns, S. C., and Schmid-Hempel, P. (1987). Evolutionary insights should not be wasted. *Oikos* **49**, 118–125.

Stephens, D. W. (1981). The logic of risk-sensitive foraging preferences. *Anim. Behav.* **29**, 628–629.

Stephens, D. W. (1987). On economically tracking a variable environment. *Theor. Popul. Biol.* **32**, 15–25.

Stephens, D. W. (1989). Variance and the value of information. *Am. Nat.* **134**, 128–140.

Stephens, D. W., and Charnov, E. L. (1982). Optimal foraging: Some simple stochastic models. *Behav. Ecol. Sociobiol.* **10**, 251–263.

Stephens, D. W., and Krebs, J. R. (1986). "Foraging Theory." Princeton Univ. Press, Princeton, New Jersey.

Stephens, D. W., Lynch, J. F., Sorensen, A. E., and Gordon, C. (1986). Preference and profitability: Theory and experiment. *Am. Nat.* **127**, 533–553.

Stone, G. N., and Willmer, P. G. (1989). Warm-up rates and body temperature in bees: The importance of body size, thermal regime and phylogeny. *J. Exp. Biol.* **147**, 303–328.

Stone, L. D. (1975). "Theory of Optimal Search." Academic Press, New York.

Strassmann, J. E. (1985). Worker mortality and the evolution of castes in the social wasp *Polistes exclamans*. *Insectes Soc.* **32**, 275–287.

Sutcliffe, G. H., and Plowright, R. C. (1988). The effects of food supply on adult size in the bumblebee *Bombus terricola* Kirby (Hymenoptera, Formicidae). *Can. Entomol.* **120**, 1051–1058.

Tamm, S. (1989). Importance of energy costs in central place foraging by hummingbirds. *Ecology* **70**, 195–202.

Taylor, F. (1977). Foraging behavior of ants: Experiments with two species of myrmecine ants. *Behav. Ecol. Sociobiol.* **2**, 147–167.

Taylor, F. (1978). Foraging behavior of ants: Theoretical considerations. *J. Theor. Biol.* **71**, 541–565.

Terada, Y., Garofalo, C. A., and Sakagami, S. F. (1975). Age-survival curves of two eusocial bees (*Apis mellifera* and *Plebeia droryana*) in a subtropical climate with notes on polyethism in *P. droryana*. *J. Apic. Res.* **14**, 161–170.

Tinbergen, N. (1951). "The Study of Instinct." Oxford Univ. Press, Oxford.

Traniello, J. F. A. (1983). Social organization and foraging success in *Lasius neoniger* (Hymenoptera: Formicidae). Behavioral and ecological aspects of recruitment communication. *Oecologia* **59**, 94–100.

Traniello, J. F. A. (1987). Individual and social modification of behavior in response to environmental factors. *In* "From Individual to Collective Behavior in Social Insects" (J. M. Pasteels and J.-L. Deneubourg, eds.), pp. 63–80. Birkhaeuser, Basel.

Traniello, J. F. A. (1988). Variation in foraging behavior among workers of the ant *Formica schaufussi*: Ecological correlates of search behavior and the modification of search pattern. *In* "Interindividual behavioral variability in social insects" (R. L. Jeanne, ed.), pp. 91–112. Westview Press, Boulder, Colorado.

Traniello, J. F. A. (1989). Foraging strategies of ants. *Annu. Rev. Entomol.* **34**, 191–210.

Trivers, R. L., and Hare, H. (1976). Haplodiploidy and the evolution of the social insects. *Science* **191**, 249–263.

Turelli, M., Gillespie, J. H., and Schoener, T. W. (1982). The fallacy of the fallacy of the averages in ecological optimization theory. *Am. Nat.* **119**, 879–884.

Van der Have, T. M., Boomsma, J. J., and Menken, S. B. J. (1988). Sex-investment ratios and relatedness in the monogynous ant *Lasius niger* L. *Evolution* (*Lawrence, Kans.*) **42**, 160–172.

VanDoorn, A., and Heringa, J. (1986). The ontogeny of a dominance hierarchy in colonies of the bumblebee *Bombus terrestris* (Hymenoptera, Apidae). *Insectes Soc.* **33**, 3–25.

Visscher, P. K. (1986). Kinship discrimination in queen rearing by honey bees (*Apis mellifera*). *Behav. Ecol. Sociobiol.* **18**, 453–460.

Visscher, P. K., and Seeley, T. D. (1982). Foraging strategy of honeybee colonies in a temperate deciduous forest. *Ecology* **63**, 1790–1801.

von Frisch, K. (1965). "Tanzsprache und Orientierung der Bienen." Springer, Berlin.

Waddington, K. D. (1985). Cost-intake information used in foraging. *J. Insect Physiol.* **31**, 891–897.

Waddington, K. D., and Holden, L. (1979). Optimal foraging: On flower selection by bees. *Am. Nat.* **114**, 179–196.

Waddington, K. D., Allen, T., and Heinrich, B. (1981). Floral preferences of bumblebees (*Bombus edwardsii*) in relation to intermittent versus continuous rewards. *Anim. Behav.* **29**, 779–785.

Walker, J., and Stamps, J. (1986). A test of optimal caste ratio theory using the ant *Camponotus* (*Colobopsis*) *impressus*. *Ecology* **67**, 1052–1062.

Wehner, R., Harkness, R., and Schmid-Hempel, P. (1983). Foraging strategies in individually searching ants. *In* "Information Processing in Animals" (M. Lindauer, ed.), Vol. 1. 1–79 Fischer, Stuttgart.

Welham, C. V. J., and Ydenberg, R. C. (1988). Net energy versus efficiency maximizing by foraging ring-billed gulls. *Behav. Ecol. Sociobiol.* **23**, 75–82.

Wells, P. H., and Giacchino, J., Jr. (1968). Relationship between the volume and the sugar concentration of loads carried by honeybees. *J. Apic. Res.* **7**, 77–82.

Wheeler, W. M. (1911). The ant colony as an organism. *J. Morphol.* **22**, 307–325.

Whitford, W. G., and Bryant, M. (1979). Behavior of a predator and its prey: The horned lizard (*Phrynosoma cornutum*) and harvester ants (*Pogonomyrmex spp.*). *Ecology* **60**, 686–694.

Wille, H., Imdorf, A., Bühlmann, G., Kilchenmann, V., and Wille, M. (1985). Beziehung zwischen Polleneintrag, Brutaufzucht und mittlerer Lebenserwartung der Arbeiterinnen in Bienenvölkern (*Apis mellifica* L.). *Mitt. Schweiz. Entomol. Ges.* **58**, 205–214.

Willmer, P. G. (1985). Thermal ecology, size effects, and the origins of communal behaviour in *Cerceris* wasps. *Behav. Ecol. Sociobiol.* **17**, 151–160.

Wilson, E. O. (1968). The ergonomics of caste in the social insects. *Am. Nat.* **102**, 41–66.

Wilson, E. O. (1971). "The Insect Societies." Harvard Univ. Press, Cambridge, Massachusetts.

Wilson, E. O. (1980). Caste and division of labor in leaf-cutter ants (Hymenoptera: Formicidae: *Atta*). II. The ergonomic optimization of leaf cutting. *Behav. Ecol. Sociobiol.* **7**, 143–156.

Wilson, E. O. (1984). The relation between caste ratios and division of labor in the ant genus *Pheidole* (Hymenoptera: Formicidae). *Behav. Ecol. Sociobiol.* **16**, 89–98.

Wilson, E. O. (1985). The sociogenesis of insect colonies. *Nature (London)* **228**, 1489–1495.

Winston, M. L. (1979). Events following queen removal in colonies of Africanized honeybees in South America. *Insectes Soc.* **26**, 373–381.

Winston, M. L. (1980). Swarming, afterswarming, and reproductive rate of unmanaged honeybee colonies. *Insect Soc.* **72**, 391–398.

Winston, M. L. (1987). "The Biology of the Honey Bee." Harvard Univ. Press, Cambridge, Massachusetts.

Winston, M. L., and Fergusson, L. A. (1985). The effect of worker loss on temporal caste structure in colonies of the honeybee (*Apis mellifera* L.). *Can. J. Zool.* **63**, 777–780.

Winston, M. L., and Katz, S. J. (1981). Longevity of cross-fostered honeybee workers of European and African races. *Can. J. Zool.* **59**, 1571–1575.

Winston, M. L., and Katz, S. J. (1982). Foraging differences between cross-fostered honeybee workers (*Apis mellifera*) of European and Africanized bees. *Behav. Ecol. Sociobiol.* **10**, 125–129.

Wolf, T. J., and Schmid-Hempel, P. (1989). Extra loads and foraging life span in honeybee workers. *J. Anim. Ecol.* **58**, 943–954.

Wolf, T. J., and Schmid-Hempel, P. (1990). Integrating individual behaviour with colony status in social insects: The case of nectar-collecting honeybees. *Behav. Ecol. Sociobiol.* **27,** 103–111.

Wolf, T. J., Schmid-Hempel, P., Ellington, C. P., and Stevenson, R. D. (1989). Physiological correlates of foraging efforts in honey-bees: Oxygen consumption and nectar load. *Funct. Ecol.* **3,** 417–424.

"Microsmatic Humans" Revisited: The Generation and Perception of Chemical Signals

Benoist Schaal

Ecole Pratique des Hautes Etudes
Laboratoire de Psycho-Biologie de l'Enfant
URA 315 CNRS
75005 Paris, France

Richard H. Porter

Department of Psychology and Human Development
Vanderbilt University
Nashville, Tennessee 37203

I.   Introduction

"Man and primates generally are microsmatic, and the sense of smell *evidently* plays a relatively minor role in their behavior" (Herrick, 1924).

A.   Overview

Major advances in our understanding of chemical communication in non-human animals have served as an impetus for systematic investigations of social olfaction in our own species. Carefully controlled experiments on a wide range of vertebrates as well as invertebrates have documented the critical role of olfactory cues for sexual behavior, parent–offspring interactions, territorial marking, social recognition, warning and alarm signals, aggression, and physical growth and development (for reviews, see Shorey, 1976; Doty, 1976, 1986; Müller-Schwarze and Mozell, 1977; Brown, 1979; Stoddart, 1980; Vandenbergh, 1983; Albone, 1984; Brown and Macdonald, 1985; Duvall *et al.*, 1986; Halpin, 1986). Even though it is commonly believed that nonhuman primates have a poor sense of smell and, therefore, rely little or not at all on this sensory modality for social interactions, research with several families (e.g., Lemuridae, Indridae, Callitrichidae, and Cebidae) indicates that biological odors may be involved in such activities as territorial marking, individual and kin recognition, and reproductive

135

behavior (Kaplan *et al.*, 1977; Rogel, 1978; Epple *et al.*, 1986; Millhollen, 1986; Epple, 1986).

Animal behaviorists have devised effective testing paradigms and quantifiable behavioral measures for studying overt responsiveness to olfactory stimuli. Assay techniques originally developed to determine the chemical composition of insect pheromones have also been used for analyzing mammalian (including human) chemical signals. Neuroanatomical and neuroendocrine manipulations of laboratory animals have afforded insights into the physiological bases of odor perception and implicated chemoreceptive inputs in addition to olfaction sensu stricto in the mediation of social interactions (Scalia and Winans, 1976; Wysocki, 1979; Meredith, 1983; Johnston, 1985).

The contributions of animal behaviorists and neuroscientists are implicit in many of the studies cited in the remainder of this article—which is intended to be an integrative review of empirical research on human olfactory communication. Particular emphasis is given to relevant work that has appeared in the scientific literature since Doty's review of this same topic in 1981. As any chemical cuing system involves the generation and transmission of chemosignals by a sender, and their detection, identification, and integration by a receiver, this article is organized in two parts. The discussion of social olfaction is preceded by a section on emission of potential chemical signals.

B.   THE CONCEPT OF MICROSMATY

Olfaction represents a critical source of environmental information in so-called "macrosmatic" mammals (e.g., rodents, carnivores, ungulates), the behavior of which could not be fully understood before a good knowledge of their olfactory functioning had been accumulated. According to traditional scientific terminology, this first category of mammalian taxa can be contrasted with the "microsmatic" species (e.g. Monotremata, Tubulidentata, Cetacea, Carnivora Pinnipedia, Primates) in which the olfactory sense was considered as a phylogenetically involuted relic having limited, if any, ethological salience. Introduced by Broca (1888), this dichotomy was initially based on neuroanatomical criteria such as the importance of the nasal annexes, the surface of the main olfactory neuroepithelium, the volume of the main olfactory bulb, and the ratio of the volume of the olfactory bulb to the entire brain or animal (Wirtz, 1950; Stephan *et al.*, 1970; Bauchot, 1981). This structurally based classification led to erroneous predictions about functional capacities of the olfactory system. In fact, we propose that this method of classification is a more valid reflection of the gaps in scientific inquiry since Broca's day than of the effective operational properties of nasal chemoreception in orienting behavior. Thus, taxa currently designated as "microsmatic" appear simply to be those in which chemoreception has been documented less in the context of normal social interactions. If we consider the taxa of vertebrates classically included in this category, it can be noted that they involve species which have been either technically difficult to raise and handle for long periods of time (e.g., Monotremata, Tubulidentata, Cetacea) or to which a hegemony of another sensory system has been somewhat dogmatically assigned (e.g., Aves, Cetacea, Primates).

A brief survey of studies of avian and cetaean olfaction will illustrate how these animals came to represent the microsmatic, or even anosmic, categories. In both cases, the sequence of investigations was comparable: first, anatomists described the structures typically associated with olfaction in other vertebrates; second, on the basis of this anatomical evidence, they inferred the sensory performance and effective use of smell in these species and, thus, strongly influenced until very recent times the orientation of subsequent sensory physiologists and behaviorists. Such a situation led to the conclusion that the sense of smell is unimportant in a majority of birds (e.g., Bang and Cob, 1968). However, electrophysiological (Tucker, 1965; Wenzel and Sieck, 1972) and behavioral studies in various species have recently invalidated this assertion (e.g., Wenzel, 1973; Goldsmith and Goldsmith, 1982; Papi, 1986; Wallraff, 1986; Clark and Mason, 1987). Similarly, the great reduction or total absence of the peripheral and central olfactory structures in cetaceans led to a belief in their general chemical insensitivity (e.g., Pilleri and Gihr, 1970). Numerous behavioral observations now suggest developed (nonolfactory) chemosensory abilities in both Odontocetes and Mysticetes (Lowell and Flanigan, 1980; Cave, 1988) and some data exist on the emission of chemical signals in dolphins (Adams and Nachtigall, 1988). These examples demonstrate that functional conclusions based on an exclusive (and often partial) anatomical analysis can lead to spurious models of the perceptual world of animals. A parallel process may have been the basis for the development of the "scientific representation" of primate, and particularly human, sensory functioning.

New facts collected in the last decades render this mode of classification obsolete. Keverne (1980, 1982, 1983) has offered two arguments dismissing the functional microsmaty of primates. First, he points out that the small number of olfactory receptors—one of the decisive criteria defining microsmaty—has no significance in itself because the same receptors respond to different odors following distinct patterns (Gesteland et al., 1965). Second, the olfactory system projects to the neocortex after relaying in the thalamus (Powell et al., 1965). In addition, an exclusive focus on olfaction omits the contribution of other chemoreceptive inputs to nasal chemoreception, namely, that of the trigeminal system (Cain, 1974; Doty et al., 1978a). Finally, although the differences between absolute olfactory thresholds of "microsmatic" versus human systems can clearly be considerable (Davis, 1973; Marshall and Moulton, 1981), the relative thresholds appear not to be so discrepant (Davis, 1973; Slotnick and Ptak, 1977). These arguments suggest that the counterproductive label of "microsmaty" should no longer be used in functional contexts for primates. As Keverne (1983) argued eloquently, "The fact that olfactory information is coded as a pattern which requires a higher order of recognition means that animals with a greater neural backup have the potential for a more sophisticated pattern recognition. Since the olfactory bulb seems to be acting mainly as a filter, and decoding of the olfactory message is a more central event, animals with a greater neocortical support system have the greatest ability to make use of this system. Primates do not therefore have a poorly developed sense of olfactory perception, and the ways in which this is employed may well be the most evolved of all species."

II.   THE CHEMOEMITTING SYSTEM

A.   A ZOOLOGICAL PERSPECTIVE

The interindividual communicative function of bodily chemicals appears to have been derived secondarily from substances serving other more primary and critical functions, such as the preservation of a healthy skin barrier and internal homeostasis, and has generally been overlooked in humans. Though the human scent organs were considered as residual in Schaffer's (1937) early inventory, this author concluded that they might give off potentially meaningful stimuli and he called for their systematic study. Since that time, a significant advance has been made in knowledge of human skin glands and natural body odor production, especially by dermatologists (e.g., Montagna and Parakkal, 1974; Hurley and Shelley, 1960; Sastry et al., 1980; Labows, 1988). Moreover, numerous data on nonhuman mammalian scent-producing organs and mechanisms have been amassed during the same period (Schaffer, 1940; Quay, 1977; Thiessen, 1977; Adams, 1980; Albone, 1984; Brown and Macdonald, 1985; Maderson, 1986). Despite considerable interspecific variation, several tentative generalizations may be drawn from those structures zoologists have demonstrated or inferred as being scent organs in mammals: (1) *Specific semiochemical involvement* is generally ascribed to any surface area of the body (save sensory structures) where the cytological structure is obviously different from surrounding tissue and which gives off secretions that are behaviorally or physiologically active in conspecifics. (2) In the great majority of cases, the chemical ecology of the skin is the result of the *mixture of several elementary exocrine substrates* which act synergistically; the concurrent production of (i) odor substrates, (ii) odor "fixatives," and (iii) adequate ecological conditions (porosity, heat, and humidity) makes the skin an ideal source of semiochemicals. (3) The odorous properties of the exocrine substrates are often revealed or enhanced by the breakdown activity of *symbiotic skin microorganisms,* whose effect is mainly *localized* in specialized areas where they find optimal ecological conditions (hairy skin folds, pouches, and cavities). (4) *Structural and functional modifications* are associated with the evolutionary specialization of particular regions or glands as semiochemical effectors, e.g., (i) enlargement of substrate-producing units and development of specialized appendages (hair) and (ii) underlying modifications in vascularization, innervation, and pigmentation. (5) The quality, intensity, and timing of semiochemical activity is *dependent on endogenous* (hormonal and metabolic stimulation, ontogeny) *and exogenous factors* (psychological and emotional stimulation). (6) The *release* of semiochemical material is effected via involuntary permanent mechanisms (e.g., elementary surface skin glands and skin flora), as well as those under more immediate physiological and behavioral control (including specialized skin glands more or less isolated from the skin surface and waste products such as urine and feces). (7) Chemically simple compounds, which apparently fit with the concept of pheromone (as revised by Beauchamp *et al.*, 1976), have been isolated from these scent organs in a very limited set of species.

In the following section, these gross generalizations regarding nonhuman semiochemical production serve as an analytic framework to assess analogous phenomena in our own species.

B. SOURCES OF POTENTIAL SEMIOCHEMICALS

1. *Elementary Semiochemical Mechanisms*

The thin hydrolipidic coat covering the 1.8 m² of the adult human skin surface is the result of four main recognized sources of secretions/excretions. At least three types of glandular structures are present from birth in the human dermal tissue in addition to epidermal materials steadily raised by the process of keratinization. The elementary skin glands have been categorized according to their morphological and functional characteristics (for more details, see Schiefferdecker, 1922; Kuno, 1956; Botelho *et al.*, 1969). Primary secretions/excretions from these sources are reviewed briefly as a requisite for understanding the formation of an individual's general or local odor profile.

Eccrine glands (EG), which represent the dominant category of skin glands in humans (counts fall between 1.6×10^6 and 4×10^6; Kuno, 1956; Szabo, 1963), are the source of eccrine sweat, the most copious skin secretion. These glands are formed by a closed coil embedded in the dermis (secretory portion) followed by a tubular duct piercing the epidermis independently of hair follicles (Adams, 1980; Quinton, 1988). The EG are densely distributed over the whole body surface, with considerable regional variation, both topographically and functionally. Decreasing density of EG was noted over different areas of the body, viz., soles ($620/cm^2$) and palms > head (forehead and parietal zones) > trunk [sagittal parts of the chest ($64/cm^2$) and the back] > arms and legs (Kuno, 1956; Sato and

Dodson, 1970). EG have been dichotomized according to the mechanism triggering their activity, some being activated mainly by thermal stimuli and others responding primarily to psychological stimuli, with very short latencies. Although these activating mechanisms are not exclusive (Ogawa, 1975) and considerable interindividual variation can occur (Sato and Sato, 1983), thermoreactive EG are situated primarily on the trunk, face, neck, and extremities, while psychoreactive EG are mainly located on the palms and soles and in the axillae (Kuno, 1956; Sato, 1977). Human eccrine sweat is a very dilute solution (over 99% water) of inorganic (sodium, chloride, bicarbonate ions) and organic compounds (e.g., urea, lactate, numerous free amino acids and proteins, albumin, globulins, prostaglandins, histamine, esterases; Sato, 1977). The average water loss (including transepidermal deperdition and eccrine secretion) approximates 1 liter per day, and eccrine secretory rate can reach 12 liters under extreme heat or exercise conditions, which exceeds greatly the secretory rate of other exocrine glands, e.g., salivary or lacrymal glands (Kuno, 1956; Sato, 1977).

The secretory portion of the *apocrine sweat glands* (AG) lies deeper in the dermis and is more circumvoluted than that of the EG. Its straight duct opens near the orifice of the pilosebaceous canal and, consequently, the topographical distribution of the AG overlaps with that of hair (Hurley and Shelley, 1960; Robertshaw, 1983). They are aggregated in several areas, including principally the axillae (where they are of greatest size and activity), areolae, and the periumbilical, pubic, genital, perineal, and circumanal regions, but can also be present on the face (eye lids and ear canals) and scalp. They produce exceedingly small amounts of a milky lipid- and protein-rich fluid, the secretion of which is elicited by psychological stimulation (at a rate of 1 to 10 μl/day; Hurley and Shelley, 1960). Intradermal injection of adrenalin or emotional stress induces episodical contractions of the neuroepithelial lining of the secretory part of the AG and provokes a flush of apocrine sweat (Montagna and Parakkal, 1974). The exact composition of this secretion is little known in its native state. Roughly, it is constituted of proteins (10%), fatty acids (propionic and isovaleric), cholesterol (1%), ammonia, and reducing sugars (Labows, 1988; Sastry *et al.*, 1980; Gower *et al.*, 1988). Chemical microanalyses have also shown the presence of a variety of odorous steroids (approximately 0.02%) in extracts of total sweat or axillary hair (see below).

A third common category of glands, *sebaceous glands* (SG), occurs profusely over much of the skin surface (except palms, soles, and the dorsal surfaces of feet) in association with hair follicles. They are largest, most dense and productive on the face (forehead) and scalp, in the midline of the back and chest, axillae, anogenital skin of both sexes, abdomen, arms, and legs (in that order; Benfenati and Brillanti, 1939; Montagna, 1963). The periphery of body orifices, viz., the eye lids, lips, areolae, prepuce, and labia minora, is endowed with SG free of hair (Hyman and Giudicci, 1963). Sebum, the primary product of SG, is a complex lipidic mixture, the qualitative and quantitative composition of which is difficult to delineate because of its early bacterial alteration and its surface contamination by lipids of epidermal or apocrine origins. The major constituents of sebum include triglycerides, wax esters, squalene, cholesterol esters, and cholesterol (Nicolaïdes, 1963; Agache and Blanc, 1982). In addition, numerous free fatty acids are produced by the oxidation of triglycerides by lipophilic bacteria residing in the follicular canal. Sebum secretion–excretion is a continuous process, its rate being governed mainly by androgens and pituitary hormones (Thody and Shuster, 1989).

In addition to sebaceous lipids, the epidermis also contributes to the skin lipidic film by the process of keratinization. During this steady degeneration of epidermal cells, the lipids which compose them are released in notable quantities ($5–10$ $\mu g/cm^2$) evenly distributed over the body (Montagna and Parakkal, 1974). These epidermal lipids are mainly composed of free sterols (cholesterol), mono-, di-, and triglycerides and phospholipids (Nicolaïdes, 1974).

The chemical substrates produced by these exocrine sources have few if any odor properties (for the human nose) in their native state. Their olfactory qualities generally result from enzymatic handling by a limited range of microorganisms normally residing in and on the epidermis (Albone et al., 1977; Jackman, 1982). In healthy individuals, this skin flora is mainly composed of bacteria (e.g., micrococci, diphtheroids, propionibacteria) and yeasts (e.g., Pityrosporum; Marples, 1965, 1969; Noble, 1981). The number and composition of the flora have been shown to be idiosyncratic, but vary with age and gender (Sommerville, 1969; Marples, 1982). In addition, the bacterial distribution over the body is uneven, in terms of both density and species. The sequestered sites carry the largest numbers of bacteria, i.e., the toeweb, axilla, umbilicus, groin, and anal–perineal regions, although the face and neck carry high densities of anaerobic diphtheroids residing in the sebaceous follicles (Montes and Wilborn, 1970; Bibel and Lovell, 1976; Marples, 1982). Each skin biotope is colonized by a particular ratio of these microorganisms, resulting in differing chemical treatment of the exudates from the skin glands. For example, the occurrence of Pityrosporum ovale, a main scalp dweller, is correlated with the production (in culture) of γ-lactones which are partially responsible for the odor of unclean hair (Labows et al., 1979a). Likewise, an individual's axillary odor is dependent on the composition of its axillary flora (Leyden et al., 1981; Labows, 1988; Rennie et al., 1988; Gower et al., 1988).

The microecological patchwork of the skin reinforces the odorous effects of the skewed distribution of the surface commensals. Regional variations in moisture, temperature, and air renewal converge to select a particular composition ratio in the local microflora. Microtopographical conditions of the skin further strengthen the localized action of the bacterial populations. The epidermal relief is composed of pores and divergent networks of furrows whose depth varies according to the area considered (Makki *et al.,* 1979; Montagna, 1985). This organization may have a role in the sebum–sweat mixing and emulsion (Jones *et al.,* 1951) and local two-dimensional spreading. In addition, the density of the furrows increases the surface of adequate housing for the commensal skin flora. Body hair, particularly the coarse hair of the scalp, axillae, and pubic and genital regions, has been shown to function similarly as a bacterial growth multiplier. In an experiment by Shelley *et al.* (1953), one axilla of male subjects was shaved, soaped for 10 min, and rinsed with water, while the other was only soaped and rinsed. As noted by two raters, the unshaved axilla recovered its typical odor after 6 hr, contrasting with the shaved side which developed a noticeable odor only between hours 24 and 48. Likewise, the bacterial degradation of triglycerides is faster and more complete in hairy as compared to nonhairy areas (Gloor and Kohler, 1977). Hair tufts may thus serve several functions in the very local production and release of body odorants: (1) skin secretions (especially those of the hair-associated glands) adhere to them, (2) they increase the surface for bacterial growth, and (3) they increase the volatilization surface and, thus, optimize the dispersion of odor molecules.

Above we have briefly listed the main sources of substrates giving off, primarily or secondarily, odorous volatiles. But, as a consequence of their high molecular weight, many compounds (e.g., long-chained lipids of sebaceous or epidermal origin) present in the native secretions cannot act as olfactants. Such involatile products can, however, be of considerable importance in the temporal dynamics of chemoemission. Their potential effect has been illustrated by the evaporation rate modeling of ^{14}C-labeled phenylacetic acid from inert metal plates which had been previously smeared with different sebumlike substances. The odorant had considerably lower evaporation rates from the sebum- or squalene-treated plates as compared to mineral oil-treated or control plates (Regnier and Goodwin, 1977). It can thus be concluded that the lipidic fraction of the skin secretions strongly influences the relative stability over time of the local olfactory characteristics. Moreover, in the experiment cited above, both *porosity* of the substratum and *relative humidity* of the environment had a dramatic effect on the evaporation rate of the odorant from the plates, an increased porosity slowing it down and a high hygrometry enhancing it. Comparable factors should apply to the release of odorants from the skin, especially in regard to the effect of the watery eccrine sweat on the evaporation of volatile molecules already present on the skin surface and to the developmental reduction of epidermal smoothness with age.

Finally, dermal vascularization is highly heterogeneous over the body and defines several surface areas of more intense metabolic activity where socially elicited thermal fluctuations can occur, e.g., the axillae, the areolae, and the abdominal and genital areas in both sexes (Marples, 1969). The surface temperature of the skin can have several interacting effects on the local production and release of potential odorants: (1) a higher heat production inflates the growth of symbiotic microorganisms and increases the rate of their enzymatic activity (Thiessen, 1977; Reichert *et al.*, 1982); (2) local increments of the cutaneous temperature augment the excretion rate of sebum (10% per 1°C) and its viscosity (Cunlife *et al.*, 1975); (3) thermal fluctuations have a notable effect on both the volatilization rate of molecules and their efficiency as olfactory stimulants. This is suggested indirectly by the fact that sebum taken from the ventral gland of the Mongolian gerbil is more readily detected by human observers when it is heated (Thiessen, 1977). Furthermore, heightened temperature of the inspired air flow produces larger electro-olfactogram responses recorded from the olfactory mucosa (Ottoson, 1956) and qualitative changes in odor perception (Berglund *et al.*, 1988).

The various chemical substrates emitted by the skin glands and modified by the skin flora, and the local superficial or deeper properties of the skin, contribute to a complex web of synergistic interrelations which are summarized in Fig. 1. Because differing body areas can be characterized by the number and composition of elementary skin glands (as well as other sources of body exudates, such as mucus, saliva, milk, and genital, urinary, and intestinal discharges), odorigenic microorganisms, and local ecological conditions, they should therefore each have a unique chemical cocktail. In the following section, regional distributions of these elementary semiochemical mechanisms on the human body are examined.

2. Significant Odor-Producing Sites of the Body

The cephalic region is endowed with many odorous sources which could play a role in the regulation of social interactions. Among these sources, the scalp, hair, and the oral cavity give off more prominent odors than other areas such as the ears, eyes, nose, and neck. As already mentioned, the face and scalp are the regions most densely supplied with highly active SG (Benfenati and Brillanti, 1939). Owing to this intense seborrhea, the scalp and hair surfaces are continuously anointed with lipids, and even after washing their reanointment occurs rapidly (Saint-Léger and Lévêque, 1982). The enzymatic activity of the resident microflora of the scalp and hair on these lipids may generate the characteristic scalp odor. This is suggested by *in vitro* incubation of *Pityrosporum ovale* (a yeast that is a major scalp resident) on sebum and subsequent gas chromatography/mass spectrometry (GC/MS) profiling of the headspace volatiles. Under these conditions, the cultures emit an odor akin to that of unwashed hair and the analysis reveals volatile aliphatic acids and numerous γ-lactones (majority of γ-decalactone; Labows *et al.*, 1979a).

Breath and mouth odor result from a complex mixture of organic compounds of plasmatic, gastric, and, mainly, oral origin, the latter arising from debris of the oral epithelium, saliva, blood, and remnants of diet. These materials are nor-

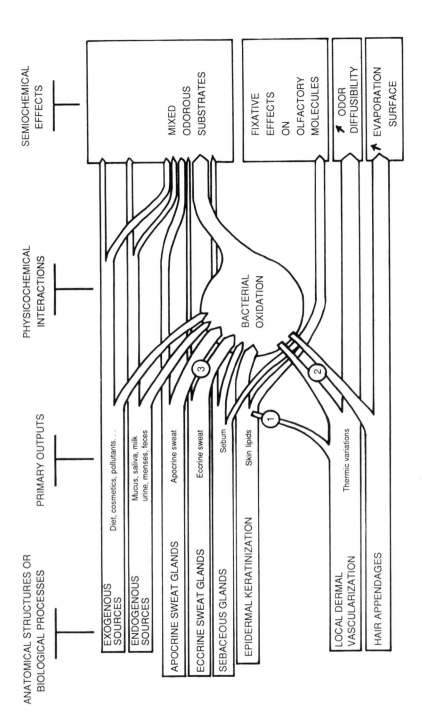

FIG. 1. Diagrammatic representation of the secretions/excretions of elementary skin glands, their partial bacterial breakdown, and several microecological factors, the complex interplay of which results in a localized olfactory label. 1, Indicates the thermic enhancement of excretion rate and fluidity of skin lipids; 2, the positive effect of skin temperature and hairiness on bacterial growth; 3, in addition to chemical substrates, eccrine and apocrine sweat provides moisture further favoring bacterial multiplication. For more details, see Section II,B,1.

mally degraded by the oral bacterial flora into volatiles, contributing to mouth odor (Tonzetich, 1978). This process can be accentuated through poor oral hygiene and bad mouth health conditions (viz., caries, gingivitis; Tonzetich, 1978; Kostelc *et al.*, 1980). The most annoying oral odors develop after optimum fermentation in periods of reduced salivary flow, e.g., in the early morning. They have been related to the presence of hydrogen sulfide, methyl mercaptan, dimethyl sulfide, dimethyl disulfide, ammonia, urea, etc. (Kostelc *et al.*, 1980). In GC/MS profiling of 224 expired air samples of 28 normal carefully selected adults, Krotoszynski *et al.* (1977) were able to identify at least 102 organic compounds, the major volatiles being acetone, isoprene, acetonitrile, and, among others, several alcohols, aldehydes, and nitrogen and sulfur compounds. These diversified breath volatiles, although present in trace amounts, may nonetheless be a good reflection of the systemic levels of an individual. It is surprising, however, that volatile steroids are absent from this profile. Androgens, corticosteroids, and progestogens are known to be transferred to saliva, and fluctuations of the level of salivary steroids reflect the plasmatic level of unbound steroids (Vining and McGinley, 1984). Bird and Gower (1983) reported the presence in trace concentrations of the volatile androstenone in saliva of men and women.

In addition to the marked odor of hair and breath, the head is the site of several waxy, mucous, or watery secretions (cerumen, caruncular secretion, nasal exudates, tears). The sometimes copious amounts of cerumen secreted in the external ear is the result of specialized AG (ceruminous glands) and SG (Shelley and Perry, 1956). It has a strong odor for dogs as well as for humans (Schaffer, 1937). The odorous constituents of the nasal exudates, the white secretion of the caruncular and eyelid SG, and tears have escaped attention. Tears have been shown, however, to include enzymes, catecholamines, and various hormones (prolactin, adrenocorticotropic hormone; Frey and Langseth, 1985), and semiochemical significance has been attributed to nasal mucus in primates (squirrel monkeys; Schwartz and Rosenblum, 1980). In addition, it has been suggested that the sebum of the numerous labial and buccal SG (Hyman and Giudicci, 1963) may function as semiochemicals during bucco-buccal kissing exchange (Nicholson, 1984).

The *palms and soles* are richly supplied with EG ($620/cm^2$; Sato, 1977). These EG have a tonic production of sweat (evidenced by variations in electrical skin resistance). In addition, they respond phasically with negligible latency to emotional and sensory stimulation (Kuno, 1956). Palms and soles are thus permanently humidified with eccrine sweat, which varies between individuals and according to ethnicity, age, and gender (younger and female subjects having higher counts or active glands than older and male counterparts; Juniper and Dykman, 1967). In addition to the above-mentioned materials given off in eccrine sweat, it is interesting to note that gonadal hormones or their metabolites might be excreted in palmar sweat. In a series of experiments using a dog trained to select progesterone, aluminum rods held in the hand by a pregnant woman were repeatedly selected by the dog in preference to similar rods held either by males or nonpregnant females (Kloek, 1961). Similarly, King *et al.* (1964) have shown that fingerprinted glass slides could be detected by dogs on the basis of their odor.

In addition, through manipulative activities, palms are the body area most easily contaminated with extraneous odorants. Soles of feet, especially when sequestered in shoes, can develop a very pungent odor, probably as a result of bacterial action (Reynolds, 1988; Marshall, 1988).

The axillae are regions of limited skin surface containing all the cutaneous mechanisms of potential semiochemical significance described in the previous section. Probably as a result of these converging functional properties, and also because they emit an obvious odor, these areas of the human body are the only ones recognized by dermatologists (Montagna, 1985), zoologists (Albone, 1984), and chemists (Sastry *et al.*, 1980) as "scent organs." As stated somewhat teleologically by Montagna (1985), "every detail of the axilla is precisely tailored to produce and distribute those substances that give human beings their distinctive odor."

The abundant and watery eccrine sweat produced in the axilla mixes with the sticky, odorigenic, apocrine secretion released under emotional stress, and with the continuously excreted sebum. The mixture of these products facilitates the emulsion of the apocrine fluid and sebum, and, hence, their spread over the whole of the axillary skin and hair surfaces. The hygrometric, thermal, and microtopographical (hair) features of the armpit favor the proliferation of selected bacterial groups using the exocrine substrates as nutrients. This intense bacterial activity generates the typical axillary odor; indeed, when collected in sterile conditions and incubated at room temperature, apocrine sweat develops no odor even after 14 days; by contrast, the same secretion captured from uncleansed axillae emits the characteristic odor after only 6 hr (Shelley *et al.*, 1953). As mentioned previously, axillary hair has an additional notable influence on this process (Shelley *et al.*, 1953).

The relationship between the axillary flora of an individual and that same person's odor characteristics was demonstrated by Leyden *et al.* (1981), who studied 229 subjects split into two groups according to the odor they gave off (i.e., "pungent" versus "faint acid"). Axillary dominance of diphtheroids and high total bacterial counts were correlated with the formation of a "pungent" odor, while lower counts and dominance of micrococci were correlated with a "faint acid" odor. This was later confirmed by *in vitro* inoculation of pure apocrine sweat with the contrasting bacterial types: micrococci produced an "acidic" odor characterized as isovaleric acid, while diphtheroids produced a stronger odor suggesting the presence of other olfactants (Labows *et al.*, 1982).

Finally, a replication by Rennie *et al.* (1988) showed that micrococci or cor-yneform domination of axillae is related to low and high axillary odor intensity, respectively.

It appears thus that the axillary chemical ecology is an exquisitely complex mosaic combining axillary exudates and numerous compounds of exogenous origin (Labows *et al.*, 1979b). Several odorigenic compounds regularly present in the axillae have been advanced as communicative cues, including numerous aliphatic acids (acetic, propionic, butyric, isovaleric, valeric, etc.; Labows *et al.*, 1982; Preti *et al.*, 1987; Zeng *et al.*, 1989) and volatile and nonvolatile steroids (cholesterol, testosterone, androstenediol, dehydroepiandrosterone, etc.; Claus and Alsing, 1976; Labows *et al.*, 1979c; Bird and Gower, 1982; Nixon *et al.*, 1988). For several reasons, the steroids excreted in axillary sweat have attracted considerable research effort: several of them, peculiarly the 16-an-drostenes, give axillary-like musky or urinous odors perceptible to humans (Kloek, 1961) at a low detection threshold (Amoore *et al.*, 1977). In addition, 5-androst-16-en-3-one (androstenone) and 5-androst-16-en-3-ol (androstenol) are known to function as releasing pheromones in the sow (Signoret, 1970) and similar effects have been hypothesized for humans (see Section III). Both of these steroids are evident in extracts of axillary hair (Nixon *et al.*, 1988) and in total axillary sweat collected on cotton pads (Gower, 1972; Brooksbank *et al.*, 1974; Claus and Alsing, 1976; Bird and Grower, 1981; Grower *et al.*, 1985; Preti *et al.*, 1987), but not in uncontaminated apocrine sweat (Labows *et al.*, 1979c) nor axillary head space (Labows *et al.*, 1979c). Consequently, these odorous steroids result from bacterial action on precursors present in apocrine sweat (Bird and Gower, 1982; Rennie *et al.*, 1988; Gower *et al.*, 1988).

The nipples and areolae are small highly specialized portions of skin of special interest because they concentrate three features of potential semiochemical rele-vance and their functional activity seems strictly confined to a particular period of the female reproductive life, viz. pregnancy and lactation. (1) Although of very limited extension, the nipple–areolar region is densely supplied with varied skin glands. The hairless nipple is supplied with AG and SG, the ducts of which open directly on the nipple's tip and not into lactiferous ducts. The latter are active and enlarge during lactation (Perkins and Miller, 1926). On the areola, a few vellus hairs (and their associated AG and SG), EG, and enlarged SG can be found (Montagna and MacPherson, 1974). Additionally, the areolar surface contains 12 to 20 so-called corpuscles of Montgomery whose prominence during the gesta-tional and lactational periods attests to their activity (Montgomery, cited in Speert, 1958). These areolar tubercles are formed by sebaceous glands intimately associ-ated with a lactiferous duct which drains miniature mammary lobules giving off a milky fluid (Montagna and Yun, 1972; Smith *et al.*, 1982). Finally, the colostrum and milk released at the nipple from the principal lactiferous ducts add their intrinsic olfactory qualities, reflecting often the dietary choices of the mother. (2)

Although its primary function may be to preserve the skin from the corrosive action of the infant's saliva, the lipidic substrate excreted from the independent SG and those associated with the Montgomery's formations may also act as odor fixatives. The intricate arrangement of sebum and milk sources in Montgomery's glands may indeed favor their mixing during sucking episodes and may thus improve the persistence over time of the olfactory complex formed on the areolar surface. (3) Finally, the presence of Haller's subareolar vascular plexus (Mitz and Lalardie, 1977) confers to this region a higher surface temperature as compared to the nipple and to the remainder of the breast. This thermal characteristic may regulate the evaporation rate of the olfactory molecules, thereby enhancing their effectiveness as semiochemicals. Interestingly, this thermal feature of the areola is triggered in anticipation by the crying infant (Vuorenkoski et al., 1969), resulting in an optimal condition for odorous learning.

The pubic area is well endowed with hair and associated AG and SG. Its olfactory properties might, however, stem rather from the closeness of inguinal and genital regions than from pubic skin glands themselves. Although well developed, pubic AG indeed seem functionless and hence do not generate odorigenic substrates comparable to that occurring in the axillary AG (Klingman and Shehadeh, 1964).

Male genitalia: The proximal parts of the penis and the scrotum are well endowed with hair and associated SG and AG, as well as with EG. On the mucocutaneous surface of the glans (especially the corona) and the internal face of the prepuce, atrichial SG can be found which Tyson considered as "glandulae odoriferae" (Schaffer, 1937). These glands secrete, directly on the surface, a lipidic matrix which contributes to an odorous accumulation in the preputial fold (Schaffer, 1937; Hyman and Giudicci, 1963). Although the origin and composition of this cheesy substance, the smegma, are not well elucidated (Kamat et al., 1960), it is known to include epithelial squames, components of urine and semen, and their secondary derivatives under the action of the local microflora.

Semen is a complex mixture generated by the testes and male accessory organs. Following ejaculation, the seminal aggregate is rapidly modified by intense enzymatic reactions, which among other consequences alter its olfactory characteristics. In addition to its inherent odor due to spermine, handling of choline and polyamines generate trimethylamine, a fishy odorant, and putrescine and 1-pyrroline, mainly responsible for the spermous odor (Albone, 1984). Humans have a very low threshold for 1-pyrroline and it has been suggested to be a "vestigial male sex pheromone" (Amoore et al., 1975). Semen also contains numerous volatile steroids (Kwan et al., 1989).

Female genitalia: The elementary skin glands are abundantly represented in this area (Ridley, 1976). The hairy skin of the outer aspect of the labia majora is endowed with EG and epitrichial AG and SG. The inner face of the labia majora, the labia minora, and the clitoris are richly supplied in hair-free AG and SG, and mucus glands (Schaffer, 1937; Hyman and Giudicci, 1963). In addition, the vulval area is anointed with clear mucus from Bartholin's and Skeen's glands.

In both sexes, the hairy skin of these regions is easily contaminated with odorigenic materials arising from urine, semen, uterine and vaginal exudates, or from odorants microbiologically fashioned from these substrates. The chronically high temperature and the moisture-retaining skin folds of these body areas (this confinement being culturally reinforced with tight clothes) indeed favor an intense bacterial proliferation. The phasic increase of the surface temperature of the abdomen and genital areas during sexual arousal (Talbot-Seeley et al., 1980) adds a radiation effect favorable to further volatilization of odorous molecules.

The *vaginal discharge* is a complex amalgam originating from the upper reproductive tract (endometrial fluid and blood, cervical mucus), the vagina itself (exfoliated cells, transudate of plasma), possibly the male ejaculate, and the numerous compounds potentially derived from these substrates by the vaginal microflora (Hafez and Evans, 1978). Quantitatively, it represents an appreciable amount of secretion: 1.89 g/day (Huggins and Preti, 1981). Considerable emphasis has been given to the odorous qualities of primate (including human) vaginal exudate as an index of pathology and as a possible means of communicating the fertile period of the ovulatory cycle (e.g., Michael et al., 1975a; Keverne, 1976; Goldfoot et al., 1976; Rogel, 1978). Michael et al. (1974, 1975b) and Preti and Huggins (1975) examined the volatile fatty acid content in vaginal secretions of normal women. They collected samples (by lavage or tampons worn for 6 hr) on alternate days during one menstrual cycle and processed them by gas chromatography. A distinct blend of aliphatic acids (acetic, propionic, butyric, isobutyric, isovaleric, and isocaproic), subsequently labeled "copulin" (Michael et al., 1975b), was demonstrated in one third of the subjects, the remaining two thirds producing only acetic acid. Considerable individual variation was noted in the content of volatile acids, with approximately 30% of the subjects being "producers," and the other "nonproducers." It is suggested that the secretions from acid producers emit a more distinctive (cheesy) odor as compared to those of the nonproducers (Huggins and Preti, 1981). The production of copulin appeared to be under hormonal control since sharp intraindividual fluctuations occur during the menstrual cycle and the use of oral contraceptives reduces volatile fatty acid production and abolishes its menstrual fluctuations (these issues continue to be debated however, see Huggins and Preti, 1981). The application of the odorogram technique (gas chromatographic analysis combined with organoleptic rating) seems to confirm qualitative variations in vaginal odors, periovulatory and menstrual odors being described as pleasant and unpleasant, respectively (Keith et al., 1975b). In addition to the aliphatic compounds of copulin, a huge array of other low-molecular-weight substances can be found in vaginal fluids, some of which (e.g., lactic acid and urea) show menstrual fluctuations (Dravnieks *et al.*, 1974; Huggins and Preti, 1981). The most objectionable vaginal odor, attributed to trimethylamine (Klaus, 1927; Brand and Galask, 1986), is produced during menses in healthy women (Neuhaus, 1961; Keith *et al.*, 1975b).

Urine is the major substrate used in most mammalian semiochemical systems. As a filtrate of the milieu intérieur, it closely reflects the physiological and metabolic state of the organism. The volatile profile of urine results from a copious amount of volatiles among which ketones, aldehydes, lactones, alcohols and phenols, pyrroles, sulfur compounds, and aliphatic acids are the most common. Less volatile substances include sexual and adrenal steroids and their metabolites (specifically androstenone–androstenol), amino acids, and amines (Zlatkis and Liebich, 1971; Sastry *et al.*, 1980; Albone, 1984). Varied determinants impart their effect on the volatile urinary profile of an individual; diet and hormonal environment are the most evident. Physiological effects are manifested through modifications of urinary chemical profiles by gender (Dirren *et al.*, 1975), age (Thompson *et al.*, 1977), and diverse pathologies (Sastry *et al.*, 1980).

The perianal area, limited posteriorly by the coccyx and anteriorly by the genitalia, is richly supplied with EG and AG. According to his comparative anatomical study, Schiefferdecker (1922) labeled this region in humans "Zirkumanalorgan." SG are diffusely scattered in association with hair, and atrichial SG occur on the mucocutaneous junction with the anal orifice (Schaffer, 1937; Hyman and Giudicci, 1963). In addition to the exudates from these numerous skin glands, fecal residues may taint the odor of this area.

While fecal odors have been shown to be critical in mammalian semiochemical systems (e.g., in the rabbit: Goodrich *et al.*, 1981; the rat: Leon 1980; and many carnivores: Albone, 1984), they have not been considered in humans, probably as a consequence of their universally recognized offensiveness (at least in adults). Nevertheless, excrements were often used in medieval official medicine, as well as in folk remedies and cosmetics in numerous human groups all over the world (Bourke, 1891). Indirect analyses have revealed strong-smelling fatty acids, sulfur compounds, and skatole (Sastry *et al.*, 1980), and recent use of the odorogram technique showed that the odor content of the feces was directly related to the nature and variety of the food items ingested (Moore *et al.*, 1984, 1985). Vegetarians might thus be easily contrasted from meat-eaters on that basis. Likewise, newborns fed on breastmilk produce feces which develop a peculiar and rather "pleasant" odor in contrast to bottle-fed newborns whose fecal scent resembles that of older weaned children. The extent to which such differences may be correlated with differences in maternal behavior has not been examined. In the same vein, flatus is rarely considered in human olfactory interactions, although it has objectionable social effects. It is essentially composed of odorless constituents such as CO_2, N_2, NH_4, H_2, but traces of ammonia, hydrogen sulfide, volatile amines, and fatty acids contribute to its stench. Flatus production is notably enhanced after the ingestion of crucifers and beans, probably as a result of anaerobic bacterial degradation (Sastry et al., 1980).

3. Summary: The Scent-Producing Network of a "Microsmatic" Species

How do the previously mentioned tentative criteria characterizing semiochemical-producing structures in other mammals apply to the human secretory/excretory structures? From the data reviewed in the previous sections, it appears that varied superficial secretory units are scattered diffusely over the whole surface of the human body, while localized dense aggregations of these units occur in at least five cutaneous sites, viz., the scalp, the axillae, the areolae, the pubogenital area (preputial and vulvar folds), and the perianal area; the oral and vaginal cavities, fecal and urinary emissions complete this odorigenic network. Four of these sites are situated on the upper half of the body (scalp, mouth, axillae, areolae) and all of these sites are accessible from the ventral side. The fact that several sites are endowed with structural and functional modifications suggests their potential semiochemical relevance: superficial appendages in the form of hair occur in three sites (scalp, axillae, pubosexual areas) and four sites are intensely vascularized, providing locally elevated thermal gradients (face, axillae, areolae, sexual areas). The spots of higher exocrine activity generally concentrate and mix the exudates of several sources, thus enhancing their potential semiochemical effects. In most of the localized sites, as well as on the totality of the skin, the odor of exocrine substances is increased by the enzymatic actions of resident bacteria. The secretion of semiochemicals at virtually all of these sites is basically dependent on endocrine activity, which in turn can be acutely sensitive to psychological–social events. The release of odorous substrates seems mostly to be passive, with the possibility of transient increases resulting from localized changes in (1) rate or quality of substrate production, (2) evaporative intensification, (3) contraction of associated myoepithelial elements, or (4) heat production by underlying vasoactivity. Several simple products resulting from bacterial degradation have been proposed as putative semiochemicals, e.g., a series of aliphatic acids of vaginal origin and androstenol–androstenone of mainly axillary origin.

It appears that human exocrine glands give off a plethora of natural products which envelope the body with a qualitatively complex, presumably distinctive, volatile label. The majority of the privileged secretory sites seem, however, to be only secondarily concerned with the production of semiochemicals, although at least one of them is often characterized as a specialized scent gland (axillae). This situation can be readily compared to that of other primate species credited with a highly active chemical communication system. For members of Lemuridae, Epple (1986) has reviewed the occurrence of specialized scent glands (in addition to the elementary skin glands). Their numbers range from only 1 (in

70% of the species considered) to 4 (in *Lemur catta*). Similarly, in the 12 species of Cebidae for which details are available, 10 have only one developed specialized scent gland. Thus, although the accumulation of distinguishable skin attributes seems to be a good predictor of the role of olfaction in behavior, the absence of well-differentiated specialized glands does not necessarily imply an inefficient chemical communication system. Without obvious specializations, the local quality and quantity of exocrine substrates and the composition and density of resident microorganisms and microecological conditions can generate a highly distinctive odoriferous profile in different regions of the body in humans. As stated by Stoddart (1988), *"Homo sapiens* exhibits many of the characteristics one would expect to find in a species which has an active olfactory communication system."

C. DEVELOPMENTAL TRENDS IN CHEMOEMISSION

1. Birth and the Development of Body Odor

The skin of the newborn infant is not totally devoid of the substances which adhered to its surface during fetal life. Rather, it is covered with a waxy film, the vernix caseosa, composed of triglycerides, cholesterol, and unsaponifiable greases (Dietel, 1978; Nicolaïdes, 1972), that results from the accumulation of lipids elaborated by the skin and exchanged with the amniotic fluid (Stalder *et al.*, 1986). It is generally held that the vernix has primary functions of preventing excessive wetting of the fetal skin and, postnatally, of reducing the risk of dehydration and facilitating the infant's movement through the birth canal (Dietel, 1978); this greasy cover might also contribute secondarily to the selective fixation of olfactory molecules diluted in the amniotic environment. The maternal diet influences the amniotic concentration of certain odorous compounds which can be retained by the vernix after birth; indeed, the neonate's skin may be strongly tainted with recognizable spicy odors after the mother ingests dishes flavored with curry, cumin, or fenugreek prior to delivery (Hauser *et al.*, 1985). However, the visual, tactile, and olfactory traces of the vernix caseosa are generally eliminated shortly after birth. In 94% of the 126 ethnic groups for which birth rituals have been described, the first practice concerns the washing of the neonate (Lozoff, 1983) and, often, subsequent anointing with artificial odorants (e.g., Schiefenhövel and Sich, 1983). The vernix caseosa thus seems to have limited semiochemical value.

The neonatal eccrine skin glands, which are active shortly after birth, are 13 times more dense in full-term newborns and 4 times more dense in 1- to 18-month-old children than in adults (counts at the thigh level; Szabo, 1963). The amount of sweat released per gland is, however, 3 times less than in mature glands (in response to the same dose of acetylcholine; Foster *et al.*, 1969). An abundant emission of eccrine sweat often occurs immediately after birth (Schwartz, 1982), but a stable eccrine function emerges some days later; thermogenic sweating begins between days 3 and 5 and is fully developed at day 8 (Uchino, 1939; Harpin and Rutter, 1982a); emotional sweating also develops in the same period (Verbov and Baxter, 1974; Harpin and Rutter, 1982b). Two factors may affect the production rate and composition of neonatal sweat: (1) the infant's state and motor activity, a distressed newborn giving off an amount of sweat comparable to that of anxious adults (Harpin and Rutter, 1982a); (2) the infant's diet (maternal or formula milk) and, for breast-fed infants, the maternal diet.

The SG are also highly active after birth; during the first postnatal week, the amount of sebum excreted reaches that of a young adult (Agache *et al.*, 1980; Rochefort, 1985). After this period, the seborrhea remains relatively low until puberty (Emanuel, 1936; Dietel, 1978). In addition, the composition of the lipidic surface film is unique to the neonatal period, with higher contents of cholesterol and its esters (Ramasastry *et al.*, 1970; Serri *et al.*, 1982).

The substrates released by both of these classes of skin glands (the AG being dormant at this age, see below) serve as nutrients for the commensal bacteria which rapidly colonize the neonatal skin surface. From birth onward, the skin harbors four groups of harmless bacteria: staphylococci, diphtheroïds, coliforms, and streptococci (Marples, 1965). The first two, most frequent, bacterial groups show a regular colonization pattern in all the neonates studied by Sarkany and Gaylarde (1967, 1968): after a drop during the first 10 postnatal hours, the density of staphylococci increases considerably during the following 2 days and reaches a plateau at day 4. The density of the diphtheroïd bacilli also reaches a steady state from day 2. It is interesting to note that the postnatal washing routines applied to the newborn do not disturb this pattern of colonization (Sarkany and Gaylarde, 1968). From the first hours after birth, the skin flora is unevenly distributed over the infant's body, with higher densities in the skin folds (axillae, groin).

Although the factors governing the initial bacterial colonization of the neonatal skin remain unclear, mother–infant contact seems important in the earliest phases of this process. Because the skin of infants delivered by Caesarean is sterile, while the skin flora of naturally born infants is similar to that of the vagina, a *bacterial labeling* of the infant by the mother's birth canal has been suggested (Sarkany and Gaylarde, 1968). In the same vein, neonates having had direct skin-to-skin contact with their mother immediately after delivery are more rapidly colonized by the maternal skin flora (Gerstner *et al.*, 1984).

In summary, several factors combine optimally for a prompt epigenesis of the neonatal chemical signature: (1) a considerable production of substrates (sebum and sweat) concomitant with a swift bacterial colonization which is unaltered by care routines; (2) the oxidative actions of the commensal flora on the exocrine substrates add new odorous compounds to those present in the native secretions; (3) the "fixative" effect of the sebum regulates the stability of the infant's olfactory label. Those three components of neonatal semiochemistry reach a steady level of functioning as early as the first postnatal week.

2. Before and After Puberty

Toward puberty there are marked structural and functional changes in the elementary chemoemitting units of the skin, the associated skin appendages, and microflora. The entire apopilosebaceous units enlarge as a result of their priming by androgens. The most obvious changes concern the development of pubic, axillary, and other body hair; pubic hair becomes evident at 11 and 13 years in (Caucasian) girls and boys, respectively, and axillary hair appears about 2 years later (Marshall and Tanner, 1969, 1970).

The SG also increase in size and sebum productivity is enhanced more than fivefold (Pochi *et al.*, 1979). Between 2 and 8 years, the skin lipids are dominated by cholesterol and its esters, the chemical markers of sebum (wax esters and squalene) occurring in lower amounts. At ages 8 to 10, the concentrations of the latter compounds rise to about two-thirds of the adult level, and sebum becomes the dominant substance in the lipidic surface film. Between 10 and 15, the skin lipid composition is similar to that to adults (Ramasastry *et al.*, 1970; Sansone-Bassano *et al.*, 1980; Serri *et al.*, 1982).

The third component of the pilosebaceous unit, the AG, increase structurally from their small and dormant prepubescent state and begin to give off apocrine sweat, whose appearance correlates with the emission of axillary odor (Kuno, 1956). Important changes of eccrine-like glandular precursors into apocrine structures take place in the axillary regions during the pubertal period, giving rise to structures designated as apoeccrine glands (Sato *et al.*, 1987). These neoformed structures can account for as many as 45% of the total axillary glands in 16–18 year olds. They are very active in secreting a serous fluid (at a rate sevenfold higher than EG; Sato and Sato, 1987) and contribute significantly to the overall axillary moisture.

The productivity of EG is also stimulated by the pubertal rise of gonadal androgens. Before puberty both sexes secrete similar amounts of eccrine sweat which are comparable to that secreted by adult females (pilocarpine-elicited secretion from the forearm; Rees and Shuster, 1981). The sex difference in sweating becomes significant only after puberty. At this age, excess plantar, palmar, and axillary sweating (hyperhidrosis) occurs often in response to thermal or mental activation (Champion, 1986).

Probably as a result of the considerable rise in the potential nutrients provided by the skin glands in early infancy and around puberty, higher counts of skin commensals have been reported in these periods (Sommerville, 1969; Leyden *et al.*, 1975). It is suggested that sebum provides a major stimulus to bacterial growth (notably to *Propionibacterium acnes*), especially on the face (Leyden *et al.*, 1975). The pubertal activation of the elementary semiochemical mechanisms of the skin goes hand in hand with the acquisition of a distinctive odor profile. The typical axillary, scalp, and foot odors are emitted as a result of bacterial handling of eccrine, apocrine, and sebaceous exudates. In addition, the activation of genital functions (menarche, seminal emission) also contributes to the release of unique odors in the sexual areas. The marked sexual dimorphism of odor-producing sources initiated at puberty is maintained through adulthood. In older years, however, the secretory activity of skin glands drops steadily (for SG, for example, see Plewig and Klingman, 1978).

D. ORGANISMIC AND ENVIRONMENTAL INFLUENCES
   ON CHEMOEMISSION

1. Genetic Influences

Differential distribution and functional properties of skin glands, and olfactory correlates, have been noted between various ethnic groups. Ellis (1905), Klineberg (1935), and Baker (1974) have collected many subjective descriptions of the olfactory impressions of early explorers and ethnographers when meeting people of different ethnic groups. According to such anecdotes, Caucasoids and Negroids were said to give off a "strong" whole body odor, while the Mongoloids emitted only a slight natural scent. Of course, such reports (even if valid) do not allow one to separate the environmental versus organismic determinants of body odors, nor to evaluate the ethnocentric biases of the ratings. Indeed, in an early experiment, the odors of black and white college students eating similar diets and otherwise living in similar environments could not be reliably discriminated (Morlan, 1950). Nevertheless, several authors have reported ethnic differences in the density, distribution, and activity of skin glands. Kuno (1956) noted differences in EG distribution between Japanese and European males, and African Bantu show greater EG density than do Caucasoids (Rook *et al.*, 1986). In a comparative study of pilocarpine-stimulated sweating of Europeans, Asian Indians, and Africans, a higher production of eccrine sweat was noted in the Europeans (McCance and Puhorit, 1969). Differential size, amount, and distribution of AG and SG have also been shown in Caucasoids and Negroids (Schiefferdecker, 1922; Homma, 1926). The most striking fact is the weak AG development in Mongoloids (as compared to both other groups): in these they are present sparsely in the axillae, rarely in the pubic and female sexual region, and are almost absent from the chest (Adachi, 1937). This trend is accentuated by differences in axillary hair density (which is greatest in Caucasoids; Ebling *et al.*, 1986) and AG activity. Kuno (1956) quantified the rate of axillary sweating in response to mental stress and noted an invariably high sweat output in 92% of the Caucasoids (Russians) in his sample as compared to three Mongoloid groups, i.e., 70% Japanese, 46% Koreans, and 37% Chinese. According to Adachi (1937), only 10% Japanese and 2–3% Chinese develop any axillary odor.

The biochemical composition of bodily secretions/excretions varies according to individuals' genetic make-up (Penrose, 1924; Kalmus, 1955). It is unlikely, for example, that any two people (with the possible exception of identical twins) produce the exact same combinations of complex skin lipids (Nicolaïdes, 1974). Indeed, variability in the amount of surface skin lipids and pH between monozygotic twins is less than that of dizygotic twins (Gloor and Schnyder, 1977). These substances may therefore endow every individual with a distinctive "chemical signature" (olfactory "fingerprint"). Relevant research with rodents has identified specific gene complexes that control the production of discriminable odors. Thus, female wild house mice respond differently to the odors of males carrying a deleterious mutation in the t complex ($t/+$ heterozygotes) and those of males lacking such a mutation ($+/+$ homozygotes) (Lenington et al., 1988). Similarly, mice can distinguish between the odors of inbred conspecifics that differ in the genes of the major histocompatability complex (MHC), but are otherwise genetically identical (Yamazaki et al., 1981). It is interesting in the present context that similar sets of linked genes are found throughout the vertebrates. In our own species, the MHC complex (HLA) is also involved with immunological functioning, with the success of organ transplants correlated with the degree of HLA similarity between donor and recipient. However, the extent to which this extremely polymorphic gene complex may serve as a basis for olfactory discrimination in humans has yet to be determined.

2. *Hormonal and Metabolic Influences*

   a. *The General Effect of Gender.* The potential semiochemical involvement of the secretory discharge of the primary sexual organs has been sketched above. In this section, we consider how the average functioning of semiochemical mechanisms differs in other ways between the sexes. Although the number and gross distribution of EG are comparable in men and women (Szabo, 1963), the two sexes differ in their perspiration rate. Males sweat more than females (McCance, 1938; Kawahata, 1960) and with 2 or 3 times shorter latencies (Shuster, 1982). This sexual difference seems universal, as it has been noted in Europeans, Africans, and Indians (McCance and Puhorit, 1969). It is apparent in postpubertal children, but is not seen before puberty, when sweat rates are similar to that of adult women (Rees and Shuster, 1981). Histological studies indicate that the mean size of the AG (especially in the axillae) is bigger in men as compared to women (Hurley and Shelley, 1960) and that the size of AG is correlated with secretory activity (Shehadeh and Klingman, 1963). Sebum excretion rate is also higher in mature males relative to females (Agache and Blanc, 1982; Shuster, 1982), and a trend in the same direction is present in prepubertal children (Agache *et al.*, 1980; but see Serri *et al.*, 1982). In addition, gender is an important determinant of the qualitative and quantitative characteristics of the skin flora. In all the body sites examined (viz., the nose, axilla, groin, hip, thigh, and toeweb), aside from the forehead, males, from puberty onward, harbored significantly more cutaneous microorganisms than females (Marples, 1982; Sommerville, 1969; Leyden *et al.*, 1975). Finally, the higher pilosity and skin texture of males create more favorable multiplication sites for bacteria. It appears thus that postpubertal males concomitantly produce greater amounts of skin secretions, carry considerably more odorigenic microflora, and grow more skin appendages favorable to odor generation.

Gender differences are also observed in the composition of body exudates of various origins. For example, odorous steroids such as androstenone, androstenol, or dehydroepiandrosterone are present in higher concentration in men's axillary sweat (Bird and Gower, 1981; Gower *et al.*, 1985; Preti *et al.*, 1987), urine (Brooksbank, 1962), or saliva (Bird and Gower, 1983). The transfer from plasma to saliva of unbound hormones (e.g., testosterone, estrogens, progesterone), the amounts of which contrast markedly between the sexes, may impart additional sex-specific odorants to saliva. Moreover, the amino acid composition leads to a reliable chromatographic differentiation of male and female urine (Zlatkis and Liebich, 1971; Dirren *et al.*, 1975).

b. The Menstrual Cycle and Pregnancy. Both of these phases of the female reproductive cycle have marked influences on cutaneous physiology. In a great proportion of women, cyclic fluctuations of the chloride concentration in eccrine sweat occur with ovulatory and premenstrual peaks (Lieberman, 1966). These menstrual variations do not seem to be restricted to mineral salts but also concern other compounds, such as odorous steroids in apocrine sweat (Preti *et al.*, 1987) and compounds excreted in skin lipids (MacDonald and Clark, 1970). Sebum excretion is suggested to fluctuate during the menstrual cycle (Hodgson-Jones *et al.*, 1952), but only slight increases during the second phase of the cycle have been confirmed (Burton and Rook, 1986).

The relationship between the production of odorous volatiles and ovarian rhythm has been investigated most extensively for localized sources of the body: the axillae and the oral and vaginal cavities. The rhythmical pattern of production of axillary androstenol and dehydroepiandrosterone sulfate, measured in four subjects across five cycles, shows a peak during the preovulatory period (Preti *et al.*, 1987). The odorous profile of breath also changes through the ovarian cycle, although great individual variation occurs. The concentration of volatile sulfur compounds present in mouth air (hydrogen sulfide, methyl mercaptan, and dimethylsulfide) shows an increment at mid-cycle and during menses (Tonzetich *et al.*, 1978). Simultaneous measures of oral volatile sulfur compounds and vaginal lactic acid and urea show an increase corresponding with the onset of the preovulatory rise of estrogens (Tonzetich *et al.*, 1978). Michael *et al.* (1975a,b) have also reported mid-cycle maxima of C_2–C_5 aliphatic acids present in the vaginal fluid, but this pattern could not be detected in other studies (Preti and Huggins, 1975).

In pregnant women, changes occur in the activity of SG. The rate of sebum excretion tends to increase during pregnancy and fall abruptly to initial levels after delivery—at least in bottle-feeding women (Burton *et al.*, 1973). During this period, the Montgomery's glands of the areolae enlarge and, in late pregnancy, begin to exude a milky fluid (Natanson and Goldschmidt, 1909). The high production of sebum noted in pregnant women is maintained in lactating women (Burton *et al.*, 1975). The emission of milk, which often occurs in an uncontrollable fashion between suckling periods, probably confers a typical odor to the breast region.

c. Physical Exercise. Physical exercise induces an intense activation of the EG on the general body surface and, to a lesser extent, on the palms, soles, and axillae (Kuno, 1956). The abrupt sweat flush brings organic nutrients, such as lactic acid, urea, and amino acids, to the surface, where microorganisms decompose them to odorous metabolites (e.g., ammonia). The wave of sweating is correlated with an increase in skin temperature (Kuno, 1956), resulting in the reduction of sebum viscosity and, hence, the facilitation of its excretion from the pilous canal and spreading over the heated and wet skin surface (Burton, 1972). These surface mechanisms alone would be sufficient to generate changes in the body odor after exercise, but other processes certainly operate.

3. Environmental Influences

a. The Chemical Niche. As outlined above, the odor developed by an individual largely reflects his internal states, but it is also affected by the totality of chemical substrates which are encountered in his ecological niche. Indeed, through ingestion, inhalation, percutaneous absorption, or surface adsorption, the environment can influence very strongly an individual's olfactory profile. These environmental factors can act either directly, by qualitative or quantitative changes in body surface processes, or indirectly, through the mediation of metabolic pathways or by both of these processes.

Diet, and more generally all ingested materials, may exert a potent influence on body odors. This action is mediated by several distinct mechanisms; the transfer of stable aromatic compounds from food, or the release of new odorous compounds formed by digestion, are the most commonly quoted qualitative influences of diet, but certain dietary compounds can also have an effect on the quantitative activation of specific exocrine or microbiological mechanisms.

Most obviously, dietary volatile precursors and odorous by-products resulting from metabolism influence the aromatic quality present in the digestive tract and wastes. Oral odors reflect an individual's diet by the direct release of volatiles after masticatory reduction, by the action of salivary enzymes and bacterial flora, by gastric belching, and by pulmonary exchanges. For example, the oral degradation of vegetables from families such as *Alliaceae* (onions, garlic) and *Cruciferaceae* (cabbage) gives off sulfur compounds with tenaceous odor properties (Kostelc et al., 1981). By respiratory release, alcoholic beverages can strongly affect the odor profile of the breath. The ingestion of foodstuffs rich in cellulose or in sulfur compounds (cabbage, beans) stimulate the proliferation of the gut microflora and lead to increased production of odorous volatiles in feces and flatus (Sastry et al., 1980).

Many of the diet-derived odorants also pass the digestive barrier and taint the whole milieu intérieur from which they can be excreted by varied exocrine pathways. The odor profile of urine can be significantly affected after the ingestion of certain vegetables (e.g., onion, garlic, asparagus, coffee) and animal products (e.g., certain cheeses, fish, cod-liver oil; Löhner, 1924; White, 1975; Sastry et al., 1980; Arnaud, 1988). More generally, urinary excretion of volatile fatty acids is increased with a carbohydrate-rich diet and decreased with a protein-rich diet (Chen et al., 1970). The diet of pregnant and lactating women can modify the odorous properties of amniotic fluid (Hauser et al., 1985; Schaal, 1988b) and colostrum and milk (Baum, 1980; Vorherr, 1974), respectively. For instance, the ingestion of garlic extract-filled capsules by lactating women induces a detectable garlic flavor in the milk extracted 2–3 hours later (Mennella and Beauchamp, 1990). In addition to these dietary influences on the qualitative profile of body odors, several alimentary compounds can trigger the activation of secretion–excretion mechanisms. For example, hot and spicy foods can elicit acute sweating from the face (gustatory sweating; Champion, 1986). Finally, cyclical fluctuations in an individual's dietary selection, related to seasonal availability of foodstuffs or hormonal rhythms (Cohen et al., 1987), constitutes another possible exogenous influence on the chemical profile of body odors.

Due to fumes released by the necessity of maintaining their microclimate, of culinary practices, of repelling pests, or by drug consumption, humans generally modify their aerial chemical niche. *Aerial chemical ecology* is another factor that can momentarily modulate skin surface processes and, to a lesser extent, metabolic processes. For example, the aromatic compounds in tobacco smoke can adhere to the skin, hair, and clothes. The major volatile constituents identified from the axillary skin surface have indeed been shown to be of exogenous (either dietary or atmospheric) origin (Labows et al., 1979b). The inhalation of tobacco smoke by active, but also by passive, smoking affects the composition of body fluids such as urine and saliva (Wald and Ritchie, 1984; Greenberg et al., 1984).

Hygienic practices (i.e., washing and bathing) transiently modify the odorous emission of the body by directly suppressing the compounds responsible for the odor or by indirect reduction of the odor-producing skin bacteria (Selwyn, 1982). The frequency of cleansing and associated use of artificial odorous materials (soap, perfumes, etc.) may attenuate the occurrence of natural surface exudates, but the individual patterns of these exudates and of the skin bacteria which transform them in odorous compounds are rapidly restored (Shelley *et al.*, 1953; Sarkany and Gaylarde, 1968).

Proximal social contacts such as those occurring in mother–infant or sexual interactions provide opportunities for mutual *olfactory labeling*. Mere mother–infant contact may allow the transfer of odorous compounds from the mother's body to the infant and vice versa. The licking of the mother's breast, neck, or face by the infant, and, reciprocally, the mother's use of saliva to wipe away stains on the child's skin are common occurrences. Intimate contacts between adults similarly favor the mutual transfer of odorous substrates of cutaneous and sexual origin. Interestingly, this mutual olfactory labeling can be effective through the transfer of odorigenic skin bacteria. As already mentioned, the mother's vaginal and skin microflora seem to regulate the initial steps of bacterial colonization of the neonate's skin and, hence, to determine partially its body odor. Such *bacterial labeling* of infants and young children by the parents is also suggested as an explanation for the age-related pattern of the microflora residing on the face (higher counts in infancy and early childhood relative to later childhood; Leyden *et al.*, 1975).

b. Psychological Influences. Emotional experiences can affect noticeably an individual's quantitative and qualitative emission of body secretions–excretions. EG, especially those of the palms, soles, and axillae, and axillary apocrine glands are highly responsive to such stimulation (Kuno, 1956). This emotional sweating is reflected in the galvanic skin response, which has been used as an index of stress among adults visiting the dentist (Early and Kleinknecht, 1978) and of children admitted to hospital (Johnson and Stockdale, 1975). Stress during medical examinations can also modify the volatiles emitted in breath (as shown by the high level of isoprene in subjects who were unfamiliar with the testing situation; Conckle *et al.*, 1975), and probably in other body exudates.

Sexual arousal has an activating effect on almost all exocrine functions of the body, in addition to the specific stimulation triggering odorous output from the primary sexual organs. In both sexes, after the sexual climax a widespread perspiratory reaction occurs in the axillary fossae, the palms and soles, the face, and the trunk (Masters and Johnson, 1966). Sharp changes are also noted in the vaginal secretions with a very short latency (30 sec) after initiation of sexual stimulation (Masters and Johnson, 1966). This occurs through the intensified vaginal blood flow and transudation of a plasma-derived fluid into the vaginal lumen. These secretory variations are believed to be linked to intensified odors (Preti and Huggins, 1977); however, the latter may not be due to qualitative modifications of the secretions but to an increased quantity of materials externalized in the vulvar area (Preti *et al.*, 1979). Keith *et al.* (1975a) also reported chromatographic and sensory changes in pre- and postcoital vaginal secretions. It is thus to be expected that sexual stimulation induces notable olfactory deviations from the baseline emission rate.

  c. Climatic and Seasonal Influences. As already discussed, the thermal and hygrometric conditions of ambient air are of prime importance in the production of eccrine sweat and in the excretion of sebum. An increase in cutaneous temperature can additionally alter the composition of surface skin lipids (Williams *et al.*, 1973). Such quantitative or qualitative differences in skin secretions are likely to give rise to seasonal contrasts in individual odorous profiles.

  Climatic factors also control the seasonal rhythmicity of many abiotic features of the environment, which in turn could drive a seasonal patterning of reproductive physiology. Recent evidence of increase axillary concentration of odorous steroid in late—as compared to early—fall (Preti *et al.*, 1987) point to the possibility of a seasonal variation in the volatiles present in the axilla.

E. POTENTIAL HUMAN SEMIOCHEMISTRY

  It appears that the externalization of potential semiochemicals is not evenly distributed throughout development. Several periods of intensified output alternate with episodes of relative quiescence. In the early years, the highly active neonatal and pubertal periods are separated by a relatively dormant phase. In adulthood, the rate and quality of bodily exudates, although relatively high and constant, is affected by short-term rhythmical fluctuations related to reproductive cycles (ovarian cycle, pregnancy) in the female and, perhaps, to a seasonal pattern in males. In old age, and especially after menopause in females, several semiochemically important mechanisms are reduced or are no longer functional. The life-cycle patterning of human body exudates, both in quantity and in composition, reflects internal physiological and metabolic changes.

  Since body exudates mirror the composition of the internal milieu, they can be efficient means for the transmission of information from the internal to external world. Natural secretions–excretions may thus constitute a chemical system carrying several categories of messages related to age, gender, reproductive phase, health status, etc. Similarly, environmentally derived odorants can convey very specific chemical cues. Do these two sources of an individual's chemical markers act competitively or synergistically? If the most prominent and finely tuned source of olfactory cues resides in internally secreted compounds, then environmental odors might increase the noise from which the meaningful (chemical) information must be extracted. Alternatively, endogenous life-cycle modifications in the chemoemission system, which are primed by endocrines, may be paralleled by age and gender differentiation of environmental influences, thereby resulting in more effective signal transmission. For example, infants and children

TABLE I

CLASS-RELEVANT DIFFERENTIATION OF POTENTIAL SEMIOCHEMICAL SUBTRATES (OR PROCESSES) EMITTED FROM VARIOUS SOURCES BY THE HUMAN BODY[a]

Potentially discernible contrasts between olfactory categories	Organismic sources of volatiles													
	Skin sources				Localized sources in both sexes							Sex-related sources		
	Eccrine sweat	Apocrine sweat	Sebum	Microbiological Factors	Saliva	Breath	Scalp	Palms	Axillae	Urinary discharge	Gut discharge	Female sexual discharge	Male sexual discharge	Mammary discharge
Ethnicity contrasts	▼	▼	▼△				▼		▼					
Kin contrasts	▼		▼△				▼	△				▼△	▼△	
Age contrasts	▼	▼△	▼△	▼△	△		▼△		▼▼	△		▼▼	▼▼	
Gender contrasts	▼	▼△	▼	▼△	△	△	▼		▼△	△		▼△	▼△	▼△
Reproductive phase contrasts														
Male		△							△	△				
Female														
Ovarian state	△	△	▼△	▼△	△	△			▼△	△		▼△	▼△	
Pregnancy status		▼	▼			△			▼▼	△		▼▼		▼
Lactation status			▼											▼
Physiological status contrasts[b]														
Metabolic effects	▼△	▼						▼	▼	△				
Muscular exercise		▼						▼	▼					
Emotional effects	▼△	▼			△	△				△	▼			
Diet contrasts	▼△	△			△	▼△		△	△	▼	▼△			▼△

▼, Quantitative effects; △, qualitative effects.

[a] For references, see Sections II, B and C.
[b] Pathological deviations excluded.

do not consume exactly the same substances that adults do, and females in many cultures differ from males in regard to tobacco consumption (Waldron *et al.*, 1988). It can be hypothesized, however, that organismic factors have more influence on the cues related to individuality, kinship, age and gender categories, and reproductive phase, while environmental factors play a major role in differentiating ethnic and cultural groups.

The previous sections allow postulation of several hypotheses concerning the communicative functions of the volatile compounds present in body exudates. According to inter- or intraindividual variations in structures, physiological condition, or activity relative to chemoemission, olfactory discrimination could occur at several levels of distinction, ranging from the ethnic group to the individual. Table I presents some biological–social dimensions along which particular individuals could be discernable on the basis of quantitative or qualitative differences in the volatile cues they emit. Unfortunately, at least to our knowledge, there appear to be no direct studies of either the sources of potential discriminable social odors nor of behavioral responses to such cues for many of the social categories listed in Table I. In the following section, data for those social categories that have most often been the subject of empirical investigations of olfactory discrimination are reviewed.

III. Responses to Chemosignals

For the most part, research on human social olfaction has been guided by two major (often overlapping) themes: (1) the role of odors in discrimination of different biological categories, and (2) the possible influence of olfactory cues on sexual behavior and reproductive physiology. Both of these subtopics are discussed in the following sections, where we have focused primarily on the communicative significance of naturally occurring body odors. Accordingly, research on responsiveness to perfumes and other artificial scents has been almost entirely neglected in this review.

A. Empirical Evidence of Olfactory Discrimination of Biological Categories

Mammalian social encounters are not distributed in a random fashion among all potentially available conspecifics. The frequency and nature of interactions between particular individuals, or members of subgroups, may be markedly different from those involving others. Such discriminative interactions are often presented as an operational definition of social recognition—a convention that will be adopted for the remainder of this article (for a fuller discussion of this issue, see Blaustein and Porter, 1990). In most orders of mammals, including rodents and carnivores, olfactory phenotypes (signatures) provide a reliable basis for social discrimination. As delineated below, it is becoming increasingly evident that humans are likewise capable of discriminating individuals (or categories of individuals) by their characteristic odors alone.

1. Gender (and Age) Discrimination

Can gender be determined accurately by individuals' body odors? This seemingly straightforward question has been addressed by several investigators with somewhat mixed results.

Wallace (1977) tested college students for their ability to learn to discriminate between the hand odors of paired stimulus individuals. Over repeated trials, accuracy rates were greater when attempting to discriminate between odors of an adult male and female rather than two individuals of the same sex. It could not be concluded that humans can distinguish male and female scents "as categories," however, especially since only one male/female stimulus pair participated in this study.

T-shirts worn and soiled by appropriate odor donors have also been used as stimuli for tests of gender discrimination. When asked to sample (sniff) two T-shirts—one that had been worn for 24 hr by a strange male, and one worn by a strange female—22 of 29 subjects correctly identified the male's shirt (Russell, 1976). Odors of the males' shirts "were usually characterized as musky and the female odours as sweet." Using a variation of the latter procedure, Hold and Schleidt (1977) instructed volunteers to wear stimulus T-shirts for 7 consecutive nights. They were also asked to wash with the same brand of children's soap each night and to avoid the use of deodorants and perfume. Each subject was tested repeatedly with an array of 10 soiled shirts and asked several questions, including Which shirts smell male? and Which smell female? Sixteen of the 50 subjects reliably discriminated between male and female odors. Female odors, in comparison to those of males, were more frequently judged as pleasant by both male and female raters. Male odors, on the other hand, were more often described as unpleasant. This experiment was subsequently replicated with a group of odor donors who followed their "normal, everyday hygienic procedures" (Schleidt, 1980). Males and females in this latter condition were less accurately discriminated than were those who had followed a strictly prescribed hygienic routine (in the previous experiment). Moreover, stimulus odors of the normal-hygiene individuals were judged to be less unpleasant, and male and female odors from this condition more alike, than for the comparison group. Males in the former condition had presumably "washed away their 'maleness' " (Schleidt and Hold, 1982).

All participants in the above gender-identification experiments by Hold and Schleidt were German. To assess the cross-cultural generality of their data, further tests were conducted with Italian and Japanese participants (Schleidt *et al.*, 1981). Once again, subjects wore stimulus T-shirts for 7 nights and followed the prescribed hygiene routine (i.e., no perfume or deodorants; washed with the same mild soap). Whereas 32% of the original German sample reliably discriminated between male and female odors, the success rate for Italians was 20%, and 6% for the Japanese. Overall, the Japanese subjects rated stimulus odors less pleasant than did the Europeans. It was suggested that the Japanese may have a more negative attitude toward body odors and lower detection thresholds than the other two ethnic groups.

According to Schleidt and Hold (1982), olfactory discrimination of gender may be dependent on fully functional apocrine sweat glands in the stimulus individuals. These authors cite an (unpublished) thesis by Yfantis (1980), in which adult females were unable to distinguish between the odors of boys and girls who had not yet reached puberty. Likewise, the gender of adolescents was not discernible by their body odors, even though those of boys were more frequently rated as unpleasant than pleasant. There were no differences in frequencies of pleasant versus unpleasant ratings for adolescent girls' odors.

In an additional experiment (Doty *et al.*, 1978b), subjects assessed the relative pleasantness, intensity, and gender of gauze pads that had been worn overnight in the axillae of five male and five female adults. All odor donors were told not to use perfume or deodorants for 1 week, and not to bathe for 24 hr preceding the study. Few of the observers correctly identified the donors' gender at a level exceeding chance expectations. These negative results were attributed to the difficulty of the task (e.g., large number of odor stimuli; pads worn for 1 night only), as well as the lack of details given to subjects regarding the number of stimuli from each sex. Gender assignments correlated strongly with intensity and pleasantness ratings of axillary odors; with an inverse relationship found between the latter two variables. Regardless of the actual sex of the donors, stronger odors were usually rated as male, while relatively weak odors were judged to be from females (see also McBurney *et al.*, 1977). Based on these data, the authors cautioned that it is unlikely that human axillary odors alone "would allow for unequivocal establishment of gender in groups made up of heterogeneous individuals with diverse hygiene habits" (see also Russell, 1983).

Results and conclusions similar to the above were obtained from analogous studies of breath odors (Doty *et al.*, 1982). Male and female subjects reliably identified the gender of individuals who were following a routine of no oral hygiene. As for the experiments with axillary cues, breath odors of males were judged stronger and less pleasant than those of females, and gender determinations were therefore likely to have been based on this intensity/pleasantness dimension.

The lack of unambiguous qualitative differences between males and females in axillary and breath odors need not imply that there are no distinctive gender-correlated scents. Rather, it is likely that odors of various substances associated with reproductive physiology could serve as the basis for gender discrimination. Semen, for example, is a possible source of odors unique to males. Similarly, in females, numerous odorous secretions emanate from the vagina, upper reproductive tract, and accessory sex organs (see Section II,B). Odors from the breasts of lactating females could provide additional sex-specific cues.

Anecdotal reports of differential reactions of wild animals to men versus women (including attacks on women by grizzly bears) are sometimes attributed to menstrual odors (March, 1980). It has even been suggested that female reproductive odors may have limited the success of mixed-sex hunting parties in hunter/gatherer societies, and thus contributed to the sexual division of labor (Dobkin de Rios and Hayden, 1985). Experiments have yet to be conducted to test the hypothesis that such secretions may indeed be sources of odors by which humans can ascertain gender.

2. Kin versus Nonkin Discrimination

a. Mothers' Recognition of Offspring. The natural history of mother–infant interactions provides unique opportunities for the members of such dyads to have access to one another's odors. Breast-feeding infants have recurring, prolonged bouts of contact with their mother's bare flesh and concomitant bodily odors. At those same times, the proximity of the mother's nostrils to the infant (e.g., the top if its head) may expose her to odors characteristic of her neonate. Olfactory phenotypes may likewise be sampled while the mother kisses or nuzzles the baby. Reports from several laboratories show that infants' odors are reliably discriminated by their mothers and can therefore serve as the basis for early individual recognition.

The initial study by Schaal and colleagues (1980) tested maternal recognition of neonates' odors on days 2 through 10 following delivery. Cotton T-shirts worn by infants for 24–48 hr served as olfactory stimuli. To protect the stimulus shirts against odor contamination when an infant was held by the mother (or others), a second garment was worn over them. During repeated test trials, blindfolded mothers were presented with three soiled shirts (that of the subject's own infant along with two others), and asked to select the one that had been worn by their baby. Mothers identified their own infant's T-shirt at rates exceeding chance expectations on days 3 through 10 postpartum. In subsequent experiments, the proportion of correct maternal responses was shown to improve gradually over the first 10 days after they gave birth (Schaal, 1986). Increasing recognition of neonatal odors over this time period did not appear to be a function of enhanced odor sensitivity since olfactory detection thresholds (for pyridine) *rose* after day 3 (Schaal *et al.*, 1986).

Corroborating results were obtained in methodologically similar tests by Porter *et al.* (1983): when given a single trial with garments from two neonates, mothers accurately identified the one that had been worn by their own baby by olfactory cues alone. Odors of their neonates' soiled garments were also discriminated by 13 of 17 women who delivered by Caesarean section and therefore had little contact with their baby prior to tests conducted within 2 days of birth. Evidence of olfactory recognition of offspring as early as 6 hr postpartum has been reported for (blindfolded) mothers who sniffed the heads of their own and comparison infants (Russell *et al.*, 1983).

As pointed out by Kaitz *et al.* (1987), since subjects in the above experiments had not been screened for olfactory deficits, the data may actually underestimate odor discrimination capabilities of intact mothers. Accordingly, very high rates of olfactory recognition of neonates were recorded when mothers suffering noticeable olfactory impairment were excluded from the subject population. Ninety percent of the screened mothers who had only 10–60 min of pretest contact with their baby correctly identified that infant's T-shirt (three-choice test). Women with a minimum of 1 hr of neonatal contact evinced an accuracy rate of 100% on similar tests of offspring-odor discrimination.

The ability of mothers to recognize their offspring's odor is not restricted solely to the early postpartum period. Soiled T-shirts from 3–8 year olds were also identified by mothers of those children (Porter and Moore, 1981). To rule out the possibility that cues other than odors might be involved in T-shirt recognition, each stimulus garment was presented to the subjects in a separate cardboard container with a small opening cut in the lid. Mothers sampled the odors of soiled T-shirts by sniffing at the lid opening, and in 17 of 18 test trials correctly discriminated between their own child's garment and an identical shirt from an unfamiliar child of the same age.

b. Infants' Discrimination of Mother's Odor. Charles Darwin (1877), in his "biographical sketch of an infant" noted that his 1-month-old baby responded with visual fixation and "protrusion of his lips" when in the proximity of the mother's breast. Although he was not able to identify the stimulus attributes of the breast that elicited these observable behavioral patterns, Darwin expressed "doubt whether they had any connection with vision," but suggested a possible involvement of the sense of smell. Empirical support for this latter hypothesis appeared approximately 100 years later. In the prototypic experiment (Macfarlane, 1975), individual infants were placed on their back and two gauze odor pads positioned above the face so that they were suspended alongside each cheek. The infant's behavior was then recorded during two successive 60-sec trials, with the position of the two stimulus pads reversed between trials. Particular experimental conditions differed according to the ages of the infants and the combinations of odor stimuli to which they were exposed.

When tested in this manner, 17 of 20 infants (2–7 days old) spent a greater amount of time with their face turned in the direction of a pad that had been worn in contact with their mother's breast than toward a simultaneously present clean control pad. Additional tests were conducted to determine whether breast odors of nursing mothers are individually discriminable. Two-day-old infants responded similarly to a breast pad from their own lactating mother and an unfamiliar nursing female. At both 6 and 8–10 days of age, however, significantly more infants oriented for a longer time period toward their mother's breast pad compared with an unfamiliar female's pad. It was concluded from such preferential responsiveness to the maternal breast pads that infants can discriminate their mother by the unique odor of her breast.

Since Macfarlane's seminal study, considerable documentation of the salience of olfactory cues for neonates' recognition of their mother has appeared. Russell (1976) observed 6-week-old infants when presented individually with a breast pad from their mother, a breast pad from an unfamiliar mother, a clean pad, or one soiled with raw cow's milk. The pad from the infant's mother held 1–2 cm under the nostrils elicited sucking and orienting behavior that was "markedly different" from the responses to the other stimuli. These same infants did not display discriminative responses to breast odors of their own versus an unfamiliar mother during earlier test trials at 2 days and 2 weeks postpartum.

Using a variation of the testing procedure originally developed by Macfarlane, however, discrimination of mother's breast odor has been observed in infants as young as 3 days postpartum (Schaal *et al.*, 1980; Schaal, 1988a). Ongoing motor activity (head and arm movements) was reduced to a greater extent when an infant's nose came into contact with its mother's breast pad compared to either a clean pad or one from an unfamiliar lactating female.

Maternal olfactory cues other than those emanating from the breast may likewise be discriminated by neonates. Thus, in the study by Schaal *et al.* (1980), motor activity of aroused infants was also inhibited when the nose made contact with a gauze pad that had been worn against the mother's neck. It is not clear whether these infants were actually responding to maternal body odors per se since many of the stimulus pads had an obvious perfume scent. A series of analogous two-choice discrimination tests was conducted to assess infants' recognition of maternal axillary odors (Cernoch and Porter, 1985). Two-week-old breast-fed infants oriented preferentially toward gauze pads that had been worn in the axillary region of their mother when paired with pads from either nonparturient or unfamiliar lactating females. In contrast, bottle fed infants of this same age appeared unable to discriminate between axillary odors of their own mother and another bottle-feeding female, or a nonparturient woman. The most plausible explanations for this marked disparity in the behavior of bottle versus breast-feeding infants are (1) lactating females may produce odor cues that are especially salient for neonates and therefore more readily discriminated; (2) because of differences in early interactions with their mother, breast-fed infants may become more rapidly familiarized with her characteristic odor than is the case for bottle-feeders. These hypotheses are discussed further in Sections III,C and IV,A.

Children's preferential responsiveness to maternal odors is not limited to the first several weeks after birth. When tested with soiled T-shirts, 3- to 5-year-old children accurately discriminated their own mother's odor and indicated that they preferred it over odors from other women (Schaal *et al.*, 1980).

    c. Discrimination of Other Kin. Olfactory discrimination of kin beyond the mother–offspring dyad has been the topic of few empirical investigations. Whereas 2-week-old breast-feeding infants discriminate their own mother's axillary odor (as seen above), father's odor from this same source did not elicit preferential orientation when paired with axillary odors from an unfamiliar adult male (Cernoch and Porter, 1985). Conflicting results have been presented in the two reports of fathers tested for their ability to identify the odors of their own infants. Ten blindfolded fathers performed at a chance level when asked to smell the heads of three infants (24–48 hr old) and chose the one they believed to be their child (Russell *et al.*, 1983). Stimulus infants "generally slept through the procedure" and had been washed prior to the test. In two-choice discrimination tests using soiled T-shirts as stimuli, however, 26 of 30 fathers correctly identified their own infant's garment (<72 hr after birth) (Porter *et al.*, 1986). The disparity between these two studies could be a function of differential difficulty of the two test situations (i.e., two-choice and three-choice discrimination tasks). Furthermore, in this context, soiled garments may be more adequate sources of salient odor cues than are recently washed heads of infants. Additional odor discrimination tests demonstrated that aunts and grandmothers reliably identified T-shirts worn by their neonatal relatives when matched with a comparable garment from an unrelated, unfamiliar infant (Porter *et al.*, 1986).

    Sibling interactions are of particular relevance to the study of social development and the evolution of social behavior (e.g., Porter, 1989). Full siblings share a mean of 50% of their alleles as a function of common descent, and are therefore as closely related (genetically) as are parents and offspring. When their age difference is not too great, interactions with siblings typically constitute a large proportion of children's social behavior. Therefore, it may not be very surprising at this point that siblings have been found to be capable of discriminating one another by olfactory cues. T-shirts worn by 3- to 8-year-old children were correctly identified by their siblings, regardless of their sex (Porter and Moore, 1981). Moreover, adult subjects reliably discriminated between the odors of their sibling from whom they had been separated from 1–30 months and a stranger of the same age and sex (Porter *et al.*, 1986).

3. Discrimination of Self and Nonkin

    Tests of self-identification by olfactory cues have generally yielded positive results, but with a great deal of intersubject variability. Hold and Schleidt (1977) presented adult subjects with a sample of 10 soiled T-shirts and asked them to choose the one that had their own smell. This procedure was repeated three times for each participant and the criterion for recognition of one's own odor was two out of three correct choices. Fourteen of the 48 subjects (31%) reliably selected their own T-shirt by its odor. Hedonic ratings of own odor were higher for women than for men; women tended to categorize their own odor as pleasant while men more frequently rated their odor as unpleasant. This experiment was later replicated with two groups of participants: those who followed their normal hygienic practices, and those who only washed with unscented soap and avoided the use of perfumes and deodorant (Schleidt, 1980). The success rates of these two groups were similar in tests for own-odor recognition (the percentages of subjects who selected their own shirt in 2/3 trials were 26 and 31, respectively). In an attempt to assess the generality of these findings, the 10-choice odor-discrimination task as described above was conducted with three ethnic groups (Schleidt et al., 1981). The percentages of German, Italian, and Japanese subjects who identified the odor of their own soiled garment (in 2 of 3 trials) were 31, 38, and 25, respectively.

Soiled T-shirts have been used in three additional studies of self-recognition by odor cues. A significant proportion of adults identified their own shirt when included with a shirt from a strange man and one from a strange woman (Russell, 1976). Furthermore, 3 of 11 college students picked their own T-shirt from a sample of 12 stimuli ($p < 0.06$) (McBurney et al., 1977). Donors rated their own shirt as "less unpleasant" than did the other participants who sampled three garments in 9 of 11 cases. In a more recent similar experiment, a greater proportion of males than females failed to identify their own soiled T-shirt in a 10-choice odor discrimination task (Lord and Kasprzak, 1989). Failure to recognize one's own odor was also more common for smokers versus nonsmokers, and among women during the early phase of menses.

The ability to discriminate individuals by their characteristic odors is not restricted solely to biological kin. Thus, the rate of correct identification of spouses' odors was similar to that for own odor in a 10-choice soiled T-shirt test (Hold and Schleidt, 1977). Although German women tended to rate their partner's odor as "pleasant," Japanese and Italian women more often categorized the odor of their spouse's shirt as "unpleasant" (Schleidt et al., 1981). Men from these same ethnic groups classified their spouse's odor as "predominantly pleasant."

There are two reports of olfactory recognition among unrelated children (Verron and Gaultier, 1976; Marlier and Schaal, 1989). In the latter study, 8 of 18 blindfolded children (4–5 years old) were able to name the preschool classmate whose neck they smelled. Once again, females displayed more reliable recognition than males, and girls were more often correctly identified by their neck odor than were boys.

Learned discrimination of the odors of unfamiliar persons was investigated by Wallace (1977). Subjects were given repeated trials in which they attempted to distinguish between hand odors of the same two adults. After each trial, they were told whether they had made the correct choice. Over 30 trials, the majority of both men and women participants correctly discriminated between the hand odors of two individuals. Accuracy levels were higher for male/female stimulus pairs than for male/male or female/female pairs, and the performance of female subjects was superior to that of males.

4. Reproductive Phase and Sexual Attractants

Perhaps the issue of most widespread interest in regard to human social olfaction concerns the possible involvement of odors in sexual attraction. That is, do adult males and/or females produce specific odor signals that are sexually arousing to members of the opposite sex?

In at least some mammalian species, the attractiveness of females' scents to males is greatest during estrus. The presumed biological function of these cues is to enhance reproductive efficiency by increasing the likelihood that males will be sexually responsive to females during those times when mating may result in fertilization. Most owners of (intact) female dogs are well aware of the dramatic effects of their pets' odorous signals (when they are in heat) on male dogs in the neighborhood.

Michael and colleagues (e.g., Michael and Keverne, 1970; Michael et al., 1971, 1975a) published an influential series of articles claiming that male rhesus monkeys are sexually responsive to endocrine-dependent vaginal secretions from conspecific females. Behavioral observations and biochemical assays implicated several volatile aliphatic acids as active components of these complex mixtures.

Although Michael's original data and conclusions have become the subject of considerable controversy and debate (e.g., Goldfoot et al., 1976; Goldfoot, 1982; Rogel, 1978), they nonetheless stimulated further research on the possible production of sexual attractants by human females. Vaginal secretions from young women with no known gynecological problems were analyzed by gas chromatography (Michael et al., 1974). The relative proportions of aliphatic acids found in these samples were similar to those of female rhesus monkeys as discussed above (Section II). Moreover, the production of these acids increased near the middle of the menstrual cycle.

If vaginal aliphatic acids function as sexual signals in humans, one would expect their secretion rates to be positively correlated with males' hedonic ratings. The necessary experiments to test this hypothesis directly have yet to be conducted, although evaluations of vaginal odors throughout the menstrual cycle have been reported (Doty et al., 1975). Vaginal secretions from consecutive phases of the menstrual cycle were collected from four women and sampled by male and female subjects. Overall, vaginal odors were rated on the unpleasant side of a continuum ranging from pleasant to unpleasant, with samples from the preovulatory and ovulatory phases of the cycle rated "slightly weaker and less unpleasant" than those from the other phases. Thus, this *in vitro* test provided no evidence that vaginal odors during ovulation are attractive (or even pleasant) to adult males.

In a more naturalistic context, Morris and Udry (1978) assessed the influence of odors of aliphatic acids (the reputed rhesus monkey female sex attractants) on overt human sexual behavior. Every night throughout three menstrual cycles, women applied a treatment solution to the skin of their chest. Neither the participating women nor their husbands were told which solution, i.e., either a mixture of six synthetic aliphatic acids or one of three control substances, they were exposed to on any given night. Responses to daily questionnaires revealed no differential effects of the aliphatic acids versus control substances on the frequency of intercourse or the sexual motivation of either partner. Exposure to similar aliphatic acids was investigated further in a study whose subjects wore surgical masks impregnated with a mixture of these substances (Cowley *et al.*, 1977). Individuals exposed to aliphatic acids differed from controls in their judgments of men and women described as job candidates. Effects of the experimental treatment were most pronounced for ratings of male candidates by female judges. The results were difficult to interpret, however, since the direction and magnitude of the treatment effects varied across candidates.

The search for male olfactory attractants has centered on two steroid compounds that are known sexual signals in pigs. Androstenol (musk-scented) and androstenone (smelling like urine) are concentrated in the saliva of boars and elicit stereotyped mating postures in sows (Melrose *et al.*, 1974; Signoret, 1970). Commercially available sprays of these substances are used by pig breeders to facilitate artificial insemination.

The several attempts to evaluate responsiveness to androstenol and androstenone have yielded mixed, sometimes contradictory results. University students wearing surgical masks impregnated with androstenol were asked to assess written descriptions of alleged job applicants (Cowley *et al.*, 1977). Overall, ratings by the androstenol group did not differ reliably from those by students wearing untreated masks, even though androstenol did appear to influence the assessments of particular candidates.

In a variation of the above experiment, Kirk-Smith *et al.* (1978) had 12 male and 12 female subjects rate photographs of people while wearing an androstenol-treated or a clean surgical mask. Photographed women were judged "sexier, more attractive, and better" by the androstenol-exposed subjects (both males and females) than by the clean-mask controls. Individuals in the androstenol condition also rated stimulus men and women as "warmer."

To assess whether moods are influenced by androstenol, subjects placed a small quantity of this substance, or a placebo, on their upper lips each morning for 1 month (Benton, 1982). According to daily self-ratings, women exposed to androstenol were more submissive than the placebo group in the middle of their menstrual cycle. Ratings of additional moods, including "sexy/unsexy" did not, however, differ between the two conditions. Some evidence of mood alterations was also noted among women who were exposed to androstenone while judging photographs and descriptions of a stimulus male college student (Filsinger et al., 1984). In comparison to women in no-odor or control-odor conditions, those exposed to androstenone rated themselves as less sexy. Male subjects' moods were not affected by androstenone, nor were ratings of sexual attractiveness of the stimulus male (by either the male or female judges).

There appears to be only one reported study of the effects of androstenol placed directly on persons of the opposite sex (Black and Biron, 1982). Individual subjects interacted briefly with a confederate wearing androstenol or a control substance. Androstenol treatment had no noticeable influence on ratings of physical attractiveness of the opposite-sex confederate by either males or females.

It has been further suggested that androstenol may function as a "spacing pheromone" among men (Gustavson et al., 1987). Limited empirical support for this claim involves the use of treated toilet stalls in men's and women's restrooms. When androstenol was present, the use of particular stalls by males was less frequent than during (untreated) baseline periods or periods of androstenone treatment. Females, on the other hand, displayed no differences in frequencies of stall choices across treatment and control periods. Using similar methods, the rates of occupancy of chairs in a dentist's office were observed after one of them had been sprayed with androstenone (Kirk-Smith and Booth, 1980). Men were reported to avoid a seating location on days when it had been treated with a high level of androstenone as compared to untreated control days. Women, in contrast, more frequently selected a particular seat if it was androstenone-sprayed (but see Doty, 1981).

On balance, the experiments reviewed above provide no basis for concluding that human males or females produce odors functionally analogous to sexual attractants in other species. The few reports of positive results from in vitro studies of responsiveness to putative "sex pheromones" form an inconsistent pattern and are offset by the failure to find any effects in more natural contexts.

This does not, however, imply that bodily odors are of no significance for human sexual preferences and behavior. As recently discussed by Kirk-Smith and Booth (1987; see also Doty, 1981; Engen, 1982; Filsinger and Fabes, 1985), the meaning of particular scents is acquired through experience (i.e., conditioning and the context in which they are perceived). Therefore, the characteristic odor of one's lover may be arousing because of its association with intimacy and sexual activity. That same olfactory signal will probably be of little relevance to others. Moreover, personal odors that arouse passion in an intimate setting may not have the same effects in a different environment.

The high pleasantness ratings given by German couples to odors of T-shirts

worn by their own partner (Hold and Schleidt, 1977; Schleidt, 1980) are likely to
be a manifestation of such acquired odor hedonics. However, it should be pointed out that, in a subsequent experiment, Japanese and Italian couples, especially
women, did not rate their partners' odors as pleasant as did their German counterparts (Schleidt et al., 1981).

Mere exposure may also contribute to the subjective evaluation of scents,
including individual odors. An odor originally perceived as neutral or even
negative may be judged more positively with continued exposure and familiarization (e.g., Cain and Johnson, 1978). Therefore, recurring interactions among the
same individuals could further enhance the hedonic value of one another's odor.

5. Diet-Primed Differences

Ultimately, a person's odor is the product of an intricate interaction between
genotypically influenced variables and environmental factors (see Sections
II,D,1 and 3). If one excludes externally applied odorants, substances that are
ingested or inhaled are the environmental agents most likely to have an effect on
body odor. Accordingly, persons who are heavy smokers of tobacco products, or
those who routinely eat highly spiced or seasoned foods, may thereby incorpo-
rate traces of those substances into their olfactory phenotypes. Within several
hours after eating a meal containing large quantities of garlic, the pungent odor
of that plant may be detected emanating from the pores on the back of the hand.
Because such environmental influences are likely to be more variable and transient than are genotypic sources of body odors, they would be expected to
provide less reliable cues of individual or group identity. Nonetheless, when
genotype is held constant, dietary differences between individuals can be detected in their body odors. Adult subjects have greater difficulty discriminating
between palm odors of identical twins who eat the same diet as opposed to twins
fed markedly different diets (Wallace, 1977). Even trained tracking dogs make
more errors when tested for their ability to discriminate between soiled T-shirts
from monozygotic twins fed similar diets compared to their performance with
garments from such twins whose diets are dissimilar (Hepper, 1988).

B. PRESUMED PRIMING EFFECTS

Aside from their hypothesized functions as sexual attractants, or as potential
sources of information regarding the gender and endocrine status of conspecifics,
bodily odors might play a further role in reproduction through their effects on
relevant physiological processes. Particular attention has been given to the possibility that temporal parameters of human menstrual cycles may be susceptible
to olfactorily mediated perturbations. Synchronized menstrual cycles among
women who live together or otherwise frequently interact with one another are a
well-documented phenomenon. Over a period of several months beginning with

the start of the academic year, differences between the time of onset of menstruation decreased significantly for university students who were roommates or close friends (McClintock, 1971; Graham and McGrew, 1980; Quadagno et al., 1981).

McClintock (1971) also noted that students in an all-female college who interacted with males less than three times a week had significantly longer cycles than women spending more time with males. For women in coeducational universities, amount of social contact with males was *not* related to menstrual cycle length (Graham and McGrew, 1980; Quadagno et al., 1981). However, women who spent a minimum of two evenings per week with males displayed heightened ovulation rates (Veith et al., 1983). As suggested by Quadagno et al. (1981), differential correlations between time with males and cycle length for women on coeducational versus all-female campuses could be a reflection of differing rates of routine casual contact with men in these two environments. The sensory basis for the observed fluctuations in menstrual cycles and ovulation was not established in the above studies, but in each instance the authors discussed the likely involvement of olfactory signals.

In experiments designed to assess directly the possible influences of chemical cues on menstrual activity, women subjects have been exposed to axillary secretions from both male and female donors. Russell et al. (1980) monitored menstrual cycles of two groups of women: one treated with an extract of underarm perspiration from a single donor female, and a control group treated with plain alcohol. A sample of the appropriate experimental or control substance was applied to the upper lip (below the nostrils) of each participant three times a week over a 4-month period. By the end of the experimental treatment, onset of menstruation for those women exposed to the underarm extract was significantly closer to that of the donor than during the pretreatment month. Prior to the beginning of exposure to the axillary extract, the mean difference between donor and subjects in onset of menstruation was 9.3 days, as compared to a posttreatment mean difference of 3.4 days. During that same time span, control subjects showed no significant changes relative to the cycle of the donor female.

Although these data were interpreted as evidence that a donor woman's odor may alter endocrine cycles of other women, the authors cautioned that the reported effects could have been mediated by physiological systems other than olfaction per se. For example, active agents in the axillary extract could have been absorbed through the skin rather than stimulating the olfactory receptors. The validity of this study has been further questioned on methodological grounds (Doty, 1981). Subjects had been informed of the purpose of the experiment prior to the start of the treatment, and the odor donor also served as one of the experimenters, thereby allowing the opportunity for the results to be biased by nonolfactory social factors.

More recently, menstrual cycle responsiveness to axillary secretions from both male and female donors has been investigated in a series of double-blind experiments. Women who believed that they had normal menstrual cycles (ranging from 26 to 32 days) were assigned to the female-extract study (Preti *et al.*, 1986), while those reporting "aberrant" cycle length participated in the male-extract experiment (Cutler *et al.*, 1986). For each of these experiments, women were treated with axillary or control (ethanol) stimuli applied to their upper lip by a technician who was unaware of the particular treatment condition for any subject. The female subjects were not informed of the true purpose of the experiment.

Over a 2-month period, the mean difference in onset of menstruation between women treated with female axillary secretions and the donors of those stimuli decreased significantly from 8.3 to 3.9 days. No reliable change in onset of menses relative to that of the donors was observed among women in the ethanol control condition. Among the women treated with male axillary secretions for a 14-week period, those who were *not* sexually active evinced reduced variability in cycle length and a significantly greater proportion of "normal length" cycles as compared to control subjects. These same comparisons did not reach statistical significance when sexually active women were included in the analyses, suggesting the possibility that regular heterosexual contact "masks the influences of male extract" (Cutler *et al.*, 1986).

The preceding two studies represent the most well-controlled attempts to date to assess the influence of bodily chemical signals (from both male and female donors) on menstrual activity. Nonetheless, because of the limited subject populations and small numbers of menstrual cycles over which data were collected, the results should be considered preliminary (see also critiques of methodological details by Wilson, 1987, 1988). Furthermore, as was the case for the above-mentioned related experiment by Russell *et al.* (1980), the reported effects could have been mediated by percutaneous absorption of the chemical extracts, rather than by airborne odorants. The authors themselves recognize the limitations of these initial studies (Cutler *et al.*, 1986) and stress the need for "more carefully designed" experiments over longer time periods (Cutler, 1988).

C.   ONTOGENETIC MECHANISMS OF SOCIAL DISCRIMINATION

Elucidation of the underlying bases of olfactory signatures provides little information regarding the mechanisms by which individuals develop the ability to decode or discriminate those phenotypic traits. A person might be identified by a genetically determined chemical fingerprint, but what are the ontogenetic processes mediating recognition of that odor?

1.   Direct Familiarization

The most obvious means by which social recognition develops is that of direct familiarization. Indeed, there is no readily apparent alternative mechanism to explain individual recognition of unrelated persons. As a result of direct exposure and interactions, individuals become familiar and are subsequently discriminated, regardless of whether they are kin or unrelated. Moreover, actual contact per se is not necessary for the mediation of recognition by this mechanism, providing that one becomes sufficiently acquainted with an individual's salient phenotypic traits. Thus, effective recognition may be accomplished through prior exposure and familiarization with a photograph, a voice over the telephone, or other characteristic signatures.

The ontogeny of the recognition of biological kin in our own species is best studied with neonates who have had only limited contact (ideally, none) with relatives (Porter, 1991). Early discriminative responsiveness to maternal axillary odors by breast-fed, but not bottle-fed infants, as discussed above, may be a function of differential familiarity with discernible olfactory cues (Cernoch and Porter, 1985). During the lengthy recurring bouts of sucking at the mother's breast, an infant is exposed to her bare flesh and may thereby become rapidly acquainted with her unique body odor. Bottle-feeders, because they do not necessarily have the same degree of early exposure to maternal chemical signatures, may require a longer time to become familiar with those odors.

Rapid familiarization could also play a meaningful role in early recognition of an offspring's odors. Mothers whose mean duration of pretest contact with their neonates ranged from only 30 to 35 min, nonetheless correctly identified the odors of those newborns (Kaitz et al., 1987; Russell et al., 1983). Mean lengths of interaction with infants preceding successful discrimination of their odors by fathers, grandmothers, and aunts were 2.6, 1.4, and 0.8 hr, respectively (Porter et al., 1986). These data argue against the need for long-term exposure to infants for the development of olfactory recognition of those same babies. To rule out the possible effect of short-term contact, however, odors of stimulus kin would have to be recognized with *no* prior direct exposure. It is interesting in this regard that 10 women who had only 1–9 min of contact with their neonates immediately following delivery failed to identify their newborn's garment in a three-choice discrimination test (Kaitz et al., 1987). The authors caution that one should not conclude that mothers require more than 9 min of exposure to their infant's odor for recognition to develop. Rather, during the brief period of early contact in the delivery room, the scent of the stimulus infants may have been masked by other strong odorants (e.g., blood, stool, amniotic fluid). Results of an additional experiment suggest that an extended period of direct contact with the neonate immediately after delivery may enhance the development of maternal recognition of that infant's odor (Schaal and Kontar, 1986). Mothers whose infant had been placed on the breast for 30–40 min beginning at birth and stimulated to suckle were more accurate at discriminating their own offspring's odor over the first 10 days postpartum than were mothers given only 5 min early contact with their newborn.

An alternative approach to the investigation of early exposure and the development of olfactory discrimination is the use of artificial odorants whose presentation can be more precisely described and controlled than that of naturally occurring body odors. Beginning on the day of birth, infants were exposed to the odor of cherry or ginger for a period of approximately 24 hr (Balogh and Porter, 1986). A gauze pad treated with the appropriate odorant was taped to the inside of each infant's bassinet, behind and slightly above their head. Following the treatment period, subjects were tested for their responses to the exposure odor and a novel odor simultaneously presented on either side of the face. Day-old girls oriented in the direction of the exposure odor for significantly longer than toward the novel stimulus. Male infants, however, did not respond differentially to the exposure and novel odors.

These data suggest that familiarization with a particular olfactory stimulus shortly after birth may be sufficient for infants (at least females) to develop preferences for that odor. The failure of boys to respond discriminatively to strong odorants to which they had been exposed might have been an artifact of the testing procedure. Boys were much more likely than girls to turn their head in one direction (most often the right) at the beginning of the test and remain in that position throughout the trial. This directional bias could have overridden any odor-mediated response tendencies in male neonates. On the other hand, these results could be an early manifestation of true life-long sex differences in olfactory perception or sensitivity; superior performance by females on odor discrimination and detection tasks has been reported with older subjects ranging from childhood to over 90 years of age (e.g., Doty, 1981; Doty et al., 1984; Koelega and Köster, 1974).

2. Familial Resemblance

To the extent that close kin share similar phenotypic traits, individuals with whom one has had no prior direct contact may still be recognized as kin. Already familiar kin (or their signatures) could be used as standards against which to compare others. Those whose salient signatures match or closely approximate the standard might thereby be discriminated. For example, a strange may be suspected of being a long-lost relative because he has the familiar "family nose." This recognition mechanism, commonly referred to as phenotype-matching, is similar to direct familiarization in that it is also based on exposure and familiarity. In this instance, however, the familiarization is of an indirect nature; individuals are discriminated not because of direct previous contact, but as a function of their phenotypic resemblance to relatives with whom one is already acquainted, or even to oneself (Porter and Blaustein, 1989).

Subjective anecdotal accounts suggest that early recognition of newborn infants may be facilitated by their olfactory resemblance to other family members. Several of the mothers and fathers who correctly identified their neonate's T-shirt in tests of olfactory recognition remarked that the selected garment had a familiar smell or one that was similar to the odor of other close relatives (e.g., the other parent or an older sibling) (Porter et al., 1983, 1986). To assess empirically the hypothesis that humans may indeed be capable of detecting olfactory resemblance among family members, adult subjects were asked to match the odors of T-shirts that had been worn by mothers and their 3- to 8-year-old children (Porter et al., 1985). Subjects in these experiments were neither related to nor familiar with the stimulus mothers and offspring. In one test trial, participants sampled the odor of a child's shirt then attempted to select the garment worn by the mother of that child from among an array of shirts from four adult females. The same subjects were also presented with the opposite task, in which they were given shirts from four children and instructed to choose the one that most closely matched the odor of a particular mother. For both test conditions, the proportion of correct choices from among the four comparison olfactory stimuli was significantly greater than expected by chance, indicating that mothers and their 3- to 8-year-old children share perceptibly similar odors.

While such odor resemblance among close kin could be a function of their overlapping genotypes, shared environments might also give rise to similar body odors in mothers and their offspring. Therefore, an additional experiment investigated whether individuals who are *not* genetically related but who share similar diets and are otherwise exposed to comparable household odors develop similar body odors. When the same procedures as for the mother–offspring odor-matching tests were used, but with stimulus shirts worn by husbands and wives, reliable pairings of spouse odors were not observed. The differential success in matching odors of mothers/offspring versus husbands/wives implies that environmental similarity may not be sufficient for nonkin to develop pronounced odor similarity. Rather, olfactory resemblance in kin appears to be mediated at least partially by underlying genotypic similarity.

Although the odors of genetic kin appear to be similar, they are not functionally identical. Parents displayed no problems in distinguishing between the odors of T-shirts from two of their own children, i.e., they correctly associated each of the soiled T-shirts with the particular child who had worn it (Porter and Moore, 1981). Since the 3- to 8-year-old siblings had been exposed to similar environmental cues, the most plausible source of odor differences among members of this kin class is genotypic variability (on average, full siblings share 50% of their alleles as a function of direct descent). Therefore, if resemblance between odor phenotypes is positively correlated with genotypic resemblance, the odors of siblings and other close kin should be more similar than the odors of nonkin, but *not* identical (with the possible exception of monozygotic twins). Thus, according to this model, olfactory familial resemblance is a function of similarity between individuals' distinct odor phenotypes, rather than to a family label per se.

Our emphasis on the genetic basis of kinship-correlated odor resemblance does not imply that such similarity is entirely impervious to environmental perturbations. It will be recalled that odors of identical twins are more easily discriminated by both conspecifics and trained dogs if those siblings had been eating dissimilar rather than identical diets (Hepper, 1988; Wallace, 1977).

IV. DISCUSSION AND CONCLUSIONS

A. FUNCTIONAL SIGNIFICANCE OF OLFACTORY RECOGNITION

Humans are capable of identifying individual conspecifics by a variety of phenotypic traits involving several sensory modalities (e.g., vision, audition, olfaction). This functional redundancy in recognizable signatures attests to the importance of social discrimination both during our day-to-day existence and from a more ultimate genetic perspective. On one hand, discrimination of individuals or group members is a necessary prerequisite for the development of social attachments and relationships, as well as of complex heterogeneous organizations or societies. Theoretical biologists further argue that an ability to recognize kin accurately would facilitate nepotistic interactions and appropriate choice of mates, and could therefore be a significant factor in the evolution of social behavior.

Olfaction is obviously not the most important modality for mediating social interactions in our own species, but this channel of communication does have properties that may be especially relevant for effective social discrimination. Olfactory signatures that have a genotypic basis should remain relatively constant over an individual's lifetime in spite of minor environmentally induced modifications. Unlike visual appearance and voice quality, which change drastically from birth through old age, characteristic odor phenotypes may be quite stable. An initial attempt to test this hypothesis involved adult full siblings that had been living apart, with no direct contact, for up to 30 months (mean = 7 months; Porter *et al.*, 1986). A statistically significant proportion of these individuals correctly identified a T-shirt soiled by their separated sibling when paired with a second shirt worn by an unfamiliar person of the same age and sex. Olfactory signatures provided a reliable (sufficiently invariant) means of recognizing familiar siblings even after the prolonged period of separation.

The temporal parameters of olfactory memory may be further conducive to long-term social recognition through this modality. While typical retention curves for visual stimuli show a steep decline over a period of several months, performance on odor recognition tests remain relatively constant even after a 12-month interval (Engen and Ross, 1973). Engen (1977, 1982) noted that performance on visual recognition tests is superior to that of odor recognition tests conducted immediately after stimulus exposure. Following an interval of 4 months, however, the accuracy rate for recognizing odors was greater than for picture recognition. According to Engen and Ross (1973), "the odor-coding process . . . is less accurate but far more enduring than coding of the major sense modalities." This hypothesis implies that once they become familiar, olfactory signatures may be discriminated for longer periods of time than other phenotypic traits. It should be emphasized, however, that odor memory and its relationship to social discrimination are not well understood at present.

From the studies reviewed above, it appears that neonates may be particularly sensitive to olfactory cues, especially those from lactating females. Discrimination of mothers' individual odors by their breast-feeding newborns is evident by 3 days postpartum (Schaal et al., 1980). This is also approximately the earliest age at which discrimination of the mother's voice has been documented (DeCasper and Fifer, 1980), and several weeks before unambiguous visual recognition of the maternal face (reviewed by Porter, 1991). Because infants are responsive to maternal odors shortly after birth, those cues might contribute to the initial stages of the developing mother–infant relationship.

Even (female) infants who had been bottle-fed since birth oriented preferentially toward breast odors of unfamiliar lactating females at 2 weeks of age (Makin and Porter, 1989). Such positive responsiveness was not observed when girls in this same feeding condition were tested with axillary odors from lactating females. Once again, boys (also bottle-feeders) did not display the same odor discrimination as girls; their responses to a breast pad from a lactating female were indistinguishable from those to a clean control pad.

It is proposed from the data currently available that lactating females of our own species emit chemical cues that serve two distinct functions: (1) unique odor signatures enable infants to discriminate their own mother (emanating from the breast and axillae); and (2) a general attractant, associated with the breast region, to which infants (at least girls) respond regardless of their feeding history and prior experience with the stimulus female. Early attraction to breast odors may in turn increase the neonate's exposure to the maternal chemical signature and potentiate the process of familiarization and the development of individual olfactory discrimination.

B. FROM BIOLOGY TO CULTURE

When applied to a species in its classical sense, the label "microsmatic" denotes that olfaction has little, if any, salience in the regulation of behavior (see Section I,B). The acuity of humans for biological odors is, however, substantiated by the laboratory experiments reviewed above. This set of data is dependent to a great extent on forced-choice procedures focusing a subject's attention onto selected olfactory features of conspecifics and thus maximizing their performance in a given context. Therefore, the results of the laboratory studies cannot be directly extrapolated to other contexts, or to normal life circumstances. Also, given the present state of the art, they predict poorly the degree of actual use of olfaction in controlling the flux of social behavior. A detailed discussion of this issue (which is beyond the scope of this article) should not overlook another corpus of information reflecting human reliance on olfactory cues in real life, viz. introspective and detailed descriptive case studies by clinical psychologists and psychiatrists (e.g., Ellis, 1905; Daly and White, 1930; Brill, 1932; Laird, 1934; Bieber, 1959; Kalogerakis, 1963; Peto, 1973), observational and representational data from given cultural groups collected by anthropologists (e.g., Roubin, 1980; Howse, 1986, 1987; Seeger, 1988) and human ethologists (e.g., Eibl-Eibesfeldt, 1984), and large-panel questionnaire studies of consumers.

For example, Todd (1979) reports the case of a 13-year-old boy who emitted a "bad body odor," a trait that induced constant stigmatizing by his classmates and resulted in social rejection and depression. When a defect in trimethylamine metabolism was diagnosed and the boy's diet strictly managed, the olfactory symptoms disappeared and subsequent social reintegration occurred. Another example concerns a mother who rejected her newborn because "he didn't smell right" (Curtis-Jenkins, 1975). In non-Western cultures, however, different attitudes to conspecific odor are exhibited by frequent sniffing directed at others. For example, in the Amazonian Yanomamö or the New Guinean Kanum-Irebe, rubbing another's body and then sniffing one's fingers are common acts (Alès, 1987, Schulze-Westrum, 1968). A detailed descriptive study of olfactory behavior in such "odor-seeking cultures," would no doubt further elucidate the olfactory modulation of behavior in our own species.

Taken together, these sources provide sufficiently persuasive evidence that body odors (resulting from natural or culturally modified substrates) make a notable contribution to the social–perceptual world of humans in both Western and non-Western societies. The universal use of extraneous odorants over the human body implies that social olfaction remains salient as a communicative channel. But does it follow necessarily that odorous materials produced by the body itself are unimportant because they are removed or masked? While this argument is implicit in many recent articles on the topic (e.g., Hall, 1969; Mykytowycz, 1985), it can be contested for at least two reasons: the suppressive activities (unless they rely on shaving or cutting off) are very short-lived, and may actually have opposite effects on body odors (e.g., bathing favors an increased rate of bacterial multiplication on the skin (Selwyn, 1982), and hence, a rapid restoration of the previous odor profile). Furthermore, the extraneous odorants used as cosmetics form a mixture with the materials already present on the skin, which may disperse their olfactory power and thus preserve individualized labels. In summary, the act of anointing one's body with artificial odors adds complexity to the odors produced by the human chemoemitting system and should be considered in any extensive theory of human olfactory communication.

The underlying motives and techniques of suppressing naturally produced odorants and adding artificially fashioned ones can be exquisitely diverse among distinct cultural groups, or among the varied life-styles within a culture. While suppressive activities are motivated by concerns of purity, cleanliness, and health, additive activities tend to be justified by more varied rationales. They can carry different meanings which are sent redundantly through other sensory channels. Three main categories of social meanings can be suggested:

1. "I am from the same/different group as yourself," group levels ranging from the culture as a whole to the nuclear family. Largey and Watson (1972) and Corbin (1982; see also König, 1972) have abundantly discussed the role of real or alleged olfactory cues in racial, social class, or urban/rural differentiation in both past and modern Western societies. Comparable examples can be found in non-Western societies: In the Nuba (Sudan), olfactory sameness is socially enforced and fosters group integration (Ebin, 1980); in the Near and Middle East, strangers are welcomed and integrated into the community after several perfuming rituals (Aubaille-Sallenave, 1987), which could be seen as olfactory allomarking practices. As a result of creating or accepting an olfactory label that is in harmony with the expectations of a given social group, individuals reduce the risks of being stigmatized.

2. Another category of potential olfactory signals focuses on basic biological differences between individuals of the group: "I am of the same/different age or sex as yourself." In certain societies, the practice of additive activities is regulated by rigid rules, thus stratifying the group members into age categories. Even if perfuming is widely used by both sexes, it seems that in most cultures, including our own, females are more fond of artificial scents than males. Furthermore, this quantitative difference is reinforced by the application of gender-stereotyped qualitatively distinct odors, which therefore enhances olfactory sexual dimorphism.

3. Finally, artificial odors can bear indications about an individual's preparedness for particular social interactions, especially relevant to sexual attraction and mate choice: "I am a potential mate for you." Seductive odors are in use almost everywhere; in Melanesia, for example, men wear a strong musky aromatic leaf during dances (Davenport, 1965); in Nauru (Oceania), women stand in steam saturated with a certain odor, a practice after which "all men fell in love of you" (Petit-Skinner, 1976); in the Yanomamö, males carry olfactory charms in their arm adornments that are intended to attract women's favors (Alès, 1987). These examples are not far from the fondness of European and American males for perfumes composed of androstenone, advertized as being an unresistible sexual attractant.

The social effects of artificial odors are not necessarily seen as antagonistic to those of self-produced odors. Rather, they may enhance olfactory signals previously produced by the organism itself. Some authors have argued that perfumes, especially when applied on erogenic zones, function as supranormal variants of natural olfactants (Freytag, 1972). A brief return to laboratory data will help us to show that artificial scents often operate in the same functional ensemble as biological odors. Indeed, manufactured fragrances can acquire a psychobiological meaning in the same way as naturally occurring odorants. Active newborns aged 3 to 10 days responded similarly to the odor of perfume present on their mother's neck and to the intact odor of their mother's breast (Schaal, 1986). Such odor contingency learning can be established very swiftly by associative processes or mere exposure. Two-week-old babies display preferential head turning responses toward the perfume that had been systematically paired with breast feeding during the 14 previous days (Schleidt and Genzel, 1990). Such an olfactory learning could even be acquired after only one 30-minute episode of contingency between an artificial odor and breast- or bottle-feeding (Sullivan, 1990). The proneness of learning of new olfactants has also been demonstrated separately from the feeding context. Lott *et al.* (1989) have shown that the presentation of a novel odor during a 15-min massage period is sufficient to bias the preferences in favor of this odor in 4- to 16-hr-old neonates. A similar shift in olfactory preferences could be obtained in 2-day-old neonates after they had been merely exposed to perfumes for the previous 24 hr while laying in their crib (Balogh and Porter, 1986). Human newborns, aside from being able to form an association between odors produced by their mother and the whole stimulatory context she provides, can also acquire similar associations with artificial odors. Such odor learning, whether mediated by social interactions or not, undoubtedly occurs further in children and adults, specifically in emotion-primed situations. Kirk-Smith *et al.* (1983) present evidence that a familiar odor (even when administered at subliminal levels) can be readily associated with a mildly stressful event and that it can elicit measurable attitudinal changes when presented at a later time. They suggest that "a natural odour could (similarly) come to acquire a signal value without a recipient being aware of an initial pairing, or its later initiation."

It is obvious that a life-long process of olfactory enculturation is at work, beginning at birth (and even before, the fetus being exposed to the aromas of maternal diet; Schaal, 1988a,b). It logically follows that artificial, but also natural, odors should be especially salient in the context of cultural groups in which they have acquired psychobiological meaning. That most individuals show a relatively positive or neutral attitude or behavior toward the odor of related/familiar conspecifics, and at the same time develop overt avoidance toward the body odor of unfamiliar people, may reflect such a phenomenon. Yet, this does not mean that culturally manipulated odor signals contribute to rigid closure of human groups and to their isolation. A multitude of human cultures indeed use environmental substances which emit subjectively similar odorants (e.g., musky or floral notes) and have developed widely overlapping olfactory categorizations, such as "what is nice smelling is good" (Loudon, 1977; Dupire, 1987; Schleidt *et al.*, 1988). Finally, the permanent chemical base produced by the body itself should remain the common denominator of the human olfactory communicative code.

V. SUMMARY

The responsiveness of humans to conspecific chemical cues as well as their rate of production of diverse potential olfactory signals suggest that it may be inappropriate to characterize members of our own species as "microsmatic."

Skin glands of presumed semiochemical significance are distributed over the entire body surface, with localized dense aggregations occurring in sites such as the axillary, scalp, areolar, and pubogenital areas. Topographical variation in the amount of glandular secretions/excretions is correlated with structural and physiological modifications that potentially enhance their communicative efficacy (e.g., increased vascularization, thick hair growth). Perceptible odors emanating from individuals are the result of a complex interaction between genetically influenced factors (e.g., distribution of skin glands, endocrine and metabolic processes) and environmental variables (diet, chemical action of microorganisms, climate, aerial chemical ecology).

Distinctive body odors provide a reliable basis for social discrimination. Thus, within hours of delivery mothers (and other family members) recognize the odor of their neonate. Newborn infants likewise respond preferentially to breast and axillary odors emanating from their own lactating mother. Olfactory cues have also been implicated in recognition of self and unrelated individuals, and in gender discrimination.

The primary ontogenetic mechanism involved in the recognition of the odors of individuals (or of other social categories) is familiarization arising from direct exposure. Recognition of kin may also be facilitated by discernible similarity (genetically mediated) in their olfactory signatures.

At present, data from studies of the possible role of olfactory cues in human sexual behavior and related endocrine processes are ambiguous and provide no clear evidence of general sex attractants produced by either sex. Odors may nonetheless contribute to sexual arousal through the association of specific scents with previous erotic experiences or particular individuals.

Acknowledgments

The authors wish to acknowledge the following sources of support for this project: Grant no. HD-15051 from the NICHD, U.R.A. 315 of the CNRS, Peabody College of Vanderbilt University, and Laboratoire de Comportement Animal, INRA-Nouzilly. NATO Collaborative Research Grant no. 366/87 and the Roudnitska Foundation provided the opportunity for the authors to prepare the final draft of this manuscript in the Virgin Falls Valley (Tennessee), the Falaise de Bagneux (Paris), and at La Jeunerie (Touraine). The assistance of Anne-Yvonne Jacquet and Claude Kervella is greatly appreciated.

References

Adachi, B. (1937). Der Rassengeruch nebst dem Rassenunterschied in Schweissdrüsen. *Z. Rassenkd.* **6**, 273–307.

Adams, N. A., and Nachtigall, P. E. (1988). Chemical communication in dolphins: Chemical constituents of the perianal gland. *Congr. Chem. Signals Vertebr., 5th,* Oxford.

Adams, M. G. (1980). Odour-producing organs of mammals. *Symp. Zool. Soc. London* **45**, 57–86.

Agache, P., and Blanc, D. (1982). Current status in sebum knowledge. *Int. J. Dermatol.* **21**, 304–315.

Agache, P., Blanc, D., Barrand, C., and Laurent, R. (1980). Sebum levels during the first year of life. *Br. J. Dermatol.* **103**, 643–649.

Albone, E. S. (1984). "Mammalian Semiochemistry." Wiley, Chichester.

Albone, E. S., Gosden, P. E., and Ware, G. C. (1977). Bacteria as a source of chemical signals in mammals. *In* "Chemical Signals in Vertebrates" (D. M. Müller-Schwarze and M. M. Mozell, eds.), Vol. 1, pp. 35–43. Plenum, New York.

Alès, C. (1987). Les parfums végétaux des Yanomamï (Indïens du Venezuela). *In* "Parfums de plantes" (G. Meurgues and F. Aubaile-Sallenave, eds.), pp. 242–246. MNHN, Paris.

Amoore, J. E., Forester, L. J., and Buttery, R. G. (1975). Specific anosmia to 1-pyrroline: The spermous primary odor. *J. Chem. Ecol.* **1**, 229–310.

Amoore, J. E., Pelosi, P., and Forester, M. J. (1977). Specific anosmias to 5-androst-16-en-3-one and ω-pentadecalactone: The urinous and musky primary odors. *Chem. Senses Flavour* **2**, 401–425.

Arnaud, M. J. (1988). The metabolism of coffee constituents. *In* "Coffee" (R. J. Clarke and R. Macrae, eds.), Vol. 3, pp. 33–55. Elsevier, Amsterdam.

Aubaile-Sallenave, F. (1987). Les parfums dans le monde musulman. *In* "Parfums de plantes" (G. Meurgues and F. Aubaile-Sallenave, eds.), pp. 165–167. MNHN, Paris.

Baker, J. R. (1974). "Race." Oxford Univ. Press, London.

Balogh, R. D., and Porter, R. H. (1986). Olfactory preferences resulting from mere exposure in human neonates. *Infant Behav. Dev.* **9**, 395–401.

Bang, B. G., and Cob, S. (1968). The size of the olfactory bulb in 109 species of birds. *Auk* **85**, 55–61.

Bauchot, R. (1981). Etude comparative des volumes relatifs des bulbes olfactifs chez les vertébrés: L'homme est-il microsmatique? *J. Psychol. Norm. Pathol.* **1**, 71–80.

Baum, J. D. (1980). Parent–offspring relations in man. *J. Reprod. Fertil.* **62**, 651–655.

Beauchamp, G. E., Doty, R. L., Moulton, D. G., and Mugford, R. A. (1976). The pheromone concept in mammalian chemical communication: A critique. *In* "Mammalian Olfaction, Reproductive Processes, and Behavior" (R. L. Doty, ed.), pp. 143–160. Academic Press, New York.

Benfenati, A., and Brillanti, F. (1939). Sulla distribuzione delle ghiandole sebacee nella cute del corpo umano. *Arch. Ital. Dermatol.* **15**, 33–41.

Benton, D. (1982). The influence of androstenol—a putative human pheromone—on mood throughout the menstrual cycle. *Biol. Psychol.* **15**, 249–256.

Berglund, B., Berglund, U., Högman, L., and Olsson, M. J. (1988). The influence of radiant heat on odor perception. *8th Bienn. Congr. Euro. Chemorecept. Res. Organ.*, p. 62. Warwick, U.K.

Bibel, D. J., and Lovell, D. J. (1976). Skin flora maps: A tool in the study of cutaneous ecology. *J. Invest. Dermatol.* **67**, 265–269.

Bieber, I. (1959). Olfaction in sexual development and adult sexual organization. *Am. J. Psychother.* **13**, 851–859.

Bird, S., and Gower, D. G. (1981). The validation and use of a radioimmunoassay for 5-androst-16-en-3-one in human axillary collection. *J. Steroid. Biochem.* **14**, 213–219.

Bird, S., and Gower, D. G. (1982). Axillary 5-androst-16-en-3-one, cholesterol and squalene in men: Preliminary evidence for 5-androst-16-en-3-one being a product of bacterial action. *J. Steroid Biochem.* **17**, 517–522.

Bird, S., and Gower, D. G. (1983). Estimation of the odorous steroid, 5-androst-16-en-3-one, in human saliva. *Experientia* **39**, 790–792.

Black, S. L., and Biron, C. (1982). Androstenol as a human pheromone: No effect on perceived physical attractiveness. *Behav. Neural Biol.* **34**, 326–330.

Blaustein, A. R., and Porter, R. H. (1990). The ubiquitous concept of recognition, with special reference to kin. *In* "Interpretation and Explanation in the Study of Behavior" (H. E. Bekoff and D. Jamieson, eds.), Vol. 1, pp. 123–148. Westview Press, Boulder, Colorado.

Botelho, S. Y., Brook, F. P., and Shelley, W. B., eds. (1969). "Exocrine Glands." Univ. of Pennsylvania Press, Philadelphia.

Bourke, J. G. (1891). "Scatologic Rites of all Nations." Lowdermilk, Washington.

Brand, J. M., and Galask, R. P. (1986). Trimethylamine: The substance mainly responsible for the fishy odor often associated with bacterial vaginosis. *Obstet. Gynecol.* **68**, 682–685.

Brill, A. A. (1932). The sense of smell in the neuroses and psychoses. *Psychoanal. Q.* **1**, 7–42.

Broca, P. (1888). "Mémoires d'Anthropologie," Vol. 5. Reinwald, Paris.

Brooksbank, B. W. L. (1962). Urinary excretion of androst-16-en-3-α-ol. Levels in normal subjects and effects of treatment with trophic hormones. *J. Endocrinol.* **24**, 435–444.

Brooksbank, B. W. L., Brown, R., and Gustafsson, J. A. (1974). The detection of 5-androst-16-en-3-ol in human male axillary sweat. *Experientia* **30**, 864–865.

Brown, R. E. (1979). Mammalian social odors: A critical review. *Adv. Study Behav.* **10**, 103–162.

Brown, R. E., and Macdonald, D. W., eds. (1985). "Social Odors in Mammals." Oxford Univ. Press, Oxford.

Burton, J. C. (1972). Factors affecting the rate of sebum excretion in man. *J. Soc. Cosmet. Chem.* **24**, 241–258.

Burton, J. C., and Rook, A. (1986). The ages of man and their dermatoses. *In* "Textbook of Dermatology" (A. Rook *et al.*, eds.), pp. 265–283. Blackwell, Oxford.

Burton, J. C., Shuster, S., Cartlidge, M., Libman, L. J., and Martell, U. (1973). Lactation, sebum excretion and melanocyte-stimulating hormone. *Nature (London)* **243**, 349–350.

Burton, J. C., Shuster, S., and Cartlidge, M. (1975). The sebotrophic effect of pregnancy. *Acta Derm.-Venereol.* **55**, 11–13.

Cain, W. S. (1974). Contribution of the trigeminal nerve to perceived odor magnitude. *Ann. N.Y. Acad. Sci.* **237**, 28–34.

Cain, W. S., and Johnson, F., Jr. (1978). Lability of odor pleasantness: Influence of mere exposure. *Perception* **7**, 459–465.

Cave, A. J. (1988). Note on olfactory activity in Mysticetes. *J. Zool.* **214**, 307–311.

Cernoch, J. M., and Porter, R. H. (1985). Recognition of maternal axillary odors by infants. *Child Dev.* **56**, 1593–1598.

Champion, R. H. (1986). Disorders of sweat glands. *In* "Textbook of Dermatology" (A. Rook *et al.*, eds.), pp. 1881–1896. Blackwell, Oxford.

Chen, S., Zieve, C., and Mahadevan, V. (1970). *J. Lab. Clin. Med.* **75**, 1628–1635.

Clark, L., and Mason, J. R. (1987). Olfactory discrimination of plant volatiles by European starlings. *Anim. Behav.* **35**, 227–235.

Claus, R., and Alsing, W. (1976). Occurrence of 5-andros-16-en-3-one, a boar pheromone, in man and its relationship to testosterone. *J. Endocrinol.* **68,** 483–484.

Cohen, I. T., Sherwin, B. B., and Fleming, A. S. (1987). Food cravings, mood and the menstrual cycle. *Horm. Behav.* **21,** 457–470.

Conckle, J. P., Camp, B. S., and Welch, B. E. (1975). Trace composition of human respiratory gas. *Arch. Environ. Health* **30,** 290–295.

Corbin, A. (1982). "Le Miasme et la Jonquille, l'Odorat et l'Imaginaire Social au 18-19ème siècle." Aubier, Paris.

Cowley, J. J., Johnson, A. L., and Brooksbank, B. W. L. (1977). The effect of two odorous compounds on performance in an assessment-of-people test. *Psychoneuroendocrinology* **2,** 159–172.

Cunlife, W. J., Burton, J. C., and Shuster, S. (1975). Effect of local temperature variation on sebum excretion rate. *Br. J. Dermatol.* **83,** 650–653.

Curtis-Jenkins, G. H. (1975). As discussant of J. S. Rosenblatt, Prepartum and postpartum regulation of maternal behavior in the rat. *Ciba Found Symp.* **33,** 34.

Cutler, W. B. (1988). Reply to Wilson (Letter to the editor). *Horm. Behav.* **22,** 272–277.

Cutler, W. B., Preti, G., Krieger, A., Huggins, G. R., Garcia, C. R., and Lawley, H. J. (1986). Human axillary secretions influence women's menstrual cycles: The role of donor extract from men. *Horm. Behav.* **20,** 463–473.

Daly, C. D., and White, R. S. (1930). Psychic reactions to olfactory stimuli (a preliminary paper). *Br. J. Med. Psychol.* **10,** 70–87.

Darwin, C. (1877). A biographical sketch of an infant. *Mind* **7,** 285–294.

Davenport, W. (1965). Sexual patterns and their regulation in a society of the southwest Pacific. *In* "Sex and Behavior" (F. A. Beach, ed.), pp. 164–207. Wiley, New York.

Davis, R. G. (1973). Olfactory psychophysical parameters in man, rat, dog and pigeon. *J. Comp. Physiol. Psychol.* **85,** 221–232.

DeCasper, A. J., and Fifer, W. P. (1980). Of human bonding: Newborns prefer their mothers' voices. *Science* **208,** 1174–1176.

Dietel, K. (1978). Morphological and functional development of the skin. *In* "Perinatal Physiology" (U. Stawe, ed.), pp. 761–773. Plenum, New York.

Dirren, H., Robinson, A. B., and Pauling, L. (1975). Sex-related patterns in the profiles of human urinary amino-acids. *Clin. Chem. (Winston-Salem, N.C.)* **21,** 1970–1975.

Dobkin de Rios, M. D., and Hayden, B. (1985). Odorous differentiation and variability in the sexual division of labor among hunter/gatherers. *J. Hum. Evol.* **14,** 219–228.

Doty, R. L., ed. (1976). "Mammalian Olfaction, Reproductive Processes, and Behavior." Academic Press, New York.

Doty, R. L. (1981). Olfactory communication in humans. *Chem. Senses* **6,** 351–376.

Doty, R. L. (1986). Odor-guided behavior in mammals. *Experientia* **42,** 257–271.

Doty, R. L., Ford, M., Preti, G., and Huggins, G. R. (1975). Changes in the intensity and pleasantness of human vaginal odors during the menstrual cycle. *Science* **190,** 1316–1318.

Doty, R. L., Brugger, W. E., Jurs, P. C., Orndorff, M. A., Snyder, P. J., and Lowry, L. D. (1978a). Intranasal trigeminal stimulation from odorous volatiles: Psychometric responses from anosmic and normal humans. *Physiol. Behav.* **20,** 175–185.

Doty, R. L., Orndorff, M. M., Leyden, J., and Kligman, A. (1978b). Communication of gender from human axillary odors: Relationship to perceived intensity and hedonicity. *Behav. Biol.* **23,** 373–380.

Doty, R. L., Green, P. A., Ram, C., and Yankell, S. L. (1982). Communication of gender from human breath odors: Relationship to perceived intensity and pleasantness. *Horm. Behav.* **16,** 13–22.

Doty, R. L., Shaman, P., Applebaum, S. L., Giberson, R., Sikorski, L., and Rosenberg, C. (1984). Smell identification ability: Changes with age. *Science* **226,** 1441–1443.

Dravnieks, A., Keith, L., Krotoszinski, B., and Shah, J. (1974). Vaginal odors: GLC assay method for evaluating odor. *J. Pharm. Sci.* **63**, 36–40.

Dupire, M. (1987). Des goûts et des odeurs: Classification et universaux. *Homme* **27**, 5–25.

Duvall, D., Müller-Schwarze, D. M., and Silverstein, R. M., eds. (1986). "Chemical Signals in Vertebrates," Vol. 4. Plenum, New York.

Early, C. E., and Kleinknecht, R. A. (1978). The palmar sweat index as a function of repression-sensitization and fear of dentistry. *J. Consult. Clin. Psychol.* **46**, 184–185.

Ebin, V. (1980). Les parfums en Afrique Noire. *In* "Hommes, Parfums et Dieux" (L. A. Roubin, ed.), p. 7. Musée de l'Homme, Paris.

Ebling, F. J., Dawber, R., and Rook, A. (1986). The hair. *In* "Textbook of Dermatology" (A. Rook *et al.*, eds.), pp. 184–185. Blackwell, Oxford.

Eibl-Eibesfeldt, I. (1984). "Die Biologie des menschlichen Verhaltens; Grundriss der Human-ethologie." Piper, Munich.

Ellis, H. (1905). "Studies in the Psychology of Sex; Sexual Selection in Man. Part II. Smell," Vol. 4. Davis, Philadelphia, Pennsylvania.

Emanuel, S. V. (1936). Quantitative determination of the sebaceous gland's function, with particular mention of the method employed. *Acta Derm.-Venereol.* **17**, 444–450.

Engen, T. (1977). Taste and smell. *In* "Handbook of Psychology and Aging" (J. E. Birren and K. W. Schaie, eds.), 554–561. Van Nostrand-Reinhold, New York.

Engen, T. (1982). "The Perception of Odors." Academic Press, New York.

Engen, T., and Ross, B. M. (1973). Long-term memory of odors with and without verbal descriptions. *J. Exp. Psychol.* **100**, 221–227.

Epple, G. (1986). Communication by chemical signals. *In* "Comparative Primate Biology" (G. Mitchell and J. Erwin, eds.), Vol. 2A, pp. 531–580. Liss, New York.

Epple, G., Belcher, A. M., and Smith, A. B. (1986). Chemical signals in callitrichid monkeys—a comparative review. *In* "Chemical Signals in Vertebrates" (D. Duvall, D. Müller-Schwarze, and R. M. Silverstein, eds.), Vol. 4. Plenum, New York.

Filsinger, E. E., and Fabes, R. A. (1985). Odor communication, pheromones, and human families. *J. Marriage Fam.* **47**, pp. 349–359.

Filsinger, E. E., Braun, J. J., Monte, W. C., and Linder, D. E. (1984). Human responses to pig sex pheromone 5-androst-16-en-3-one. *J. Comp. Psychol.* **98**, 219–222.

Foster, K. G., Key, E. N., and Katz, G. (1969). Response of sweat glands of neonates to thermal stimuli and to intradermal acetylcholine. *J. Physiol. (London)* **203**, 13–21.

Frey, W. H., and Langseth, M. (1985). "Crying, the Mystery of Tears." Winston Press, Minneapolis, Minnesota.

Freytag, H. (1972). Die Bedeutung des Parfüms innerhalb des Adaptationsmoddells der Kosmetic. *J. Soc. Cosmet. Chem.* **23**, 811–822.

Gerstner, G., Gitsch, E., Enzelsberger, H., Metka, H., and Rotter, M. (1984). Bakterielle Besiedlung des Nabels und der Nase von Neugeborenen mit oder ohne primären Hautkontakt beim Anlegen unmittelbar postpartum. *Gynaekol. Rundsch.* **24**, 24–30.

Gesteland, R. C., Lettvin, J. Y., and Pitts, W. H. (1965). Chemical transmission in the nose of the frog. *J. Physiol. (London)* **181**, 525–559.

Gloor, M., and Kohler, H. (1977). On the physiology and biochemistry of the scalp and hair lipids. *Arch. Dermatol. Res.* **257**, 273–277.

Gloor, M., and Schnyder, U. W. (1977). Vererbung funktioneller Eigenschaften der Haut. *Hautarzt* **28**, 231–234.

Goldfoot, D. A. (1982). Multiple channels of communication in rhesus monkeys: Role of olfactory cues. *In* "Primate Communication" (C. T. Snowdon, C. H. Brown, and M. R. Petersen, eds.), pp. 413–428. Cambridge Univ. press, Cambridge.

Goldfoot, D. A., Kravetz, M. A., Goy, R. W., and Freeman, S. K. (1976). Lack of effect of vaginal lavages and aliphatic acids on ejaculatory responses in rhesus monkeys: Behavioral and chemical analyses. *Horm. Behav.* **7**, 1–28.

Goldsmith, K. M., and Goldsmith, T. H. (1982). Sense of smell in the black-chinned hummingbird. *Condor* **84**, 237–238.

Goodrich, B. S., Hesterman, E. R., Shaw, K. S., and Mykytowycs, R. (1981). Identification of some volatile compounds in the odor of fecal pellets of the rabbit, *Oryctolagus cuniculus J. Chem. Ecol.* **7**, 817–827.

Gower, D. G. (1972). 16-Unsaturated C19 steroids: A review of their chemistry, biochemistry and possible physiological role. *J. Steroid Biochem.* **3**, 45–103.

Gower, D. G., Bird, S., Sharma, P., and House, F. R. (1985). Axillary 5-androst-16-en-3-one in men and women: Relationships with olfactory acuity to odorous 16-androstenes. *Experientia* **41**, 1134–1136.

Gower, D. G., Nixon, A., and Mallett, A. I. (1988). The significance of odorous steroids in axillary odour. *In* "Perfumery: The Psychology and Biology of Fragrance" (S. Van Toller and G. H. Dodd, eds.), pp. 47–76. Chapman & Hall, London.

Graham, C. A., and McGrew, W. C. (1980). Menstrual synchrony in female undergraduates living on a co-educational campus. *Psychoneuroendocrinology* **5**, 245–252.

Greenberg, R. A., Haley, N. J., Etzel, R. A., and Loda, F. A. (1984). Measuring the response of infants to tobacco smoke: Nicotine and cotidine in urine and saliva. *N. Engl. J. Med.* **310**, 1075–1078.

Gustavson, A. R., Dawson, M. E., and Bonett, D. G. (1987). Androstenol, a putative human pheromone, affects human (*Homo sapiens*) male choice performance. *J. Comp. Psychol.* **101**, 210–212.

Hafez, E. S. E., and Evans, T. N., eds. (1978). "The Human Vagina." North-Holland Publ., Amsterdam.

Hall, E. T. (1969). "The Hidden Dimension." Doubleday, New York.

Halpin, Z. (1986). Individual odors among mammals: Origins and functions. *Adv. Study Behav.* **16**, 39–70.

Harpin, V. A., and Rutter, N. (1982a). Development of emotional sweating in the newborn infant. *Arch. Dis. Child.* **57**, 691–695.

Harpin, V. A., and Rutter, N. (1982b). Sweating in preterm babies. *J. Pediatr.* **100**, 614–619.

Hauser, G. J., Chitayat, D., Berns, L., Braver, D., and Muhlbauer, B. (1985). Peculiar odours in newborns and maternal prenatal ingestion of spicy food. *Eur. J. Pediatr.* **144**, 403.

Hepper, P. G. (1988). The discrimination of human odour by the dog. *Perception* **17**, 549–564.

Herrick, C. J. (1924). "Neurological Foundations of Behavior." Holt, New York.

Hodgson-Jones, I. S., Mackenna, R. M., and Wheatley, V. (1952). The study of human sebaceous activity. *Acta Derm.-Venereol.* **32**(S29), 155–161.

Hold, B., and Schleidt, M. (1977). The importance of human odour in non-verbal communication. *Z. Tierpsychol.* **43**, 225–238.

Homma, F. C. (1926). On apocrine sweat glands in White and Negro men and women. *Bull. Johns Hopkins Hosp.* **38**, 365–371.

Howse, D. (1986). Le sens sans parole: Vers une anthropologie de l'odorat. *Anthropol. Soc.* **10**, 29–45.

Howse, D. (1987). Olfaction and transition: An essay on the ritual uses of smell. *Can. Rev. Soc. Anthropol.* **24**, 398–416.

Huggins, G. R., and Preti, G. (1981). Vaginal odors and secretions. *Clin. Obstet. Gynecol.* **24**, 355–377.

Hurley, H. J., Jr., and Shelley, W. B. (1960). "The Human Apocrine Sweat Gland in Health and Disease." Thomas, Springfield, Illinois.

Hyman, A. B., and Giudicci, A. A. (1963). Ectopic sebaceous glands. *In* "Advances in the Biology of Skin" (W. Montagna, R. A. Ellis, and A. F. Silver, eds.), pp. 78–93. Pergamon, Oxford.

Jackman, P. S. (1982). Body odours—The role of skin bacteria. *Semin. Dermatol.* 1, 143–148.

Johnson, P. A., and Stockdale, D. F. (1975). Effect of puppet therapy on palmar sweating of hospitalized children. *Johns Hopkins Med. J.* **137**, 1–5.

Johnston, R. E. (1985). Olfactory and vomeronasal mechanisms of communication. *In* "Taste, Olfaction, and the Central Nervous System" (D. W. Pfaff, ed.), pp. 322–346. Rockefeller Univ. Press, New York.

Jones, K. K., Spencer, M. C., and Sanchez, S. A. (1951). The estimation of the rate of the secretion of sebum in man. *J. Invest. Dermatol.* **17**, 213–221.

Juniper, K., and Dykman, R. A. (1967). Skin resistance, sweat-gland counts, salivary flow, and gastric secretion: Age, race and sex differences, and intercorrelations. *Psychophysiology* **4**, 216–222.

Kaitz, M., Good, A., Rokem, A. M., and Eidelman, A. I. (1987). Mother's recognition of their newborns by olfactory cues. *Dev. Psychobiol.* **20**, 587–591.

Kalmus, H. (1955). The discrimination by the nose of the dog of individual human odours and in particular of the odours of twins. *Br. J. Anim. Behav.* **5**, 25–31.

Kalogerakis, M. G. (1963). The role of olfaction in sexual development. *Psychosom. Med.* **25**, 420–432.

Kamat, V. B., Panse, T. B., and Khanolkar, V. R. (1960). Constituents of human smegma. *Proc.— Indian Acad. Sci., Sect.B* **52**, 1–8.

Kaplan, J. N., Cubicciotti, D., and Redican, W. K. (1977). Olfactory discrimination of squirrel monkey mothers by their infants. *Dev. Psychobiol.* **10**, 447–453.

Kawahata, A. (1960). Sex differences in sweating. *In* "Essential Problems in "Climatic Physiology" (E. H. Oga, K. Ogata, and S. Itoh, eds.), pp. 169–184. Nakado Publ., Kyoto.

Keith, L., Dravnieks, A., and Krotoszinski, B. (1975a). Olfactory study: Human pheromones. *Arch. Gynaekol.* **218**, 203–204.

Keith, L., Stromberg, P., Krotoszinski, B., Shah, J., and Dravnieks, A. (1975b). The odors of the human vagina. *Arch. Gynaekol.* **220**, 1–10.

Keverne, E. B. (1976). Sexual attractants in primates. *J. Cosmet. Chem.* **27**, 257–269.

Keverne, E. B. (1980). Olfaction in the behaviour of non-human primates. *Symp. Zool. Soc. London* **45**, 313–327.

Keverne, E. B. (1982). Olfaction and the reproductive behavior of nonhuman primates. *In* "Primate Communication" (C. T. Snowdon, C. H. Brown, and M. R. Petersen, eds.), pp. 396–412. Cambridge Univ. Press, Cambridge.

Keverne, E. B. (1983). Chemical communication in primate reproduction. *In* "Pheromones and Reproduction in Mammals" (J. G. Vandenbergh, ed.), pp. 79–92. Academic Press, New York.

King, J. E., Becker, R. F., and Markee, J. E. (1964). Studies in olfactory discrimination in dogs. 3. Ability to detect human odor trace. *J. Anim. Behav.* **12**, 311–315.

Kirk-Smith, M. D., and Booth, D. A. (1980). Effects of androstenone on choice of location in other's presence. *In* "Olfaction and Taste" (H. Van Der Starre, ed.), Vol. 7, pp. 397–400. IRL Press, London.

Kirk-Smith, M. D., and Booth, D. A. (1987). Chemoreception in human behaviour: Experimental analysis of the social effects of fragrances. *Chem. Senses* **12**, 159–166.

Kirk-Smith, M. D., Booth, D. A., Carroll, D., and Davies, P. (1978). Human social attitudes affected by androstenol. *Res. Commun. Psychol., Psychiatry Behav.* **3**, 379–384.

Kirk-Smith, M. D., Van Toller, S., and Dodd, G. H. (1983). Unconscious odor conditioning in human subjects. *Biol. Psychol.* **17**, 221–231.

Klaus, K. (1927). Beitrag zur Biochemie der Menstruation. *Biochem. Z.* **185**, 3–10.

Klineberg, O. (1935). "Race Differences." Harper, New York.

Klingman, A. M., and Shehadeh, N. (1964). Pubic apocrine glands and odor. *Arch. Dermatol.* **89**, 461–463.

Kloek, J. (1961). The smell of some steroid sex hormones and their metabolites: Reflections and experiments concerning the significance of smell for the mutual relations of the sexes. *Psychiatr., Neurol., Neurochir.* **64**, 309–344.

Koelega, H. S., and Köster, E. P. (1974). Some experiments on sex differences in odor perception. *Ann. N.Y. Acad. Sci.* **237**, 234–246.

König, R. (1972). Kulturanthropologische Betrachtung zum Problem der Parfümierung. *J. Soc. Cosmet. Chem.* **23**, 823–829.

Kostelc, J. G., Preti, G., Zelson, P. R., Stoller, N. H., and Tonzetich, T. J. (1980). Salivary volatiles as indicators of periodontitis. *J. Periodontol.* **15**, 185–192.

Kostelc, J. G., Preti, G., Zelson, P. R., Tonzetich, T. J., and Huggins, G. R. (1981). Volatiles of exogenous origin from the human oral cavity. *J. Chromatogr.* **226**, 315–323.

Krotoszinski, B., Gabriel, G., and O'Neill, H. (1977). Characterization of human expired air: A promising investigative and diagnostic technique. *J. Chromatogr. Sci.* **15**, 239–244.

Kuno, Y. (1956). "Human Perspiration." Thomas, Springfield, Illinois.

Kwan, T. K., Trafford, D. J., Martin, H. L., and Gower, D. B. (1989). Odorous androst-16-enes and other C19 steroids in human semen. *Biochem. Soc. Trans.* **17**, 749–750.

Labows, J. N. (1988). Odor detection, generation, and etiology in the axilla. *In* "Antiperspirants and Deodorants" (C. B. Felger and K. Laden, eds.), pp. 321–343. Dekker, New York.

Labows, J. N., McGinley, K., Leyden, J. J., and Webster, G. F. (1979a). Characteristic γ-lactone odor production of the genus Pityrosporum. *Appl. Environ. Microbiol.* **38**, 412–415.

Labows, J. N., Preti, G., Hoelzle, E., Leyden, J., and Klingman, A. (1979b). Analysis of human axillary volatiles: Compounds of exogenous origin. *J. Chromatogr.* **163**, 294–299.

Labows, J. N., Preti, G., Hoelzle, E., Leyden, J., and Klingman, A. (1979c). Analysis of human apocrine secretions. *Steroids* **34**, 249–259.

Labows, J. N., McGinley, K., and Klingman, A. (1982). Perspectives on axillary odor. *J. Soc. Cosmet. Chem.* **34**, 193–202.

Laird, D. A. (1934). Some normal odor effects and associations of psychoanalytic significance. *Psychoanal. Rev.* **21**, 194–200.

Largey, G. P., and Watson, D. R. (1972). The sociology of odors. *Am. J. Sociol.* **77**, 1021–1034.

Lenington, S., Egid, K., and Williams, J. (1988). Analysis of a genetic recognition system in wild house mice. *Behav. Genet.* **18**, 549–564.

Leon, M. (1980). Maternal pheromone. *Physiol. Behav.* **13**, 441–453.

Leyden, J. J., McGinley, K. J., Mills, O. H., and Klingman, A. M. (1975). Age-related changes in the resident bacterial flora of the human face. *J. Invest. Dermatol.* **65**, 379–381.

Leyden, J. J., McGinley, K. J., Hoelzle, E., Labows, J. N., and Klingman, A. M. (1981). The microbiology of the human axilla and its relationship to axillary odor. *J. Invest. Dermatol.* **77**, 413–416.

Lieberman, J. (1966). Cyclic fluctuation of sweat electrolytes in women. *JAMA, J. Am. Med. Assoc.* **195**, 117–123.

Löhner, L. (1924). Über menschliche Individual- und Regionalgerüche. *Pfluegers Arch. Gesamte Physiol. Menschen Tiere* **202**, 25–45.

Lord, T., and Kasprzak, M. (1989). Identification of self through olfaction. *Percept. Mot. Skills* **69**, 219–224.

Lott, I. T., Sullivan, R. M., and McPherson, D. (1989). Associative olfactory learning occurs in the neonate. *Neurology* **39**(S3), 110.

Loudon, J. B. (1977). On body products. *In* "The Anthropology of the Body" (J. Blacking, ed.), pp. 161–178. Academic Press, New York.

Lowell, W. R., and Flanigan, W. F. (1980). Marine mammal chemoreception. *Mammal. Rev.* **10,** 53–59.

Lozoff, B. (1983). Birth and bonding in nonindustrial societies. *Dev. Med. Child Neurol.* **25,** 595–600.

MacDonald, I., and Clark, G. (1970). Variations in the levels of cholesterol and triglycerids in the skin surface during the menstrual cycle. *Br. J. Dermatol.* **83,** 473–476.

Macfarlane, A. (1975). Olfaction in the development of social preferences in the human neonate. *Ciba Found. Symp.* **33,** 103–113.

Maderson, P. F. (1986). The tetrapod epidermis: A system protoadapted as a semiochemichal source. *In* "Chemical Signals in Vertebrates" (D. Duvall, D. Müller-Schwarze, and R. M. Silverstein, eds.), Vol. 4, pp. 13–25. Plenum, New York.

Makin, J. W., and Porter, R. H. (1989). Attractiveness of lactating females' breast odors to neonates. *Child Dev.* **60,** 803–810.

Makki, S., Barbenel, J. C., and Agache, P. (1979). Quantitative method for the assessment of the microtopography of human skin. *Acta Derm.-Venereol.* **59,** 285–291.

March, K. S. (1980). Deer, bears and blood: A note on non-human animal response to menstrual odor. *Am. Anthropol.* **82,** 125–127.

Marlier, L., and Schaal, B. (1989). Olfactory, tactile and auditory cues in the recognition of individuality in children. *Int. Ethol. Conf., 21st,* Utrecht, 108.

Marples, M. J. (1965). "The Ecology of Human Skin." Thomas, Springfield, Illinois.

Marples, M. J. (1969). Life on human skin. *Sci. Am.* **220,** 108–115.

Marples, R. (1982). The normal flora of different sites in the young adult. *Curr. Med. Res. Opin.* **7**(S2), 67–70.

Marshall, D. A., and Moulton, D. G. (1981). Olfactory sensitivity to α-ionone in humans and dogs. *Chem. Senses* **6,** 53–61.

Marshall, J. *et al.* (1988). A comparative study of the cutaneous microflora of normal feet with low and high level of odor. *Appl. J. Bacteriol.* 61–68.

Marshall, W. A., and Tanner, J. M. (1969). Variation in the pattern of pubertal changes in girls. *Arch. Dis. Child.* **44,** 291–303.

Marshall, W. A., and Tanner, J. M. (1970). Variation in the pattern of pubertal changes in boys. *Arch. Dis. Child.* **45,** 13–23.

Masters, W. H., and Johnson, V. (1966). "The Human Sexual Response." Little, Brown, Boston, Massachusetts.

McBurney, D. H., Levine, J. M., and Cavanaugh, P. H. (1977). Psychophysical and social ratings of human body odor. *Pers. Soc. Psychol. Bull.* **3,** 135–138.

McCance, R. A. (1938). Individual variations in response to high temperatures. *Lancet* (July 23), ■ 190–191.

McCance, R. A., and Puhorit, G. (1969). Ethnic differences in the response of the sweat glands to pilocarpine. *Nature (London)* **221,** 378–379.

McClintock, M. K. (1971). Menstrual synchrony and suppression. *Nature (London)* **229,** 244–245.

Melrose, D. R., Reed, H. C. B., and Patterson, R. L. S. (1974). Androgen steroids as an aid to the detection of oestrus in pig artificial insemination. *Br. Vet. J.* **130,** 61–67.

Mennella, J. A., and Beauchamp, G. K. (1990). The effect of maternal diet on breast milk odors and the nursling's behavior. Annual Meeting of the International Society for Developmental Psychobiology. Cambridge, England.

Meredith, M. (1983). Sensory physiology of pheromone communication. *In* "Pheromones and Reproduction in Mammals" (J. G. Vandenbergh, ed.), pp. 199–252. Academic Press, New York.

Michael, R. P., and Keverne, E. B. (1970). Primate sex pheromone of vaginal origin. *Nature (London)* **225,** 84–85.

194   BENOIST SCHAAL AND RICHARD H. PORTER

Michael, R. P., Keverne, E. B., and Bonsall, R. W. (1971). Pheromones: Isolation of male sex attractants from a female primate. *Science* **172**, 964–966.

Michael, R. P., Bonsall, R. W., and Warner, P. (1974). Human vaginal secretions: Volatile fatty acid content. *Science* **186**, 1217–1219.

Michael, R. P., Bonsall, R. W., and Warner, P. (1975a). Primate sexual pheromones. *In* "Olfaction and Taste V" (D. A. Denton and J. P. Coghlan, eds.), pp. 417–424, Academic Press, New York.

Michael, R. P., Bonsall, R. W., and Kutner, M. (1975b). Volatile fatty acids, "copulins," in human vaginal secretions. *Psychoneuroendocrinology* **1**, 153–163.

Millhollen, A. (1986). Territorial scent marking by two sympatric lemur species. *In* "Chemical Signals in Vertebrates" (D. Duvall, D. Müller-Schwarze, and R. M. Silverstein, eds.), Vol. 4. Plenum, New York.

Mitz, V., and Lalardrie, J. P. (1977). A propos de la vascularisation et de l'innervation sensitive du sein. *Senologia* **2**, 33–39.

Montagna, W. (1963). The sebaceous glands in man. *In* "Advances in the Biology of Skin" (W. Montagna, R. A. Ellis, and A. F. Silver, eds.), pp. 19–31. Pergamon, Oxford.

Montagna, W. (1985). The evolution of human skin. *J. Hum. Evol.* **14**, 3–22.

Montagna, W., and MacPherson, E. E. (1974). Some neglected aspects of the anatomy of human breasts. *J. Invest. Dermatol.* **63**, 10–16.

Montagna, W., and Parakkal, P. (1974). "The Structure and Function of Skin." Academic Press, New York.

Montagna, W., and Yun, J. S. (1972). The glands of Montgomery. *Br. J. Dermatol.* **86**, 126–133.

Montes, L. F., and Wilborn, W. H. (1970). Anatomical location of normal skin flora. *Arch. Dermatol.* **101**, 145–159.

Moore, J. G., Krotoszynski, B. K., and O'Neill, H. (1984). Fecal odorgrams. *Dig. Dis. Sci.* **29**, 907–911.

Moore, J. G., Straight, R. C., Osborne, D. N., and Wayne, A. (1985). Olfactory, gas chromatographic and mass spectral analyses of fecal volatiles traced to ingested licorice and apple. *Biochem. Biophys. Res. Commun.* **131**, 339–346.

Morlan, G. K. (1950). An experiment on the identification of body odor. *J. Genet. Psychol.* **77**, 257–263.

Morris, N. M., and Udry, J. R. (1978). Pheromonal influences on human sexual behaviour: An experimental search. *J. Biosocial Sci.* **10**, 147–157.

Müller-Schwarze, D. M., and Mozell, M., eds. (1977). "Chemical Signals in Mammals," Vol. 1. Plenum, New York.

Mykytowicz, R. (1985). Olfaction—a link with the past. *J. Hum. Evol.* **14**, 75–90.

Natanson, K., and Goldschmidt, W. (1909). Über das morphologische Verhalten der Montgomeryschen Drüsen. *Monatsschr. Geburtshilfe Gynaekol.* **30**, 34–43.

Neuhaus, W. (1961). Dr Eigengeruch des Menschen, seine Wahrnehmung, Bedeutung und Beeinflussung. *Muench. Med. Wochenschr.* **103**, 1752–1755.

Nicholson, B. (1984). Does kissing aid human bonding by semiochemical addiction? *Br. J. Dermatol.* **111**, 623–627.

Nicolaïdes, N. (1963). Human skin surface lipids—origin, composition and possible function. *In* "Advances in the Biology of Skin" (W. Montagna, R. A. Ellis, and A. F. Silver, eds.), pp. 167–187. Pergamon, Oxford.

Nicolaïdes, N. (1972). The fatty acids of wax esters and sterol esters from vernix caseosa and from human skin. *Lipids* **8**, 506–517.

Nicolaïdes, N. (1974). Skin lipids: Their biochemical uniqueness. *Science* **186**, 19–26.

Nixon, A., Mallett, A. I., and Gower, D. B. (1988). Simultaneous quantification of five odorous steroids (16-androstenes) in the axillary hair of men. *J. Steroid Biochem.* **29**, 505–510.

Noble, W. C. (1981). "Microbiology of the Human Skin." Lloyd-Luke Ltd., London.

Ogawa, T. (1975). Thermal influences on palmar sweating and mental influences on generalized sweating in man. *Jpn. J. Physiol.* **25**, 525–535.

Ottoson, D. (1956). Analysis of electrical activity of the olfactory epithelium. *Acta Physiol. Scand.* **35**(S122), 1–183.

Papi, F. (1986). Pigeon migration: Solved problems and open questions. *Monit. Zool. Ital.* **20**, 471–517.

Penrose, L. S. (1924). Human biochemical genetics. *Adv. Sci.* **10**, 56–64.

Perkins, O. C., and Miller, A. M. (1926). Sebaceous glands in the human nipple. *Am. J. Obstet. Gynecol.* **11**, 789–794.

Petit-Skinner, S. (1976). Nauru ou la civilisation de l'odorat. *Obj. Mondes (Paris)* **16**, 125–128.

Peto, A. (1973). The olfactory forerunner of the superego: Its role in normalcy, neurosis and fetishism. *Int. J. Psycho-Anal.* **54**, 323–330.

Pilleri, G., and Gihr, M. (1970). The central nervous system of the Mysticete and Odontocete whales. *In* "Investigations on Cetacea" (G. Pillery, ed.), Vol. 2, pp. 89–127. Brain Anatomy Institute, Bern.

Plewig, G., and Klingman, A. (1978). Proliferative activity of the sebaceous glands in the aged. *J. Invest. Dermatol.* **70**, 314–320.

Pochi, P. E., Strauss, S. S., and Downing, D. T. (1979). Age-related changes in sebaceous activity. *J. Invest. Dermatol.* **73**, 108–112.

Porter, R. H. (1989). Littermate influences on behavioral and physiological development in spiny mice. *In* "Contemporary Issues in Comparative Psychology" (D. A. Dewsbury, ed.). Sinauer Assoc., Sunderland, Massachusetts.

Porter, R. H. (1991). Mutual mother–infant recognition in humans. *In* "Kin Recognition" (P. G. Hepper, ed.). Cambridge Univ. Press, Cambridge (in press).

Porter, R. H., and Blaustein, A. R. (1989). Mechanisms and ecological correlates of kin recognition. *Sci. Prog. (Oxford)* **73**, 53–66.

Porter, R. H., and Moore, J. D. (1981). Human kin recognition by olfactory cues. *Physiol. Behav.* **27**, 493–495.

Porter, R. H., Cernoch, J. M., and McLaughlin, F. J. (1983). Maternal recognition of neonates through olfactory cues. *Physiol. Behav.* **30**, 151–154.

Porter, R. H., Cernoch, J. M., and Balogh, R. D. (1985). Odor signatures and kin recognition. *Physiol. Behav.* **34**, 445–448.

Porter, R. H., Balogh, R. D., Cernoch, J. M., and Franchi, C. (1986). Recognition of kin through characteristic body odors. *Chem. Senses* **11**, 389–395.

Powell, T. P., Cowan, W. M., and Raisman, G. (1965). The central olfactory connections. *J. Anat.* **99**, 791–813.

Preti, G., and Huggins, G. R. (1975). Cyclical changes in volatile acidic metabolites in human vaginal secretions and their relation to ovulation. *J. Chem. Ecol.* **1**, 361–368.

Preti, G., and Huggins, G. R. (1977). Unpleasant vaginal odor induced by sexual arousal. *J. Am. Med. Assoc.* **237**, 1735.

Preti, G., Huggins, G. R., and Silverberg, G. Y. (1979). Alterations in the organic compounds of vaginal secretions caused by sexual arousal. *Fertil. Steril.* **32**, 47–54.

Preti, G., Cutler, W. B., Garcia, C. R., Huggins, G. R., and Lawley, H. J. (1986). Human axillary secretions influence women's menstrual cycles: The role of donor extract from females. *Horm. Behav.* **20**, 474–482.

Preti, G., Cutler, W. B., Christensen, C. M., Lawley, H., Huggins, G. R., and Garcia, C. R. (1987). Human axillary extracts: Analysis of compounds from samples which influence menstrual timing. *J. Chem. Ecol.* **13**, 717–731.

Quadagno, D. M., Shubeita, H. E., Deck, J., and Francoeur, D. (1981). Influence of male social contacts, exercise and all-female living conditions on the menstrual cycle. *Psychoneuroendocrinology* **6**, 239–244.

Quay, Q. W. (1977). Structure and function of skin glands. *In* "Chemical Signals in Vertebrates" (D. M. Müller-Schwarze and M. M. Mozell, eds.), Vol. 1, pp. 1–15. Plenum, New York.

Quinton, P. M. (1988). Structure and function of eccrine sweat glands in humans. *In* "Antiperspirants and Deodorants" (K. Laden and C. B. Felger, eds.), pp. 57–88. Dekker, New York.

Ramasastry, P., Downing, D. T., Pochi, P. E., and Strauss, J. S. (1970). Chemical composition of human skin surface lipids from birth to puberty. *J. Invest. Dermatol.* **54,** 139–144.

Rees, J., and Shuster, S. (1981). Pubertal induction of sweat gland activity. *Clin. Sci.* **60,** 689–692.

Regnier, F. E., and Goodwin, M. (1977). On the chemical and environmental modulation of pheromone release from vertebrate scent marks. *In* "Chemical Signals in Vertebrates" (D. M. Müller-Schwarze and M. M. Mozell, eds.), Vol. 1, pp. 115–133. Plenum, New York.

Reichert, U., Saint-Léger, D., and Schaefer, H. (1982). Skin surface chemistry and microbial infection. *Semin. Dermatol.* **1,** 91–100.

Rennie, P. J., Holland, K. T., Mallett, A. I., Watkins, W. J., and Gower, D. G. (1988). 16-Androstene steroid content of apocrine sweat and microbiology of the human axilla. *Conf. Chem. Signals Vertebr., 5th,* Oxford.

Reynolds, R. D. (1988). Foot odor. *Am. Fam. Physician* **37,** 58.

Ridley, C. M. (1976). "The Vulva." Saunders, London.

Robertshaw, D. (1983). Sweat and heat exchange in man and other mammals. *J. Hum. Evol.* **14,** 63–73.

Rochefort, A. (1985). Etude concommitante des sécrétions sébacées du nouveau-né et de la reconnaissance olfactive du nouveau-né par sa mère. Unpublished DEA Thesis, University of Besançon.

Rogel, M. J. (1978). A critical evaluation of the possibility of higher primate reproductive and sexual pheromones. *Psychol. Bull.* **85,** 810–830.

Rook, A., Savin, J. A., and Wilkinson, D. S. (1986). The prevalence, incidence and ecology of diseases of the skin. *In* "Textbook of Dermatology" (A. Rook *et al.,* eds.), pp. 39–53. Blackwell, Oxford.

Roubin, L. A., ed. (1980). "Hommes, parfums et dieux." Musée de l'Homme, Paris.

Russell, M. J. (1976). Human olfactory communication. *Nature (London)* **260,** 520–522.

Russell, M. J. (1983). Human olfactory communication. *In* "Chemical Signals in Vertebrates" (D. M. Müller-Schwarze and R. M. Silverstein, eds.), Vol. 3, pp. 259–273. Plenum, New York.

Russell, M. J., Switz, G. M., and Thompson, K. (1980). Olfactory influences on the human menstrual cycle. *Pharmacol., Biochem. Behav.* **13,** 737–738.

Russell, M. J., Mendelson, T., and Peeke, H. V. S. (1983). Mothers' identification of their infant's odors. *Ethol. Sociobiol.* **4,** 29–31.

Saint-Léger, D., and Lévêque, J. L. (1982). A comparative study of refatting kinetics on the scalp and forehead. *Br. J. Dermatol.* **106,** 669–675.

Sansone-Bassano, G., Cummings, B., Seeler, A. K., and Reisner, R. M. (1980). Composition of human skin surface lipids from birth to puberty. *Br. J. Dermatol.* **103,** 131–137.

Sarkany, I., and Gaylarde, C. C. (1967). Skin flora of the newborn. *Lancet* (March 18), 589–590.

Sarkany, I., and Gaylarde, C. C. (1968). Bacterial colonization of the skin of the newborn. *J. Pathol. Bacteriol.* **95,** 115–122.

Sastry, S. D., Buck, K. T., Janak, J., Dressler, M., and Preti, G. (1980). Volatiles emitted by humans. *In* "Biochemical Applications of Mass Spectrometry" (G. R. Waller and O. C. Dermer, eds.), 1st Suppl. Vol., pp. 1085–1129. Wiley, New York.

Sato, K. (1977). The physiology, pharmacology and biochemistry of the eccrine sweat gland. *Rev. Physiol. Biochem. Pharmacol.* **79,** 51–131.

Sato, K., and Dodson, R. L. (1970). Regional and individual variations in the function of the human eccrine sweat gland. *J. Invest. Dermatol.* **54,** 443–449.

Sato, K., and Sato, F. (1983). Individual variation in structure and function of human eccrine sweat glands. *Am. J. Physiol.* **245,** R203–R208.

Sato, K., and Sato, F. (1987). Sweat secretion by human axillary apoeccrine sweat glands in vitro. *Am. J. Physiol.* **252**, R181–R187.

Sato, K., Leidal, R., and Saton, F. (1987). Morphology and development of an apoeccrine sweat gland in human axillae. *Am. J. Physiol.* **252**, R166–R180.

Scalia, F., and Winans, S. S. (1976). New perspectives on the morphology of the olfactory system: Olfactory and vomeronasal pathways in mammals. *In* "Mammalian Olfaction, Reproductive Processes, and Behavior" (R. L. Doty, ed.), pp. 7–28. Academic Press, New York.

Schaal, B. (1986). Presumed olfactory exchanges between mother and neonate in humans. *In* "Ethology and Psychology" (J. Le Camus and J. Cosnier, eds.), pp. 101–110. Privat- I.E.C., Toulouse.

Schaal, B. (1988a). Olfaction in infants and children: Developmental and functional perspectives. *Chem. Senses* **13**, 145–190.

Schaal, B. (1988b). Discontinuité natale et continuité chimio-sensorielle: Modèles animaux et hypothèses pour l'homme. *Année Biol.* **27**, 1–41.

Schaal, B., and Kontar, F. (1986). The development of the mother's ability to identify her infant's odor: Effect of individual and experiential variables *World Congr. Infant Psychiatry, 3rd,* Stockholm, Sweden.

Schaal, B., Montagner, H., Hertling, E., Bolzoni, D., Moyse, A., and Quichon, R. (1980). Les stimulations olfactives dans les relations entre l'enfant et la mère. *Reprod. Nutr. Dev.* **20**, 843–858.

Schaal, B., Rochefort, A., and Cismaresco, A. S. (1986). Mother's olfactory recognition of her newborn: Relations to mother's olfactory detection threshold and to infant's sebum excretion level. *Abstr. Int. Conf. Hum. Ethol. 5th,* Tützing, West Germany, p. 61.

Schaffer, J. (1937). Die Duftorgane des Menschen. *Wien. Klin. Wochenschr.* **20**, 790–796.

Schaffer, J. (1940). "Die Hautdrüsen Organe der Saügetiere." Urban-Schwarzenberg, Berlin.

Schiefenhövel, W., and Sich, D., eds. (1983). Die Geburt aus Ethnomedizinischer Aussicht. *Curare* **S1**, 1–299.

Schiefferdecker, P. (1922). Die Hautdrüsen des Menschen und der Saügetiere. *Zoologica* (*N.Y.*) **72**, 1–154.

Schleidt, M. (1980). Personal odor and nonverbal communication. *Ethol. Sociobiol.* **1**, 225–231.

Schledt, M., and Genzel, C. (1990). The significance of mother's perfume for infants in the first weeks of their life. *Ethol. Sociobiol.* **11**, 145–154.

Schleidt, M., and Hold, B. (1982). Human odour and identity. *In* "Olfaction and Endocrine Regulation" (W. Breipohl, ed.), pp. 181–194. IRL Press, London.

Schleidt, M., Hold, B., and Attili, G. (1981). A cross-cultural study on the attitude towards personal odors. *J. Chem. Ecol.* **7**, 19–31.

Schleidt, M., Neumann, P., and Morishita, H. (1988). Pleasure and disgust: Memories and associations of pleasant and unpleasant odours in Germany and Japan. *Chem. Senses* **13**, 279–293.

Schulze-Westrum, T. (1968). Ergebnisse einer zoologisch-völkerkündlichen Expedition zu den Papuas. *Umschau* **68**, 295–300.

Schwartz, C. G., and Rosenblum, L. A. (1980). Novelty, arousal and nasal marking in the squirrel monkey. *Behav. Neural Biol.* **28**, 116–122.

Schwartz, V. (1982). The development of the sweat glands and their function. *In* "Scientific Foundations of Paediatrics" (J. A. Davis and J. Dobbing, eds.), Vol. 2, pp. 741–744. International Ideas, London.

Seeger, A. (1988). Anthropology and odor: From Manhattan to Mato Grosso. *Perfum. Flavor.* **13**, 41–48.

Selwyn, S. (1982). The evolution of cleansing and antimicrobial care of the skin. *Curr. Med. Res. Opin.* **7**(S2), 61–66.

Serri, F., Fabrizi, G., and Urbani, S. (1982). Skin surface lipid composition in different age groups in infancy and childhood. *Curr. Med. Res. Opin.* **7**(S2), 23–25.

Shehadeh, N., and Klingman, A. (1963). The bacteria responsible for axillary odor. *J. Invest. Dermatol.* **41**, 3–10.

Shelley, W. B., and Perry, E. T. (1956). The physiology of the apocrine (ceruminous) gland of the human ear canal. *J. Invest. Dermatol.* **26**, 13–20.

Shelley, W. B., Hurley, H. J., and Nichols, A. C. (1953). Axillary odor: Experimental study of the role of bacteria, apocrine sweat and deodorants. *Arch. Dermatol. Syphilol.* **68**, 430–446.

Shorey, H. H. (1976). "Animal Communication by Pheromones." Academic Press, New York.

Shuster, S. (1982). Mature thoughts on mature skin. *Curr. Med. Res. Opin.* **7**(S2), 75–82.

Signoret, J. P. (1970). Reproductive behaviour of pigs. *J. Reprod. Fertil.* (S11), 105–117.

Slotnick, B. M., and Ptak, J. E. (1977). Olfactory intensity-difference thresholds in rats and humans. *Physiol. Behav.* **19**, 795–802.

Smith, D. M., Peters, T. G., and Donegan, W. L. (1982). Montgomery's areolar tubercles. *Arch. Pathol. Lab. Med.* **106**, 60–63.

Sommerville, D. A. (1969). The normal flora of the skin in different age groups. *Br. J. Dermatol.* **8**, 248–258.

Speert, H. (1958). "Essays in Eponymy, Obstetric and Gynecologic Milestones." Macmillan, New York.

Stalder, J. F., Saint-Léger, D., and François, A. M. (1986). Variations topographiques de la composition du vernix caseosa. Congrès de Dermatologie, Nantes.

Stephan, H., Bauchot, R., and Andy, O. J. (1970). Data on size of the brain and of various brain parts in insectivores and primates. *In* "The Primate Brain" (C. R. Noback and W. Montagna, eds.), pp. 289–297. Appleton-Century-Crofts, New York.

Stoddart, D. M. (1980). "The Ecology of Vertebrate Olfaction." Chapman & Hall, London.

Stoddart, D. M. (1988). Human odor culture: a zoological perspective. *In* "Perfumery: The Psychology and Biology of Fragrance" (S. Van Toller and G. H. Dodd, eds.), pp. 3–17. Chapman & Hall, London.

Sullivan, R. M. (1990). Newborn human infants exhibit CR's to an odor previously paired with either breast or bottle feeding. Annual Meeting of the International Society for Developmental Psychobiology. Cambridge, England.

Szabo, G. (1963). The number of eccrine sweat glands in human skin. *In* "Advances in the Biology of Skin" (W. Montagna, R. A. Ellis, and A. F. Silver, eds.), Vol. 3, pp. 3–10. Pergamon, Oxford.

Talbot-Seeley, T., Abramson, P. R., Perry, L. B., Rothblatt, A. B., and Seeley, D. M. (1980). Thermographic measurement of sexual arousal: A methodological note. *Arch. Sex. Behav.* **9**, 77–86.

Thiessen, D. D. (1977). Thermoenergetics and the evolution of pheromone communication. *Prog. Psychobiol. Psychol. Biol.* **7**, 91–191.

Thody, A. J., and Shuster, S. (1989). Control and function of sebaceous glands. *Physiol. Rev.* **69**, 383–416.

Thompson, J. A., Miles, B. S., and Fennessey, P. V. (1977). Urinary organic acids quantitated by age groups in a healthy pediatric population. *Clin. Chem. (Winston-Salem, N.C.)* **23**, 1734–1738.

Todd, W. A. (1979). Psychosocial problems as a major complication of an adolescent with trimethylaminuria. *J. Pediatr.* **94**, 936–937.

Tonzetich, J. (1978). Oral malodor: An indicator of health status and oral cleanliness. *Int. Dent. J.* **28**, 309–319.

Tonzetich, J., Preti, G., and Huggins, G. R. (1978). Changes in the concentration of volatile sulphur compounds of mouth air during the menstrual cycle. *J. Int. Med. Res.* **6**, 245–254.

Tucker, D. (1965). Electrophysiological evidence of olfactory function in birds. *Nature (London)* **207**, 34–36.

Uchino, S. (1939). Sweating in newborn infants. *Sanfujinka Kiyo* **22**, 238–245.

Vandenbergh, J. G., ed. (1983). "Pheromones and Reproduction in Mammals." Academic Press, New York.

Veith, J. L., Buck, M., Getzlaf, S., Van Dalfsen, P., and Slade, S. (1983). Exposure to men influences the occurrence of ovulation in women. *Physiol. Behav.* **31**, 313–315.

Verbov, J., and Baxter, J. (1974). Onset of palmar sweating in newborn infants. *Br. J. Dermatol.* **90**, 269–276.

Verron, H., and Gaultier, C. (1976). Processus olfactifs et structures relationnelles. *Psychol. Fr.* **21**, 205–209.

Vining, R. F., and McGinley, R. A. (1984). Transport of steroids from blood to saliva. *In* "Ninth Tenovus Workshop: Immunoassay of Steroids in Saliva" (G. F. Read *et al.*, eds.). Alpha-Omega, Cardiff, Wales.

Vorherr, H. (1974). "The Breast: Morphology, Physiology, and Lactation." Academic Press, New York.

Vuorenkoski, V., Wasz-Höckert, O., Koivisto, E., and Lind, J. (1969). The effect of cry stimulus on the temperature of the lactating breast of primipara, a thermographic study. *Experientia* **25**, 1286–1287.

Wald, N., and Ritchie, C. (1984). Validation of studies on lung cancer in non smokers married to smokers. *Lancet* **1**, 1067.

Waldron, I., Bratelli, G., Carriker, L., Sung, W. E., Vögeli, C., and Waldman, E. (1988). Gender differences in tobacco use in Africa, Asia, the Pacific and Latin America. *Soc. Sci. Med.* **27**, 1269–1275.

Wallace, P. (1977). Individual discrimination of humans by odor. *Physiol. Behav.* **19**, 577–579.

Wallraff, H. G. (1986). Relevance of olfaction and atmospheric odors to pigeon homing. *In* "Orientation in Space" (G. Beugnon, ed.), pp. 71–80. Privat-I.E.C., Toulouse.

Wenzel, B. M. (1973). Chemoreception. *In* "Avian Biology" (D. S. Farner and J. R. King, eds.), Vol. 3, pp. 389–415. Academic Press, New York.

Wenzel, B. M., and Sieck, M. (1972). Olfactory perception and bulbar electrical activity in several avian species. *Physiol. Behav.* 9, 287–294.

White, R. H. (1975). Occurence of methylthioesters in urine of humans after they have eaten asparagus. *Science* **189**, 810–811.

Williams, M., Cotterill, W. J., Williamson, B., Forster, R. A., Cotteril, J. A., and Edwards, J. (1973). The effect of local temperature changes on sebum excretion rate and forehead surface lipid composition. *Br. J. Dermatol.* **88**, 257–262.

Wilson, H. C. (1987). Female axillary secretions influence women's menstrual cycles: A critique. *Horm. Behav.* **21**, 536–546.

Wilson, H. C. (1988). Male axillary secretions influence women's menstrual cycles: A critique. *Horm. Behav.* **22**, 266–271.

Wirtz, K. (1950). Studien über die cerebralisation: Zur quantitativen Rangordnung bei Säugetieren. *Acta Anat.* **9**, 134–196.

Wysocki, C. J. (1979). Neurobehavioral evidence for the involvement of the vomeronasal system in mammalian reproduction. *Neurosci. Biobehav. Rev.* **3**, 301–341.

Yamazaki, K., Yamaguchi, M., Beauchamp, G. K., Bard, J., Boyse, E. A., and Thomas L. (1981). Chemosensation: An aspect of the uniqueness of the individual. *In* "Biochemistry of Taste and Olfaction" (R. H. Cagan and M. R. Kare, eds.). Academic Press, New York.

Yfantis, C. (1980). Geruchserkennen zwischen Mutter und Kind. Unpublished Master's Thesis, University of München.

Zeng, X., Preti, G., Lawley, H. J., and Leyden, J. (1989). Isolation and structural characterization of pungent odor from a unique natural source: The human axillae. *196th Natl. Meet. Am. Chem. Soc.*

Zlatkis, A., and Liebich, H. M. (1971). Profile of volatile metabolites in human urine. *Clin. Chem. (Winston-Salem, N.C.)* **17**, 592–594.

Lekking in Birds and Mammals: Behavioral and Evolutionary Issues

R. Haven Wiley

DEPARTMENT OF BIOLOGY
UNIVERSITY OF NORTH CAROLINA AT CHAPEL HILL
CHAPEL HILL, NORTH CAROLINA 27599

I. Introduction

Of all animal societies perhaps the most bizarre are leks. These aggregations of displaying males are visited by females solely for copulation. To some they have represented the vindication of Darwin's theory of sexual selection (Darwin, 1871; Selous, 1927). To others they have seemed simply baffling. "Leks . . . challenge the whole enterprise of behavioral ecology. There are no answers as yet . . . " to questions about their evolution (Gould, 1982). Generalities in our understanding of leks have been slow to emerge. As a consequence of this challenge, a great deal of research has focused on leks in the past two decades. This review attempts to organize the results of this work in a way to suggest directions for the future.

Even the problem of what species to include in a discussion of lekking has no simple answer. Criteria for leks (Wiley, 1974; Bradbury, 1981) focus on three features: (1) lack of any parental care by males, as well as any direct contributions of males to feeding or protecting their mates; (2) lack of any association of displaying males with resources, such as food, shelter for young, or nesting substrates, that affect female reproductive success; and (3) aggregation of displaying males. Females visit leks solely for copulation and then leave to raise their offspring without any association with a male. Males contribute nothing except sperm to their offspring. In all known cases that fit the above criteria, the males in any one aggregation differ markedly in their mating success.

These features of social organization, however, do not occur as an invariant syndrome. Extremely unequal distributions of matings among males recur in many species that lack male parental care, and the features of leks mentioned above occur in various combinations in other species (Table I). In particular, some closely related species or even populations of the same species that share the first two features differ in the dispersion of displaying males, which may be

TABLE I
CLASSIFICATION OF MATING SYSTEMS WITH LITTLE OR NO MALE
PARENTAL CARE[a]

	Receptive females	
Mating locations	Aggregated	Dispersed
Associated with resources	Colonial resource-defense polygyny	Dispersed resource-defense polygyny
Not associated with resources	Leks	Dispersed display sites

[a]Excluding mating systems in which males defend individual females or groups of females (harems) for relatively long periods of time.

either aggregated in leks or dispersed on solitary display sites. Although this review focuses on species that fit the three criteria given above for leks, there are allusions to species with dispersed display sites where appropriate.

Lekking has evolved independently in many groups of birds (Payne, 1984; Höglund, 1989) and mammals (Bradbury, 1977; Gosling, 1986; Clutton-Brock et al., 1988a), and mating systems that fit the three basic criteria also appear among frogs, fish, and insects. This review, however, focuses on birds and mammals, groups for which the most intensive studies of lekking are available (scientific names of species mentioned in the text can be found in Section XIII).

The current interest in leks arises from the restriction of males' reproductive contributions solely to sperm. This situation distills the complexities of sexual selection. Females get nothing but genes from mates; so any choice of mates by females evolves without complications introduced by males' associations with resources used by females or by males' contributions to the survival or reproduction of offspring or mates. The interest of lekking species for the study of sexual selection, first recognized by Darwin (1871), was emphasized near the turn of the century by the pioneering English naturalist Edmund Selous (1927). The term "lek" derives from ordinary Scandinavian words meaning play and, by extension, courtship.

Despite the continuing interest in the evolution of leks, I emphasize in this review a distinction between behavioral and evolutionary mechanisms. Previously, I have argued that social organization of any sort requires investigation on three levels (Wiley, 1981). The lowest level of investigation, one that attempts no explanation, produces a description of the patterns or structure in individuals' social relationships throughout their lives, a step analogous to anatomy in other branches of biology. The next level of investigation identifies the genetic, physiological, and behavioral mechanisms that produce these patterns in social relationships. These mechanisms, operating throughout an individual's life, of course, amount to the epigenesis of the individual's social behavior. Ultimately, any complete biological understanding requires an investigation of the evolutionary mechanisms that have produced the present genetic composition of the population.

In the case of mating systems, including leks, this hierarchical approach separates, in particular, female choice from sexual selection. The first is a behavioral mechanism that can generate patterns of mating between individuals; the second, often a consequence of differences in mating success produced by particular behaviors, is a mechanism of the propagation of genes in a population. In some cases these approaches are conflated and in others pursued almost in isolation. In the end, however, structural, behavioral, and evolutionary approaches are no doubt mutualistic in advancing our knowledge. Each suggests issues for those interested in the others.

To clarify the relationships of these approaches in studies of leks, in this review I first consider some general patterns in the social structure of leks, in particular the constancy and variability in the locations of leks and the nonuniform distribution of matings. Then I examine the behavioral interactions that could produce these patterns. Next I turn to general evolutionary issues raised by lekking species, including possibilities for sexual selection, and finally to evolutionary scenarios, complex hypotheses for the evolutionary origins of lekking.

II. Patterns in Lek Behavior

As a first step in understanding leks, this section examines two patterns described repeatedly for lekking birds and mammals: constancy in the locations of leks and nonuniform distributions of matings among males.

A. Constancy in Locations of Leks in Successive Years

Almost every investigation of a lekking species has noted that leks tend to recur from year to year in similar locations. To establish how much locations vary, however, it is necessary to determine the locations of leks over large areas and spans of years. In one such study, Patterson (1952) mapped the locations of all leks of sage grouse in 526 km^2 in Wyoming for 3 years. In the first year, there were 28 leks, with 14 to 400 males each (mean, 78 males). In the second and third years, all leks recurred in locations occupied the preceding year. In the third year, after the population declined by 26%, leks included 2 to 295 males. Because annual mortality of male sage grouse is high (Section IX), probably 75% of the males at leks in the third year had not been present 2 years earlier. Bradbury et al. (1989a) also reported that leks of this species recurred from year to year in the same locations, with significant rank correlations between numbers of males present at each lek in successive years. Likewise, 20 leks of sharp-tailed grouse in Alberta all recurred on the same sites in three successive seasons (Rippin and Boag, 1974a). In other populations of this species, however, more change has occurred. In North Dakota, only 73 of 178 leks remained active more than 5 years (F. R. Henderson and W. W. Jackson, cited by Bergerud and Gratson, 1988), and in Wisconsin 14 of 25 leks remained active on the same site in 3 successive years (Gratson, 1988). Constancy in locations of leks evidently varies among populations of the same species, but often a substantial majority of leks remain in the same locations from one year to the next.

The appearance of new leks and disappearance of former ones often accompany marked increases or decreases in populations (Schwartz, 1945; Dalke *et al.*, 1963). Those leks that disappear and those that appear in new locations also tend to include few males. Tropical lekking species rarely undergo major changes in population densities within periods of a few years, and locations of most leks are correspondingly stable (Lill, 1974a,b, 1976; Snow, 1974; Stiles and Wolf, 1979).

Mammalian leks also show constancy in locations. Fallow deer, with a rutting season confined to about 1 month each year, usually form leks at similar locations in successive years (Clutton-Brock *et al.*, 1988a; Appollonio *et al.*, 1989a,b). In Uganda kob, reproduction occurs year-round. A male holds his position on a lek for periods of several weeks, during which he has little opportunity to feed, and then is replaced by a male from outside the lek. Individual males thus cycle between periods of lekking and periods away from leks when they forage and regain their condition (Buechner and Roth, 1974). Of 15 leks, 10 remained active in the same locations for at least 14 years (Buechner and Roth, 1974). These leks thus clearly exemplify constancy of location with continual turnover of male membership.

Species with dispersed display sites also show constancy in the locations of sites with successive males in occupation. In these species, since often only one male is regularly associated with a display site, stable locations might result entirely from each male's faithfulness to a site. For example, in most tropical species, longevities of males are high enough that display sites are often occupied by one male for several years in a row, longer than the durations of most field studies (Snow, 1970; Vellenga, 1980b; McDonald, 1989a,b). Nevertheless, in both satin bowerbirds and several genera of manakins display sites can have a succession of different males in residence (Snow, 1962a; Lill, 1974a,b; Vellenga, 1980b; McDonald, 1989a,b). In species with high annual mortality, like forest grouse, it is easier to determine the proportion of display sites occupied by a succession of different males. In both ruffed grouse and blue grouse, about a third of all display sites are occupied perennially by successions of males; another third are occupied intermittently, and the remainder in any one year have had no previous occupation (Gullion and Marshall, 1968; Gullion, 1967, 1981; Lewis and Zwickel, 1981; Lewis, 1981).

A prerequisite for constancy in the locations of leks is a stable habitat and thus, stable spatial patterns of resources and movements of individuals (Bradbury *et al.*, 1989a). Leks are often associated with particular features of habitats, such as sparse or short vegetation (de Vos, 1983; Gosling, 1986; Gosling and Petrie, 1990), streams (Stiles and Wolf, 1979), steep slopes (Snow, 1970), low ridges (Schwartz, 1945), or depressions (Wiley, 1973a; Bradbury *et al.*, 1989a). Yet, even though leks often occur in locations with particular vegetational and micro-topographical features, no report has ever concluded that these tendencies completely explain the locations of displaying males in any lekking species (Section VII,C).

B.   MOVEMENTS OF LEKS WITHIN A SEASON

A number of studies have documented that the males on a lek have moved to new locations (Stiles and Wolf, 1979; Gibson and Bradbury, 1987; Gratson, 1988; Appollonio *et al.*, 1990). In some cases, these movements were temporary relocations during a single morning's activity (Lumsden, 1965, 1968; Koivisto, 1965); in other cases, they involved permanent relocations that occurred either abruptly or by stages from day to day. In some cases, such moves suggest an attraction of males to females in new locations (Section IV). In other cases, these shifts occur in response to changes in habitat near leks, as when lekking grouse move from sites with relatively tall grass or shrubs to recently burned areas (Anderson, 1969; Sexton and Gillespie, 1979; Cannon and Knopf, 1981; Gates, 1985). Black grouse in Finland often form leks on frozen lakes in early spring, only to move to nearby openings on shore as the ice thaws (Koivisto, 1965). These cases emphasize again that a stable habitat is necessary for constancy in locations of leks.

C.   VARIATION IN AGGREGATION OF MALES

Another source of variation in lekking species results from differences in dispersion of males within or between populations. Among ruffs in a population in Finland, males switched between attending leks, waiting in areas used by females for feeding, and actively pursuing females (Lank and Smith, 1987). The number of males at leks was higher on days with higher temperatures, and thus lower energy requirements, and on days following those with greater numbers of females copulating. Males on leks copulated 4–5 times more frequently than those away from leks. Male buff-breasted sandpipers in Alaska shift from aggregation at leks early in the season to dispersed display later, in accordance with changes in the dispersion of females (Pruett-Jones, 1988). In Lawes' parotia about 30% of males display solitarily and have about the same success in mating as aggregated males (Pruett-Jones and Pruett-Jones, 1990). Solitarily displaying males occur in small numbers in many species that regularly form leks (Hamerstrom and Hamerstrom, 1973; Lill, 1974a; Rolstad and Wegge, 1987) and in some cases copulate successfully (Kruijt et al., 1972; Sexton, 1979; de Vos, 1983).

Intraspecific variation in sizes and spacing of leks often correlates with differences in population density. Thus, the sparse population of black grouse in the Netherlands, before its extirpation, formed smaller leks with greater average spacing of males within a lek than in denser populations in Scandinavia (de Vos, 1983). The same contrast applies to white-bearded manakins in Suriname and Trinidad. The less dense populations in Suriname average fewer males at a lek, wider spacing of leks and greater distances between males within leks (Olson and McDowell, 1983). In two antelopes, Uganda kob and topi, clustering of male territories into leks occurs in areas with dense populations (Leuthold, 1966; Montfort-Braham, 1975; Gosling, 1986; Gosling and Petrie, 1990). Fallow deer have especially plastic mating systems, including harems, groups of mixed sex with several males in a dominance hierarchy, solitary territories, and leks (Langbein and Thirgood, 1989). These variations are in part related to the densities of males and females in a population, as well as to the synchrony of females' estrus and perhaps to habitat (Schaal, 1986; Langbein and Thirgood, 1989). For many species, there is no information on the nature of the differences in males' and females' behavior that produce differences in the sizes and spacing of leks. Yet, these intraspecific variations could provide insights into the advantages and disadvantages of lekking for individual males and females.

D. MATING CENTERS

Sage grouse, perhaps the species with the most extreme development of lekking, is remarkable both for the very large numbers of males that congregate at some leks, 400 or more (Scott, 1942; Patterson, 1952), and for the compact groups of females, sometimes over 40 at a time, that gather at particular places within a lek. The latter feature of this species has occasioned substantial disagreement among observers. Scott (1942), in his report on sage grouse, noted that both the location of a lek itself and the sites where copulations occurred within a lek remained constant during any one season and from year to year. Subsequent observers of sage grouse have included those agreeing that mating tends to recur in the same locations within leks (Patterson, 1952; Wiley, 1973a) and those denying this pattern (Lumsden, 1968; Gibson and Bradbury, 1986; Hartzler and Jenni, 1988).

The evidence against stable mating centers comes in part from observations that some leks themselves move in the course of a single season (Section II,B). In addition, there is evidence that copulations on sage grouse leks do not always occur at a single site during a season (Lumsden, 1968; Hjorth, 1970; Hartzler,

1972; Wiley, 1973a; Bradbury and Gibson, 1983; Hartzler and Jenni, 1988). Three of these reports, however, come from a single lek, Ford's Creek Lek, near Grass Range, Montana. In 1965, Lumsden used cannon-nets to capture males and females on this lek; others had trapped birds here in preceding years (Lumsden, 1968). Lumsden noted that this lek was unusual in having two clusters of males about 800 m apart. During his observations following cannon-netting, marked males used broadly overlapping areas on the lek and females gathered at 20 different locations. He also noted that males moved their positions in response to his activities following netting or trapping on the lek. In 1968, I found that males on this lek occupied largely exclusive territories (Wiley, 1973a). Females likewise favored particular sites, but one such site was discontinued and another initiated in the course of the 2 weeks of frequent mating. Hartzler, who observed Ford's Creek Lek for the three seasons 1969–1971, again found that males had territories and that copulations did not occur at a single location on the lek during any one season (Hartzler and Jenni, 1988). There were some striking differences in locations of copulations between years, although the locations of some concentrations of matings corresponded between years. Hartzler trapped males on this lek in the first year of his study and reported that several which he could identify before trapping returned to their previous locations.

Thus, both observers after Lumsden agreed that males defended territories on this lek, and all three observers agreed that copulations were not restricted to a single location within a season. Gibson and Bradbury (1986) have cited Hartzler's data as their primary evidence against stable mating centers. In addition, Hjorth (1970) reported that matings occurred in four males' territories on a lek in Montana with only six regularly attending males. In contrast, at larger leks not subjected to netting or trapping, Scott (1942), Patterson (1952), and Wiley (1973a) observed that mating occurred predominantly, although not exclusively, in a small area within a lek. Maps of the locations of copulations indicated that these areas, about 10 m in diameter, approximated the size of a central male's territory but did not necessarily coincide with any one male's boundaries nor with the geometric center of the lek (Wiley, 1973a). The conclusion seems inescapable that leks of sage grouse vary in the stability of mating centers, at least within any one season.

There are two possibilities, not mutually exclusive, for explaining these differences in the stability of mating locations. First, the disturbance of a lek by cannon-netting or trapping might disrupt the birds' behavior, perhaps that of both sexes (Section II,F); such disruption might carry over for a number of years, if males and females tend to return to similar locations in successive years or to follow more experienced individuals (Section V). Mating centers have shifted locations when disturbed (Wiley, 1973a) or when covered by a snow drift (Scott, 1942). Second, it seems likely that leks might vary in the stability of individuals' locations, both those of males and those at which females copulate, regardless of possible disturbances. It is plausible, for instance, that smaller leks might be less stable than larger ones (Section VI).

As for the locations of copulations on sage grouse leks in successive years, most evidence is anecdotal. Results of mapping the locations of copulations in successive years have so far only been published for Ford's Creek Lek (Hartzler and Jenni, 1988); there is no similar comparison between years for a lek in which mating locations have remained stable within a season.

In other species as well, few studies have mapped the locations of copulations, as well as males' display sites or boundaries, in successive seasons. On one lek of common capercaillie, two mating centers each shifted location once in the course of 4 years (LeClerq, 1988). In one population of sharp-tailed grouse, mating centers recurred at the same locations within several leks for 3 years (Kermott, 1982; p. 34), but in another with exceptionally high annual mortality mating centers shifted 10–20 m between years (Landel, 1989). Within a large lek of Guianan cock-of-the-rock, individual display courts varied in mating success from year to year, but the most successful courts were clustered in the same part of the lek in each of 4 years (Trail, 1984; p. 159). In lekking fallow deer, copulations also tend to recur in the same locations in successive years (Clutton-Brock et al., 1988a; Appollonio et al., 1989b). On topi leks, worn patches in the most successful territories persist from year to year (Gosling and Petrie, 1990).

Sage grouse sometimes form extremely large leks, with as many as 200–400 males. On such leks, females have several sites at which they congregate and copulate (Scott, 1942; Patterson, 1952; Wiley, 1973a). Roughly one such focus for females occurs for each 50–70 males present by the end of the mating season. This arrangement suggests that such a large lek actually constitutes a "superlek," an aggregation of aggregations, with each basic unit having a maximum of 60 or so males. Such superleks have also been reported for other species (Bradbury, 1977).

E. DISTRIBUTION OF COPULATIONS AMONG MALES

A pattern reported universally by observers of leks is the nonuniform distribution of matings among males. While widely recognized in a qualitative way, there is relatively little quantitative information. To obtain the necessary data requires unbiased observation of a random or representative sample of males. For species in open habitats with brief mating seasons, it is possible to obtain nearly complete observation of behavior, and to examine the possibility that scattered copulations are more often overlooked than clustered ones. For species with prolonged mating seasons and those with leks in dense habitats, it is necessary to plan focal-individual observations on a schedule that avoids suspected biases.

Only for a few species are there adequate data to compare different leks, years, or populations. To present these distributions in a uniform format, it is useful to graph them as cumulative proportions of copulations against cumulative proportions of males attending a lek (Figs. 1–4). These graphs make it clear that within any one season the distribution of copulations among males on a lek is highly skewed. They also suggest the possibility of inter- or intraspecific variations in the distribution of mating on leks. The greater skew in sage grouse than in black grouse agrees with a proposal that mating distributions might be less uniform in grouse with greater sexual dimorphism or larger leks (Wiley, 1974).

Distributions of matings within one season would not be reflected in distributions of lifetime mating success, if a male's success varied from year to year (Clutton-Brock, 1983). However, successful male black grouse tended to remain successful from year to year, at least until near the ends of their lives (Kruijt and de Vos, 1988). Consistent success in mating from year to year has also been reported for male common capercaillie (Wegge and Larsen, 1987; LeClerq, 1988) and Guianan cock-of-the-rock (Trail, 1984, p. 91). The distribution of lifetime mating success in these cases might not differ markedly from that within a single season.

A further issue in interpreting these distributions is the contribution of genetic and environmental influences on mating success (Sutherland, 1985a,b, 1987; Hubbell and Johnson, 1987). One aspect of this issue is particularly relevant to lekking species. Distributions of matings within one season are based on an assortment of males of different ages. If mating success varies with age (Section

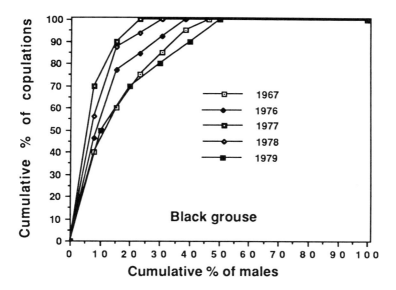

FIG. 1. Distributions of matings among males at one lek of black grouse in 5 years (Kruijt and de Vos, 1988).

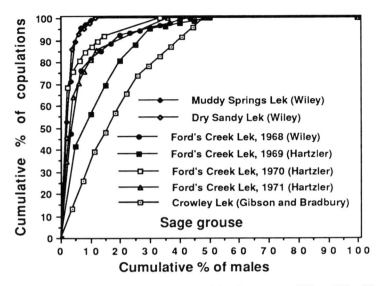

FIG. 2. Distributions of matings among males on leks of sage grouse (Wiley, 1973a; Gibson and Bradbury, 1985; Hartzler and Jenni, 1988).

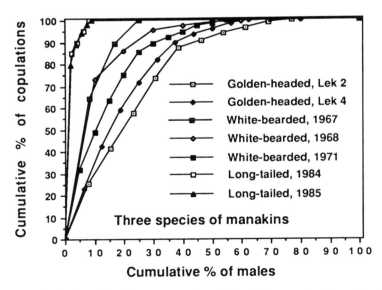

FIG. 3. Distributions of matings among males on leks of three species of manakins (golden-headed, Lill, 1976; white-bearded, Lill, 1974a; long-tailed, McDonald, 1989b).

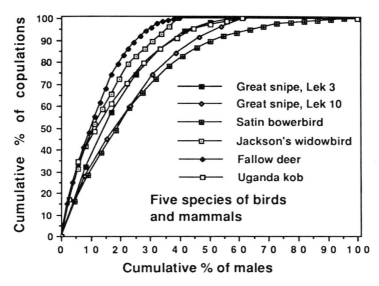

FIG. 4. Distributions of matings among males on leks of four species of birds and mammals and in satin bowerbirds, a species with dispersed display sites (great snipe, Höglund and Lundberg, 1987; satin bowerbird, Borgia, 1985b; Jackson's widowbird, Andersson, 1989; fallow deer, Clutton-Brock *et al.*, 1988a; Uganda kob, Floody and Arnold, 1975).

III,B), lumping males of different ages will exaggerate the deviation from uniformity in lifetime reproductive success. Comparisons of different species or populations might reflect the degree to which young males attend leks and thus are included in the totals for lekking males.

It is not clear to what extent lekking is associated with unusually skewed distributions of male mating success. Polygynous species in general have greater variance in male mating success than do monogamous species (Clutton-Brock, 1983; Payne, 1984). To assess the effect of lekking itself, as opposed to polygyny in general, would require a comparison of distributions of male mating success in lekking species and in species with resource-defense polygyny, harem polygyny, or dispersed display sites. In a comparison of male black grouse, red deer, and northern elephant seals (Kruijt and de Vos, 1988; Clutton-Brock *et al.*, 1988b; LeBoeuf and Reiter, 1988), among those surviving to reproductive age, the proportion failing to mate at least once is lowest in red deer and highest in elephant seals. Thus, nonuniformity in distributions of matings among males of lekking species might not be exceptional among polygynous species overall.

Sexual differences in size, coloration, and elaboration of secondary sexual characters also tend to be associated with polygamy, although exceptions are numerous (Clutton-Brock *et al.*, 1977; Payne, 1984). On the other hand, lekking species seem not to have greater sexual dimorphism in comparison to species with other forms of polygyny. Höglund's (1989) comparative review showed no association of sexual dimorphism in size or coloration with lekking, but his study only classified species into two categories of dimorphism and lumped all species without leks regardless of other distinctions in mating system. Among species of grouse, sexual dimorphism in size is allometric: the ratio of male to female mass increases with increasing female mass. The smallest and least dimorphic species include those that are usually monogamous. The two largest and most dimorphic have leks, but species with leks and those with dispersed display sites do not differ clearly in either mass or dimorphism (Wiley, 1974). Some lekking species lack any notable sexual differences either in mass or secondary sexual characters (Stiles and Wolf, 1979; Payne, 1984; Trail, 1990; Höglund et al., 1990). In conclusion, it remains unclear whether or not lekking species stand out from related species with dispersed display sites, or other forms of polygyny, in distributions of male mating success and in sexual dimorphism.

F. GENERAL METHODOLOGICAL PROBLEMS IN STUDYING LEKS

Studies of leks, like other behavioral studies, involve some intrusion of the observers, but leks present some special problems not often explicitly discussed. For example, many studies have used small blinds erected within or near leks. Males often appear reluctant to shift their locations and eventually accept a blind on a lek, even to the extent that they walk within 1 m or perch atop it (Schwartz, 1945; Hamerstrom and Hamerstrom, 1973). Females, on the other hand, shift their locations more readily and, in any case, have less time during their few visits to habituate. Females have been found to avoid a newly erected blind (Wiley, 1973a) and might avoid permanent ones as well. Clearly, even subtle reactions of females could alter the locations of matings on leks.

Capturing individuals for marking is often most easily accomplished on or near leks (Lumsden, 1968; Robel, 1966, 1967; Gibson and Bradbury, 1985). Studies of leks are exceptional among field studies of behavior in the temptation to capture individuals near locations with such significance for the subjects' social behavior. In some cases, it has been possible to capture and mark individuals away from leks during the nonbreeding season, and this is probably the optimal procedure (Lill, 1974a,b, 1976; Hamerstrom and Hamerstrom, 1973; de Vos, 1983; Kruijt and de Vos, 1988). Recognition of individuals for behavioral studies can sometimes instead rely on minor natural variations in appearance (Hjorth, 1970; Wiley, 1973a; Hamerstrom and Hamerstrom, 1973; Gosling and Petrie, 1990).

There are few studies of the effects of disturbing individuals on their leks. Dalke et al. (1963) reported that less than half of the male sage grouse returned to a lek after cannon-netting. Although older males were more likely to return than yearlings, even some of them disappeared. For black grouse, radio packages increased mortality of both sexes for a week following capture. Survivors beyond this time, however, appeared to fare as well as controls (Angelstam, 1984). Some male black grouse caught on leks in the Netherlands did not return for 1–2 days; those with central positions lost all or parts of their territories while those with peripheral positions did not (Kruijt *et al.*, 1972).

The difficulties of studying leks without disturbance, in conjunction with variation in the patterns of lekking within any one species, create a basic conundrum that all students of leks must confront. There is an unavoidable choice between intensive investigation of one or a few leks, on the one hand, and extensive but less thorough assessment of variation among leks, on the other. In the end, we need both kinds of information.

III. Behavioral Interactions of Males

Any social structure is generated by individuals' responses to each other. Of course, each of these responses invites further explanation in terms of physiological, ontogenetic, and genetic mechanisms. The first step, however, in understanding the social structure of leks is to examine the responses of the individuals involved: the responses of males to each other, of males to females, of females to males, and of females to each other.

A. Territoriality and Dominance

The interactions of males attending leks typically include elements both of territoriality and of dominance relationships. Different investigators studying the same species have often emphasized one or the other aspect of males' interactions, without clear indications that they actually observed different behavior. An example comes from studies of greater prairie chickens by two groups. Hamerstrom and Hamerstrom (1960, 1973) discussed males' relationships almost entirely in terms of territoriality. They described males defending small areas with well-defined, but flexible, boundaries at which neighbors engaged in ritualized encounters and sometimes escalated fights. In contrast, Robel and colleagues (Robel, 1964, 1966, 1967; Robel and Ballard, 1974) described the relationships of males in terms of differences in aggressiveness. In 2 years, the males most successful in mating also ranged over the largest areas on the lek. Although Robel referred to these areas as "territories," they were in fact ranges determined by plotting the males' locations at 15-min intervals.

These differences are resolved by considering the males' behavior in the presence and absence of females. When there are no females visiting a lek, males occupy small discrete territories with definite boundaries from which all intruding rivals are normally evicted. On the other hand, when females are present, males often leave their territories to approach the females. In these conditions, relationships more closely resemble those of a dominance hierarchy without clear reference to location. Despite these movements of males, copulations usually occur within males' territories as defined by boundary encounters (Hamerstrom and Hamerstrom, 1960, 1973). Robel (1967, p. 113) described successful males "escorting females to the center of activity [of the lek] prior to copulation."

Greater prairie chickens seem to represent an extreme among grouse in movements of males on a lek, although movements of displaying males away from their territories occur in other lekking grouse as well (Koivisto, 1965; Lumsden, 1965, 1968; Moss, 1980). As in prairie chickens, dominance relationships among male sage grouse become clearer after they move away from their previously established territories (Gibson and Bradbury, 1987).

The combination of dominance and territoriality applies to males of other lekking species as well. A territory is often defined as an area within which an individual dominates its rivals and has nearly exclusive access to resources (Waser and Wiley, 1979). Even without exclusive use of an area, dominance relationships can vary with individuals' locations (Brown, 1963; Piper and Wiley, 1989). Furthermore, in some cases not all territorial locations are equal. When better competitors defend better locations, the result is an "ideal despotic distribution" (Fretwell, 1972) or "polarized territoriality" (Wiley, 1973a). In this case, individuals are ranked in the end by the value of their locations, even though they interact primarily with immediate neighbors. Thus the questions are, To what extent do lekking males show evidence of ranking, even when they maintain nearly exclusive areas? and To what extent does location influence interactions, even when males' movements overlap?

Evidence for dominance relationships without respect to location comes from several tropical lekking species. Male long-tailed manakins use overlapping sets of display sites so that each display site is visited regularly by 3–15 males (McDonald, 1989a). At each site, dominance is clearly established between the two or three most frequent males. The top-ranking (alpha) male at one site tends also to dominate opponents at 1–3 nearby sites. In this case, individual males rise in dominance at the sites they use as more dominant males disappear (McDonald, 1989b). Male capuchinbirds also congregate for display without indications of territoriality; one male in each group dominates the others in access to the perch used for copulation (Snow, 1972; Trail, 1990). Limited observations of Goldie's bird of paradise, a species restricted to several small islands at the eastern end of New Guinea, suggest similar dominance relationships among males sharing a display site (LeCroy et al., 1980; see also Snow and Goodwin, 1974).

Clear indications of dominance relationships also appear among male satin bowerbirds, which construct bowers of woven sticks at their dispersed display sites. Males steal bright decorations and sticks from each others' bowers, and some males are much more successful at defending their bowers and stealing from neighbors than are others (Borgia, 1985a,b; Borgia and Gore, 1986). In addition, at artificial food sources away from their display sites, supplantations indicate a dominance hierarchy among males (Borgia, 1985a, 1986). It remains unclear, however, whether or not dominance at feeding sites is related to success in protecting bowers from rivals. Males' relationships might also influence the locations of their display sites, as males sometimes take over more successful individuals' sites when the latter disappear (Vellenga, 1980b). Bowerbirds, like manakins and capuchinbirds, have low annual mortality, so even studies extending over a number of years have obtained little information on turnover of males.

Studies of lekking grouse have also revealed that males continue their social relationships away from leks and during seasons with little activity at leks (Lumsden, 1965; Koivisto, 1965; Robel, 1969; Angelstam, 1984). The clearest description of this behavior pertains to male black grouse from a lek in the Netherlands (Kruijt et al., 1972; de Vos, 1983; Kruijt and de Vos, 1988). These males tended to associate with each other elsewhere as well. When feeding, males seldom interacted, but they regularly interrupted any responses of other males to females. These interruptions were performed mostly by those males with peripheral territories at the lek, as if their zones of dominance over rivals extended radially outward from the lek. Furthermore, this site-dependent dominance or territoriality was polarized, as males took central positions on leks when they were available (Section III,B). Male common capercaillie also have large ranges that extend radially outward from leks, but the relationships of males in these areas is unknown (Hjorth, 1970; Wegge and Larsen, 1987; LeClerq, 1988).

Continuity in the relationships of males is also indicated by the observation that male grouse often maintain their spatial arrangements to some extent even when they move away from a lek to approach nearby females (Sections II,B and IV; Koivisto, 1965; Lumsden, 1968; Gibson and Bradbury, 1987). Continuing relationships of males throughout the year might also lead to low levels of aggression among males early in the season, as often observed (Wiley, 1973a; Moyles and Boag, 1981; Hartzler and Jenni, 1988; but see Koivisto, 1965).

Territorial relationships of males within leks are clearest when all males, even those generally unsuccessful in mating, can copulate successfully provided they get a chance at locations within their territories (Buechner, 1961; Buechner and Schloeth, 1965; Hjorth, 1970; Wiley, 1973a; Floody and Arnold, 1975; Bradbury, 1977; Beehler, 1983b; Kruijt and de Vos, 1988; Hartzler and Jenni, 1988; Andersson, 1989). In these cases, males generally adhere to territorial boundaries even in the presence of receptive females. In sage grouse, territorial boundaries often remain stable for periods of weeks, and males dominate all intruders in their territories even when females are on the lek. Males with little overall success in mating nevertheless copulate without interruption at locations inside their territories, provided females stay away from boundary zones one to a few meters wide (Wiley, 1973a; Hartzler and Jenni, 1988). Within the boundary zone between territories, neighboring males interrupt each others' copulations reciprocally. Males with high overall success tend to have many females that solicit well inside their territories. Less successful males either have few females solicit inside their territories or attempt most of their copulations near their boundaries with more successful neighbors and thus have higher probabilities of interruption (Wiley, 1973a). In black grouse as well, copulations near territorial boundaries are more likely to be interrupted by neighbors (Kruijt et al., 1972).

Success in interrupting copulations has been taken as evidence of a male's dominance on a lek (Scott, 1942; Lumsden, 1965; Foster, 1983). The preceding discussion, however, indicates that asymmetries in interruptions do not necessarily reflect dominance relationships in a simple way. If females tend to mate within particular males' territories, the neighbors of these males would have the greatest opportunities for interruptions. In Guianan cocks-of-the-rock, it is indeed the neighbors of the most successful males that interrupt the most copulations (Trail and Koutnik, 1986). The neighbors of successful males might also attempt most of their copulations near their territorial boundaries, where they would have a higher risk of disruption by neighbors (Wiley, 1973a).

Even when males can copulate without challenge within their territories, there are often indications of overall dominance relationships among those on a lek. The tendency of males to move their positions on leks toward the center, where most matings take place, recurs in a number of lekking species (Section III,B). In addition, boundary encounters when females are present on a lek are often asymmetrical. Those males farther from females tend to encroach on the territories of their neighbors closer to females, so that the former more often provoke encounters to which the latter respond and the latter more often terminate encounters in order to return to the females (Wiley, 1973a; Kruijt et al., 1972; Kermott, 1982, p. 110). These patterns suggest that males in locations nearer females prevent other males from occupying those positions, so that males are in fact ranked by their territorial positions.

Hartzler and Jenni (1988) argued that polarized territoriality of this sort could not apply to the Ford's Creek Lek. The shifting locations of females on this lek make stable polarity in territorial relationships unlikely. Nevertheless, their maps indicate that some males did move their boundaries from one year to the next to include parts of areas where frequent copulation occurred the preceding year. Hartzler and Jenni (1988) also emphasize the relatively slow reoccupation of vacancies on grouse leks (Kruijt et al., 1972; Wiley, 1973a). However, the settled relationships of neighboring males could also explain why interactions do not increase markedly when a vacancy appears. It would pay peripheral males to wait before they leap, if, as in black grouse, central males easily evict intruders after absences from the lek (Kruijt et al., 1972; see also Snow, 1962a).

In conclusion, in most species males' relationships on leks do not conform completely either to dominance, without influence of location, or to territoriality, without indications of ranking. The combined influences of ranking and location on males' relationships have rarely been considered explicitly. In particular, more information is needed on asymmetries in the territorial relationships of males on a lek and on site-dependent dominance among males away from leks.

B. Age as a Factor in the Social Relationships of Males

In most lekking species, as in many other polygynous species (Selander, 1972; Clutton-Brock et al., 1977; Clutton-Brock, 1983; Alatalo et al., 1988), young males have less developed secondary sexual characteristics than do older males. Male manakins retain a drab, female-like plumage for 3 years before attaining full development of bright male plumage (Snow, 1962a,b; Lill, 1974a, 1976; Foster, 1977a, 1981, 1987; McDonald, 1989a,b). Similar sequences of male plumages occur in many cotingas, both in species with leks and those with dispersed display sites (Snow, 1982). Male birds of paradise with leks and bowerbirds with dispersed display sites retain immature plumage even longer (Gilliard, 1969; Vellenga, 1980b). Male fallow deer and reduncinine antelope, including the lekking species, require several years to attain full body mass and antler size (Buechner and Roth, 1974; Clutton-Brock et al., 1988a). Although female hammer-headed bats can breed at an age of 6 months, males do not attain full development of their enlarged larynx and active sperm until 18 months (Bradbury, 1977).

Among lekking grouse, males in their first year often have less developed tail feathers and other secondary sexual characters, although these distinctions are sometimes subtle or unreliable (Patterson, 1952; Eng, 1963; Dalke et al., 1963; Koivisto, 1965). They are also smaller on average than older males (Beck and Braun, 1978). In common capercaillie, the largest grouse, growth to full size takes at least 2 years (Moss, 1987a,b). In addition, in sage grouse the esophageal sac used to produce characteristic sounds does not develop as rapidly during a male's first spring as in later years, so that first-year males attain full development only after the females begin to appear regularly on leks (Eng, 1963; Lumsden, 1968; Wiley, 1973a,b).

A similar delay in seasonal development applies to second-year male blue grouse, a species with dispersed display sites (Bendell, 1955). On the other hand, sexually monomorphic lekking species, such as hermit-hummingbirds (Stiles and Wolf, 1979), lack any age-related differences in males' morphology. For these species, it is not known whether or not young males' seasonal development lags behind that of older males.

In those species with delayed development of full size or secondary sexual characteristics in males, recognizably younger males often visit leks but do not participate fully in lekking activities. In manakins, males retaining some female-like plumage briefly visit older males' display sites at leks (Snow, 1962a; Lill, 1974b, 1976; Foster, 1981; McDonald, 1989a). They sometimes claim these sites when the older males vacate them during the annual molt, but they are evicted quickly when the older males return (Snow, 1962a). In black grouse, yearling males intruding on a lek often evoke little attention from established males, unless they begin to display (Kruijt et al., 1972; de Vos, 1983). Young male sage grouse often join groups of females visiting leks and thus temporarily escape notice by territorial males (Wiley, 1973a). Young male fallow deer infiltrate leks in the interstices of older males' territories (Clutton-Brock et al., 1988a).

In sage grouse, younger males do not usually establish territories on leks until after females begin to visit regularly (Patterson, 1952; Eng, 1963; Emmons and Braun, 1984). They display for brief periods at first and do not occupy any one area consistently (Wiley, 1973a; Hartzler and Jenni, 1988). Seasonal delay in regular attendance of yearling males at leks has not been well documented in other lekking grouse, although it has been noted for common capercaillie (Dement'ev and Gladkov, 1967). In Norway, males of this species do not establish stable territories until the end of their second spring (Wegge and Larsen, 1987).

Young males of lekking species often have less stable locations for display than do older males. In several species of grouse, yearlings are known to visit several leks while older males with few exceptions attend only one (Dalke et al., 1963; Koivisto, 1965; Robel, 1967; Robel et al., 1970; de Vos, 1983; Emmons and Braun, 1984; Wegge and Larsen, 1987). First-year males normally establish territories at the peripheries of existing leks (Robel, 1967; Robel and Ballard, 1974; Koivisto, 1965; Wiley, 1973a; Kruijt et al., 1972; de Vos, 1983; Moyles and Boag, 1981). Although yearling male black grouse in the Netherlands sometimes established territories late in the season in the central parts of leks, these males had all lost their territories by the following season, so that all 2-year old males held peripheral territories (de Vos, 1983). In lekking species other than grouse, young males also visit more than one lek before establishing stable positions (Buechner and Roth, 1974; McDonald, 1989a,b) and display from peripheral positions (Beehler, 1983b; Trail, 1984, p. 160). In Trinidad, immature male white-bearded manakins displayed at a "practice lek" separate from the leks used by older males where copulations occurred (Snow, 1962a). In sage grouse, yearling males also sometimes display near groups of females at locations away from leks (Dunn and Braun, 1986).

In species with solitary display sites, like the bearded bellbird and several forest-inhabiting grouse, yearling males also display either less than older males or not at all and often tend to take positions near the peripheries of established older males' territories (Snow, 1973; Gullion, 1967, 1981; Bendell and Elliott, 1967; Bendell et al., 1972; Zwickel, 1972; Hannon et al., 1979; Ellison, 1971). Yearling male blue grouse preferentially settle near those display sites of older males visited more frequently by females (Lewis and Zwickel, 1980, 1981; Jamieson and Zwickel, 1983).

In studies of lekking grouse, first-year males either have never copulated successfully (Koivisto, 1965; Robel, 1967; Wiley, 1973a; Moyles and Boag, 1981; Hartzler and Jenni, 1988) or have only copulated infrequently (de Vos, 1983; Hjorth, 1970; Hartzler and Jenni, 1988). Hamerstrom and Hamerstrom (1973) found that 18% of copulations by male greater prairie chickens during a 22-year study were performed by yearling males. Their extensive data on the age structure of this population based on marked individuals suggest that on average 34% of males were yearlings. Assuming that yearling and older males were observed equivalently, copulation rates/male averaged about 2.3 times higher for older males. This pattern of little or no copulation by males in their first breeding season, and sometimes even later, recurs in all lekking species: in fallow deer and kob (Buechner and Roth, 1974; Clutton-Brock et al., 1988a; Appolonio et al., 1989a,b), in ruff (Hogan-Warburg, 1966), in manakins and cock-of-the-rock (Snow, 1962a; Lill, 1974a, 1976; Trail, 1985a), and in hermit-hummingbirds (Stiles and Wolf, 1979; Snow, 1974). It also applies to species with dispersed display sites (Snow, 1973; Payne and Payne, 1977; Borgia, 1986).

The possibility that young males' behavior is simply an alternative tactic for copulation seems unlikely, although the tendency of some yearling males to mingle with groups of females might suggest this possibility. In sage grouse, yearling males that join groups of females on leks have never been seen to copulate. The current evidence suggests that young males in these species instead make less commitment to competition for territories and mates. Nevertheless, a male should in general take any adventitious opportunity for copulation; infrequent copulations by first-year males probably need no other explanation.

Do behavioral interactions with older males control the development of reproductive physiology and morphology in younger males? Social interactions with older, dominant males might inhibit reproduction by younger subordinates (see Vandenbergh, 1971); alternatively, young males might fail to develop full reproductive behavior and physiology regardless of interactions with older males (see Wiley and Hartnett, 1976). An investigation of this behavioral and physiological question would involve comparisons of first-year males subject to interactions with older males and others not subject to such interactions. Removals of older males from leks would also provide relevant information, but no fully satisfactory experiments along these lines are available for lekking species. Systematic removal of older males from leks of the common capercaillie suggested that the seasonal development of young males was to some extent independent of their interactions with older males (Kirikov cited by Dement'ev and Gladkov, 1967, p. 97). This experiment, however, did not preclude interactions between age classes away from the lek.

Interactions with older males might have more influence on where, rather than when, younger males establish themselves. Two studies that removed central males from leks of greater prairie chickens and sharp-tailed grouse showed that additional males established themselves on these leks primarily at peripheral locations, while nearby undepleted leks did not acquire additional males (Ballard and Robel, 1974; Rippin and Boag, 1974a,b). It is probable that the recruits in these studies were previously unestablished yearling males, although they were not examined in the hand as required to determine the ages of males in these two species. Radio-tracking, however, showed that young males often visited several leks at this time (Robel *et al.*, 1970), and no males previously established on nearby leks moved to the experimentally depleted ones (Rippin and Boag, 1974a). In grouse, the formation of new leks in response to increasing populations can also involve mostly yearling males (Cannon and Knopf, 1981).

It seems plausible that young males of lekking species prospect for optimal locations to establish themselves. For instance, yearling male sharp-tailed grouse are attracted to leks used by large numbers of females, even when male mortality on these leks is higher than elsewhere (R. L. Brown, reviewed by Bergerud and Gratson, 1988, p. 503). Male black grouse tend to establish territories at locations where they interact with females or other males (de Vos, 1983), and the same might apply to yearling male sage grouse (Emmons and Braun, 1984).

These patterns in the behavior of immature males in lekking grouse are remarkably similar to extensively documented patterns in blue grouse, a species with dispersed display sites. Yearling males' testes develop later in the season and never reach the same size on average as do those of older males, although yearlings do produce viable sperm (Bendell, 1955; Hannon *et al.*, 1979). Yearlings also arrive in breeding areas later than do older males, at about the same time that females arrive, and preferentially localize their activities at the periphery of older males' territories, particularly those territories that most frequently have females nearby (Bendell and Elliott, 1967; Bendell *et al.*, 1972; Zwickel, 1972; Lewis and Zwickel, 1980, 1981; Jamieson and Zwickel, 1983). When older males are removed from their territories, yearlings occupy the vacancies, although some yearlings remain nonterritorial despite the persistence of vacancies (Bendell and Elliott, 1967; Bendell *et al.*, 1972; Zwickel, 1972). Nevertheless, these territorial yearlings do not develop gonads any larger than those of nonterritorial yearlings collected at the same time (Hannon *et al.*, 1979).

Age-related differences in behavior might continue even after males have reached full adult development. Long-tailed manakins provide a clear example (McDonald, 1989a,b). Males with fully developed plumage become regular attendants at display sites of more senior, dominant males, which perform nearly all the copulations. Only after persisting in subordinate status until the dominant male disappears can a younger male acquire dominance at a small zone with 1–3 display sites. Survival is high in this species, so that males of known age have never become dominant at display sites before age 8. Band-tailed manakins have a similar succession of males from subordinate to dominant status in a display territory; final stages of courtship are again performed only by dominant males. In this species, however, one of two cases of succession involved a reversal of the relationships of the two top-ranking males in a territory; in the other case, succession of the second in rank followed disappearance of the dominant male (Robbins, 1985). In these two species, succession to mating status occurs among males ranked in a dominance hierarchy.

Alternatively, succession could occur by movements of males from less to more advantageous locations. In species like some lekking grouse, in which first-year males establish territories at the peripheries of leks and established males tend to retain their territories from year to year (Kruijt et al., 1972; Evans, 1969; de Vos, 1983; Hartzler and Jenni, 1988), young males might well have to wait for vacancies to obtain better locations. In some cases, social interactions at leks might produce a stochastic progression of males toward central locations where most copulations occur (Kruijt et al., 1972; Wiley, 1973a, 1978). Such a process would generate a correlation of mating success with seniority and age. This correlation, however, would presumably not be strong, because the irregular geometry of most leks and the stochastic nature of mortality would create considerable variation in the progression of males. In addition, individual differences in males' capabilities and physiological condition would introduce further variation.

Seventeen years of data on marked black grouse at one lek in the Netherlands showed that males were progressively more likely to occupy central territories and to have higher mating success with increased age at least through age 5; thereafter males appeared to lose vigor, so that they often lost their territories and declined in mating success. The mean rate of copulation for males in their third through fifth years was 2.8/year, approximately a 4-fold increase over that for males in their first or second years. The former were also nearly twice as likely to hold central territories (42 and 23%, respectively) (Kruijt and de Vos, 1988), where most copulations occurred (Kruijt and Hogan, 1967). Males in fact were four times more likely to shift territorial boundaries toward the center of a lek than toward the periphery (de Vos, 1983). Males that moved had always been unsuccessful in their previous locations. In confirmation of the greater competition for central positions, vacancies of central territories were filled more quickly than vacancies of peripheral territories (Kruijt et al., 1972).

For the common capercaillie, Wegge and Larsen (1987) reported that males only exceptionally moved to fill vacancies. The areas involved, however, are ranges extending 0.5–1 km from the lek. Because the ranges of different males regularly visiting a lek were, for the most part, exclusive, Wegge and Larsen (1987) called them territories, although evidence of defense or dominance was not obtained. The spatial organization of males within the lek was not investigated. On the other hand, they reported that 3-year-old males had larger ranges located farther from the lek than did older males (mean areas 61 and 26 ha, respectively); the youngest male known to have mated was 4 years old. These findings suggest the possibility of succession in status, but perhaps not associated with changes of location.

On relatively large leks of sage grouse, males have been found to move their territories into vacancies closer to a mating center. In each of four instances, a neighboring male located farther from females moved its territory into a vacancy over periods of several days (Wiley, 1973a). In contrast, at the Ford's Creek Lek, which lacked a stable mating center (Section II,D), there was no clear movement of territories toward positions frequented by females and no improvement of mating success with age after a male's second year (Hartzler and Jenni, 1988). The question of territorial succession in sage grouse cannot be answered without more observations on vacancies and movements of territories on a number of leks.

Movements of territories to fill vacancies closer to the center of a lek have also been observed in hermit-hummingbirds (Stiles and Wolf, 1979), white-bearded manakins (Snow, 1962a), and Uganda kob (Floody and Arnold, 1975). On leks of kob and topi, mating tends to occur in central territories (Floody and Arnold, 1975; Fryxell, 1987; Gosling and Petrie, 1990). In Guianan cock-of-the-rock, males progress from being intruders on leks, to holding peripheral and eventually central territories (Trail, 1984, pp. 157–158). Among mature males, individuals tended to move their small territories around a display court closer to successful males, but these moves were not restricted to occupation of neighboring vacancies. Males that moved their territories, whether previously successful or unsuccessful, were less likely to mate in the following year than were comparable males that did not move. However, once a male mated successfully, he became much less likely to move again. In this species it thus seems probable that a male's success in mating depends both on the location of his court within a lek and on his occupation of it for several years during which females become familiar with him. Mating success of marked males increased on average with age (Trail, 1984).

The clearest evidence for territorial succession in lekking species comes from experimental removals of central males. In greater prairie chickens, for instance, after removal of 2–3 males in central positions on leks with 7–9 established males, the remaining birds that previously had peripheral positions shifted their ranges to more central positions where copulations occurred (Ballard and Robel, 1974). This study, however, failed to collect information on the boundaries of males' territories, as revealed by aggressive interactions, as opposed to their ranges on the lek. On a lek of white-bearded manakins, when two successful males were removed, neighbors occupied the vacancies, either immediately or eventually, and copulated successfully (Lill, 1974a).

Removals of central male sharp-tailed grouse from two leks induced similar changes (Rippin and Boag, 1974a,b); vacancies created in the center of a lek were first filled by males originally located adjacent to the center and then, after these were removed, by males originally in peripheral locations. Evans (1969) provides a clear illustration of the movement of a male sharp-tailed grouse's territory toward the center of a lek; in this case, the movement consisted of a partial withdrawal from the male's original territory during the autumn and complete withdrawal by the following spring. Hjorth (1970) also illustrates a shift in territorial boundaries, in which two yearling neighbors divided an area vacated by a 2-year-old male after he was trapped on the lek. In this case, the two yearlings both copulated in their newly acquired areas. In general, copulations tend to occur near the centers of leks in this species (Lumsden, 1965; Hjorth, 1970, p. 412; Kermott, 1982).

This pattern of territorial succession in sharp-tailed grouse was confirmed by Moyles and Boag (1981). Males began to establish territories in the first autumn, although some were not permanently established at a lek until their second autumn. These young males first took peripheral positions on leks, where they displayed little aggression or constancy in attendance at first. They then moved their positions to occupy vacancies toward the center of a lek, so that mating success depended in part on seniority at a lek. By mapping males' territories on a lek in three successive years, Kermott (1982) also documented this process. In five cases, males with peripheral territories acquired central territories in adjoining locations in subsequent years; no transitions from central to peripheral territories occurred.

An increase in aggressiveness is not usually sufficient to change the territorial locations of male sharp-tailed grouse. Trobec and Oring (1972) implanted testosterone pellets in five males on one lek in May, late in the breeding season. Although the implanted males engaged in more aggressive interactions, predominantly with more centrally located males, none managed to evict an opponent or to enlarge its territory. Trobec and Oring's finding thus suggests that current behavioral interactions do not alone explain social relationships and the distribution of mating success on leks. Leks evidently exhibit "social inertia" (Guhl, 1968).

Hormonal manipulations of males on leks would bear further investigation. In birds with relatively large, all-purpose territories, males implanted with testosterone in some cases increase the sizes of their territories and in some cases do not (Watson and Parr, 1981; Wingfield, 1984). In sharp-tailed grouse, there is one well described case of an unusually aggressive yearling male that obtained a central territory and mated successfully (Kermott, 1982, p. 66). It seems possible that hormonal manipulations would have the greatest effect early in the season before territorial boundaries are set.

In some species with dispersed display sites, males also move to occupy sites vacated by successful males (Payne and Payne, 1977; Shaw, 1984). For instance, in village indigobirds, following removal or disappearance of five successful males, less successful males relocated to claim the vacated sites (Payne and Payne, 1977). In three cases, their subsequent mating success was not followed. In the other two cases, respectively, a newcomer copulated successfully within a few days and a series of males all failed to copulate. Future experiments of this sort, with adequate replication, might compare removals of successful and unsuccessful males.

This review of the behavioral interactions of males on leks shows how sparse the available evidence remains. We lack a study that incorporates all of the following: (1) observations of several leks, (2) mapping of territorial boundaries and copulations based on complete observations or unbiased sampling, (3) permanently identified individuals followed for most of their lives, and (4) adequately replicated experimental manipulations.

C.   COOPERATION AND COORDINATION OF MALES

Perhaps the most striking form of male–male interaction on leks occurs in those species in which two or more males coordinate their efforts. The unique case of the ruff apparently involves cooperation of two male morphs, those with predominantly white ruffs and head tufts and those with any of various darker colors. When white males, termed "satellites," visit leks, they display submissive behavior to resident territorial males (Hogan-Warburg, 1966). Although a resident attempts to drive away satellites once females are present on his territory, satellites nevertheless obtain some copulations (Hogan-Warburg, 1966; van Rhijn, 1973). Individual satellites seem to form associations with particular territories on a lek, but these associations might result simply from their attraction to territories in which females gather. Because the coloration of the breeding plumage is retained throughout life and thus presumably has a genetic basis, the persistence of this polymorphism requires some form of balancing selection (Hogan-Warburg, 1966; van Rhijn, 1973, 1983, 1985). Hogan-Warburg (1966) argued that satellites on small leks are more successful and contribute more to the success of resident males. It has also been proposed that the presence of a satellite on a resident's territory increases the chances that a female will copulate (Hogan-Warburg, 1966; Shepard, 1975). van Rhijn (1973) could not confirm these suggestions and instead proposed that the presence of a satellite male enhances the attraction of females to a resident's territory (van Rhijn, 1973, 1985). Although there is little quantitative evidence to evaluate any of these points, there are indications that residents and satellites might interact cooperatively to enhance mating success by both males and also that competition occurs between them as well.

No other lekking species has comparable male polymorphism. Coordination of displays, however, raises similar issues of cooperation and competition. In the long-tailed manakin (Foster, 1977a; McDonald, 1989a,b) and its congeners with similar displays (Snow, 1977; Foster, 1981), the strikingly coordinated efforts of two males are related to succession of males in dominance at display sites. In these species, two males produce a loud call in unison when females are not present nearby. In long-tailed manakins, the rate of coordinated calling correlates with female visits to a display site (McDonald, 1989a). When a female arrives, the two males engage in a coordinated dance, which consists of alternating performances of similar actions. The subordinate male of the pair, however, always retires before the final preliminaries to copulation, which is always performed by the dominant male. The subordinate might realize some eventual benefit, because when a dominant male disappears, the subordinate becomes the new dominant at the same site (McDonald, 1989a,b). This succession, however, does not necessarily result in immediate benefits for the new dominant, as visits by females in one case decreased markedly in the first year. These birds have such low mortality, however, that data are slow to accumulate on the consequences of takeovers. The possibility of eventual benefits from inheriting a display site could help to explain a subordinate's assistance in attracting and stimulating females by means of coordinated vocalization and display.

In several other tropical lekking birds, males also coordinate displays (Snow, 1963; Foster, 1977, 1981; LeCroy et al., 1980; Robbins, 1983, 1985; Prum, 1985, 1986; Prum and Johnson, 1987). Some of these cases involve two males performing similar displays in stereotyped alternation, as in the wire-tailed manakin (Schwartz and Snow, 1978), and in other cases performing synchronized or alternating calls, as in the calls of some birds of paradise of the genus *Paradisaea* (Gilliard, 1969, p. 410; Dinsmore, 1970; LeCroy, 1981). Male capuchinbirds time their loud calls to avoid overlap with other males on their lek (Snow, 1972). Remarkable coordination also occurs in sharp-tailed grouse, although it is not emphasized in reports on this species (Lumsden, 1965; Hjorth, 1970; Kermott and Oring, 1975). Males have specially modified tail feathers that are scraped together to produce a stacatto rattle. At intervals all males on a lek cease and stand in place; after a pause of several seconds, they resume abruptly, producing a dramatic acoustic effect.

These instances of coordination might represent males' attempts to outdo each other in competitive display, or they might represent collective signals that attract females, or both (Avery, 1984). The brief synchronized silences during tail-rattling by sharp-tailed grouse are difficult to interpret solely in terms of competitive display by individual males. Instead, these coordinated displays might represent cooperative efforts to attract and stimulate females. Since male sharp-tailed grouse tend to move their territorial locations toward the center of the lek, where most copulations occur, cooperation in display might have evolved in conjunction with succession of social positions, as in long-tailed manakins.

Less striking forms of coordination occur in other species in the form of contagious display. This possibility has again received little attention, although observers occasionally note its occurrence (Snow, 1962a; Snow and Goodwin, 1974). Display by one male tends to stimulate display by nearby males. This form of coordination in display is easily explained by competition among individual males. No male would do well to be outdone by its neighbor, if it could help it. Nevertheless, it is not inconceivable that the collective aspects of simultaneous display by aggregations of males might also have some influence on females that displays by individual males would not (Section V,D).

If coordinated or contagious display represents a form of reciprocal altruism (Avery, 1984), all males involved must realize some increased expectation of mating success in the long run. In addition, there must be some means of denying advantages to noncooperators (Axelrod and Hamilton, 1981). Territorial succession or succession in dominance could provide both of these essentials, if noncooperators were less likely to improve their locations or status (see Wiley and Rabenold, 1984). These possibilities for lekking species have not received attention.

IV. RESPONSES OF MALES TO FEMALES

An aspect of the behavioral mechanisms of lekking that has received little systematic attention is the response of males to females. In part this neglect results from observations that males congregate and establish territories in the absence of females.

Almost every report on lekking species, as well as on species with dispersed display sites, indicates that males visit leks both earlier and later in the season than do females. In nonmigratory lekking species, males often visit leks throughout the year except during periods of molting and physiological stress. Thus, males of lekking grouse visit their leks from the earliest mild days in late winter or early spring until their period of molt in late summer and then, in most species, again during the autumn until severe weather begins (Patterson, 1952; Lumsden, 1965; Koivisto, 1965; Hammerstrom and Hammerstrom, 1973; de Vos, 1983; Vehrencamp et al., 1989). In tropical species, males also visit their leks almost throughout the year except during molt (Snow, 1962a,b; Trail, 1984). Attendance at leks, however, drops or ceases during periods of short food supply (Snow, 1962a), which can be an annual occurrence in seasonal climates (Foster, 1977b; Worthington, 1982). Male fallow deer, which occupy their territories on leks continuously during the brief rut, nevertheless attend both several days earlier and later than do females (Clutton-Brock et al., 1988a; Appollonio et al., 1989a). Males of tropical lekking antelope also visit their leks throughout the year, except during seasons of sparse food in highly seasonal environments

(Buechner and Roth, 1974; Schuster, 1976). The pattern thus suggests that males of many lekking species spend as much of their time as possible at their leks and leave only as necessary for food or during periods of increased susceptibility to predators such as during molt.

The same principal applies to daily attendance as well. Males of lekking deer and reduncinine antelope continuously occupy their territories at leks for periods of several weeks, with little food (Buechner and Roth, 1974; Floody and Arnold, 1975; Fryxell, 1987; Clutton-Brock *et al.*, 1988a). Males of lekking birds, hammer-headed bats, and topi leave their leks daily in order to feed (Bradbury, 1977; Gosling and Petrie, 1990). Nevertheless, in all species, males attend their leks for longer periods each day than do females. Once again, males appear to spend as much time as possible on their leks and leave primarily when necessary for feeding and drinking.

Although males interact with each other for long periods in the absence of females, they respond in several obvious ways to females. These responses include (1) movements toward females, (2) changes in tactics and rates of display, and (3) copulation.

The first of these responses is clear when males on leks move as a group to approach nearby females (Section II,B). This tendency to approach females is confirmed by responses of males to groups of taxidermic mounts of females. Male sharp-tailed grouse were attracted to sites as much as 100–200 m away from established leks by mounted females, although no information was provided about the ages or previous territorial histories of the males that responded (Bergerud and Gratson, 1988). According to Bergerud and Gratson (1988), R. L. Eng found that taxidermic mounts of females also attracted male sage grouse away from an established lek. In three experiments with black grouse in the Netherlands, de Vos (1983, pp. 38–42) showed that nonterritorial and yearling males in particular were attracted to taxidermic mounts of females or to caged decoys. Displaying to a female appeared to stimulate a male to establish a territory that included the female's location. There were indications, however, that a male's attachment to the site waned gradually in the absence of further interactions with females.

The result might differ when taxidermic mounts of females are placed within territories on a lek. In an experiment in 1969, I found that four mounted females in normal postures inside a territory on the periphery of a large lek, about 50 m from an active mating center, resulted in no clear attraction of other males. On a lek of sharp-tailed grouse, Kermott (1982, p. 115) also found that a taxidermic mount, although energetically courted when placed within a male's territory, would not induce neighboring males to leave their territories even when the resident male was temporarily absent.

The way in which groups of males approach females depends on the responses of individual males. In lekking grouse, males with no females in their territories spend most of their time displaying on the sides of their territories closest to females elsewhere on the lek (Kruijt et al., 1972; Wiley, 1973a). These males tend to encroach across their boundaries with neighbors that are closer to females. Each male thus spends most of his time displaying as close as possible to the females and at intervals interrupts his displays to dash across his territory to encounter encroaching neighbors also trying to approach the females (Wiley, 1973a; Kermott, 1982, p. 110). Similar tendencies evidently also apply to black grouse and Uganda kob, in which aggressive interactions are most frequent along territorial boundaries nearest locations where females gather and copulations occur (Kruijt et al., 1972; Floody and Arnold, 1975). These tendencies could easily result in a group of males moving as a unit away from their usual locations to approach nearby females. The nearest peripheral male only needs to move outward away from the other males and toward the females; the immediate neighbors could then also move toward the females, and so forth.

Lekking males often change their tactics of display depending on the presence of females on the lek or even their distance from females' locations within a lek. Many species have displays that in part permit accurate location of a lek or display site by nearby females, such as the various jumps and short flights performed by some species of lekking grouse (Lumsden, 1965; Hjorth, 1970; Kruijt et al., 1972), ruffs (Hogan-Warburg, 1966; van Rhijn, 1973), buff-breasted sandpipers (Myers, 1979), and Jackson's widowbirds (Andersson, 1989) and certain calls or mechanical sounds produced by tropical lekking birds and bats (Bradbury, 1977; Snow, 1973; McDonald, 1989a). The "flutter jump" displays of several species of lekking grouse are released particularly by females flying near a lek or by their calls (Hamerstrom and Hamerstrom, 1960; Koivisto, 1965; Kermott, 1982, p. 25). The performance of these displays decreases once females have arrived near a male. Sometimes males on a lek at a distance from females continue these displays after other males closer to females have desisted.

Proximity to females in general tends to increase rates and intensity of display. During the 2 hrs. following sunrise, when females are most numerous on leks, male sage grouse with females in their territories usually performed "strut" displays at rates of 6–6.5/min; in comparison, males with no females in either their own or neighboring territories usually displayed at rates of 1–1.5/min (Wiley, 1973a). Males with females in neighboring territories, but not in their own, displayed at intermediate, and highly variable, rates. During the middle of April in 2 years, Hartzler and Jenni (1988) report 21 and 22% increases in rates of display when male sage grouse had females within 3 m (6.6 and 6.2 displays/min) in comparison to when they did not (5.4 and 5.1 displays/min). As territories were roughly 5–10 m in diameter, females within 3 m would be either within the male's own territory or near the boundary of a neighbor's territory. Although few measurements are available, many other observers note in passing that lekking males increase their rates of display when females are nearby (Snow,

1962a; Robel, 1964; Hogan-Warburg, 1966; Kruijt *et al.*, 1972; Lill, 1974a, 1976; Beehler, 1983b; Trail, 1984, p. 223; LeClerq, 1988).

Once females have approached closely, males of lekking species generally switch to a series of intricate movements around the females and sometimes different vocalizations or sounds. These close-range tactics have been particularly well described for several species of manakins (Snow, 1962a; Lill, 1974a, 1976; McDonald, 1989a), ruff (Hogan-Warburg, 1966; van Rhijn, 1973; Shepard, 1975), and black grouse (Kruijt *et al.*, 1972). Male ruffs crouch and freeze when females enter their territories. The act of rising from this position seems to trigger solicitation for copulation in females (Shepard, 1975). In black grouse, males repeatedly perform "rookooing" displays while moving in circular or semicircular paths around the female. These movements sometimes appear to herd females farther into the male's territory and sometimes appear to represent a gradual testing of the female to determine whether or not she will hold still for mounting and copulating. When a female leaves a male's territory, the male often performs a characteristic movement of turning directly away from her, presenting his undertail coverts and "rookooing" toward locations of previous copulations in his territory, a tactic that sometimes appears to attract the female back (Kruijt *et al.*, 1972).

Quantitative study of these movements has proved difficult, as a consequence of their complexity, but would repay more effort. Kruijt (1967) adopted the innovation of placing a taxidermic mount of a female in normal walking posture on a small sled that could be pulled back and forth with a simple rope and pulley. During my work with sage grouse, borrowing Kruijt's idea, I filmed four males as they interacted with a stuffed female on a small, moveable sled. The subjects were all in their second year or later, and they occupied neighboring territories but had different levels of mating success. The tests were conducted on days when females had visited the lek but at times during the morning after all females had left the subjects' territories and all neighboring territories. These experiments showed that male sage grouse have tactics for display that closely resemble those described for black grouse, although they are not often so apparent in the birds' normal behavior because females so frequently associate in groups. All males in this small sample responded vigorously to the model without any major differences in tactics.

The ultimate response of a male to a female on a lek is copulation. Males of lekking birds, like males of many other birds, eventually attempt to mount and copulate with any motionless female and probably virtually any motionless object of approximately the correct size (Lill, 1974a). More interesting are the apparent restraints on males' copulatory responses to females, in view of the enormous time and effort spent obtaining a chance to copulate. Forced copulations, in which males aggressively subdue resisting females, are not reported for any lekking species. Many investigators emphasize that the decision to copulate is the female's (Selous, 1927; Wiley, 1973a; Lill, 1974a, 1976; Bradbury, 1977; Beehler, 1983b, 1987a; Kruijt and de Vos, 1988; Clutton-Brock *et al.,* 1988a; McDonald, 1989a; Trail and Adams, 1989). In all lekking species, copulation is invariably preceded by the female adopting a special solicitation posture. Any female that is not ready to copulate simply scoots away when approached too closely by a displaying male. When this happens, males do not pursue but instead resume display. Even males that never copulate within a season refrain from aggressive attempts at copulation.

It is interesting to note that there are two reports of abnormal female sage grouse that have aggressively attempted copulation with other females (Scott, 1942; Wiley, 1973a). These females matched others in plumage and size and joined groups of females on the lek. Unlike other females, they repeatedly attacked nearby females, especially soliciting ones, grabbed their necks, mounted, and attempted to copulate like a male. The victims, some of which lost beakfuls of feathers to the assailant, struggled away from these attacks as quickly as possible.

This abnormal behavior illustrates two points: attempts at forced copulation are within the realm of possibilities for at least this lekking species, and even aggressive attempts at copulation in these circumstances are not successful without the partner's cooperation. For ducks, it has been argued that females eventually submit to forced copulations to avoid physical injury (McKinney *et al.,* 1983). In contrast, male sage grouse, even those that are otherwise unsuccessful in mating, do not attempt forced copulations, and females apparently do not submit. In general, males of lekking species, despite strong responses of other sorts to nearby females, normally act with restraint in attempting copulation.

V. RESPONSES OF FEMALES TO MALES

Much attention in investigations of lekking species has focused on the responses of females to males, in order to identify the mechanisms for female choice of mating partners. Most of these studies have sought correlations between measures of males' morphology or behavior and their mating success or visits by females. Before considering these findings, it is useful to examine the behavior of females in approaching and visiting leks.

A. INTRODUCTION TO THE BEHAVIOR OF FEMALES AT LEKS

In all lekking species, females usually visit a lek on several days before copulation (Lumsden, 1965; Kruijt and Hogan, 1967; Clutton-Brock *et al.,* 1988a; McDonald, 1989a; Pruett-Jones and Pruett-Jones, 1990). Furthermore, during these visits to a lek, a female often visits more than one male's territory. Even in the case of a lek of fallow deer, in which the most successful males held territories on the side from which females approached in their regular daily movements, most females visited several males before mating (Apollonio *et al.*, 1989b).

The manner in which females approach a lek in some cases suggests that they obtain an overview before making any close approaches to individual males. Thus, female manakins, cocks-of-the-rock, and birds of paradise in tropical forests usually first perch in trees above or near the congregation of males' display perches and then visit several males in succession (Gilliard, 1962; Lill, 1974a, 1976; Trail, 1985a; Beehler, 1983b; Trail and Adams, 1989). Female sage grouse often arrive at a lek in dim light before sunrise, at a time when males display almost continuously. In typical approaches, females fly directly over the aggregation of displaying males (Wiley, 1973a). While in flight over the lek, they utter a distinctive call. Female sharp-tailed grouse approaching a lek also utter a distinctive call, which appears to stimulate male display (Lumsden, 1965). Female black grouse tend to land in central territories on a lek or, if they have landed in the periphery, to walk immediately toward the center (Kruijt and Hogan, 1967).

After landing near the periphery of the lek, female sage grouse proceed, as it becomes light enough to see well, to walk toward the center and to join other females (Wiley, 1973a). While thus walking, females tend to avoid displaying males; they are less likely to stop walking near a displaying male than near another female (Wiley, 1973a). Female black grouse also walk slowly among the displaying males and avoid those that approach them (Kruijt and Hogan, 1967). Aside from the evidence of their presence on the lek, the females appear superficially indifferent to the males, until they begin to adopt solicitation postures. Female kob and topi entering a lek likewise tend to avoid males and to approach other females (Gosling and Petrie, 1990; Balmford, 1990).

Females of lekking grouse usually mate only once before laying a clutch (Lumsden, 1965; Kruijt and Hogan, 1967; Robel, 1970; Hamerstrom and Hamerstrom, 1973; Robel and Ballard, 1974; Wiley, 1973a). Kruijt and de Vos (1988) reported that about 20% of females mate two or three times in a season, usually with the same male. This usual equivalence of one copulation with one clutch allows easy interpretation of the mating success of lekking male grouse. In ruffs, on the other hand, females often copulate with more than one male during a single visit to a lek (Hogan-Warburg, 1966; van Rhijn, 1973), and in golden-headed manakins females copulate up to 6 times over a period of 1–3 days for each clutch (Lill, 1976).

Studies of marked or radio-equipped females have often revealed that some of them visit more than one lek in a season. In golden-headed manakins over a third of known females were observed visiting two leks less than 200 m apart, although observations at each lek covered only half of the time; nevertheless, 98% of females seen at two leks mated at only one of them and 94% of females showed strong or absolute preferences for single males (Lill, 1976). Female grouse and birds of paradise also often visit more than one lek in a season (Robel *et al.,* 1970; Kruijt *et al.,* 1972; Pruett-Jones and Pruett-Jones, 1990). Radio-tracked female sage grouse have home ranges large enough to include an average of 2.2 leks (Bradbury *et al.,* 1989b).

On the other hand, some females show remarkable faithfulness to a particular male or location when copulating more than once (Kruijt and de Vos, 1988; Lill, 1974a, 1976; Trail and Adams, 1989; Pruett-Jones and Pruett-Jones, 1990; Balmford, 1990). In white-bearded and golden-headed manakins, females often returned directly to the same display site and partner and copulated with few preliminaries when they were renesting within any one season. Future work must address questions about possible differences in the behavior of females at the different leks they visit and in the age or previous experience of females that visit more than one lek or male and those that do not. Nevertheless, it is clear that females visit a number of males and often more than one lek before mating.

The highly unequal distribution of matings among males on leks and the absence of forced copulations indicate that females must in some way largely concur in decisions about mating. There are four possibilities for the mechanism of this concurrence: (1) females could use similar criteria in selecting males with particular individually distinctive features; (2) females could use similar criteria based on the overall distribution of males or stimulation on a lek; (3) females could use similar criteria in choosing a location with particular environmental features, such as microtopography or vegetation; and (4) females could copy each other. Individual females might use a combination of these mechanisms, perhaps in some hierarchical order; concurrence in choice would be preserved if all females combined these mechanisms in the same way.

The first and second possibilities are considered in the immediately following sections. The third possibility has no support: even though leks tend to occur in locations with certain topographic or vegetational features (Section II,A), no report has ever suggested that these features were sufficient to specify the locations of leks or of copulations within leks. Nevertheless, it remains possible that females are not completely inattentive to vegetational or other environmental features in their mating decisions. The fourth possibility is the subject of Section VI.

B.   RESPONSES TO THE OVERALL ARRANGEMENT OF MALES

There is circumstantial evidence that females might use the overall spatial arrangement of males in choosing a place to copulate. Females in many lekking species copulate more often in central than in peripheral portions of a lek, although not necessarily at its geometric center (Koivisto, 1965; Robel, 1966;

Wiley, 1973a; Lill, 1974a; Floody and Arnold, 1975; Kermott, 1982; Trail, 1984; Fryxell, 1987; Hartzler and Jenni, 1988; Clutton-Brock *et al.*, 1988a; Gosling and Petrie, 1990). In black grouse, central territories (those with neighbors on all sides) attract more females, and males with central territories are more likely to copulate (Kruijt and Hogan, 1967; Kruijt *et al.*, 1972). On leks of greater prairie chickens, records from a 22-year study showed that copulations occurred over twice as frequently in central as in peripheral territories, although there were more males with peripheral territories (Hamerstrom and Hamerstrom, 1973). Hogan-Warburg (1966) found examples of successful males located near the peripheries of leks of ruffs, but Shepard (1975) reported a tendency for females to solicit for copulations in central territories on two of the three leks she studied. However, the small numbers of resident males on these leks made it difficult to identify central and peripheral territories. These correlations of mating with central locations on leks could, of course, result either from aggregation of males around sites where mating occurred or from females' preferences for central locations.

Central territories on leks tend to be smaller than peripheral ones, as reported in numerous studies. It is thus also possible that females might be attracted to dense congregations of males, rather than to central portions of a lek as such. In leks of golden-headed manakins, densely clustered males have higher mean mating success than more dispersed males nearby (Lill, 1976). As these clusters remained in similar locations from year to year, however, it was not possible to exclude the preference of females for the location of a cluster. Female black grouse and village indigobirds also appear attracted to places with more densely clustered males (Kruijt *et al.*, 1972; Payne and Payne, 1977).

Despite the tendency for females to copulate in central or denser portions of a lek, it is usually clear that not all males in these locations have equal mating success (Kruijt *et al.*, 1972; Wiley, 1973a; Lill, 1976; Payne and Payne, 1977; Hartzler and Jenni, 1988). Because males on neighboring territories often differ markedly in success and because leks often have somewhat irregular shapes, mating success of males on leks usually lacks any fixed relationship with distance from particular locations. Gibson and Bradbury (1985), for instance, found no significant correlation between mating success (numbers of copulations) of individual males and the distances of the centers of their territories from the geometric center of copulations. Mating status (whether or not each male mated at least once) also had no significant relationship, in a logistic regression, with distance from the center of copulations. In addition, two studies have found no indication of a significant linear regression of mating success on distance from the geometric center of males' territories (Gibson and Bradbury, 1985; Andersson, 1989). Nevertheless, it remains possible that females do respond, even if not linearly or symmetrically with distance, to the center of the distribution of males or to the greater density of central males in their initial orientation on a lek.

C.   PREFERENCES FOR FEATURES OF INDIVIDUAL MALES

For lekking species, most evidence of female preferences for individual males' features comes from correlations between features of males' behavior or morphology and their mating success. There are two problems with these correlational studies: (1) any significant correlation between two variables might actually result from the influences of some third unidentified variable; and (2) the direction of causality is often difficult to resolve, even if we accept some causal relationship between the two variables. The first problem is minimized by multivariate analysis of the many possible influences on mating success, in order to control for correlations and interactions among the independent variables (Lande and Arnold, 1983; Gibson, 1987). The second problem is difficult to eliminate entirely without experimentation.

These two problems might differ in the degree to which they confound interpretation of correlations with male morphology and behavior, respectively. Correlations of male behavior with mating success could result either (1) because females approach and copulate with males that have particular features of behavior, or (2) because males alter their behavior when females, perhaps especially those receptive to courtship, approach them. A third alternative, perhaps the most realistic, is that both kinds of causality occur: females tend to approach and copulate with males that respond to them in particular ways. In contrast, correlations of male morphology with mating success or female visits do not in general face this problem of interpretation, as morphology remains essentially constant during the course of a female's visits before copulation. This correlation, on the other hand, often encounters the possibility of a third causative variable, in particular, age.

A final caveat in interpretation of correlations is a problem of any exploratory analysis: when large numbers of possibilities are considered, some statistically significant results are expected by chance. In the absence of some antecedent hypothesis about which correlations should prove significant and which should not, it can even prove difficult to specify exactly how many possibilities have been considered at some stage of the investigation.

Most correlational studies of male mating success or of female visits to males have uncovered significant correlations with some of the variables considered. Morphological variables are notably less frequent among the significant correlations than are behavioral variables (Table II), at least when analysis excludes immature males. Some of the behavioral correlates seem almost certainly the result of females' choices rather than their cause. For instance, the correlation of mating success with frequency of boundary encounters with neighbors (Kruijt *et al.*, 1972; Wiley, 1973a; Lill, 1976; Kermott, 1982, p. 109) is reasonably explained by the attraction of males toward the boundaries of, or even into, neighboring territories with females in them.

Some behavioral correlates of mating success, like display rates, seem es-

TABLE II

CORRELATES OF MALE MATING SUCCESS IN BIRDS AND MAMMALS WITH LEKS OR DISPERSED
DISPLAY SITES

	Attributes of males	
Species (ref.)	Correlated with mating success	Not correlated with mating success
Black grouse (Kruijt et al., 1972)	Circling-in movements	
Black grouse (Kruijt and de Vos, 1988)	Rookooing phrase duration[a]	
Sage grouse (Wiley, 1973b)		Strut displays[a] Boundary encounters[a] Fights
Sage grouse (Gibson and Bradbury, 1985)	Attendance Strut displays[a] Principal component of acoustic features Three separate acoustic features	Territory size Distance to geometric center of males Distance to geometric center of matings Body mass Two principal components of size
Sage grouse (Hartzler and Jenni, 1988)	Strut displays during peak of female visits[a]	Strut displays before females visited
Great snipe (Höglund and Lundberg, 1987)	Display fights[a] Central location	Attendance White tail feathers Principal component of size Mass Fights Principal component of acoustic features
White-bearded manakin (Lill, 1974a)		Mass Wing length Displays Fanning displays/female visit Snap-jump bouts/female visit Territorial defense Display court size Saplings used for display
Golden-headed manakin (Lill, 1976)	Territorial invasion by others Invading others' territories	Body mass Wing length Display fights Agonistic interaction Calls/display fight
Long-tailed manakin (McDonald, 1989a)	Toledo calls Butterfly displays[a]	Tail length Hops

(continued)

TABLE II
(*Continued*)

Species (ref.)	Attributes of males	
	Correlated with mating success	Not correlated with mating success
Satin bowerbird (Borgia, 1985b)	Blue feathers Two other kinds of bower decorations Size and density of sticks in bowers Quality of bower	Four other kinds of bower decorations
Lawes' parotia (Pruett-Jones and Pruett-Jones, 1990)	Display probability	Display rate Vocalization rate Attendance Five measures of size
Jackson's widowbird (Andersson, 1989)	Tail length Jump displays	Jump height Attendance Display court quality Collar diameter Body mass Three measures of size Distance to geometric center of males
Village indigobird (Payne and Payne, 1977)	Songs[b] Attendance	Body mass Hovering displays or other displays
Fallow deer (Clutton-Brock *et al.*, 1988a)	Early start in rut Central territory Fighting success Groaning rate Antler length Hind foot length	
Fallow deer (Apollonio *et al.*, 1989a)	Attendance Territory position Age Fights	Fighting success Courtship duration
Uganda kob (Floody and Arnold, 1975)	Agonistic encounters	
Uganda kob (Balmford, 1990)	Fighting Whistle bouts Ear length Body mass	Other measures of morphology

[a]Corrected for effects of exposure to females, or evidence presented that stimulation by females has little effect.

[b]Corrected for effects of copulation but not for effects of female visits.

pecially plausible as bases for female preferences; these correlations, however, are prime candidates for the reverse (or reciprocal) causation. As reviewed above (Section IV), a male sage grouse increases its rate of display markedly when there is a female in a neighboring territory and even more when there is a female within his own territory. As similar findings are reported for many lekking species, the problem for interpreting correlations is severe. Since most of the variance in measures of males' display rates is associated with differences in their exposure to females, detection of any residual differences in males' displays involves extraction of a small signal from a lot of noise.

In such cases, the exact procedures for removing the noise can prove to be critical. Even when it is reasonable to expect that behavioral differences among individual males on a lek would influence mating success, either directly or indirectly, the difficulty of identifying these differences on the basis of correlational studies suggests that special caution is required in reaching conclusions.

The sensitivity of such analyses to procedural details might explain the diverse results reported for sage grouse (Wiley, 1973a; Gibson and Bradbury, 1985; Hartzler and Jenni, 1988). At Ford's Creek Lek in Montana, Wiley (1973a) examined the rates of display of male grouse in 10-min periods during which a focal male had one or more females either within his territory, in a neighboring male's territory, or in neither, as determined by examining time-lapse films. The idea was to examine males' rates of display under conditions of comparable access to females. The study included 6 males with 4–20 samples each in which females were within the subject's territory. These males obtained 0–41 copulations during the entire season. There were no differences between males that successfully copulated at least once and those that did not, nor any correlations of display rates with total numbers of copulations among successful males, except that the most successful male displayed at a significantly lower mean rate when females were in his territory than did another male that never copulated. The lower mean rate of this successful male resulted from several outlying samples with much lower rates, perhaps a result of fatigue from continual display (see also Scott, 1942). There were no notable differences in display rates among these males in the other two conditions of access to females. The small sample size in this study would not, however, permit detection of small differences among males.

Hartzler and Jenni (1988) and Gibson and Bradbury (1985) reported significant correlations between display rate and mating success. In comparison to Wiley's study, their methods resulted in larger samples of males for comparison but less specific information about access to females. Instead of classifying males by the locations of females with respect to their territorial boundaries, they recorded the distance to the nearest female during 5- or 10-min samples of males' displays. Hartzler calculated display rates for each male when females were closer than 3 m and when females were farther away, during three periods in

April in each of 2 years; he then compared males that had copulated at least five times and those that had not. In five of the six periods, more successful males displayed at higher mean rates than less successful ones and in three of them the difference was statistically significant ($p < 0.05$, Mann-Whitney U Tests on data in their Tables 7.5 and 7.6; Hartzler and Jenni do not report statistical tests for these data). In four of the six periods, more successful males also displayed at higher mean rates less than successful ones when females were more than 3 m away. Among males that copulated at least once, there was no significant correlation of mating success with display rate.

Gibson and Bradbury (1985) controlled for proximity to females by obtaining the linear regression of display rates on distance to the nearest female and time of morning and then using the residual for each sample as a measure of the corrected display rate (145 total samples, 19 males). Whether or not a male copulated at least once was then taken as a dichotomous response variable and mean corrected display rate was taken as an explanatory variable in a logistic regression; statistical significance was high for an association of display rate with mating success. Attendance at the lek and the first principal component of acoustical measures of the display also had significant associations with mating, but three morphological measures did not. Only one variable, the third principal component of acoustical measures, correlated with number of copulations among those males that mated at least once.

Sage grouse provide a good example of how sensitive the results of such an analysis might be to the procedures for controlling males' exposure to females. In particular, arbitrarily categorizing distances to females or employing linear regression on distances to nearest females would not provide adequate controls for exposure to females if males' responses to females changed nonlinearly with distance. Consider, for example, the consequences of males responded especially vigorously to females inside their territorial boundaries. Male sage grouse consistently near females tend to be either those with high mating success or their immediate neighbors, which often display close to boundaries nearest females. These neighbors, although close to females, might both copulate much less frequently and display less, either because males respond more intensely to females within their territories, regardless of distance, or because males without females in their territories more often interrupt their bouts of display to defend their other boundaries.

Alternatively, consider the consequences of males' responses to females were an accelerating, rather than linear, function of proximity to the nearest female. In this case, those males that copulated most frequently and thus were consistently close to females would have high residuals in linear regressions of display rate on distance to females. In both of these hypothetical examples, nonlinear relationships between display rates and distances to females result in significant associations of display rates with mating success, in the absence of any real differences in individual males' responses to females. A further confounding possibility is that males might respond more to receptive females than to others, as suggested by Lill's (1974a) finding that male white-bearded manakins display more to previous mates returning in the course of subsequent nesting attempts than to other females.

The ruff, another lekking species that has received some quantitative study by several investigators, provides a further example of disagreement on the determinants of mating success. When a female enters a male's territory, he often adopts a motionless squatting position, interrupted at intervals by partial rising and stereotyped turning. In the Netherlands, Hogan-Warburg (1966) reported that females often adopted solicitation postures when males rose from squatting. In Sweden, Shepard (1975) reported that the proportion of all solicitations on a lek obtained by any one male was related to the frequency of his actions while females were on his territory. van Rhijn (1973), on the other hand, presented evidence that females were significantly less likely to solicit for copulation when the territorial male's activity was high. These studies also fail to agree on whether or not the presence of a satellite male in a resident's territory stimulates a female to copulate, but none presents a quantitative analysis of this question. Although these studies all focus on the behavior of males with females inside their territories, they do not consider the possibility that males are more responsive to receptive females than to other visitors. Statistical analysis in the studies of Hogan-Warburg and van Rhijn is based on small samples, possibly unrepresentative, and in some cases involves repeated measures on the same individuals. The study by Shepard lacks statistical analysis of critical points.

Among species for which there is only one report on correlates of mating success, assessments of possible reverse, or reciprocal, causation have varied. In their investigation of village indigobirds, Payne and Payne (1977) reported a consistent correlation in 2 years between time spent singing and mating success. Time spent singing did not differ between hours in which a male copulated and those, at the same time but on other days in which he did not. There was no assessment, however, of the possibility that females' visits, not just copulations, affect a male's time spent singing. Such an effect might even extend over several days. At a lek of black grouse in the Netherlands, the male with the highest number of copulations in each of 3 years had significantly shorter durations (and thus higher rates) of phrases in the rookooing display when females were within 30 m than did other males (Kruijt and de Vos, 1988). When no females were present on the lek, all males averaged longer durations, but the differences among males remained. Furthermore, one male with lower copulatory success in later years also had longer phrases then. This study, like others discussed above, lacked a full assessment of the responses of males to females.

Other studies reporting correlations between display rates and mating success have taken no steps to determine the direction of causation (Höglund and Lund-

berg, 1987; Andersson, 1989; also probability of display, Pruett-Jones and Pruett-Jones, 1990). Andersson (1989) discounted the possibility that rates of males'
flight displays varied in response to females, because all males seemed to display
when females were nearby. Variation in males' display rates with proximity to
females was not documented.

The trend for behavioral, rather than morphological, differences among males
to correlate with mating success (Table II) alone suggests that males' responses to
females might explain these correlations. Morphology, unlike behavior, does not
change from moment to moment in response to females. Morphology on the
other hand often correlates with age (Section III,B). In view of the major changes
found in male behavior in response to females (Section IV), interpretation of
correlations between behavior and mating success must include thorough investigation of the temporal and spatial aspects of males' responses to females, before
conclusions are reached about females' responses to males.

In the end, correlations provide problematic evidence for females' response to
males. The best approach to demonstrating these responses is experimentation
(see Andersson, 1982a; Moller, 1988). In lekking species, a number of reports
that females are attracted to playback of males' vocalizations suggest that experimental analysis of females' discriminations among individual males might be
feasible. Gibson (1989) reported that female sage grouse are attracted to playback of the sounds of a male's displays presented inside the territory of an
unsuccessful male. This experiment included no comparisons between displays
of successful and unsuccessful males, nor between different species or types of
sounds. Others have reported, with less documentation, attraction of female
greater prairie chickens to playback or imitations of male vocalizations (Hamerstrom and Hamerstrom, 1960; Silvy and Robel, 1967). Female black grouse,
on the other hand, were not attracted to playback at a location away from a
current lek (Kruijt et al., 1972).

Despite the difficulty of establishing the fact in the field, it remains plausible
that a male's effort in displaying influences his mating success, either indirectly
through influences on other males or directly through influences on females.
Effort might include rates of display, intensity of display, and attendance at leks
for longer periods during the day and the season instead of foraging. Attendance
is one of the features of male behavior that recurs as a correlate of mating success
(Table II; Kermott, 1982; Beehler, 1983b; Trail, 1984, p. 99; Gibson and Bradbury, 1985; Andersson, 1989). Another of Gibson and Bradbury's correlates of
mating success in sage grouse, the first principal component of acoustical measures, depended on three features of the sounds that accompany the "strut"
display, all of which correlated with whether or not a male copulated. These
sounds might also reflect the effort expended in display. They result from the
abrupt escape of air from the males' esophageal sac, which is compressed by the
musculature of the overlying skin during the display (Clarke et al., 1942; Honess

and Allred, 1942; Wiley, 1973b). The compression of the sac probably determines the velocity of the escaping air and thus the frequencies of the associated pops and whistle. This connection would make the frequency of the whistle an index of the effort of the displaying male, one that is less ambiguous, given uncertainty about the male's distance, than the intensity of the sound. These high frequencies are also absent from the displays of yearling males (Wiley, 1973b). Although much remains to be confirmed here, there is a possibility that these acoustical components provide an unbluffable index of the intensity of a male's display, just the sort of attribute that could provide a female with reliable information about a male's vigor.

D. RESPONSES TO COLLECTIVE FEATURES
OF AGGREGATED MALES

If females respond to some collective features of aggregated males when approaching leks, then larger leks, or leks of some minimal size, might attract more females than smaller ones. Although larger leks in general do attract more females than smaller ones, the evidence that larger aggregations of males attract disproportionately more females is mixed (for example, see Cade, 1981). In Uganda kob, average rates of copulation increased with the number of males on a lek, but reached an asymptote at 10 or more males (Balmford, 1990). During a 12-year study of greater prairie-chickens (Hamerstrom and Hamerstrom, 1955), visits by females increased monotonically with the number of males on a lek, but the increase was not in proportion to the number of males. Copulations increased nearly in proportion to the number of visiting females, but only for leks with 15 or fewer males; on larger leks the number of copulations decreased with lek size. Thus, in this case, large leks attracted disproportionately few females and had an even smaller share of copulations. In comparisons of a large and a small lek of golden-headed manakins in 2 years, Lill (1976) found no consistent differences in numbers of copulations or visits by females in proportion to numbers of males.

It is not plausible that an aggregation of males could produce an advertising signal detectable over a disproportionately wide area (Bradbury, 1981). For instance, a long-range acoustic signal produced in exact unison by two males would be doubled in intensity (increased by 3 dB) at the source; this intensity would increase the distance at which it could be detected by a factor of $\sqrt{2}$ (assuming constant background noise and excess attenuation) and would thus exactly double the area over which it could be detected. Although males of some lekking species produce loud calls in unison (Section III,C), there is no evidence at present that these calls are in exact, phase-locked unison; anything less would result in less than proportionate increase in the area of detection for aggregations of males.

Additional males would also result in more continuous broadcast of signals from a lek, particularly if males tended to avoid overlap with each others' calls (Section III,C). Greater continuity of display could result in greater probability of detection at long ranges, but detection by females is again not likely to increase in proportion to the number of males involved.

Even if there is no disproportionate increase in the effectiveness of advertisement by larger leks, the possibility remains that females respond to some collective aspect of the stimuli from a lek. The temporal or spatial patterns of the signals from an aggregation of males (Section III,C) might provide cues for females choosing leks. At the moment there is no clear information concerning this possibility. In addition, the numbers of males and females at leks do not provide a critical test of females' preferences for different sizes of leks. Despite such preferences, approximate equality of female/male ratios across leks could result from compensating adjustments in the settlement of males (Sections IV and VII,A). Experiments would provide clearer evidence for any preferences for larger leks.

VI.   INTERACTIONS OF FEMALES

The strongly nonuniform distribution of matings among males on a lek is difficult to explain solely as a result of dyadic interactions of males with independently acting females. As Bradbury and Gibson (1983) and Bradbury et al. (1985) have demonstrated with simulations, the observed correlations of male morphological or behavioral features with copulatory success are not high enough to produce the observed skew in copulatory success, provided one assumes that each female independently chooses a mate on the basis of males' morphological or behavioral features.

Several possibilities might produce greater agreement in females' choices than that generated by these simulations (Bradbury et al., 1985). Females might base their discriminations on extremely subtle but stable individual differences among males (for instance, 95% correct choices for much less than 10% differences in males' features), or the variance in the distribution of males' features might be greater than reported. These two possibilities seem unlikely, without new evidence. Females might also base their discriminations on multiple cues provided by males. If individual females combined separate assessments of several different features of males, then the redundancy provided by multiple, cues could improve accuracy of discrimination. Finally, some females might copy choices made by others.

The problem of concordance in female choice is similar to the problem of linearity in dominance hierarchies (Landau, 1951; Chase, 1974; Bradbury et al., 1985). Here, the observed correlations of individuals' morphological or behavioral traits with their rankings are not strong enough to produce hierarchies as linear as those observed, on the assumption that each dyadic dominance relationship is settled independently. The fundamental problem is that the observed correlations between individuals' characteristics and their social status are inadequate to produce a high degree of concordance in the responses of individuals acting independently. On the other hand, interdependence of individuals' responses, such as by copying each other, can produce very high levels of concordance (Losey et al., 1986).

In lekking species, interdependence of males–female associations for copulation could conceivably arise in two ways. First, interactions among the males could ensure that only one male in an aggregation could successfully mate, regardless of any preferences of females. If, for instance, only one male on a lek had opportunities to mate without interruption, as a result of males' interactions with each other, then only this male would copulate successfully. Such a situation might arise particularly in those species with frequent interruptions of copulations. It must be recognized, however, that overall rates of interruptions are not directly relevant to the issue here. The question is whether or not all males have exclusive areas in which they could copulate without interruption provided females gave them the chance.

When two or more males sharing a display site establish clear dominance relationships, as in long-tailed manakins and capuchinbirds, then copulations at this site are monopolized by the top-ranking male without interruptions by subordinates (Foster, 1977a; LeCroy et al., 1980; McDonald, 1989a,b; Trail, 1990). In these cases, the high concordance among females in mating partners at any one site results from the males' relationships. Differences in mating success among sites, however, require other explanations.

In greater prairie chickens and some manakins, interruptions might contribute to nonuniform mating distributions (Robel, 1966; Lill, 1976; Foster, 1981, 1983). In golden-headed manakins, for instance, mating success was found to correlate with rates of disrupting other males' interactions with females (Lill, 1976). In Guianan cock-of-the-rock, on the other hand, males' success in copulation was not related to the proportion of their copulations disrupted; the proportion of females' visits disrupted was in fact greater for those males that received more visits (Trail and Koutnik, 1986). Persistent disruption in this species was directed against more successful neighbors. Yet only occasionally did a male succeed in copulating with a female he had disrupted. As a rule, females in lekking species appear to have control over where and with whom they copulate (Section IV). In such cases, male–male interactions would have little if any influence on the concordance in females' choice of mates.

Alternatively, this concordance could result from interactions among females, in particular copying. In the extreme case of no errors in copying, if each female copulated only with a male that she had seen copulate previously, then all females would select the same partner (provided both that any one female might start the process when she had seen no other female copulate for a long time and that females had opportunities to observe others' copulations).

Copying of mating partners might occur either immediately or after a delay. For long-tailed manakins, anecdotal observations suggest that a female observing another copulate tended to return to copulate at the same site, and thus with the same male, within a few days (McDonald, 1989a). At lek of fallow deer in England, such effects were immediate. Females often moved into the territory of a male while he was mating; as a consequence, a male sometimes mated several times in quick succession (Clutton-Brock et al., 1988a). In the ruff, females usually form groups on leks; a soliciting or copulating female attracts other females and stimulates them to solicit in the same territory (Hogan-Warburg, 1966).

Less direct copying of other females could also tend to produce concordance in mating associations. For instance, females might simply follow or approach other females (Kruijt and Hogan, 1967; Balmford, 1990). In sage grouse, females on leks are likely to stop walking close to other females (Wiley, 1973a), an attraction that would contribute to the formation of compact congregations of females in one or a few males' territories (Scott, 1942; Patterson, 1952; Wiley, 1973a; Lumsden, 1961, 1968; Moss, 1980). In golden-headed manakins, about 20% of females' visits to males' territories occurred simultaneously with other females and 48% of females were observed to engage in at least one simultaneous visit. This latter figure might actually be low, as observations were conducted on alternate days at each of two leks. Although only a minority of copulations occurred during simultaneous visits, Lill's (1976) data do not indicate whether observing a copulation might affect a female's subsequent behavior. Female Lawes' parotias also often visit leks in groups (Pruett-Jones and Pruett-Jones, 1990). Copying of females could also occur indirectly, if females attended persistent cues, such as odors or trampled spots left by previous females (see Wiley, 1973a; Clutton-Brock et al., 1988a; Gosling and Petrie, 1990; Balmford, 1990).

Copying by females could affect mate choices in two ways. Females might tend to copy others indiscriminately on each occasion they choose a mate. Alternatively, younger or less experienced individuals might selectively copy older or experienced ones, while experienced females repeated previous choices of particular males or locations. In the case of lekking birds, there are some suggestions that opportunities exist for females' preferences to pass from older birds to younger ones. In lekking grouse, younger females tend to visit leks somewhat later than, but overlapping with, older females. In sage grouse, in which large numbers of females often congregate at leks during a 10 to 15-day period (Wiley, 1973a; Hartzler and Jenni, 1988), and females tend to visit leks on one or more days before mating, females that are at least 2 years old begin to arrive 4–5 days earlier than yearlings and have started mating by the time yearling females begin to visit (Dalke *et al.*, 1963; Gates, 1985; Petersen and Braun, 1990). Yearling females are also more likely to visit more than one lek (Petersen, 1980). In long-tailed manakins as well, younger females visit more display sites than older ones (McDonald, 1989a,b).

There are also suggestions that females making return visits to a lek move more directly to the location at which they copulate than do females with less experience on the lek (Kruijt and Hogan, 1967; Lill, 1974a). Female Guianan cocks-of-the-rock returning in a subsequent year visited fewer males on fewer days than did females not known to be returning, perhaps an indication that they acted more on their previous experience. In only 33% of cases, however, did they actually return to the same male for copulation (Trail and Adams, 1989). The majority of female Lawes' parotias mate with the same male both within and between seasons (Pruett-Jones and Pruett-Jones, 1990). On the other hand, in golden-headed manakins, three of four females observed mating in 2 successive years switched to a different lek (Lill, 1976). These data are too few for any general conclusions about the proportions of females that return to the same male or location for mating in successive years.

If older females tend to rely on previous experience in selecting mating part-ners, rather than to copy, while younger females tend to copy, then traditions of female preferences could persist across years. Such a process would be analo-gous to "oblique" cultural transmission (transmission from older to younger individuals, other than parent–offspring) as modeled by Cavalli-Sforza and Fel-dman (1981). Variation among groups of individuals as a result of sampling or transmission error is enhanced by oblique as opposed to vertical (parent–off-spring) transmission, and especially by "teacher/leader" transmission (one-to-many oblique transmission). Could switches in successful males on leks, within or between seasons, result in part from such fads in female preferences, as Trail (1984, pp. 109–110) suggested for Guianan cocks-of-the-rock? Such switches might occur with greater frequency on smaller leks.

It is clear from this discussion that much remains to be learned about the behavior of females on leks. Many possibilities need further investigation. Copy-ing, immediate or eventual, between females could help to explain the concor-dance in mating associations on a lek and perhaps also generate correlations between male features and mating success. If older females relied relatively more on previous experience and younger females more on copying, these patterns might also persist from year to year on a lek. On the other hand, copying between females within a lek would not guarantee high concordance in associations of male features with mating success between different leks. This is another pos-sible explanation for differences in correlational studies of mating success on different populations of the same species (Section III,C).

VII. Locations of Leks

Recent discussions of leks have raised the question of whether it is males or females that determine the spacing and locations of leks. One suggestion is that males take positions allowing maximal access to females, whose movements are determined by considerations other than the locations of potential mates (Emlen and Oring, 1977; Parker, 1978; Bradbury, 1981; Gosling, 1986). Females might also prefer large aggregations of males, in order to increase their choice of mates (Alexander, 1975). Other proposals include aggregation of unsuccessful males around successful ones so that they can intercept some females attracted to the preferred males (Bradbury and Gibson, 1983; Beehler and Foster, 1988; Gosling and Petrie, 1990), and aggregation of males in locations that offer maximal protection from predators both for themselves and visiting females (Koivisto, 1965; Wittenberger, 1978; Gosling, 1986). Males or females might also prefer traditional locations. For each of these possibilities, locations of leks, like social relationships within leks, depend on interactions of individuals and their responses to the environment.

A. Female Choice Models

Females could influence the sizes and spacing of leks if each simply chose her mate from the largest aggregation of males within her range. Simulations of this process show that, if males adjust their locations to maximize access to females, they are forced into leks separated by approximately the diameter of females' ranges (Bradbury, 1981). Recent studies indicate, however, that leks are usually more closely spaced than predicted by this model. Radio-tracked female sage grouse have ranges considerably larger than the distances between leks in the same population (Gibson and Bradbury, 1986; Bradbury et al., 1989b). Three of seven radio-marked females did not visit the leks nearest their nests sites but did visit ones farther away (Bradbury et al., 1989b). In other species as well, females appear to have ranges substantially greater than the spacing of leks (van Rhijn, 1983; Wegge and Rolstad, 1986; Svedarsky, 1988). Modifications of this model to include a female's costs of travel and delays before mating, however, result in distances between leks that are less than the diameters of female ranges (Gibson et al., 1990).

Bradbury et al. (1989b) report that, in comparison to a Poisson distribution for random settlement of males at leks, the distribution of lek sizes in three populations of sage grouse consistently showed an excess of very large and very small leks. This tendency to aggregate could result from females' preferences for larger leks, but any attraction of individuals to members of the same or opposite sex could also have the same effect. More direct evidence that females prefer larger leks is lacking (Section V,D).

B. HOT-SPOT MODELS

Another mechanism for the location of leks involves aggregation of males at hot spots for access to females. These models assume overlapping ranges of females, which mate with any males that they encounter, and settlement of males in positions with maximal access to mates (Bradbury and Gibson, 1983; Bradbury *et al.*, 1986). As a result of this process, the concentration of males at a site can exceed the concentration of female traffic there, because males settling at sites with high female traffic reduce the availability of unmated females at nearby locations with less traffic. Various alternatives (ideal free or ideal despotic settlement of males, random or uniform distributions of females' ranges) generate quantitatively different results, but all lead to predictions that aggregation of males, as measured by the sizes and spacing of leks, should correlate with the diameters, and hence overlap, of females' ranges. A critical test of this prediction would require information from a series of populations of the same or similar species. Even then, an observed correlation between the sizes of females' ranges and the sizes or spacing of leks could have two interpretations. Either leks increase in size with overlap in females' ranges as predicted by the model, or females' ranges expand when leks are larger and farther apart for other reasons.

There is, however, more direct evidence that movements of females influence the locations of leks. First, in some species lekking males on occasion leave their positions and move as a group to approach nearby females (Section II,B). Second, when females have well-defined routes of travel during daily or seasonal migrations, leks are often located along these routes (topi, Montfort-Braham, 1975; Gosling, 1986; Gosling *et al.*, 1987; hammer-headed bats, Bradbury, 1977; fallow deer, Schaal, 1986; Appollonio *et al.*, 1989b; sage grouse, Patterson, 1952; Dalke *et al.*, 1963; Bradbury *et al.*, 1989a,b; ruff, van Rhijn, 1983, 1985). Leks of topi tend to occur where females congregate to rest at midday (Gosling and Petrie, 1990). In the case of Kafue lechwe, leks shift location progressively as the population withdraws from alluvial areas during the peak of the rainy season (Schuster, 1976). Indirect evidence suggests that some male sage grouse likewise change leks as females move from wintering to nesting areas (Bradbury *et al.*, 1989b). White bellbirds apparently also shift their display sites in response to females' movements to higher elevations at the start of the breeding season (Snow, 1973). Perhaps the most convincing evidence for the importance of female traffic comes from a lek of fallow deer that moved to a new location in response to a change in the movements of females (Appollonio *et al.*, 1990). After parts of the forest were cut, females followed a different route in their daily travels to feeding grounds. A lek located on the former route gradually disbanded, as the males moved to a previously unoccupied location on the new route. This example illustrates the fundamental principle that males cease to visit a lek to which no females come, although not necessarily immediately.

Attraction to females probably also influences male recruitment to leks. Young males in lekking species often visit several leks before establishing stable positions (Section III,B), and it is not improbable that these prospectors might assess the number of females attracted to a lek in relation to the number of previously established males. Attendance of males at leks of sage grouse sometimes shifts markedly with changes in the presence of females nearby (Bradbury et al., 1989b). It would be instructive to compare such data for yearling and older males.

Of course, where males go to find females depends strongly on where females go when ready to mate. Simulations of hot-spot models have assumed that females make no special movements in seeking mates (Bradbury et al., 1986). In some species, however, females are known to undertake movements specifically to visit leks or display sites, although not necessarily over great distances (Beehler, 1987b; van Rhijn, 1983; Wegge and Rolstad, 1986; Clutton-Brock et al., 1988a; Balmford, 1990).

C. HOTSHOT MODELS AND SITE-SPECIFIC PREFERENCES OF FEMALES

The hotshot model proposes that males intrinsically less successful in attracting females congregate around more successful males in order to intercept arriving females. It can thus explain why males display in aggregations, rather than at dispersed sites, even if females lack any preference for groups of males or particular locations. A necessary assumption, of course, is that females choose mates on the basis of individual differences among males.

The aggregation of unsuccessful males as satellites around successful ones could result either (1) from each male's own experience in attracting females or (2) from an evolved response by intrinsically inferior males. In the first case, males would be expected to try first to attract females on their own before moving close to a successful male. Solitary males are reported for a number of lekking species, and they sometimes copulate as frequently as lekking males (Kruijt et al., 1972; de Vos, 1983; Pruett-Jones and Pruett-Jones, 1990). Although there are no reports that males first display solitarily and then move to a lek, males often first take positions at the periphery of a lek and move if they are unsuccessful (Section III,B).

In the second case, males would be expected to establish either solitary display sites or ones near successful males in accordance with stable differences in their intrinsic abilities to attract females, which could depend on size, vigor, or ornamentation. Effects of age on mating success would complicate this picture: males temporarily likely to be unsuccessful because of age might initially take positions as satellites near successful males; once they reached an optimal age for attracting females, they should then, depending on their intrinsic abilities, either establish their own display site (which in some instances might involve replacing a successful male) or remain a satellite of a successful male. Some aspects of lek behavior provide circumstantial evidence for such mechanisms, including the usual pattern of higher mating success by central males (Section III,B) and even the traditional locations of many leks with a succession of successful males (Section II,A; Beehler and Foster, 1988). On the other hand, reports of newly established leks suggest that young males predominate (Section III,B).

It is difficult to establish, as hotshot models predict, that less successful males on leks obtain matings as a result of parasitizing the attraction of females to more successful males rather than as a result of variation in females' preferences. For instance, forced copulations do not generally occur on leks (Section IV). It is possible that females might lose patience as a result of having to wait too long or being interrupted too often while attempting to mate with their preferred partner and might thus mate with other males on the lek. In Guianan cocks-of-the-rock, some males appear to obtain a few copulations in this way, although unsuccessful males, despite their interruptions of copulations by successful neighbors, are more often persistently rejected by females (Trail and Adams, 1989). It is also possible, in those species like sage grouse in which 20–40 females sometimes gather in one or two males' territories, that neighboring males obtain some copulations while a more successful rival is preoccupied elsewhere in his territory.

An alternative explanation for the aggregation of males would require that females have a preference for mating in particular locations, as a result either of individual preferences or of copying other females (Section VI). The constancy in locations of leks and, in some cases, of mating centers within leks (Section II,A and D) might arise because (1) females prefer to mate at particular locations, (2) females are consistently attracted to a particular male, as long as he survives, or (3) preferred males tend to succeed each other at a particular site.

Experimental removals of males can separate female preferences for locations as opposed to individual males (see Warner, 1987, 1988). Two limited experiments along these lines with lekking birds have resulted in individual cases of females that returned to the same site to copulate, even in the temporary absence of any male (Lill, 1974a; Payne and Payne, 1977). Female Uganda kob tend to return to the same territory in successive visits to a lek, despite changes in the resident males (Balmford, 1990). These cases suggest that females in lekking species can develop site-specific preferences for mating without reference to particular males. On the other hand, at a lek of Guianan cocks-of-the-rock, experimental obliteration of one successful male's display court resulted in no apparent decrease in his mating success following a shift in his location to an adjacent unoccupied position (Trail, 1984, pp. 162, 231).

If females tended to mate at particular locations, males would be expected to congregate there either to compete individually for females or to await succession to an optimal location (Section III,B). In either case, less successful males should try to obtain as many copulations as they can. This behavior would prove difficult to distinguish from that predicted by hotshot models.

D. HABITAT PREFERENCES AND PREDATION

Leks tend to occur in particular topographic locations or habitats. In some species, the habitat associations might result from females' preferences either for areas relatively safe from predators or near feeding grounds or routes of travel. Female fallow deer apparently prefer to mate at sites away from feeding grounds where interference with copulations by subordinate males is less frequent (Clutton-Brock *et al.*, 1988a). Females might also prefer to mate at locations away from feeding grounds in order to reduce competition with males for food (Brown, 1964; Crook, 1965; Wrangham, 1980). Black grouse, although often occupying habitats along the edges of woodland, prefer locations as open as possible for leks, perhaps for protection from predators (Koivisto, 1965) or to reduce attraction of predators to nesting areas (Kruijt *et al.*, 1972; Bergerud, 1988). Leks of sage grouse, topi, and Uganda kob are also characteristically located in areas of sparse vegetation (Patterson, 1952; Wiley, 1973a; Bradbury *et al.*, 1989b; Balmford, 1990; Gosling and Petrie, 1990).

Several reports have suggested that predation occurs very infrequently on leks (Berger *et al.*, 1963; Hamerstrom *et al.*, 1965; Lill, 1974b, 1976; Oring, 1982; Kruijt and de Vos, 1988). However, studies in areas with little human disturbance suggest that predation on leks is not insignificant (Patterson, 1952; Koivisto, 1965; Wiley, 1973a; Hartzler, 1974; Trail, 1987; Bradbury *et al.*, 1989a). On a lek of the Guianan cock-of-the-rock, Trail (1987) observed two kills by raptors and two by snakes in about 250 days of observation, although attacks by raptors occurred on average about once every 5 days. This lek averaged 55 males, which maintained year-round territories on it, so the annual mortality of displaying males on this lek amounted to approximately 10%, about a third of total annual mortality.

Lekking males of many species exhibit sudden, dramatic escape behavior at the appearance of major predators and often apparently spontaneously as a result of false alarms (Patterson, 1952; Koivisto, 1965; Wiley, 1973a; Hartzler, 1974; Beehler, 1987a; Trail, 1987; Bradbury *et al.*, 1989a), an indication that risks of predation have affected the evolution of males' behavior. In addition, certain predators, like golden eagles preying on sage grouse, goshawks on black grouse, and ornate hawk-eagles on Guianan cocks-of-the-rock, make highly specialized attacks on leks. It was my impression that golden eagles knew the locations of sage grouse leks in advance; they attacked suddenly over a nearby ridge, flying at full speed close to the ground in the dim light at dawn (Wiley, 1973a). Accounts of other lekking species suggest similarly purposive behavior by major predators (Koivisto, 1965; Trail, 1987).

Although predation seems to influence the behavior, including habitat prefer-ences, of individuals on leks, there is little evidence that aggregation of males in itself provides protection from predators. For instance, in populations of sage grouse in California, attacks by predators were disproportionately frequent on larger leks, although there was no significant relationship of male mortality with size of lek (Bradbury *et al.*, 1989a). The crucial comparison, however, might be between solitary males and groups of even a few. In Uganda kob, leks attract more predators than do solitary males, but again there is no difference in male mortality (Balmford, 1990; but see Fryxell, 1987). Enhanced detection of preda-tors by males on leks apparently compensates for attraction of predators. There seem to be no reports of females falling to predators on leks; in some species, most females' visits and copulations occur at times when attacks by predators are less frequent than at other times (Koivisto, 1965; Wiley, 1973a; Hartzler, 1974).

One difficulty with all studies of predation at leks, however, is the possibility that an observer's presence might alarm or distract predators and reduce the rates of predation. Nevertheless, although particular features of vegetation or topogra-phy might attract one or both sexes because they provide protection from preda-tors, this process seems not to provide a complete explanation for aggregation at specific sites.

VIII. Sexual Selection in Lekking Species

This review has made a point of distinguishing behavioral mechanisms from evolutionary ones. Female choice and sexual selection illustrate the complexity in the interactions of these two levels of analysis well. Female choice refers to individual females' behavioral preferences for copulating in particular circum-stances; sexual selection refers to differences in transmission of genes that influ-ence males' copulatory success (Borgia, 1979; Wade, 1979; Wade and Arnold, 1980; Arnold, 1983).

The relationships between female choice and sexual selection constitute the central interest of lekking species, inasmuch as the sexes do not interact, in general, except during the chain of events leading to copulation. The following sections identify some general issues in the study of sexual selection and apply them to lekking birds and mammals.

A. Passive Attraction

The first consideration concerns the nature of female choice. Parker (1982, 1983) has proposed that "passive attraction" of females could produce sexual selection without female choice. Attraction is "passive" when receptive females approach the most salient males, those that females perceive, for instance, to have the loudest calls or most noticeable coloration. Of course, signals that appear loudest to a female at a particular time do not necessarily have high intensity at the source, since the loudest male could by chance simply be the closest to the female. Nevertheless, assuming random or uniform distributions of females, any male that produced more intense calls at source would be perceived loudest by a disproportionate number of females. "Active choice," on the other hand, requires that females reject some males regardless of the salience of their signals (Parker, 1983).

The strength of a particular stimulus for a female depends on the capacities of her sense organs (Halliday, 1983; Sullivan, 1989) and her processing of sensory input. Although the terms suggest some essential distinction, "active" rejection and "passive" attraction both involve sensory filtering or discrimination. Acceptance of the most intense stimulus (or one above some threshold) necessarily involves rejection of other, less intense stimuli. Redefining passive choice as mating with the closest male or the first one encountered (Searcy and Andersson, 1986) does not avoid the problem. Imagine, for instance, that choice of a mating partner involved no more than copulation with the first male detected following onset of receptivity (at some time not affected by exposure to males). Even in this case, the properties of male behavior and female sensory mechanisms would determine which males were detected (produced stimulation above some threshold) and which were not. Regardless of whether her behavior depended on peripheral or central sensory filtering, a female's responses would involve discrimination among males' traits.

Female discrimination among potential mates, by whatever mechanism, is reducible to a problem in signal detection (Wiley, 1983). In its simplest form, a mechanism for detecting a signal receives an input, in the form of a signal with noise (either from random variation or masking energy), and then either responds or does not according to some criterion. Any response of a female involves a criterion for acceptance or rejection of a stimulus. A criterion might be relative for simultaneously compared signals (such as loudest call or longest tail), or absolute for sequentially processed signals (such as a call meeting certain frequency specifications or a tail exceeding a definite length). A criterion could be simple or complex, stringent or lax. The mechanism might involve only the properties of the peripheral sense organs or also the cognitive properties of the central nervous system. The issue to which Parker's (1983) argument draws attention is not whether or not females choose mates, but whether or not they necessarily have exacting criteria for their choices. In all cases, a females' responses have evolutionary consequences for males' traits.

Natterjack toads provide a case of relatively nonspecific criteria for mate choice by females (Arak, 1983, 1988). Larger males with louder calls and larger defended areas in breeding ponds obtain more mates. However, females do not make discriminations based on the acoustic attributes of calls; instead, they evidently accept any conspecific male they encounter once they reach the breeding pool, usually a male with a large defended area. Loud calls and large size presumably contribute to defending a large area.

Do leks of any birds or mammals resemble this situation? In one report that might suggest it, Robel (1967) showed that male greater prairie chickens with larger ranges on leks obtained more matings. Most copulations occurred within the males' much smaller territories, however (Section III,A). Evidently successful males ranged more widely over the lek to approach females and then accompanied them back to their territories for copulation. Another presumptive case for females' mating with the first males they encounter is provided by a lek of fallow deer in Italy, in which the most successful males occupied territories where females entered the lek; females, however, visited several males before mating (Appollonio et al., 1989b). In general, females of lekking birds and mammals visit a number of males on a lek before mating (Section V,A).

B.   DIRECT AND INDIRECT FEMALE CHOICE

Even when mating opportunities are determined mostly by interactions among males, as in Natterjack toads, the behavior of females would always, perhaps even in the case of forced copulations, affect how male–male competition influences mating. Female tendencies to mate in particular locations, in groups, or in synchrony, could all influence which males would have access to them for copulation. This point suggests a distinction between direct and indirect female choice. In the case of direct choice, females mate with particular males because of their preferences for particular features of stimulation produced directly by individual males. In the case of indirect choice, females mate with particular males because of other aspects of their preferences for situations in which to mate.

Three possibilities for indirect choice seem particularly relevant to lekking species: preferences for mating in aggregations of males, for mating in particular locations, and for copying other females. Females' tendencies to mate in aggregations of males, as a result of responses to collective properties of aggregates rather than to features of individual males (Section V,D), would allow male competition to determine mating opportunities. Females might also prefer to mate near the centers of aggregations, which would further restrict mating as a result of male competition. If females preferred to mate at a particular site (Section VII,B), this preference would create male competition to occupy that site. Preferences either for aggregations or for particular sites could result from females' copying more experienced females (Section VI).

All of these possibilities for indirect female preferences could lead to sexual selection for male characteristics that is just as intense as that from direct preferences. Indirect preferences could also lead to exaggeration of collective or coordinated display in aggregations and male competition within aggregations. Yet, none of these consequences would require differences in females' responses to stimulation produced by individual males.

C. INTER- AND INTRASPECIFIC CHOICE

Considering female choice as a form of signal detection tends to weaken the distinction between inter- and intraspecific aspects of female choice. Instead, these apparent alternatives represent points on a continuum of criteria for responses. Consider a varying stimulus, as a result of a signal plus noise, along a dimension of stimulus parameters. It is reasonable to assume that, along most stimulus dimensions, differences between hetero- and conspecific males are greater than those among conspecific males. Suppose a female solicits copulation when stimulation meets some criterion (Real, 1990). Her discrimination between hetero- and conspecific males is then analogous to discrimination among conspecific males, except that the signal/noise ratio is likely to be higher.

When females have only brief associations with males before copulating, as in most lekking species, the possibility of error in discriminating between suitable and unsuitable mates increases (Wiley, 1983). A relatively high probability of errors in recognition of conspecific mates is suggested by the high frequency of hybrids reported for species with ephemeral associations of mates (Sibley, 1957; Gilliard, 1969). Consequently, particularly in lekking species with brief mating seasons, sexual dimorphism in species-specific courtship signals might evolve in part to reduce errors in females' choices of conspecific mates.

The interpretation of frequencies of hybrids, however, is problematic, because strong sexual dimorphism might make hybrids more noticeable to ornithologists. Further tests of this hypothesis might compare frequencies of both female and male hybrids in species with brief as opposed to prolonged associations of sexes prior to mating and in species with monomorphic as opposed to dimorphic plumage. It is perhaps significant that manakins, with their prolonged breeding seasons and repeated visits by females to leks over periods of months, do not seem to have high rates of hybridization (Parkes, 1961). Experimental studies of females' responses to features of conspecific and heterospecific males might well complement studies of their responses to variation in features of conspecific males.

A clear case of two sympatric lekking species with unusually high levels of hybridization is provided by greater prairie chickens and sharp-tailed grouse in central North America (Johnsgard and Wood, 1968). Overlap of their ranges has increased as a result of human activities in the past 150 years. The two species lack bold plumage patterns, but they differ distinctly in the coloration of the large bare patches of skin over the esophageal pouch, in overall size, in the development of specially modified feathers, and in their sounds and actions during display (Hamerstrom and Hamerstrom, 1960; Lumsden, 1965; Hjorth, 1970; Kermott and Oring, 1975; Sparling, 1983), differences great enough that the two species were long classified as belonging to separate genera. In zones of overlap, however, hybrids often represent 10% of all individuals and, in some populations, even higher proportions (Johnsgard and Wood, 1968). Mixed leks are more common (as much as 17% of leks) in populations with more nearly equal proportions of the two species, but the proportion of mixed leks is far below that expected by random assortment of males. There have been no reports of copulations by hybrid males. A high incidence of hybridization between lekking species suggests that some females either lack precision in their discrimination of suitable mates or rely on indirect mechanisms of mate choice.

D. Costs and Benefits Relevant to Sexual Selection

The possibility of errors in females' choices implies that some preferences are better (more likely to propagate to subsequent generations) than others. The costs and benefits of females' preferences, and of males' features affected by these preferences, are at the heart of current theoretical work on sexual selection. Fisher's (1915, 1930) verbal argument for sexual selection proposed that female preferences for traits that were initially advantageous for males could lead eventually to the evolution of disadvantageous exaggeration in an accelerating, or run-away, process. Eventually, this exaggeration would be halted by compensating reduction in survival of males and perhaps by a switch in female preferences to other features of males. To crystalize issues, however, recent discussions have identified Fisherian evolution with the spread of traits disadvantageous for male survival as a result of arbitrary female preferences, ones with no effect on the female's own reproductive success or survival. In his discussion of females' "aesthetic" sense in the evolution of bird song, Darwin (1871) also indicated that sexual selection might result from arbitrary female preferences.

Mathematical analyses of Fisherian evolution, based either on two-locus models (O'Donald, 1980; Kirkpatrick, 1982) or on models of polygenic traits (Lande, 1981; Heisler, 1984, 1985), have shown that the run-away process occurs as a result of (1) the enhanced mating success of males with the preferred traits and (2) the genetic correlation between genes for the female preference and the male trait, a consequence of the assortative mating between individuals with these genes. In general, evolution of such traits results in a line of equilibrial frequencies of alleles for the male trait and the female preference (or, in the polygenic models, a line of equilibrial values for the male and female phenotypes). Along this line, the disadvantages of decreased survival by males are just balanced by the advantages of increased mating success (Arnold, 1987; Kirkpatrick, 1987).

Both the polygenic and the two-locus haploid models suggest that genetic drift is important in the evolution of exaggerated male traits. In both models, populations at stable equilibria evolve only by perturbations away from equilibria by genetic drift. In polygenic models, unstable equilibria occur under conditions of strong genetic covariance between the male trait and the female preference (Lande, 1981). The result is rapid evolution of both phenotypes toward extreme values. Such strong covariance could normally arise only in the course of sexual selection or by drift in small populations. Instability is also more likely when females prefer male features not directly subject to selection for viability (Heisler, 1985). In all cases, aside from any effects of genetic drift, female preferences are most likely to evolve when they reinforce directional selection for viability (Heisler, 1984, 1985).

In two-locus haploid models, when females sample males sequentially and when the preference for the male trait is not absolute, genetic drift must overcome a threshold in the frequency of the female preference allele before the frequency of the male trait allele exceeds zero (O'Donald, 1980; Kirkpatrick, 1982; Seger, 1985). This threshold decreases, so that chances for the spread of disadvantageous male traits increase (1) when females prefer a less disadvantageous trait (Kirkpatrick, 1982; Seger, 1985) and (2) when females' preferences are more nearly absolute (females with the preference allele more often mate with males carrying the trait allele).

When females with the preference allele sample a group of males simultaneously and choose the best, the line of equilibria in the two-locus haploid model is in part unstable (Seger, 1985). In this best-of-N model, rapid evolution becomes possible. This situation appears superficially to apply to leks. However, the model indicates that unstable equilibria are most likely when samples of males are very small (in general less than 10) and randomly assembled. Systematic assembly of males, so that preferred males were overdispersed, would tend to stabilize the line of equilibra. Leks seem unlikely to represent random assemblages of males.

Fisherian evolution thus appears to depend primarily on genetic drift in small disjunct or colonizing populations to accomplish large changes in disadvantageous male traits. In these conditions, any one deme might have constantly shifting behavioral mechanisms of female choice, fluctuations that could even lead to premating reproductive isolation and speciation (Lande, 1981, 1982). This situation could well have occurred in the evolutionary history of many species. Species groups like the birds of paradise provide likely examples, but speciation by this process could just as well occur in species without leks. There is also no indication yet that leks themselves represent genetic subdivision of populations (Dunn and Braun, 1985). Consequently, it is not clear that lekking in itself predisposes species to Fisherian evolution.

A female preference for a male trait would spread without genetic drift if it reinforced directional selection for increased viability in both sexes (Heisler, 1984), or even only in females. Thus, a preference for vigorous males might result in female offspring that would survive or reproduce more successfully (Andersson, 1986). Increased viability of female progeny increases the chances for female preferences to spread, because it counteracts any disadvantages arising from lower survival of male progeny or from immediate costs to females (Pomiankowski, 1987a). Conceivably, the opposite might also obtain: genes for male vigor might in some cases reduce female viability. Preferences for "good genes" for female descendants are often contrasted with Fisherian arbitrary preferences (Borgia, 1979, 1987; Kirkpatrick, 1987; Maynard Smith, 1987).

This review of current thinking about costs and benefits relevant to sexual selection suggests that these fall into three categories: (1) those expressed in males with genes for the preferred trait, (2) those expressed in females with genes for the male trait, and (3) those expressed in females with genes for the preference. These effects can be distinguished clearly in mathematical models. As a result of the genetic correlation between genes for the preference and those for the male trait, however, the latter two categories would prove difficult to separate in the field, since their effects would appear, in the absence of detailed knowledge of genotypes, as summed effects on females expressing a preference. Fisherian evolution represents one extreme, in which only costs of type 1 are considered. "Good genes" models emphasize benefits of type 2. "Polygamy threshold" (Orians, 1969; Davies, 1989) and "sexy son" models (Weatherhead and Robertson, 1979) emphasize, respectively, benefits and costs of type 3. In reality, all three kinds of these effects are likely to occur, to different degrees, as a consequence of female choice in any mating system. With this background, we can consider the situation as it is now understood in lekking species.

E.   COSTS TO SUCCESSFUL MALES

If some aspect of female behavior results directly or indirectly in increased mating success for some males on leks, it is important to determine the costs in terms of reduced survival, if any, associated with these benefits of increased mating success. No study has yet demonstrated changes in survival as a result of experimental manipulations of males' behavior or morphology. Nevertheless, costs seem plausible for lekking males, since they do little or no feeding for substantial proportions of the year and of each day they are present on a lek (Section IV). The consequences of attendance are perhaps greatest in the least favorable seasons of the year, rather than during periods when females are present, which tend to coincide with more favorable seasons. Thus, for grouse, attendance during late winter mornings, long before females arrive, might represent a considerable metabolic sacrifice. Males also spend considerable effort in displaying while on leks, particularly during periods when females are visiting or likely to visit. Because males usually display at higher rates when females are nearby, successful males should incur greater metabolic costs than unsuccessful ones (for example, Given, 1988).

These expectations based on behavioral observations have recently been confirmed for sage grouse by Vehrencamp *et al.* (1989). By using doubly labeled water, they found that metabolic energy expenditure was twice as high for males attending leks as for those not attending and that successful males (those observed to copulate at least once) had metabolic energy expenditures twice as high as unsuccessful males. On the other hand, they found that successful males lost less mass/day between captures during the mating season than did unsuccessful males. Thus, increased energy expenditure by successful males was more than completely compensated for, possibly as a result of their feeding strategies when away from the lek. Although male sage grouse have maximal reserves of lipids just preceding the breeding season, these reserves can provide only a small fraction of the energy required for display throughout the season (Hupp and Braun, 1989). The decrease in their lipid reserves and body mass during the breeding season suggests that these reserves might nevertheless provide the margin for especially demanding effort (Beck and Braun, 1978; Hupp and Braun, 1989).

Although Vehrencamp *et al.* (1989) also state that they found no differences in mortality between successful and unsuccessful males, a power test would be necessary to establish the precision of this negative conclusion. In addition to any increase in mortality as a consequence of the time and energy required for persistent display, conspicuous display would often increase a male's risks of predation (for example, Ryan *et al.*, 1982). For black grouse in the Netherlands, data are available for the mortality of mature males (at least 3 years old) during March through August in relation to their territorial status and positions. Males with central territories ($n = 27$), which were more likely to mate successfully, had 11% mortality, those with peripheral territories ($n = 47$) 17%, and those that had never had a territory ($n = 13$) 15%; none of these differences is statistically significant (de Vos, 1983). Peripheral males on sharp-tailed grouse leks also had higher disappearance rates, although some of this effect might have resulted from movements of young males to other leks (Moyles and Boag, 1981). Among male Guianan cocks-of-the-rock, males that mated successfully had annual mortality of 24%, compared to 20% for those that did not mate, again not a statistically significant difference (Trail, 1987). On leks of Uganda kob, peripheral males have higher mortality than central males, but there is no correlation between predation rate and mating success on individual territories (Balmford, 1990). Even when mortality of fully adult males is not clearly related to their mating success, lower mortality in younger males (Section IX) suggests that full commitment to display incurs increased mortality.

Males of species with extreme sexual dimorphism in size might also face higher costs as a result of greater metabolic demands for growth. Presumably, these costs explain the finding that juvenile males of the two most sexually dimorphic grouse, sage grouse and common capercaillie, suffer higher mortality in the first months of life than do females in habitats or in years with poor conditions for growth (Wegge, 1980; Moss, 1980; Swenson, 1986).

The finding that successful adult males on leks do not always have higher mortality would be expected if these males were more vigorous to begin with (Parker, 1983; Andersson, 1982b, 1986; Zeh and Zeh, 1988). Parker suggests that males differing in vigor might adjust their allocations of effort in order to maintain constant mortality and variable commitments to display. Alternatively, they might maintain constant commitment to display but have variable mortality. The best indication of overall vigor is thus, as Andersson (1986) proposed, the product of survival and mating success. Sage grouse appear to adjust mating effort while holding survival constant, although imprecision in information about survival makes it difficult to reach a firm conclusion (Vehrencamp et al., 1989). Constant mortality across a range of mating effort does not imply that display and attendance at leks do not influence mortality, since each individual male would presumably survive better if it did not attend a lek or display as much as it did.

Another difficulty in properly assessing the costs of male mating effort comes from the extremely nonuniform distributions of matings. Most of the variation in mating success occurs among "successful males," those that copulate at least once. How closely any costs correlate with mating success among these males is not clear. One relevant measure here is the correlation between display rates and mating success, uncorrected for proximity or access to females (Hartzler and Jenni, 1988; Kruijt and de Vos, 1988; Andersson, 1989). Although such measurements are often statistically significant, the correlations are not particularly high.

F. COSTS AND BENEFITS TO FEMALES

Costs to a female mating on a lek are not likely to be high. Predation on leks is low (Section VII,D) and, although difficult to compare, perhaps no higher than away from leks. Although females in some cases go out of their way to visit leks, the distances traveled for these visits tend to be relatively short (Section V). Females spend little time visiting leks. They rarely fight seriously or engage in strenuous activity there, although females at leks sometimes supplant or threaten each other (Lumsden, 1965, 1968; Hogan-Warburg, 1966; Kruijt and Hogan, 1967; Wiley, 1973a; Kermott, 1982, p. 28). Robel (1970) proposed that these interactions prevented or postponed copulation by some female greater prairie chickens and thus might regulate populations. This possibility seems unlikely. On grouse leks, aggressive behavior toward other females is usually performed by females that have solicited for copulation (Kruijt and Hogan, 1967; Lumsden, 1968; Wiley, 1973a; Robel's report also suggests that aggression by females is associated with readiness to copulate). Since females ready to copulate initiate aggression, rather than receive it, aggression among females probably does not prevent or postpone copulation.

By mating at a lek, a female gives up any possibility of male parental care. This situation does not necessarily impose costs on females. Reducing the frequency of parental visits to nests might have benefits if predation were thereby reduced. For tropical birds that feed their young with fruit, the relationships between predation rates, clutch sizes, and frequencies of parental visits to the nest could favor a shift to single parental care, although this possibility needs more analysis (Snow, 1962a; Snow and Snow, 1979; Willis, 1979; Ricklefs, 1980; Beehler, 1983a, 1987a; Beehler and Pruett-Jones, 1983). For monogamous grouse, the presence of a guarding male appears to have no influence on a female's survival or reproductive success, except possibly when predator densities are high (Martin, 1984; Hannon, 1984; Martin and Cooke, 1987).

In the absence of any advantage from male parental care, females of lekking species might benefit by mating in locations separated from nesting areas, so that displaying males cannot attract predators to themselves and their nests (Kruijt *et al.*, 1972). In support of this idea, Bergerud (1988) provides evidence that most nests of lekking grouse are located approximately half-way between leks, but this result would be obtained if females simply distributed their nests uniformly or randomly and visited the nearest lek for mating. Phillips (1990) instead proposes that females should nest at an intermediate distance from leks, a prediction based on untested assumptions about predators' movements. Data from one of three species of grouse provide tentative support for this idea, but more information is needed for a definite conclusion.

These potential immediate consequences of choosing to mate at a lek have little relevance to a female's choice of a mate within a lek. Since a female's subsequent reproductive activities always occur away from the lek, her choice within a lek could directly influence her immediate reproductive success only if males differed in their ability to fertilize eggs. This possibility might apply, especially to female grouse, which usually mate only once for a clutch, but there is little evidence on this point (Avery, 1984). Perhaps a more important consequence of choosing a mate within a lek is exposure to infectious diseases or parasites during copulation (Section X). Even when slight, immediate costs for female preferences have the important theoretical consequence of drastically reducing the possibilities for Fisherian evolution (Pomiankowski, 1988).

Increased viability for a females' offspring represents another potential benefit from choosing mates. If females' preferences result, directly or indirectly, in mating with vigorous males, the viability of their female, as well as male progeny might increase. Indirect choice for vigorous males could result from female preferences for mating in aggregations of males, particularly near the centers of aggregations, or in particular locations (Section V,B). Such preferences could lead to competition among males and result in matings with the most vigorous among them. Direct choice of individual males' features has received much more attention in recent investigations of leks. In some cases, these features might correlate with male vigor, as secondary sexual features, morphological or behavioral, seem more sensitive to male condition than other traits (Andersson, 1986). Examples of such condition-dependent male traits could include long feathers, the growth of which might depend on nutritional state (Alatalo *et al.*, 1988), synthesis of substances for bright coloration (Hamilton and Zuk, 1982), antlers (Clutton-Brock *et al.*, 1982; Clutton-Brock, 1982), higher display rates, or indications of greater display intensity.

These male features, however, raise problems for the evolution of female preferences. Since commitments to display and survival presumably involve trade-offs for any one male, females with brief exposure to males before making direct choices among them could be deceived by males making short-term adjustments in these trade-offs (Andersson, 1986; Zeh and Zeh, 1988). Indirect, rather than direct, female preferences might provide more reliable mechanisms to produce benefits for female descendants. Any direct preferences for features of individual males might focus on traits necessarily related to overall, long-term viability (Kodric-Brown and Brown, 1984). It is perhaps significant that correlates of high mating success often include attendance at leks, rates of display, and features of displays that might provide unequivocal indications of vigor (Section V,C).

A general problem in applying "good genes" models to lekking species arises from the divergent lives males and females in these species lead. One would expect that a similar genetic basis for male and female vigor would be most likely when the two sexes had the most similar ecology (Clutton-Brock, 1983). One aspect of female preferences that would often increase the viability of progeny of both sexes is avoidance of hybridization (Section VIII,C). A preference for conspecific males in fact represents an extreme form of a preference for "good genes," one in which the consequences of error are sometimes categorical.

G. HANDICAPS

"Good genes" models of sexual selection are in part a development of Zahavi's (1975) proposal that females should prefer males with "handicaps" to assure honest advertisement of male quality. Rather than simply choose the most vigorous displayer, females should prefer the most vigorous displayer in relation to a permanent disability, one that interferes with chances for feeding or avoiding predators. It is possible to imagine a variety of kinds of handicaps with different effects on the viability of males; in all cases, however, males of high viability (V) that lack the handicap (h) survive best, and those with low viability (v) that have the handicap (H) survive worst (Fig. 5). Different proposals for handicaps vary in

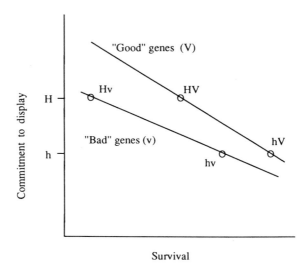

FIG. 5. Examples of the relationship of survival and display to illustrate the possibilities for males with "good" genes (genotype V) and those with "bad" genes (v) at two commitments to display, H and h. Hv males have the lowest survival, hV males the highest. HV and hv males have intermediate levels of survival; which of the two is higher depends on the shape, slopes, and positions of the lines in relation to the difference in commitment to display.

their ranking of HV and hv males between these extremes (Maynard Smith, 1987; Pomiankowski, 1987b, 1988).

Genes for male handicaps could of course spread, provided the frequency of a female preference for the handicap exceeded the necessary threshold for Fisherian evolution of disadvantageous male traits (Section VIII,D). The question therefore is, Can genes for a handicap spread even when the female preference is rare? Recent investigations of haploid genetic models have shown that, provided genetic variance for overall viability is maintained, the handicap gene either goes to fixation or is eliminated (Kirkpatrick, 1986a, b;Pomiankowski, 1987b, 1988). The line of equilibria for the preferred male trait (the handicap, in this case) and the female preference, as found in Fisherian evolution, is eliminated. This same result emerges when a handicap correlates with direct contributions by males to their mates' reproductive success, even when variation in these contributions is not heritable (Heywood, 1989). More reliable and less costly handicaps are more likely to spread (Pomiankowski, 1988). Nevertheless, a handicap still cannot spread unless the frequency of the female preference exceeds a threshold.

All males, regardless of overt handicaps, must make trade-offs in their commitments to mating success and survival. If these trade-offs differ among males, so that some males have lower survival for a given mating effort, these differences can be thought of as arising from covert handicaps. Because of the possibility of temporary adjustments of trade-offs, these covert handicaps do not allow a female with brief exposure to males to detect with much certainty those with high overall viability. An overt, permanent handicap improves her situation, by assuring that the consequences of successful display for survival were averaged over longer periods. The additional handicap means that fewer males could achieve any particular level of survival for a given commitment to display. As a consequence, errors in detecting males with "good" genes would decrease. If females had some criterion for commitment to display by a male before mating with him, then an overt, permanent handicap would increase a female's chances of detecting a male with high overall viability.

If we take a handicap in a general sense to be a male trait that increases a females' chances of detecting males with "good" genes, possibilities include long-term morphological commitments that require substantial investment of energy, skill in foraging, or vigilance against predators. Many of the morphological elaborations in males of lekking and other polygamous species might qualify. Some striking patterns, however, suggest that these features might not have high costs in many cases. First, in some species, secondary sexual morphology that increases conspicuousness, and thus might increase risks of predation, can be concealed for the most part when not actually in use for display. Prime examples are the three species of lekking grouse in North America. Away from a lek, males are, aside from overall size, hardly more conspicuous than a female, because most of the elaborate and conspicuous plumage is either on the lower side of the body or can be concealed with camouflaged feathers.

Second, modifications of beaks, jaws, legs, and wings are exceptional among secondary sexual characters in birds and mammals. Yet the clearest form of a handicap would involve modifications of those structures that directly contribute to collecting food or evading predators. In lekking birds, modifications of tail or body feathers are far more frequent and more extreme than modifications of wing feathers. One case of modified wing feathers, the stiffened secondaries of manakins in the genus *Manacus* (Snow, 1962a), does not result in a change in the shape of the wing. Sexual selection thus appears to have resulted in elaboration of male morphology in ways that tend to minimize direct impacts on males' abilities to evade predators and to forage. Exaggerated male traits thus seem not to have evolved solely because of costs that could improve a female's ability to discriminate males with high viability.

It is also worth noting that a female's discrimination of males that differ in genetic quality also depends on her criterion for mating. Thus, a female can reduce her errors in discriminating among males either (1) by attending to a signal, like a handicap, with greater variance in expression by males or (2) by attending to subtler differences in a signal with less variance.

H. CONCLUSION

Female choice of mates always involves some element of discrimination between males with "good" and those with "bad" genes, because mate choice, at a minimum, always requires species recognition to avoid dysgenic hybridization. The possibility of errors in female discrimination thus favors preferences for species-specific behavior or morphology. Simple considerations of signal detection suggest that, when the possibility of errors is high, females should prefer distinctive species-specific features of males. Since females of many lekking species, like those of other polygynous species, interact with conspecific males during relatively brief periods of their lives, advantages of female preferences for distinctive signals could explain, at least in part, the elaboration of morphology and behavior in males of these species. Furthermore, it seems probable that male traits preferred by females to permit species recognition would in general reduce male survival, since commitments to display and to survival must involve some trade-off for any male. Thus, selection for species recognition would fit models for the evolution of female preferences for male traits with immediate disadvantages for males but eventual advantages as a result of greater viability of progeny.

It is a bigger challenge to understand the evolution of female choice among conspecific males. Much recent work has focused on direct female preferences for particular features of conspecific males. There has been little attention to indirect female preferences. There is also no information from natural situations on the actual advantages or disadvantages of preferences to females and their descendants (Section X). On the theoretical side, models of Fisherian evolution suggest that arbitrary female preferences for disadvantageous male traits cannot usually spread in large populations. It remains a question for the future whether this result means that populations of lekking, and other polygynous, species are more subdivided than currently thought or that arbitrary preferences are the exception rather than the rule.

IX. EVOLUTIONARY CONSEQUENCES OF AGE STRUCTURE
IN LEKKING SPECIES

A tendency for older males to achieve higher mating success raises a number of issues in the evolution of mating systems. In lekking species, there are two aspects of age-related male mating success (Section III,B). First, it is a universal finding that males do not develop full adult morphology nor fully participate in activities on leks until an age later than that at which females begin to reproduce. Second, circumstantial evidence suggests that mating success might tend to increase with age to some extent, even after males have attained full morphological development. These patterns are also evident in other polygamous species, in cluding those with dispersed display sites and those with harem or resource-associated polygamy (Clutton-Brock *et al.,* 1988b; LeBoeuf and Reiter, 1988). For lekking species the evidence is generally stronger for the first of the above patterns than for the second, probably in part because the morphological distinctiveness of the youngest males makes this pattern easier to confirm. Regardless of the generality of the second pattern, the first in itself prompts all the essential questions.

One immediate consequence is that age-related trends in mating success of males in general reduce the variance in individuals' lifetime reproductive success (Clutton-Brock, 1983). In essence, it is inappropriate to extrapolate from the distribution of annual reproductive success in a sample of males of heterogeneous ages to a distribution of lifetime reproductive success (Section I,E).

Age-related mating success also raises questions about the use of lifetime reproductive success as a measure of the propagation of genes. The spread of genes in a population is fundamentally a question of differences in rates of propagation. Only by assuming constant generation times can one use lifetime reproductive success as a measure of rates of propagation of genes in a population. In general, comparisons of fitness require full calculations of differences in their Malthusian parameters. (Fisher, 1930; Charlesworth, 1980). Later onset of reproduction lowers rates of increase, unless there are compensating increases in survival or later fecundity. In order to attain a rate of increase matching that of genes associated with earlier reproduction, those associated with later onset of reproduction must have compensating advantages in eventual fecundity or early survival (Wiley, 1981). This problem arises for both of the patterns of age-related mating success noted above for polygamous and, in particular, for lekking species.

In discussing the evolution of these patterns, two points need emphasis. First, explanations for later onset of reproduction based on behavioral and physiological mechanisms are not adequate evolutionary explanations. Demonstrations that older males dominate younger males, or that they inhibit their physiological development, fit this category. In fact, proximate regulation of age-related reproduction by interactions among males of different ages varies among species (Section III,B).

Second, surprisingly minor demographic changes can favor later reproduction. To see this point, consider two populations, one in which males begin to mate at age one and another in which they begin at age three. Further imagine that, in both cases, females begin to reproduce at age one and that all males older than the age at onset of mating have equal probability of success. Genes affecting males in the two populations have the same rate of increase, because the population with later onset of mating also has a lower breeding sex ratio (breeding males/breeding females). The increase in eventual fecundity of males exactly compensates for their delay in breeding (Wiley, 1974). Notice, first, that a population composed of males with later onset of reproduction would have a highly nonuniform distribution of matings across all males. Second, although males of any one age probably never have equal success in mating, an assumption of nearly equal expectations of mating success for males of a particular age is not necessarily unrealistic. Much variation in mating success presumably arises by chance or by environmental influences on development.

This simplified example suggests that small differences in the consequences of early or late reproduction can favor one strategy or the other. Thus, in a population of early breeders, a gene associated with a tendency to reproduce slightly later on average would spread if it resulted on average in a sufficient increase in survival or in fecundity once reproduction began; conversely, the opposite conditions would result in the spread of a gene for earlier reproduction in a population of late breeders. Males with genes for later reproduction at first must compete for mates with the more numerous males that begin reproduction earlier. As genes for later reproduction spread and a steadily greater proportion of males begin reproduction later, fewer males would compete effectively for mates in any one season. As a consequence, expected fecundity of males with later onset of reproduction would increase. In other words, selection for later onset of reproduction has positive frequency dependence, so that conditions for the spread of a gene for later reproduction improve progressively once started.

What could cause the evolution of such age-related behavior in lekking species? Female preferences are the crucial factor, in either one of two ways: (1) preferences for exaggerated, energetic display could create survival advantages for later breeding; or (2) preferences, direct or indirect, for older males as such would create fecundity advantages for later breeding.

Satisfactory evidence for either of these possibilities is currently lacking. It is worthwhile nevertheless to consider the requirements for obtaining such evidence. Consider the question of whether or not males might realize an advantage in survival by postponing full mating effort until later in life (Wiley, 1974). This suggestion was examined by Wittenberger (1978), who reasoned as follows: if males with late onset of mating survive better, then males should have higher survival than females and sex ratios should be skewed in favor of males. Late onset of mating is associated with sexual dimorphism in size in grouse (Wiley, 1974); hunters' bags provide an estimate of sex ratios in grouse populations; therefore, if late onset of mating in males increases survival, hunters' bags should show greater male-biased sex ratios in sexually dimorphic species. In fact, he shows that sex ratios in hunters' bags do correlate with sexual dimorphism in size, but in the direction opposite to the prediction. Hence, he rejects the hypothesis that advantages in survival explain delayed maturation in male grouse.

This analysis is flawed in two ways that illustrate the care needed in conducting this sort of demographic comparison. A superficial problem arises from considering hunters' bags as random samples of populations. In fact, hunters appear to kill disproportionate numbers of males in highly dimorphic species of grouse, probably because they are easier targets and despite their inedibility (Helminen, 1963; Rajala, 1974; Lindén, 1981; Braun, 1984). The difference in over... survival of the sexes is thus even greater than sex ratios in hunters' bags suggest.

A more serious problem arises from comparing male and female survival in order to evaluate possible evolutionary advantages of the later onset of breeding by males. In fact, differences in survival between the sexes are not relevant to this question. Instead, we need to compare survival of otherwise equivalent males that begin reproductive effort at different ages. Since there are probably individual differences in vigor, stronger males might optimize the trade-off between survival and mating in different ways than weaker males (Section VIII,E and G). Nevertheless, there could well be some variation in age of full mating effort among males, not confounded completely by differences in vigor, that could serve for tests of the hypothesis. Better still, experimental manipulations of access to mates, mortality risks, or display effort might reveal the nature of trade-offs between survival and mating.

Studies of marked populations of lekking grouse, both in hunted and in unhunted populations, suggest that mortality of older males is higher than that of younger males, an indirect indication that full commitment to lekking behavior might in fact incur a cost in survival. In the protected population of black grouse in the Netherlands, 8% of males in their first and second years disappeared during spring and summer ($n = 88$), the period of most intense display and molt, while 20% of males in their third through fifth years disappeared in this season ($n = 138$) (de Vos, 1983). In boreal Sweden, territorial adult male black grouse suffered 31% mortality during spring, as determined by radio-tracking, while no nonterritorial yearling males died in this period (total $n = 54$). The former but not the latter males also incurred rapid loss of weight during spring (Angelstam, 1984). A large sample of male greater prairie chickens marked during their first winter ($n = 398$) revealed that mortality, in this unhunted population, in the years following a male's first, second, third, and fourth or later springs was 49, 49, 61, and 71%, respectively (Hamerstrom and Hamerstrom, 1973). In contrast, the mortality of females decreased slightly with age, in keeping with the absence of major changes in reproductive effort by females. In sage grouse, the same patterns appear. Adult males have higher mortality than immature males (approximately 55 and 45%, respectively), despite a disproportionate kill of young males by hunters. Yearling females have slightly higher mortality than older females, but not significantly so (Zablan and Braun, 1990). Yearling males also lose proportionately less weight than do older males during the breeding season (4.7 and 2.2%, respectively; Beck and Braun, 1978). For white-eared kob, some circumstantial evidence indicates that males in the age classes most active at leks suffer higher mortality than other age classes (Fryxell, 1987).

In blue grouse, a species with dispersed display sites, Lewis and Zwickel (1982) have estimated the consequences of delayed reproduction for both survival and breeding. Among 75 males of known age, none held display territories in their first year, but 78% did in their second year. Of the latter, 48% held territories on sites that were permanently occupied by a succession of males. Males on these permanent sites had slightly higher average annual survival, in comparison to males on transient sites (75 and 67%, respectively, although males on both kinds of sites had 86% survival as 2-year-olds). Of 2-year-olds without territories, 80% survived. Of those, 45% obtained permanent sites in their third year and the remainder took transient sites. Permanent sites, which are more likely to have females nearby, appear to offer advantages for mating. Using these figures, a 2-year-old postponing display could expect a 36% chance of obtaining a permanent site the following year (0.80 × 0.45) and a 44% chance of obtaining a transient site (0.80 × 0.55). Waiting would yield greater lifetime reproductive success in comparison to settling on a transient territory at age 2, provided the expected annual mating success on a permanent site was at least 28% greater than on a transient site. Although incomplete, this study provides an example of the kinds of information needed to assess the evolutionary advantages of waiting for advantageous situations for breeding (see also Wiley and Rabenold, 1984).

As this example illustrates, the evolution of later onset of mating could result from either increased survival or later fecundity. In lekking species, both of these effects are likely to depend on female preferences in mating. How should we view the evolution of later onset of full mating effort in males in relation to sexual selection? As reviewed in Section VIII,D, the consequences of female preferences divide into those that affect the survival and fecundity of males, those that affect the females making a choice, and those that affect female descendants. Female preferences for more energetic display, if arbitrary, would tend to increase the costs for displaying males; adaptive adjustments of age-related mating effort by males would then serve to minimize these costs.

In species with larger differences between the sexes in ecology and life history patterns, genes for male viability seem less likely to affect female viability although their effects in females are probably never completely lacking (Section VIII,F). In these species, preferences for older males as such, either direct or indirect, would thus have less influence on genetic quality of female descendants than in species with more similarities in the lives of the sexes. Yet, it is in those species with the greatest differences in the ecology and morphology of the sexes that a few older males are most likely to mate. These considerations lead to a tentative suggestion that age-related mating effort of males is more likely to have evolved as a consequence of female preferences for energetic commitment to display, either directly or indirectly, rather than as a response to female preferences for older males as such.

X. Maintenance of Genetic Variance: The Paradox of the Lek

A problem that confounds evolutionary explanations of lekking behavior in terms of female choice is the "paradox of the lek" (Borgia, 1979; Taylor and Williams, 1982). The problem is a general one for sexual selection. As with other forms of directional selection, genetic variance for the selected trait generally decreases (Williams, 1975; Maynard Smith, 1978; Jones, 1987). If enough females prefer males with certain traits, genes associated with those traits spread and eventually go to fixation, thereby removing any further selection for female choice, either as result of genetic advantages for offspring or as a result of assortative mating. For instance, O'Donald's (1980) simulations of sexual selection for disadvantageous male traits revealed that, as the frequency of the gene for the male trait approached 1.0, selection for the gene for female choice decreased to zero.

In O'Donald's (1980) simulations, only persistent back mutation of the gene for the male trait maintained the gene for female choice. Mutational variation at a single locus, however, does not produce significant selection for female choice (Taylor and Williams, 1982). For highly polygenic male traits, on the other hand, it is possible that deleterious mutations in any of numerous genes could provide slight, but effective, levels of selection for female preferences (Lande, 1976; Charlesworth, 1988). Mathematical models of sexual selection also show that genes for an arbitrary female preference and for the corresponding male trait can reach a stable equilibrium with polymorphism in one or both genes (Section VIII,D).

If females could discriminate among males on the basis of overall viability, then balancing selection for overall viability might maintain genetic variance despite the directional selection produced by female mating preferences. There are several possibilities (Felsenstein, 1976; Maynard Smith, 1989): (1) heterosis; (2) frequency-dependent selection, including selection on host–parasite interactions; (3) variation in intensities of selection in space or time; and (4) counteracting selection at different levels of organization, during different stages of life, or on different components of viability. Any of these possibilities might apply to lekking species.

Variation in selection in time or space can maintain genetic variance under special conditions. In the case of variation in space, maintenance of balanced polymorphism is sensitive to population subdivision and dispersal. So far, there is no evidence that lekking species, or polygynous species in general, differ systematically in these regards from other species (Dunn and Braun, 1985). If so, species with strong sexual selection either (1) do not differ much from other species in overall intensity of directional selection or (2) have genetic variance maintained by some other mechanism.

In the case of selection varying in time, directional selection should usually lead to eventual fixation of alleles with the highest long-term fitnesses (Maynard Smith, 1989, pp. 65–76) and thus to loss of genetic variation. Nevertheless, if selection coefficients reversed in sign at intervals of one to a few generations, polymorphism could persist. Selection coefficients for genes affecting interactions with physical features of the environment or with some biotic features, such as competitors or predators, are perhaps unlikely to reverse in sign over intervals of a few generations. The effects of the physical environment, competitors, and predators simply do not often change that dramatically and rapidly.

Interactions with parasites might satisfy these conditions (Hamilton, 1982; Hamilton and Zuk, 1982), since parasites usually have much shorter generations than their hosts and thus might evolve rapidly to counteract their hosts' defenses. Host–parasite interactions could thus result in frequency-dependent selection: the most frequent adaptations of the host would be matched by rapid evolution of counteradaptations by parasites (Maynard Smith, 1989). Genes conferring resistance to parasites and disease might thus differ markedly over periods of a few generations. Their frequencies could either fluctuate or persist in a stable equilibrium determined by frequency-dependent selection. In either case, female preferences for males resistant to parasites, as indicated by vigor in display or elaboration of ornament, might evolve particularly in species with high morbidity from parasites (Hamilton and Zuk, 1982; Kirkpatrick, 1986b; Read, 1987).

The possibility that females might prefer males with signs of resistance to parasites has prompted investigations of parasite loads in relation to mating success in various species (Schall and Dearing, 1987; Kennedy et al., 1987; Zuk, 1988; Clayton, 1990). Several studies have reported that heavily parasitized males display less than other males (Schall and Dearing, 1987; Kennedy et al., 1987). In sage grouse, one study reported that attendance at a lek, display rates, and success in mating were lower for males with higher numbers of lice or a hematozoan parasite (Boyce, 1990; Johnson and Boyce, 1990; Spurrier et al., 1990); another study found no relation between mating success and either a different hematozoan or hematocrit (Gibson, 1990). Numbers of hematozoan parasites in Lawes' parotias correlated negatively, but not significantly, with mating success, and more heavily parasitized males displayed for significantly shorter periods during the season (Pruett-Jones and Pruett-Jones, 1990). Male satin bowerbirds that mated successfully had fewer external parasites than those that did not, but there were no correlations between numbers of parasites and either quality of a male's plumage or his condition (as measured by mass/wing length) (Borgia and Collis, 1989). Despite these erratic results, the persistent trends in lekking species for correlations among (1) mating success, (2) vigor or persistence of display, and (3) parasite loads (see also Section V,C) suggest that parasites might influence the evolution of female choice.

Comparison of males within a population, however, does not provide a strong test for the hypothesis that transient adaptation to parasites maintains genetic variance and female choice. Sufficiently ill males would presumably have low persistence and vigor in display and low attendance at leks. Infection is in essence a form of covert handicap that affects the trade-offs males make between mating and survival. Consequently, if female preferences, direct or indirect, for vigorous or persistent display evolved for reasons other than rapid adaptation to parasites, females would incidentally tend to avoid parasitized males. Even if selection favored preferences for males with genes conferring resistance to parasites, these preferences, like other preferences for good genes, would not avoid the paradox of the lek unless the genetic basis for resistance shifted over periods of a few generations.

Circumstantial evidence for transient adaptations to parasites might include shifts in the kinds of parasites affecting males from generation to generation. Johnson and Boyce (1990) report, for example, that the incidence of hematozoans in male sage grouse varies among populations and between years. For definitive conclusions, however, it is necessary to demonstrate that the sexes are similarly exposed to the parasites under study and to verify changes in the genetic basis for resistance.

Other possibilities for maintaining selection for female preferences do not require genetic variation for male traits at all. If females incurred a fixed cost for indiscriminate mating, then this cost could alone maintain selection for female preferences even when genes for the preferred male trait had reached fixation. Selection against dysgenic hybridization might provide a fixed cost of this sort (Sections VIII,C and H). Even after female choice had eliminated most or all genetic variance for species-specific morphology and displays, selection for female choice would persist. The significance of discrimination against heterospecific males is that the "bad" genes persist, in the form of males of a separate species, even in the absence of genetic variance among conspecific males.

Immediate costs to females from indiscriminate mating could also maintain selection for female preferences, even though the preferred males' traits had no genetic basis. Possibilities include risks of copulation, such as predation, injury by males during competition for mates, and infection by parasitized males, as well as disruption of copulation and incomplete fertilization of eggs (Reynolds and Gross, 1990). For example, a female might realize higher immediate survival or fecundity by mating in the center of a group of males or with a dominant or vigorous male. Most of these possibilities, however, seem unlikely or remain unexamined for lekking species. For instance, injury of females is not reported, and in many species disruption of copulations is not restricted to unsuccessful males (Sections III,A). Risks of predation on females at leks in comparison to elsewhere remain unknown (Section VII,D), but seem unlikely to explain the degree of skew in mating distributions within a lek. Selection on females to reduce the immediate risk of parasitism might explain the lower mating success of heavily parastized males, particularly when parasite loads fail to correlate with either ornamentation or condition of males (Borgia and Collis, 1989).

The parasite loads of males at different ages have received little attention. In satin bowerbirds, older males have fewer external parasites (Borgia and Collis, 1989), but Gibson (1990) reported no differences with age for a hematozoan parasite in sage grouse. Age-dependent infection could result from acquired immunity or selective mortality. In either case, it could favor female preferences for older males, as a result either of obtaining good genes or reducing the risks of copulation.

It is important to emphasize that the persistence of selection for female preferences could depend on a combination of balancing or transient selection for viability and selection against risky copulation or dysgenic hybridization.

XI. EVOLUTIONARY SCENARIOS FOR THE ORIGINS OF LEKKING

There have been many proposals for conditions that lead to the evolution of leks as opposed to other mating systems. Since these proposals in general aim to provide more or less complete explanations for the evolution of lekking, they are appropriately termed evolutionary scenarios. As complex hypotheses, each makes a number of assumptions about behavioral mechanisms and evolutionary processes.

Evolutionary scenarios raise a number of general problems. One is the difficulty of enumerating a mutually exclusive set of possibilities, in part because their complexity often leads to finely divided variants. More important, evaluation of any hypothesis requires attention to its assumptions as well as its predictions, a point more easily forgotten in evaluating complex scenarios than when dealing with simpler hypotheses. The following sections summarize current scenarios for the evolution of lekking in relation to behavioral mechanisms and evolutionary issues.

A. PREDATOR AVOIDANCE AND INTERSEXUAL COMPETITION

Protection from predation is the critical component in some scenarios for the origin of leks. In grouse, the association of lekking with display in open habitats and of dispersed display sites with display in forests suggests that aggregation at leks might reduce predation in open areas (Koivisto, 1965; Wiley, 1974). Protection from predators might benefit females near displaying males as well as the males themselves (Wittenberger, 1978; Gosling, 1986). Aside from the observation that predation occurs infrequently on leks, little is known about rates of predation on solitary and aggregated males or females in different habitats (Section VII,C).

Lekking in birds other than grouse is not clearly related to habitat or other conditions that might affect exposure to predators, although the presence of other males nearby might of course increase the chances of detecting predators in any habitat. It would be instructive to collect information on levels of vigilance and persistence of display by solitary males and males on leks of different sizes.

The tendencies for males in some species to move their positions toward the centers of leks (Section III,B) and of matings to occur in central portions of leks (Section II,D) suggest that leks might function in part as selfish herds (Hamilton, 1971). Critical evidence for this possibility would come from rates of predation at different positions on leks (Section VIII,E). Regardless of other influences on the evolution of leks, risks of predation merit attention, as they bear on the costs of male display and of female choice.

Another suggestion is the possibility that females prefer to mate in locations away from feeding or nesting areas in order to minimize their competition with males for food or their exposure to predators attracted to males (Section VII,D). This suggestion alone does not explain either the aggregation of males or the nonuniform distribution of matings.

B. DISPROPORTIONATE ATTRACTION AND MALE BUFFETS

This proposal explains the advantage of male aggregation by a disproportionate attraction of females to groups of displaying males. Some versions of this scenario propose that larger leks simply produce auditory signals that carry farther and thus attract females from a larger area, not in itself an adequate explanation for attraction of females (Section V,D). A more plausible scenario would involve female preferences for synchronized or coordinated displays (Section III,C).

Attraction of females to synchronized or coordinated displays might plausibly provide a means of choosing vigorous males either between or within leks. Age might also contribute, if developing coordinated displays required prolonged social interaction. Evolutionary stability of such cooperative relations between males would require either (1) kinship among males at a lek, for which there is no suggestion in lekking species, or (2) reciprocity based on individual recognition or age-related succession (Section III,B and C; Axelrod and Hamilton, 1981; Wiley and Rabenold, 1984).

Another possibility is that females choose to mate at aggregations of males because of responses to collective features of aggregated display, the spatial density of displaying males, or the overall continuity of displays. These preferences might carry over to choices among males within a lek. The advantages of mating in a group of males might come from the ease of comparing males (Section IX,D), reduced waiting time for matings (Parker, 1978), or reliability of indirect choice of mates in obtaining optimal partners (Section XI,E). On the other hand, arbitrary preferences for mating in aggregations could in itself lead to Fisherian evolution of leks (Queller, 1987).

A related scenario, termed the female choice model, although perhaps "male buffet" is more descriptive, proposes that females prefer to mate in aggregations of males for convenience in choosing among individual males (Alexander, 1975; Emlen and Oring, 1977; Bradbury, 1981; Oring, 1982). This proposal thus requires mechanisms, not necessarily similar, for females' attraction to groups of displaying males and then for choosing, by direct or indirect means, among those assembled.

C. HOT SPOTS

In the hot-spot model for the evolution of leks, male aggregation results from males' displaying at locations that maximize their probable access to females. Simulations of this process have produced predictions for the spacing of leks, movements of females, and sizes of females' ranges, which in some cases agree with observed patterns (Section VII,B). More direct evidence from a number of species shows that leks often occur in locations with convenient access for females. In some cases, leks have disbanded and reformed elsewhere as a result of changes in movements of females (Sections II,B and IV). Furthermore, observations suggest that males in their first mating season might choose to join a lek as a result of experience with the numbers of females and males there previously (Section III,B). Thus, most of the assumptions of the hot-spot model seem plausible in modified form. One unrealistic assumption, however, concerns the movement of females. If females visit more than one lek or otherwise choose among them before mating, or if they follow other females to leks and then tend to return, females would not necessarily mate with the closest displaying male.

D. HOTSHOTS

The hotshot model proposes that females make direct choices among males and that unsuccessful males then move their locations near successful ones in order to intercept approaching females (Beehler and Foster, 1988; Gosling and Petrie, 1990). These mechanisms could lead to some constancy in location of leks, since, following the disappearance of the most preferred male, the next preferred is likely already to be established nearby. The optimal tactics for males in this case, however, are not clear (Section VII,B). In addition, a tendency of females to find replacement mates nearby amounts to a partial constraint on preferences for mating, a significant modification of this model. Hotshot scenarios, in any form, confront the problem of explaining the near unanimity of female preferences on the assumption of independent, direct choices by females (Section V,A).

A variant of the hotshot scenario proposes that females base their preferences for mating partners on the chances of interruption during copulation (Foster, 1983). Either by trial and error or by observing other females, a female might thus choose the most competitive, vigorous male in a group. In some species, however, the most successful males are not necessarily those that are least likely to be interrupted (Section III,A). This scenario could explain the high uniformity observed in females' choices, either as a consequence of females' observing previous attempts at copulation or as a consequence of relationships among males.

E. MATING SUCCESSION

Another class of scenarios for the evolution of leks, appropriately termed mating succession models, could also generate high uniformity in females' preferences, in this case by indirect choice of males by females. In these scenarios, each female tends to return to one location to mate; she might identify this location initially in any of several possible ways, by following more experienced females, by observing other females copulating without interruption (Section VI), by attraction to collective features of displaying groups (Section V,B and D), or by preferences for vigorous display or other features of male display (Section V,C). The site-faithfulness of females might apply only within an individual female's life or might be transmitted by tradition from older to younger females (Section VI). As a consequence, it would pay for males to establish dominance or territories at these preferred locations. The tendencies for males to aggregate would presumably increase if females' preferences for locations were traditional. If females' preferences for locations were highly focused, males might also move their territories gradually toward preferred sites and thus eventually, provided they remained competitive and survived, succeed to mating positions (Section II,B). Alternatively, less specific preferences of females for locations might result in succession in dominance, rather than in territorial locations. In either case, the preferences of females for a location, whether traditional and highly focused or not, could result indirectly in matings with older or more competitive males and hence, perhaps, ones with higher overall vitality.

F. COMPARISONS OF SCENARIOS

All of the more complete scenarios, those explaining both the aggregation of display and the nonuniformity of matings within aggregations, are also complex enough to admit a substantial number of variants. These variants, and the scenarios themselves, differ in their assumptions about the nature of mechanisms controlling the behavior of males and females. In some cases, scenarios grade into each other as the mechanisms become more complex. Thus, hotshot and mating succession models, in some of their variants, converge closely. Other scenarios, in some variants, are not mutually exclusive. Hotspot models, in the form of constraints on females' searches, and disproportionate attraction models could combine with hotshot or mating succession models. Predation reduction and intersexual competition models might combine with any of the others.

When expressed in simplistic form, each of these scenarios can probably be rejected for any lekking species; when expressed in realistic complexity, probably few or none can be rejected with current information. This conundrum arises from the complex variants each scenario can accommodate. The crucial distinctions are often the behavioral mechanisms that actually control the interactions of individuals. It is here that more research is needed. In addition to further investigation of female preferences for features of individual males, future work on the behavior of lekking species should include attention to (1) interactions between females, (2) female preferences for particular locations (including the spatial scale of such preferences), (3) female preferences for collective features of aggregated displays, (4) territoriality and dominance in relationships of males on leks and away from them, (5) age-related differences in the behavior of both males and females.

Recurring themes throughout this review suggest some general recommendations for further research on lekking species: (1) Quantitative analysis of social interactions is an essential base for any investigation. (2) Understanding behavioral mechanisms eventually requires experimentation. (3) Accurate understanding of behavioral mechanisms is essential for discussion of evolutionary issues and for comparison of evolutionary scenarios. (4) Age-related social behavior of males and females needs investigation. (5) Demography, in particular the demographic consequences of behavioral alternatives, also needs documentation. (6) Comparative studies should focus on variations in lekking behavior within species and also between related species. (7) Even wider comparisons are needed between lekking species and those with other mating systems, particular species with dispersed display sites lacking association with resources.

The many questions raised in this review result in part from the early stage of our current understanding of leks and in part from the complexity, both logical and logistical, of investigations of lekking species. In our push to find generalities, we should not neglect a fascination with the intricacies of lekking. We need to understand variations among and within species, as well as to identify general paradigms. Griffin (1976, p. 9) has cautioned against the "simplicity filters" that students of animal behavior sometimes adopt. While simple hypotheses necessarily bear investigation first, we must move beyond them, if we wish to comprehend the complexities of animal behavior.

XII. Summary

For species in which females have no associations with males except for brief periods preceding copulation, mating at leks probably enhances a female's discrimination of optimal mates, ones advantageous either for increasing the viability of her offspring or perhaps for reducing the immediate risks of copulation. The behavioral mechanisms by which this discrimination occurs are not yet well established for any species and might well differ among species or even among populations of the same species. These mechanisms might involve interactions among females, including learned traditions, as well as interactions among males and between females and males. Sexual selection could result from indirect, as well as direct, consequences of female preferences. The costs of display and ornamentation for males at leks are indicated by higher mortality of adult than younger males and greater energy expenditure by successful males. Advantages to females of choosing mates at leks remain mostly undocumented.

A general feature of mating at leks is a later onset of successful reproduction by males than by females. Age-related mating success of males on leks continues, at least in some cases, beyond the age at which fully developed morphology is attained and is, again at least in some cases, related to territorial succession or succession in dominance. Female preferences for mating at particular locations could provide the basis for either of these forms of mating succession and result indirectly in mating with older or more vigorous males.

Strong directional selection as a result of female preferences, either direct or indirect, tends to deplete genetic variation for the preferred male traits. This situation in turn reduces selection for the female preferences based on discriminations among conspecific males, the so-called paradox of the lek. Transient selection for resistance to parasites could maintain genetic variance for male traits, but evidence necessary to establish this possibility for lekking species is incomplete. The paradox of the lek does not arise when there are fixed costs of indiscriminate mating by females, such as immediate risks during copulation or dysgenic hybridization.

These generalities apply equally well to any species with brief interactions between the sexes and no associations of males with resources used by females. In particular, they apply to species with dispersed, rather than aggregated, display sites. In some taxa, the evolution of dispersed versus aggregated display appears related to risks of predation in different habitats; in others, this variation has no apparent explanation at present. All of these species in which copulation occurs at display sites lacking resources, whether aggregated as leks or dispersed, isolate clearly the issues of evolution by sexual selection and thus merit our continuing attention.

XIII. Scientific Names of Species Mentioned in the Text

Bat, hammer-headed (*Hypsignathus monstrosus*)
Bellbird, bearded (*Procnias avero*)
Bellbird, white (*Procnias alba*)
Bird of paradise, Goldie's (*Paradisaea decora*)
Bowerbird, satin (*Ptilinorhynchus violaceus*)
Capercaillie, common (*Tetrao urogallus*)
Capuchinbird (*Perissocephalus tricolor*)
Cock-of-the-rock, Guianan (*Rupicola rupicola*)
Deer, fallow (*Cervus dama*)
Deer, red (*Cervus cervus*)
Eagle, golden (*Aquila chrysaetos*)
Goshawk (*Accipiter gentilis*)
Grouse, black (*Tetrao tetrix*)
Grouse, blue (*Dendragapus obscurus*)
Grouse, ruffed (*Bonasa umbellus*)
Grouse, sage (*Centrocercus urophasianus*)
Grouse, sharp-tailed (*Tympanuchus phasianellus*)
Hawk-eagle, ornate (*Spizaetus ornatus*)
Hermit-hummingbirds (*Phaethornis* spp.)
Indigobird, village (*Vidua chalybeata*)
Kob, Uganda (*Kobus kob thomasi*)
Kob, white-eared (*Kobus kob leucotis*)
Lechwe, Kafue (*Kobus leche kafuensis*)
Manakin, band-tailed (*Pipra fasciicauda*)
Manakin, golden-headed (*Pipra erythrocephala*)
Manakin, lance-tailed (*Chiroxiphia lanceolata*)
Manakin, long-tailed (*Chiroxiphia caudata*)
Manakin, white-bearded (*Manacus manacus*)
Manakin, wire-tailed (*Pipra filicauda*)
Parotia, Lawes' (*Parotia lawesi*)
Prairie chicken, greater (*Tympanuchus cupido*)
Ruff (*Philomachus pugnax*)
Sandpiper, buff-breasted (*Tryngites subruficollis*)
Seal, northern elephant (*Mirounga angustirostris*)
Snipe, great (*Gallinago media*)

Toad, natterjack (*Bufo calamita*)
Topi (*Damaliscus lunatus*)
Widowbird, Jackson's (*Euplectes jacksoni*)

Acknowledgments

I thank J. Poston for his collaboration in preparing the figures and in revising the manuscript. For stimulating discussions of lekking in birds and mammals, I am indebted to the research groups in behavioral ecology at the University of North Carolina and University of Cambridge. For specific comments on the manuscript and discussions of their own work on lekking species, I thank especially A. Balmford, G. Borgia, M. Boyce, J. Bradbury, C. Braun, T. Clutton-Brock, M. Festa-Bianchet, R. Gibson, M. Gosling, H. Kermott, J. Kruijt, H. Landel, H. Mueller, L. Real, P. Trail, and S. Vehrencamp.

References

Alatalo, R. V., Höglund, J., and Lundberg, A. (1988). Patterns of variation in tail ornament size in birds. *Biol. J. Linn. Soc.* **34**, 363–374.

Alexander, R. D. (1975). Natural selection and specialized chorusing behavior in acoustical insects. *In* "Insects, Science and Society" (D. Pimentel, ed.), pp. 35–77. Academic Press, New York.

Anderson, R. K. (1969). Prairie chicken responses to changing booming-ground cover type and height. *J. Wildl. Manage.* **33**, 636–643.

Andersson, M. (1982a). Female choice selects for extreme tail length in a widowbird. *Nature (London)* **299**, 818–820.

Andersson, M. (1982b). Sexual selection, natural selection and quality advertisement. *Biol. J. Linn Soc.* **17**, 375–393.

Andersson, M. (1986). Evolution of condition-dependent ornaments and mating preferences: Sexual selection based on viability differences. *Evolution (Lawrence, Kans.)* **40**, 804–816.

Andersson, S. (1989). Sexual selection and cues for female choice in leks of Jackson's widowbird *Euplectes jacksoni*. *Behav. Ecol. Sociobiol.* **25**, 403–410.

Angelstam, P. (1984). Sexual and seasonal differences in mortality of the black grouse *Tetrao tetrix* in boreal Sweden. *Ornis Scand.* **15**, 123–134.

Apollonio, M., Festa-Bianchet, M., and Mari, F. (1989a). Correlates of copulatory success in a fallow deer lek. *Behav. Ecol. Sociobiol.* **25**, 89–97.

Apollonio, M., Festa-Bianchet, M., Mari, F., and Riva, M. (1989b). Site-specific asymmetries in male copulatory success in a fallow deer lek. *Anim. Behav.* **37**, 1007–1032.

Apollonio, M., Festa-Bianchet, M., Mari, F., Bruno, E., and Locati, M. (1990). In preparation.

Arak, A. (1983). Male–male competition and mate choice in anuran amphibians. *In* "Mate Choice" (P. P. G. Bateson, ed.), pp. 181–210. Cambridge Univ. Press, Cambridge.

Arak, A. (1988). Callers and satellites in the natterjack toad: Evolutionarily stable decision rules. *Anim. Behav.* **26**, 416–432.

Arnold, S. J. (1983). Sexual selection: The interface of theory and empiricism. *In* "Mate Choice" (P. P. G. Bateson, ed.), pp. 67–107. Cambridge Univ. Press, Cambridge.

Arnold, S. J. (1987). Quantitative genetic models of sexual selection: A review. *In* "The Evolution of Sex and its Consequences" (S. C. Stearns, ed.), pp. 283–315. Birkhaeuser, Basel.

Avery, M. I. (1984). Lekking in birds: Choice, competition and reproductive constraints. *Ibis* **126,** 177–187.

Axelrod, R., and Hamilton, W. D. (1981). The evolution of cooperation. *Science* **211,** 1390–1396.

Ballard, W. B., and Robel, R. J. (1974). Reproductive importance of dominant male greater prairie chickens. *Auk* **91,** 75–85.

Beck, T. D. I., and Braun, C. E. (1978). Weights of Colorado sage grouse. *Condor* **80,** 241–243.

Beehler, B. M. (1983a). Frugivory and polygamy in birds of paradise. *Auk* **100,** 1–12.

Beehler, B. M. (1983b). Lek behavior of the lesser bird of paradise. *Auk* **100,** 992–995.

Beehler, B. M. (1987a). Birds of paradise and mating system theory—predictions and observations. *Emu* **87,** 78–89.

Beehler, B. M. (1987b). Ecology and behavior of the buff-tailed sicklebill. *Auk* **104,** 48–55.

Beehler, B. M., and Foster, M. S. (1988). Hotshots, hotspots, and female preference in the organization of lek mating systems. *Am. Nat.* **131,** 203–219.

Beehler, B. M., and Pruett-Jones, S. G. (1983). Display dispersion and diet of male birds of paradise: A comparison of nine species. *Behav. Ecol. Sociobiol.* **13,** 229–238.

Bendell, J. F. (1955). Age, molt and weight characteristics of blue grouse. *Condor* **57,** 354–361.

Bendell, J. F., and Elliott, P. W. (1967). Behaviour and the regulation of numbers in blue grouse. *Can. Wildl. Serv. Rep.* **4,** 1–76.

Bendell, J. F., King, D. G., and Mossop, D. H. (1972). Removal and repopulation of blue grouse in a declining population. *J. Wildl. Manage.* **36,** 1153–1165.

Berger, D. D., Hamerstrom, F., and Hamerstrom, F. N., Jr. (1963). The effect of raptors on prairie chickens on booming grounds. *J. Wildl. Manage.* **27,** 778–791.

Bergerud, A. T. (1988). Mating systems in grouse. *In* "Adaptive Strategies and Population Ecology of Northern Grouse" (A. T. Bergerud and M. W. Gratson, eds.), Vol. 2, pp. 439–472. Univ. of Minnesota Press, Minneapolis.

Bergerud, A. T., and Gratson, M. W. (1988). Survival and breeding strategies of grouse. *In* "Adaptive Strategies and Population Ecology of Northern Grouse" (A. T. Bergerud and M. W. Gratson, eds.), Vol. 2, pp. 473–577. Univ. of Minnesota Press, Minneapolis.

Borgia, G. (1979). Sexual selection and the evolution of mating systems. *In* "Sexual Selection and Reproductive Competition in Insects" (M. S. Blum and N. A. Blum, eds.), pp. 19–80. Academic Press, New York.

Borgia, G. (1985a). Bower destruction and sexual competition in the satin bowerbird (*Ptilonorhynchus violaceus*). *Behav. Ecol. Sociobiol.* **18,** 91–100.

Borgia, G. (1985b). Bower quality, number of decorations and mating success of male satin bowerbirds (*Ptilonorhynchus violaceus*): An experimental analysis. *Anim. Behav.* **33,** 266–271.

Borgia, G. (1986). Sexual selection in bowerbirds. *Sci. Am.* **254,** 92–101.

Borgia, G. (1987). A critical review of sexual selection models. *In* "Sexual Selection: Testing the Alternatives" (J. W. Bradbury and M. B. Andersson, eds.), pp. 55–66. Wiley, New York.

Borgia, G., and Collis, K. (1989). Female choice for parasite-free male satin bowerbirds and the evolution of bright male plumage. *Behav. Ecol. Sociobiol.* **25,** 445–454.

Borgia, G., and Gore, M. (1986). Feather stealing in the satin bowerbird (*Ptilonorhynchus violaceus*): Male competition and the quality of display. *Anim. Behav.* **34,** 727–738.

Boyce, M. S. (1990). The red queen visits sage grouse leks. *Am. Zool.,* **30,** 263–270.

Bradbury, J. W. (1977). Lek mating behavior in the hammer-headed bat. *Z. Tierpsychol.* **45,** 225–255.

Bradbury, J. W. (1981). The evolution of leks. *In* "Natural Selection and Social Behavior" (R. D. Alexander and D. W. Tinkle, eds.), pp. 138–169. Chiron Press, New York.

Bradbury, J. W., and Gibson, R. M. (1983). Leks and mate choice. *In* "Mate Choice" (P. P. G. Bateson, ed.), pp. 109–138. Cambridge Univ. Press, Cambridge.

Bradbury, J. W., Vehrencamp, S. L., and Gibson, R. M. (1985). Leks and the unanimity of female choice. *In* "Evolution: Essays in Honour of John Maynard Smith" (P. J. Greenwood, P. H. Harvey, and M. Slatkin, eds.), pp. 301–314. Cambridge Univ. Press, Cambridge.

Bradbury, J. W., Gibson, R. M., and Tsai, I. M. (1986). Hotspots and the evolution of leks. *Anim. Behav.* **34,** 1694–1709.

Bradbury, J. W., Vehrencamp, S. L., and Gibson, R. M. (1989a). Dispersion of displaying male sage grouse. I. Patterns of temporal variation. *Behav. Ecol. Sociobiol.* **24,** 1–14.

Bradbury, J. W., Gibson, R. M., McCarthy, C. E., and Vehrencamp, S. L. (1989b). Dispersion of displaying male sage grouse. II. The role of female dispersion. *Behav. Ecol. Sociobiol.* **24,** 15–24.

Braun, C. E. (1984). Attributes of a hunted sage grouse population in Colorado, U.S.A. *Int. Grouse Symp., World Pheasant Assoc.* **3,** 148–162.

Brown, J. L. (1963). Aggressiveness, dominance and social organization in the Steller jay. *Condor* **65,** 460–484.

Brown, J. L. (1964). The evolution of diversity in avian territorial systems. *Wilson Bull.* **76,** 160–168.

Buechner, H. K. (1961). Territorial behavior in Uganda kob. *Science* **133,** 698–699.

Buechner, H. K., and Roth, H. D. (1974). The lek system in Uganda kob antelope. *Am. Zool.* **14,** 145–162.

Buechner, H. K., and Schloeth, R. E. (1965). Ceremonial mating behaviour in Uganda kob (*Adenota kob thomasi* Neumann). *Z. Tierpsychol.* **22,** 209–225.

Cade, W. H. (1981). Field cricket spacing and the phonotaxis of crickets and parasitoid flies to clumped and isolated cricket songs. *Z. Tierpsychol.* **55,** 365–375.

Cannon, R. W., and Knopf, F. L. (1981). Lek numbers as a trend index to prairie grouse populations. *J. Wildl. Manage.* **45,** 776–778.

Cavalli-Sforza, L. L., and Feldman, M. W. (1981). "Cultural Transmission and Evolution: A Quantitative Approach." Princeton Univ. Press, Princeton.

Charlesworth, B. (1980). "Evolution in Age-structured Populations." Cambridge Univ. Press, Cambridge.

Charlesworth, B. (1988). The heritability of fitness. *In* "Sexual Selection: Testing the Alternatives" (J. W. Bradbury and M. B. Andersson, eds.). pp. 21–40. Wiley, New York.

Chase, I. D. (1974). Models of hierarchy formation in animal societies. *Behav. Sci.* **19,** 374–382.

Clarke, L. F., Rahn, H., and Martin, M. D. (1942). Seasonal and sexual dimorphic variations in the so-called "air sac" region of the sage grouse. *Wyo. Game Fish Dep. Bull.* **2,** 13–27.

Clayton, D. H. (1990). Mate choice in experimentally parasitized rock doves: lousy males lose. *Am. Zool.* **30,** 251–262.

Clutton-Brock, T. H. (1982). The functions of antlers. *Behaviour* **79,** 108–125.

Clutton-Brock, T. H. (1983). Selection in relation to sex. *In* "Evolution from Molecules to Men" (D. S. Bendall, ed.), pp. 457–481. Cambridge Univ. Press, Cambridge.

Clutton-Brock, T. H., Harvey, P. H., and Rudder, B. (1977). Sexual dimorphism, socionomic sex ratio and body weight in primates. *Nature (London)* **269,** 797–800.

Clutton-Brock, T. H., Guiness, F. E., and Albon, S. D. (1982). "Red Deer: The Behavior and Ecology of Two Sexes": Univ. of Chicago Press, Chicago, Illinois.

Clutton-Brock, T. H., Green, D., Hiraiwa-Hasegawa, H., and Albon, S. D. (1988a). Passing the buck: Resource defence, lek breeding and mate choice in fallow deer. *Behav. Ecol. Sociobiol.* **23,** 281–296.

Clutton-Brock, T. H., Albon, S. D., and Guiness, F. E. (1988b). Reproductive success in male and female red deer. *In* "Reproductive Success" (T. H. Clutton-Brock, ed.), pp. 325–343. Univ. of Chicago Press, Chicago, Illinois.

Crook, J. H. (1965). The adaptive significance of avian social organisation. *Symp. Zool. Soc. London* **14**, 181–218.

Dalke, P. D., Pyrah, D. B., Stanton, D. C., Crawford, J. C., and Schlatterer, E. (1963). Ecology, productivity, and management of sage grouse in Idaho. *J. Wildl. Manage.* **27**, 810–841.

Darwin, C. (1871). "The Descent of Man, and Selection in Relation to Sex." John Murray, London.

Davies, N. B. (1989). Sexual conflict and the polygamy threshold. *Anim. Behav.* **38**, 226–235.

Dement'ev, G. P., and Gladkov, N. A., eds. (1967). "Birds of the Soviet Union," Vol. 6. Israel Program for Scientific Translations, Jerusalem.

de Vos, G. J. (1983). Social behavior of black grouse: An observational and experimental field study. *Ardea* **71**, 1–103.

Dinsmore, J. J. (1970). Courtship behavior of the greater bird of paradise. *Auk* **87**, 305–321.

Dunn, P. O., and Braun, C. E. (1985). Natal dispersal and lek fidelity of sage grouse. *Auk* **102**, 621–627.

Dunn, P. O., and Braun, C. E. (1986). Late summer-spring movements of juvenile sage grouse. *Wilson Bull.* **98**, 83–92.

Ellison, L. N. (1971). Territoriality in Alaskan spruce grouse. *Auk* **88**, 652–664.

Emlen, S., and Oring, L. (1977). Ecology, sexual selection, and the evolution of mating systems. *Science* **197**, 215–223.

Emmons, S. R., and Braun, C. E. (1984). Lek attendance of male sage grouse. *J. Wildl. Manage.* **48**, 1023–1028.

Eng, R. L. (1963). Observations on the breeding biology of male sage grouse. *J. Wildl. Manage.* **27**, 841–846.

Evans, R. M. (1969). Territorial stability in sharp-tailed grouse. *Wilson Bull.* **81**, 75–78.

Felsenstein, J. (1976). The theoretical population genetics of variable selection and migration. *Annu. Rev. Genet.* **10**, 253–280.

Fisher, R. A. (1915). The evolution of sexual preference. *Eugen. Rev.* **7**, 184–192.

Fisher, R. A. (1930). "The Genetical Theory of Natural Selection." Oxford Univ. Press (Clarendon), London and New York.

Floody, O. R., and Arnold, A. P. (1975). Uganda kob (*Adenota kob thomasii*): Territoriality and the spatial distributions of sexual and agonistic behaviors at a territorial ground. *Z. Tierpsychol.* **37**, 192–212.

Foster, M. S. (1977a). Odd couples in manakins: A study of social organization and cooperative breeding in *Chiroxiphia linearis*. *Am. Nat.* **111**, 845–853.

Foster, M. S. (1977b). Ecological and nutritional effects of food scarcity on a tropical frugivorous bird and its fruit source. *Ecology* **58**, 73–85.

Foster, M. S. (1981). Cooperative behavior and social organization of the swallow-tailed manakin (*Chiroxiphia caudata*). *Behav. Ecol. Sociobiol.* **9**, 167–177.

Foster, M. S. (1983). Disruption, dispersion, and dominance in lek-breeding birds. *Am. Nat.* **122**, 53–72.

Foster, M. S. (1987). Delayed maturation, neoteny, and social system differences in two manakins of the genus Chiroxiphia. *Evolution (Lawrence, Kans.)* **41**, 547–558.

Fretwell, S. D. (1972). "Populations in a Seasonal Environment." Princeton Univ. Press, Princeton, New Jersey.

Fryxell, J. (1987). Lek breeding and territorial aggression in white-eared kob. *Ethology* **75**, 211–220.

Gates, R. J. (1985). Observations on the formation of a sage grouse lek. *Wilson Bull.* **97**, 219–221.

Gibson, R. M. (1987). Bivariate versus multivariate analyses of sexual selection in red deer. *Anim. Behav.* **35**, 292–305.

Gibson, R. M. (1989). Field playback of male display attracts females in lek breeding sage grouse. *Behav. Ecol. Sociobiol.* **24**, 439–443.

Gibson, R. M. (1990). Relationships between blood parasites, mating success and phenotypic cues in male sage grouse (*Centrocercus urophasianus*). *Am. Zool.* **30**, 271–278.

Gibson, R. M., and Bradbury, J. W. (1985). Sexual selection in lekking sage grouse: Phenotypic correlates of male mating success. *Behav. Ecol. Sociobiol.* **18**, 117–123.

Gibson, R. M., and Bradbury, J. W. (1986). Male and female mating strategies on sage grouse lek. *In* "Ecological Aspects of Social Evolution" (D. I. Rubenstein and R. W. Wrangham, eds.), pp. 379–398. Princeton Univ. Press, Princeton, New Jersey.

Gibson, R. M., and Bradbury, J. W. (1987). Lek organization in sage grouse: Variations on a territorial theme. *Auk* **104**, 77–84.

Gibson, R. M., Taylor, C. E., and Jefferson, D. R. (1990). Lek formation by female choice: A simulation study. *Behav. Ecol.* **1**, 36–42.

Gilliard, E. T. (1962). On the breeding behavior of the cock-of-the-rock (Aves, *Rupicola rupicola*). *Bull. Am. Mus. Nat. Hist.* **124**, 31–68.

Gilliard, E. T. (1969). "Birds of Paradise and Bowerbirds." Natural History Press, Garden City, New York.

Given, M. F. (1988). Growth rate and the cost of calling activity in male carpenter frogs. *Rana virgatipes. Behav. Ecol. Sociobiol.* **22**, 153–160.

Gosling, L. M. (1986). The evolution of mating strategies in male antelopes. *In* "Ecological Aspects of Social Evolution" (D. I. Rubenstein and R. W. Wrangham, eds.), pp. 244–281. Princeton Univ. Press, Princeton, New Jersey.

Gosling, L. M., and Petrie, M. (1990). Lekking in topi: A consequence of satellite behaviour by small males at hotspots. *Anim. Behav.* **40**, 272–287.

Gosling, L. M., Petrie, M., and Rainy, M. E. (1987). Lekking in topi: A high-cost, specialist strategy. *Anim. Behav.* **35**, 616–618.

Gould, J. L. (1982). "Ethology." Norton, New York.

Gratson, M. W. (1988). Spatial patterns, movements, and cover selection by sharp-tailed grouse. *In* "Adaptive Strategies and Population Ecology of Northern Grouse" (A. T. Bergerud and M. W. Gratson, eds.), Vol. 1, pp. 158–192. Univ. of Minnesota Press, Minneapolis.

Griffin, D. R. (1976). "The Question of Animal Awareness." Rockefeller Univ. Press, New York.

Guhl, A. M. (1968). Social inertia and social stability in chickens. *Anim. Behav.* **16**, 219–232.

Gullion, G. W. (1967). Selection and use of drumming sites by male ruffed grouse. *Auk* **84**, 87–112.

Gullion, G. W. (1981). Non-drumming males in ruffed grouse populations. *Wilson Bull.* **93**, 372–382.

Gullion, G. W., and Marshall, W. H. (1968). Survival of ruffed grouse in a boreal forest. *Living Bird* **7**, 117–167.

Halliday, T. R. (1983). The study of mate choice. *In* "Mate Choice" (P. P. G. Bateson, ed.), pp. 3–32. Cambridge Univ. Press, Cambridge.

Hamerstrom, F., and Hamerstrom, F. (1955). Population density and behavior in Wisconsin prairie chickens (*Tympanuchus cupido pinnatus*). *Proc. Int. Ornithol. Congr.* **11**, 459–466.

Hamerstrom, F., and Hamerstrom, F. (1960). Comparability of some social displays of grouse. *Proc. Int. Ornithol. Congr.* **12**, 274–293.

Hamerstrom, F., and Hamerstrom, F. (1973). The prairie chicken in Wisconsin. *Wis., Dep. Nat. Res., Tech. Bull.* **64**, 1–52.

Hamerstrom, F., Berger, D. D., and Hamerstrom, F. N., Jr. (1965). The effect of mammals on prairie chickens on booming grounds. *J. Wildl. Manage.* **29**, 536–542.

Hamilton, W. D. (1971). Geometry for the selfish herd. *J. Theor. Biol.* **31**, 295–311.

Hamilton, W. D. (1982). Pathogens as causes of genetic diversity in their host populations. *In* "Population Biology of Infectious Diseases" (R. M. Anderson and R. M. May, eds.), pp. 269–296. Springer-Verlag, New York.

Hamilton, W. D., and Zuk, M. (1982). Heritable true fitness and bright birds: A role for parasites? *Science* **218**, 384–387.

Hannon, S. J. (1984). Factors limiting polygyny in the willow ptarmigan. *Anim. Behav.* **32**, 153–161.

Hannon, S. J., Simard, B. R., Zwickel, F. C., and Bendell, J. F. (1979). Differences in the gonadal cycles of adult and yearling blue grouse. *Can. J. Zool.* **57**, 1283–1289.

Hartzler, J. E. (1972). An analysis of sage grouse lek behavior. Ph.D. Dissertation, University of Montana, Missoula.

Hartzler, J. E. (1974). Predation and the daily timing of sage grouse leks. *Auk* **91**, 532–536.

Hartzler, J. E., and Jenni, D. A. (1988). Mate choice by female sage grouse. *In* "Adaptive Strategies and Population Ecology of Northern Grouse" (A. T. Bergerud and M. W. Gratson, eds.), Vol. 1, pp. 240–269. Univ. of Minnesota Press, Minneapolis.

Heisler, I. L. (1984). A quantitative genetic model for the origin of mating preferences. *Evolution (Lawrence, Kans.)* **38**, 1283–1295.

Heisler, I. L. (1985). Quantitative genetic models of female choice based on "arbitrary" male characters. *Heredity* **55**, 187–198.

Helminen, M. (1963). Composition of the Finnish populations of capercaillie, *Tetrao urogallus,* and black grouse, *Lyrurus tetrix,* in the autumns of 1952–1961, as revealed by a study of wings. *Pap. Game Res., Helsinki,* 23.

Heywood, J. S. (1989). Sexual selection by the handicap mechanism. *Evolution (Lawrence, Kans.)* **43**, 1387–1397.

Hjorth, I. (1970). Reproductive behaviour in Tetraonidae. *Viltrevy* **7**, 184–596.

Hogan-Warburg, A. J. (1966). Social behavior of the ruff, *Philomachus pugnax* (L.). *Ardea* **54**, 109–229.

Höglund, J. (1989). Size and plumage dimorphism in lek-breeding birds: A comparative analysis. *Am. Nat.* **134**, 72–87.

Höglund, J., and Lundberg, A. (1987). Sexual selection in a monomorphic lek-breeding bird: Correlates of male mating success in the great snipe Gallinago media. *Behav. Ecol. Sociobiol.* **21**, 211–216.

Höglund, J., Kalas, J. A., and Lofaldli, L. (1990). Sexual dimorphism in the lekking great snipe. *Ornis Scand.* **21**, 1–6.

Honess, R. F., and Allred, W. J. (1942). Structure and function of the neck muscles in inflation and deflation of the esophagus in the sage cock. *Wyo. Game Fish Dep., Bull.* **2**, 5–12.

Hubbell, S. P., and Johnson, L. K. (1987). Environmental variance in lifetime mating success, mate choice, and sexual selection. *Am. Nat.* **130**, 91–112.

Hupp, J. W., and Braun, C. E. (1989). Endogenous reserves of adult male sage grouse during courtship. *Condor* **91**, 266–271.

Jamieson, I. G., and Zwickel, F. C. (1983). Spatial patterns of yearling male blue grouse and their relation to recruitment into the breeding population. *Auk* **100**, 653–657.

Johnsgard, P. A., and Wood, R. W. (1968). Distributional changes and interactions between prairie chickens and sharp-tailed grouse in the Midwest. *Wilson Bull.* **80**, 173–188.

Johnson, L. L., and Boyce, M. S. (1990). Female choice of males with low parasite loads in sage grouse. *In* "Ecology, Behavior and Evolution of Bird-Parasite Interactions" (J. Loye, C. van Riper, III, and M. Zuk, eds.). Oxford Univ. Press, Oxford. In press.

Jones, J. S. (1987). The heritability of fitness: Bad news for "good genes"? *Trends Ecol. Evol.* **2**, 35–38.

Kennedy, C., Endler, J., Poynton, S., and McMinn, H. (1987). Parasite load predicts mate choice in guppies. *Behav. Ecol. Sociobiol.* **21**, 291–295.

Kermott, L. H. (1982). Breeding behavior in the sharp-tailed grouse. Ph.D. Dissertation, University of Minnesota, Minneapolis.

Kermott, L. H., and Oring, L. W. (1975). Acoustical communication of male sharp-tailed grouse (*Pedioecetes phasianellus*) on a North Dakota dancing ground. *Anim. Behav.* **23**, 315–386.

Kirkpatrick, M. (1982). Sexual selection and the evolution of female choice. *Evolution (Lawrence, Kans.)* **36**, 1–12.

Kirkpatrick, M. (1986a). The handicap mechanism of sexual selection does not function. *Am. Nat.* **127**, 222–240.

Kirkpatrick, M. (1986b). Sexual selection and cycling parasites: A simulation study of Hamilton's hypothesis. *J. Theor. Biol.* **119**, 263–271.

Kirkpatrick, M. (1987). Sexual selection by female choice in polygynous animals. *Annu. Rev. Ecol. Syst.* **18**, 43–70.

Kodric-Brown, A., and Brown, L. H. (1984). Truth in advertising: The kinds of traits favored by sexual selection. *Am. Nat.* **124**, 309–323.

Koivisto, I. (1965). Behavior of the black grouse, *Lyrurus tetrix* (L.), during spring display. *Finn. Game Res.* **26**, 1–60.

Kruijt, J. P. (1967). Reproductive behaviour of black grouse (*Lyrurus tetrix*) (16-mm film). Stichting Film en Wetenschap, Utrecht, Holland.

Kruijt, J. P., and de Vos, G. J. (1988). Individual variation in reproductive success in male black grouse, *Tetrao tetrix* L. *In* "Reproductive Success" (T. H. Clutton-Brock, ed.), pp. 279–290. Univ. of Chicago Press, Chicago, Illinois.

Kruijt, J. P., and Hogan, J. A. (1967). Social behaviour on the lek in black grouse, *Lyrurus tetrix tetrix* (L.). *Ardea* **55**, 203–240.

Kruijt, J. P., de Vos, G. J., and Bossema, I. (1972). The arena system of black grouse. *Proc. Int. Ornithol. Congr.* **15**, 399–423.

Landau, H. G. (1951). On dominance relations and the structure of animal societies. I. Effect of inherent characteristics. *Bull. Math. Biophys.* **13**, 1–19.

Lande, R. (1976). The maintenance of genetic variability by mutation in a polygenic character with linked loci. *Genet. Res.* **26**, 221–235.

Lande, R. (1981). Models of speciation by sexual selection on polygenic traits. *Proc. Natl. Acad. Sci. U.S.A.* **78**, 3721–3725.

Lande, R. (1982). Rapid origin of sexual isolation and character divergence within a cline. *Evolution (Lawrence, Kans.)* **36**, 213–223.

Lande, R., and Arnold, S. J. (1983). The measurement of selection on correlated characters. *Evolution* **37**, 1210–1226.

Landel, H. F. (1989). A study of female and male mating behavior and female mate choice in the sharp-tailed grouse, *Tympanuchus phasianellus jamesi*. Ph.D. Dissertation, Purdue University, West Lafayette, Indiana.

Langbein, J., and Thirgood, S. J. (1989). Variation in mating system of fallow deer (*Dama dama*) in relation to ecology. *Ethology* **83**, 195–214.

Lank, D. B., and Smith, C. M. (1987). Conditional lekking in ruff (*Philomachus pugnax*) *Behav. Ecol. Sociobiol.* **20**, 137–145.

LeBoeuf, B. J., and Reiter, J. (1988). Lifetime reproductive success in northern elephant seals. *In* "Reproductive Success" (T. H. Clutton-Brock, ed.), pp. 344–362. Univ. of Chicago Press, Chicago, Illinois.

LeClerq, B. (1988). "Le grand coq de bruyère ou grand tétras." Editions Sang de la Terre, Paris.

LeCroy, M. (1981). The genus *Paradisaea:* Display and evolution. *Am. Mus. Novit.* **2714**, 1–52.

LeCroy, M., Kulupi, A., and Peckover, W. S. (1980). Goldie's bird-of-paradise: Display, natural history, and traditional relationships of people to the bird. *Wilson Bull.* **92**, 289–301.

Leuthold, W. (1966). Variations in territorial behavior of Uganda kob, *Adenota kob thomasi* (Neumann 1896). *Behaviour* **27**, 214–257.

Lewis, R. A. (1981). Characteristics of persistent and transient territorial sites of male blue grouse. *J. Wildl. Manage.* **45,** 1048–1051.

Lewis, R. A., and Zwickel, F. C. (1980). Removal and replacement of male blue grouse on persistent and transient territorial sites. *Can. J. Zool.* **58,** 1417–1423.

Lewis, R. A., and Zwickel, F. C. (1981). Differential use of territorial sites by male blue grouse. *Condor* **83,** 171–176.

Lewis, R. A., and Zwickel, F. C. (1982). Survival and delayed breeding in male blue grouse. *Can. J. Zool.* **60,** 1881–1884.

Lill, A. (1974a). Sexual behavior of the lek-forming white-bearded manakin (*Manacus manacus trinitatus* Hartert). *Z. Tierpsychol.* **36,** 1–36.

Lill, A. (1974b). Social organization and space utilization in the lek-forming white-bearded manakin, *M. manacus trinitatis. Z. Tierpsychol.* **36,** 513–530.

Lill, A. (1976). Lek behavior in the golden-headed manakin, *Pipra erythrocephala,* in Trinidad (West Indies). *Adv. Ethol.* **18,** 1–83.

Lindén, H. (1981). Hunting and tetraonid populations in Finland. *Finn. Game Res.* **39,** 69–78.

Losey, G. S., Jr., Stanton, F. G., Telecky, T. M., Tyler, W. A., III, and the Zoology 691 Graduate Seminar Class (1986). Copying others, an evolutionary stable strategy for mate choice: A model. *Am. Nat.* **128,** 653–664.

Lumsden, H. G. (1961). The display of the capercaillie. *Br. Birds* **54,** 257–272.

Lumsden, H. G. (1965). Displays of the sharp tail grouse. *Ont., Dep. Lands For., Res. Rep.* **66,** 1–68.

Lumsden, H. G. (1968). The displays of the sage grouse. *Ont., Dep. Lands For. Res. Rep. (Wild.)* **83,** 1–94.

Martin, K. (1984). Reproductive defence priorities of male willow ptarmigan (*Lagopus lagopus*): Enhancing mate survival or extending paternity options? *Behav. Ecol. Sociobiol.* **16,** 57–63.

Martin, K., and Cooke, F. (1987). Bi-parental care in willow ptarmigan: A luxury? *Anim. Behav.* **35,** 369–379.

Maynard Smith, J. (1976). Sexual selection and the handicap principle. *J. Theor. Biol.* **57,** 239–242.

Maynard Smith, J. (1978). "The Evolution of Sex." Cambridge Univ. Press, Cambridge.

Maynard Smith, J. (1985). Sexual selection, handicaps and true fitness. *J. Theor. Biol.* **115,** 1–8.

Maynard Smith, J. (1987). Sexual selection—a classification of models. *In* "Sexual Selection: Testing the Alternatives" (J. W. Bradbury and M. B. Andersson, eds.), pp. 9–20. Wiley, New York.

Maynard Smith, J. (1989). "Evolutionary Genetics." Oxford Univ. Press, Oxford.

McDonald, D. B. (1989a). Correlates of male mating success in a lekking bird with male–male cooperation. *Anim. Behav.* **37,** 1007–1022.

McDonald, D. B. (1989b). Cooperation under sexual selection: Age-graded changes in a lekking bird. *Am. Nat.* **134,** 709–730.

McKinney, F., Derrickson, S. R., and Mineau, P. (1983). Forced copulation in waterfowl. *Behaviour* **86,** 250–294.

Moller, A. P. (1988). Female choice selects for male sexual ornaments in the monogamous swallow. *Nature (London)* **332,** 640–642.

Montfort-Braham, N. (1975). Variations dans la structure social du topi, *Damaliscus korrigum* Ogilby, au Parc National de l'Akagera, Rwanda. *Z. Tierpsychol.* **39,** 332–364.

Moss, R. (1980). Why are capercaillie cocks so big? *Br. Birds* **73,** 440–447.

Moss, R. (1987a). Demography of capercaillie *Tetrao urogallus* in north-east Scotland. I. Determining the age of Scottish capercaillie from skull and head measurements. *Ornis Scand.* **18,** 129–134.

Moss, R. (1987b). Demography of capercaillie *Tetrao urogallus* in north-east Scotland. II. Age and sex distribution. *Ornis Scand.* **18,** 135–140.

Moyles, D. L. J., and Boag, D. A. (1981). Where, when, and how male sharp-tailed grouse establish territories on arenas? *Can. J. Zool.* **59**, 1576–1581.

Myers, J. P. (1979). Leks, sex and buff-breasted sandpipers. *Am. Birds* **33**, 823–825.

O'Donald, P. (1980). "Genetic Models of Sexual Selection." Cambridge Univ. Press, Cambridge.

Olson, D. H., and McDowell, M. K. (1983). A comparison of white-bearded manakin (*Manacus manacus*) populations and lek systems in Suriname and Trinidad. *Auk* **100**, 739–742.

Orians, G. H. (1969). On the evolution of mating systems in birds and mammals. *Am. Nat.* **103**, 589–603.

Oring, L. W. (1982). Avian mating systems. *Avian Biol.* **6**, 1–92.

Parker, G. A. (1978). Evolution of competitive mate searching. *Annu. Rev. Entomol.* **23**, 173–196.

Parker, G. A. (1982). Phenotype-limited evolutionarily stable strategies. *In* "Current Problems in Sociobiology" (B. R. Bertram, T. H. Clutton-Brock, R. I. M. Dunbar, D. I. Rubenstein, and R. Wrangham, eds.), pp. 173–201. Cambridge Univ. Press, Cambridge.

Parker, G. A. (1983). Mate quality and mating decisions. *In* "Mate Choice" (P. P. G. Bateson, ed.), pp. 141–166. Cambridge Univ. Press, Cambridge.

Parkes, K. C. (1961). Intergeneric hybrids in the family Pipridae. *Condor* **63**, 345–350.

Patterson, R. L. (1952). "The Sage Grouse in Wyoming." Sage Books, Denver, Colorado.

Payne, R. B. (1984). Sexual selection, lek and arena behavior, and sexual size dimorphism in birds. *Ornithol. Monogr.* **33**, 1–52.

Payne, R. B., and Payne, K. (1977). Social organization and mating success in local song populations of village indigobirds, *Vidua chalybeata. Z. Tierpsychol.* **45**, 113–173.

Petersen, B. E. (1980). Breeding and nesting ecology of female sage grouse in North Park, Colorado. M.S. Thesis, Colorado State University, Fort Collins.

Petersen, B. E., and Braun, C. E. (1990). In preparation.

Piper, W. H., and Wiley, R. H. (1989). Correlates of dominance in wintering white-throated sparrows: Age, sex, and location. *Anim. Behav.* **37**, 298–310.

Pomiankowski, A. N. (1987a). The costs of choice in sexual selection. *J. Theor. Biol.* **128**, 195–218.

Pomiankowski, A. N. (1987b). Sexual selection: The handicap principle does work—sometimes. *Proc. R. Soc. London, Ser. B* **231**, 123–145.

Pomiankowski, A. N. (1988). The evolution of female mate preferences for male genetic quality. *Oxford Surv. Evol. Biol.* **5**, 136–184.

Pruett-Jones, S. G. (1988). Lekking versus solitary display: Temporal variations in dispersion in the buff-breasted sandpiper. *Anim. Behav.* **36**, 1740–1752.

Pruett-Jones, S. G., and Pruett-Jones, M. A. (1990). Sexual selection through female choice in Lawes' parotia, a lek-mating bird of paradise. *Evolution (Lawrence, Kans.)* **44**, 486–501.

Prum, R. O. (1985). Observations of the white-fronted manakin (*Pipra serena*) in Suriname. *Auk* **102**, 384–387.

Prum, R. O. (1986). The displays of the white-throated manakin *Corapipo gutturalis* in Suriname. *Ibis* **128**, 91–102.

Prum, R. O., and Johnson, A. E. (1987). Display behavior, foraging ecology, and systematics of the golden-winged manakin (*Masius chrysopterus*). *Wilson Bull.* **99**, 521–539.

Queller, D. C. (1987). The evolution of leks through female choice. *Anim. Behav.* **35**, 1424–1432.

Rajala, P. (1974). The structure and reproduction of Finnish populations of capercaillie, *Tetrao urogallus*, and black grouse, *Lyrurus tetrix*, on the basis of late summer census data from 1963–66. *Finn. Game Res.* **35**, 1–51.

Read, A. F. (1987). Comparative evidence supports the Hamilton and Zuk hypothesis on parasites and sexual selection. *Nature (London)* **328**, 68–70.

Real, L. A. (1990). Search theory and mate choice. I. Models of single sex discrimination. *Am. Nat.* (in press).

Reynolds, J. D., and Gross, M. R. (1990). Costs and benefits of female mate choice: Is there a lek paradox? *Am. Nat.* **136,** 230–243.

Ricklefs, R. (1980). Commentary. *Condor* **82,** 476–477.

Rippin, A. B., and Boag, D. A. (1974a). Recruitment to populations of male sharp-tailed grouse. *J. Wildl. Manage.* **38,** 616–621.

Rippin, A. B., and Boag, D. A. (1974b). Spatial organization among male sharp-tailed grouse on arenas. *Can. J. Zool.* **52,** 591–597.

Robbins, M. B. (1983). The display repertoire of the band-tailed manakin (*Pipra fasciicauda*). *Wilson Bull.* **95,** 321–342.

Robbins, M. B. (1985). Social organization of the band-tailed manakin (*Pipra fasciicauda*). *Condor* **87,** 449–456.

Robel, R. J. (1964). Quantitative indices to activity and territoriality of booming *Tympanuchus cupido pinnatus* in Kansas. *Trans. Kans. Acad. Sci.* **67,** 702–711.

Robel, R. J. (1966). Booming territory size and mating success of the greater prairie chicken. (*Tympanuchus cupido pinnatus*). *Anim. Behav.* **14,** 328–331.

Robel, R. J. (1967). Significance of booming grounds of greater prairie chickens. *Proc. Am. Philos. Soc.* **111,** 109–114.

Robel, R. J. (1969). Movements and flock stratification within a population of blackcocks in Scotland. *J. Anim. Ecol.* **38,** 755–763.

Robel, R. J. (1970). Possible role of behavior in regulating greater prairie chicken populations. *J. Wildl. Manage.* **34,** 306–312.

Robel, R. J., and Ballard, W. B., Jr. (1974). Lek social organization and reproductive success in the greater prairie chicken. *Am. Zool.* **14,** 121–128.

Robel, R. J., Briggs, J. N., Cebula, J. J., Silvy, N. J., Viers, C. E., and Watt, P. G. (1970). Greater prairie chicken ranges, movements, and habitat usage in Kansas. *J. Wildl. Manage.* **34,** 286–306.

Rolstad, J., and Wegge, P. (1987). Habitat characteristics of capercaillie *Tetrao urogallus* display grounds in southeastern Norway. *Holarctic Ecol.* **10,** 210–229.

Ryan, M. J., Tuttle, M. D., and Rand, A. S. (1982). Bat predation and sexual advertisement in a neotropical anuran. *Am. Nat.* **119,** 136–139.

Schaal, A. (1986). Mise en évidence d'un comportement de reproduction en arène chez la daim d'Europe (*Dama dama*). *C. R. Seances Acad. Sci. Ser. 3* **303,** 729–732.

Schall, J. J., and Dearing, M. D. (1987). Malarial parasitism and male competition for mates in the western fence lizard, *Sceloporus occidentalis. Oecologia* **73,** 389–392.

Schuster, R. H. (1976). Lekking behavior in Kafue lechwe. *Science* **192,** 1240–1242.

Schwartz, C. W. (1945). The ecology of the prairie chicken in Missouri. *Univ. Mo. Stud.* **20**(1), 1–99.

Schwartz, P., and Snow, D. W. (1978). Display and related behavior of the wire-tailed manakin. *Living Bird* **17,** 51–78.

Scott, J. W. (1942). Mating behavior of the sage grouse. *Auk* **59,** 477–498.

Searcy, W. A., and Andersson, M. (1986). Sexual selection and the evolution of male song. *Annu. Rev. Ecol. Syst.* **17,** 507–533.

Seger, J. (1985). Unifying genetic models for the evolution of female choice. *Evolution (Lawrence, Kans.)* **39,** 1185–1193.

Selander, R. K. (1972). Sexual selection and dimorphism in birds. In "Sexual Selection and the Descent of Man: 1871–1971" (B. Campbell, ed.), pp. 180–230. Aldine, Chicago, Illinois.

Selous, E. (1927). "Realities of Bird Life." Constable, London.

Sexton, D. A. (1979). Off-lek copulation in sharp-tailed grouse. *Wilson Bull.* **91,** 150–151.

Sexton, D. A., and Gillespie, M. M. (1979). Effects of fire on the location of a sharp-tailed grouse arena. *Can. Field-Nat.* **93,** 74–76.

Shaw, P. (1984). The social behaviour of the pin-tailed whydah *Vidua macroura* in northern Ghana. *Ibis* **126**, 463–473.

Shepard, J. M. (1975). Factors influencing female choice in the lek mating system of the ruff. *Living Bird* **14**, 87–111.

Sibley, C. G. (1957). The evolutionary and taxonomic significance of sexual dimorphism and hybridization in birds. *Condor* **59**, 166–191.

Silvy, N. J., and Robel, R. J. (1967). Recordings used to increase trapping success of booming greater prairie chickens. *J. Wildl. Manage.* **31**, 370–373.

Snow, B. K. (1970). A field study of the bearded bellbird in Trinidad. *Ibis* **112**, 299–329.

Snow, B. K. (1972). A field study of the calfbird *Perissocephalus tricolor*. *Ibis* **114**, 139–162.

Snow, B. K. (1973). Notes on the behavior of the white bellbird. *Auk* **90**, 743–751.

Snow, B. K. (1974). Lek behaviour and breeding of Guy's hermit hummingbird *Phaethornis guy*. *Ibis* **116**, 278–297.

Snow, B. K., and Snow, D. W. (1979). The ochre-bellied flycatcher and the evolution of lek behavior. *Condor* **81**, 286–292.

Snow, D. W. (1962a). A field study of the black and white manakin, *Manacus manacus*, in Trinidad. *Zoologica (N.Y.)* **47**, 65–104.

Snow, D. W. (1962b). A field study of the golden-headed manakin, *Pipra erythrocephala*, in Trinidad, W. I. *Zoologica (N.Y.)* **47**, 183–198.

Snow, D. W. (1963). The display of the blue-backed manakin, *Chiroxiphia pareola*, in Tobago, West Indies. *Zoologica (N.Y.)* **48**, 167–176.

Snow, D. W. (1977). Duetting and other synchronized displays of the blue-backed manakins, Chiroxiphia spp. *In* "Evolutionary Ecology" (B. Stonehouse and C. Perrins, eds.), pp. 239–251. University Park Press, Baltimore, Maryland.

Snow, D. W. (1982). "The Cotingas." British Museum (Natural History) and Cornell Univ. Press, Ithaca, New York.

Snow, D. W., and Goodwin, D. (1974). The black and gold cotinga. *Auk* **91**, 360–369.

Sparling, D. W. (1983). Quantitative analysis of prairie grouse vocalizations. *Condor* **85**, 30–42.

Spurrier, M. F., Boyce, M. S., and Manly, B. F. J. (1990). Effects of parasites on mate choice by captive sage grouse, *Centrocercus urophasianus*. *In* "Ecology, Behavior and Evolution of Bird–Parasite Interactions" (J. Loye, C. van Riper, III, and M. Zuk, eds.). Oxford Univ. Press, Oxford. In press.

Stiles, F. G., and Wolf, L. L. (1979). Ecology and evolution of lek mating behavior in the long-tailed hermit hummingbird. *Ornithol. Monogr.* **27**, 1–78.

Sullivan, B. K. (1989). Passive and active female choice: A comment. *Anim. Behav.* **37**, 692–694.

Sutherland, W. J. (1985a). Chance can produce a sex difference in variance in mating success and explain Bateman's data. *Anim. Behav.* **33**, 1349–1352.

Sutherland, W. J. (1985b). Measures of sexual selection. *Oxford Surv. Ecol. Biol.* **2**, 90–101.

Sutherland, W. J. (1987). Random and deterministic components of variance in mating success. *In* "Sexual Selection: Testing the Alternatives" (J. W. Bradbury and M. B. Andersson, eds.), pp. 209–219. Wiley, New York.

Svedarsky, W. D. (1988). Reproductive ecology of female greater prairie chickens in Minnesota. *In* "Adaptive Strategies and Population Ecology of Northern Grouse" (A. T. Bergerud and M. W. Gratson, eds.), Vol. 1, pp. 193–239. Univ. of Minnesota Press, Minneapolis.

Swenson, J. E. (1986). Differential survival by sex in juvenile sage grouse and gray partridge. *Ornis Scand.* **17**, 14–17.

Taylor, P. D., and Williams, G. C. (1982). The lek paradox is not resolved. *Theor. Popul. Biol.* **22**, 392–409.

Trail, P. W. (1984). The lek mating system of the Guianan cock-of-the-rock: A field study of sexual selection. Ph.D. Dissertation, Cornell University, Ithaca, New York.

Trail, P. W. (1985a). Territoriality and dominance in the lek-breeding Guianan cock-of-the-rock. *Natl. Geogr. Res.* **1**, 112–123.

Trail, P. W. (1985b). Courtship disruption modifies mate choice in a lek-breeding bird. *Science* **227**, 778–780.

Trail, P. W. (1987). Predation and antipredator behavior at Guianan cock-of-the-rock leks. *Auk* **104**, 496–507.

Trail, P. W. (1990). Why should lek-breeders be monomorphic? *Evolution (Lawrence, Kans.)* (in press).

Trail, P. W., and Adams, E. S. (1989). Active mate choice at cock-of-the-rock leks: Tactics of sampling and comparison. *Behav. Ecol. Sociobiol.* **25**, 283–292.

Trail, P. W., and Koutnik, D. L. (1986). Courtship disruption at the lek in the Guianan cock-of-the-rock. *Ethology* **73**, 197–218.

Trobec, R., and Oring, L. (1972). Effects of testosterone propionate implantation on lek behavior of sharp-tailed grouse. *Am. Midl. Nat.* **87**, 531–536.

Vandenbergh, J. G. (1971). The influence of the social environment on sexual maturation in male mice. *J. Reprod. Fertil.* **24**, 383–390.

van Rhijn, J. (1973). Behavioral dimorphism in male ruffs, *Philomachus pugnax. Behaviour* **47**, 153–229.

van Rhijn, J. (1983). On maintenance and origin of alternative mating strategies in the ruff *Philomachus pugnax. Ibis* **125**, 482–498.

van Rhijn, J. (1985). A scenario for the evolution of social organization in ruffs *Philomachus pugnax* and other charadriiform species. *Ardea* **73**, 25–37.

Vehrencamp, S. L., Bradbury, J. W., and Gibson, R. M. (1989). The energetic cost of display in male sage grouse. *Anim. Behav.* **38**, 885–896.

Vellenga, R. E. (1980a). Moults of the satin bowerbird *Ptilonorhynchus violaceus. Emu* **80**, 49–54.

Vellenga, R. E. (1980b). Distribution of bowers of the satin bowerbird at Leura, NSW, with notes on parental care, development and independence of the young. *Emu* **80**, 87–102.

Wade, M. J. (1979). Sexual selection and variance in reproductive success. *Am. Nat.* **114**, 742–746.

Wade, M. J., and Arnold, S. J. (1980). The intensity of sexual selection in relation to male sexual behavior, female choice, and sperm precedence. *Anim. Behav.* **28**, 446–461.

Warner, R. R. (1987). Female choice of sites versus mates in a coral reef fish, *Thalassoma bifasciatum. Anim. Behav.* **35**, 1470–1478.

Warner, R. R. (1988). Traditionality of mating site preferences in a coral reef fish. *Nature (London)* **335**, 719–721.

Waser, P. M., and Wiley, R. H. (1979). Mechanisms and evolution of spacing in animals. *In* "Handbook of Behavioral Neurobiology" (P. Marler and J. G. Vandenbergh, eds.), Vol. 3, pp. 159–223. Plenum, New York.

Watson, A., and Parr, R. (1981). Hormone implants affecting territory size and aggressive and sexual behaviour in red grouse. *Ornis Scand.* **12**, 55–61.

Weatherhead, P. J., and Robertson, R. J. (1979). Offspring quality and the polygyny threshold: The "sexy son hypothesis." *Am. Nat.* **113**, 201–208.

Wegge, P. (1980). Distorted sex ratio among small broods in a declining capercaillie population. *Ornis Scand.* **11**, 106–109.

Wegge, P., and Larsen, B. B. (1987). Spacing of adult and subadult male common capercaillie during the breeding season. *Auk* **104**, 481–490.

Wegge, P., and Rolstad, J. (1986). Size and spacing of capercaillie leks in relation to social behavior and habitat. *Behav. Ecol. Sociobiol.* **19**, 401–408.

Wiley, R. H. (1973a). Territoriality and non-random mating in sage grouse, *Centrocercus urophasianus. Anim. Behav. Monogr.* **6**, 85–169.

Wiley, R. H. (1973b). The strut display of male sage grouse: A "fixed" action pattern. *Behaviour* **47**, 129–152.

Wiley, R. H. (1974). Evolution of social organization and life-history patterns among grouse. *Q. Rev. Biol.* **49**, 201–227.

Wiley, R. H. (1978). The lek mating system of the sage grouse. *Sci. Am.* **238**(5), 114–125.

Wiley, R. H. (1981). Social structure and individual ontogenies: Problems of description, mechanism and evolution. *In* "Perspectives in Ethology" (P. P. G. Bateson and P. H. Klopfer, eds.), Vol. 4, pp. 105–133. Plenum, New York.

Wiley, R. H. (1983). The evolution of communication: Information and manipulation. *In* "Animal Behaviour" (T. R. Halliday and P. J. B. Slater, eds.), Vol. 2, pp. 156–189. Blackwell, Oxford.

Wiley, R. H., and Hartnett, S. A. (1976). Effects of interactions with older males on behavior and reproductive development in first-year male red-winged blackbirds *Agealius phoeniceus*. *J. Exp. Zool.* **196**, 231–242.

Wiley, R. H., and Rabenold, K. N. (1984). The evolution of cooperative breeding by delayed reciprocity and queuing for favorable social positions. *Evolution (Lawrence, Kans.)* **38**, 609–621.

Williams, G. C. (1975). "Sex and Evolution." Princeton Univ. Press, Princeton, New Jersey.

Willis, E. O. (1979). Commentary. *Condor* **81**, 324.

Wingfield, J. C. (1984). Environmental and endocrine control of reproduction in the song sparrow, *Melospiza melodia*. II. Agonistic interactions as environmental information stimulating secretion of testosterone. *Gen. Comp. Endocrinol.* **56**, 417–424.

Wittenberger, J. F. (1978). The evolution of mating systems in grouse. *Condor* **80**, 126–137.

Worthington, A. (1982). Population sizes and breeding rhythms of two species of manakins in relation to food supply. *In* "The Ecology of a Tropical Forest: Seasonal Rhythms and Long-Term Changes" (E. G. Leigh, Jr., A. S. Rand, and D. M. Windsor, eds.), pp. 213–225. Smithsonian Inst. Press, Washington, D.C.

Wrangham, R. W. (1980). Female choice of least costly mates: A possible factor in the evolution of leks. *Z. Tierpsychol.* **54**, 352–367.

Zablan, M., and Braun, C. E. (1990). In preparation.

Zahavi, A. (1975). Mate selection—a selection for a handicap. *J. Theor. Biol.* **53**, 205–214.

Zeh, D. W., and Zeh, J. A. (1988). Condition-dependent sex ornaments and field tests of sexual selection theory. *Am. Nat.* **132**, 454–459.

Zuk, M. (1988). Parasite load, body size, and age of wild-caught male field crickets (Orthoptera: Gryllidae): Effects on sexual selection. *Evolution (Lawrence, Kans.)* **42**, 969–976.

Zwickel, F. C. (1972). Removal and repopulation of blue grouse in an increasing population. *J. Wildl. Manage.* **36**, 1141–1152.

Index

Contents of Previous Volumes